THE SCRIPPS NEWSPAPERS
GO TO WAR, 1914–18

THE HISTORY OF COMMUNICATION

Robert W. McChesney
and John C. Nerone, editors

A list of books in the series appears at the end of this book.

DALE E. ZACHER

The Scripps Newspapers Go to War, 1914–18

UNIVERSITY OF ILLINOIS PRESS
URBANA AND CHICAGO

© 2008 by Dale E. Zacher
All rights reserved
Manufactured in the United States of America
C 5 4 3 2 I
♾ This book is printed on acid-free paper.

Library of Congress Cataloging-in-Publication Data
Zacher, Dale.
The Scripps newspapers go to war, 1914–18 /
Dale Zacher.
   p.   cm. — (The history of communication)
Includes bibliographical references and index.
ISBN-13: 978-0-252-03158-8 (cloth : alk. paper)
ISBN-10: 0-252-03158-X (cloth : alk. paper)
   1. World War, 1914–1918—Press coverage—United States.
2. E.W. Scripps Company—History.
I. Title.
D632.Z33   2008
070.4'499403—dc22   2006100928

For Yu-li, Luke,
and Daniel

Contents

Acknowledgments ix

Introduction 1

1. The Concern: June 27, 1914 13
2. Seeds Get Planted: June 1914 to May 1915 32
3. Harsh Realities: May to November 1915 58
4. "Genuine Enthusiastic Support": November 1915 to November 1916 81
5. Democracy versus Autocracy: December 1916 to July 1917 106
6. "To Advocate a Policy and to Yourself Meet Its Requirements": July to December 1917 137
7. Reconsidering an "Ostrich Type of Patriotism": 1918 172

Conclusion: "Harder . . . to Be of Public Service" 211

Notes 225

Bibliography 279

Index 281

Acknowledgments

I began doing research for this book as a project in Journalism 811 while a graduate student at Ohio University in 1994. What first was a short study of the Scripps newspapers in the 1916 election evolved into my doctoral dissertation and now this book. It has been a long journey, and I am endebted to dozens of people who helped me through all of the stages as the manuscript was written, revised, and updated.

I had great professors at Ohio University who influenced this project in many ways. In particular, my thanks to John Gilliom and David Mould for their encouragement and input as members of my dissertation committee. A special thanks to Joe Bernt, another committee member, who is a great sounding board for ideas about Scripps history. He has always been willing to help me since my first days at Ohio University, and I am very grateful.

My biggest thanks, though, goes to Pat Washburn, who chaired my dissertation and comprehensive exam committees, and who was the single biggest reason I decided to come to the E. W. Scripps School of Journalism as a master's student in 1993. From my acceptance letter to my last days there, he made me feel like I was the most important student ever to attend the graduate program. His warm welcome, great sense of humor, and professional attitude were very reassuring for me as I moved from the prairies of North Dakota to the foothills of Athens, Ohio. His patience, advice, and encouragement on this project over the many years, too, made him the best mentor I could have.

I did most of the writing of this book while teaching at Creighton University and the University of North Dakota (UND). My thanks to my colleagues at these institutions, especially Stephen Rendahl at UND, once a teacher from my undergraduate days, who kindly helped motivate me to finish the last parts of what was then a dissertation.

Gerald Baldasty, University of Washington, and Dwight Teeter, University of Tennessee helped me immensely in reshaping the manuscript into this book. Their insights and suggestions made this a much stronger study. Thanks, too, to the excellent staff at University of Illinois Press, especially Kerry Callahan and Rebecca Crist.

I would also like to thank the many librarians and archivists who helped me as I researched this project. Most of the research was done at the Robert E. and Jean R. Mahn Center for Archives and Special Collections at Alden Library at Ohio University, where George Bain and his staff did a great job of helping me find the many nuggets in the voluminous gold mine of Scripps correspondence. The Scripps-Howard Foundation and the Scripps family also deserve my gratitude for donating the Scripps papers to Ohio University and for funding the collection so scholars can use it.

Finally, I wish to dedicate this study to my family for waiting patiently while I read and typed away, and giving me encouragement and help all along. This book is dedicated to Yu-li, Luke, and Daniel, who provided my greatest motivation and support.

THE SCRIPPS NEWSPAPERS
GO TO WAR, 1914–18

Introduction

In the winter of 1919, sixty-five-year-old Edward Willis Scripps (generally known as E.W.) was thinking about his mortality and the future of his chain of newspapers and news services. "This might be as good a time as another to take up and get out of the way some business that ought to be settled before . . . I get much older," he wrote one of his personal attorneys, Thomas Sidlow, on December 11, 1919. Scripps hoped to set up a legal arrangement that would allow him to keep "centralized and continued control" while ensuring that any heir to his fortune was "capable, willing and anxious to conduct the business."[1]

The latter point was no small one. Scripps was concerned about how his heirs would run his newspapers after his death, and he was not sure if his two sons were up to the job. "I want to safeguard, as far as possible and for as long a time as possible, the continuation of the policy which I inaugurated and which I have striven always to maintain," he told Sidlow.

That policy, long engrained in the news operations of the Scripps newspapers, was focused on strongly supporting social justice issues, especially those affecting the working classes, while remaining politically independent. In the 1878 inaugural issue of the *Cleveland Press*, his first newspaper, Scripps pledged to support good politicians and good policies regardless of the political party that produced them. "It is no part of a newspaper's business to array itself on the side of this or that party, or fight or lie or wrangle for it," he told his readers. Comparing the journalistic process to a jury trial, Scripps said his newspaper simply would obtain the facts as best it could, be a "witness" for those facts, and let the public "find the verdict."[2]

For the next three decades, that commitment to be an independent champion of the working classes paid off handsomely, making millions for Scripps and allowing him to expand his chain nationwide. The Scripps chain—known by the in-house nickname "the Concern"[3]—arguably, in the days before radio and television, was the nation's first national news organization.[4] In 1919 it consisted of twenty-one newspapers in twelve states, the Newspaper Enterprise Association (NEA; a syndicated news service also sold to non-Scripps papers), and United Press (UP; the second largest American wire service). By 1914 the Concern had earned a national reputation for what were termed "progressive" causes, especially those concerning working men and women, and hoped to broaden its editorial influence nationally.

World War I, however, would challenge the values and assumptions in that 1878 editorial as never before. First, the war seemed to undermine the idealistic roles presented in Scripps's trial metaphor. Was not the Concern more of a "judge" of facts than a "witness" to them? Could the "jury" of readers be trusted to find the truth among the facts or did it need to be led to the truth as determined by the Concern? Second, the Scripps pledge to remain politically neutral was broken brazenly when it gave, for the first time, its national, unified support to one candidate—Woodrow Wilson. In doing so, the Concern felt it had lost any freedom it had to criticize his administration later, hurting its credibility with its working class readers and opening it to charges that Wilson repaid Scripps with draft deferments for his sons.

The war also negatively affected the relationship Scripps had with his two surviving sons, Jim and Robert, and made E.W. fear they would not work together after his death. The familial battles ultimately affected the news operation of the Scripps papers, hurting morale and leadership at a critical time. The family disagreements during the war period ultimately burst out and caused a split in the Scripps chain in the early 1920s.

Three Levels of Answers

Research for this book began with what seemed like a straightforward question: how and why did the Scripps newspaper chain, a large media company with news outlets spread across the country and with many working-class readers, cover World War I—one of the most divisive wars in American history? The intention was to use the Scripps chain's experiences to write a history never done before—a detailed case study of the daily news operations of a large media company during the war years of 1914–18. With a wire service, a growing syndication arm, and a national spread of newspapers, the Concern is great material for a systematic, multifaceted study of how and why this war was covered.

But it was soon became obvious that any case study of the Scripps newspaper chain could not simply focus on the content it produced or the organizational logistics it faced in covering a global war. One also must know about the family who owned the news organization and how that family reacted to the war, for these things affected how the war was covered. Just as important, the chain's politics and devotion to championing the social justice causes of the working classes were shaped by the war and helped shape the war coverage. This study, designed originally to find out how the Scripps papers covered World War I—and why they did so in that way—also revealed significant findings about how the war changed the Concern.

This book, then, becomes a story revealed at three levels, with each providing meaning and context to the others. At one level, the logistics and organizational considerations of covering a major war—the finances and the content of what readers saw—are revealed and analyzed. Most major newspapers, the primary mass media of the day, faced the same issues in covering the war, so this level of the story helps the general understanding of how they did so.

The other two levels are unique to the Scripps chain but critical to understanding the first level. Much of this book is a family history of a father and two sons fighting to define their roles and the direction of the chain. Because family was so important and Scripps wanted his sons to take over before he died, the war period becomes a key chapter in the corporate management history of the Scripps newspaper chain.

The third level of the story relates to the social justice spirit E. W. Scripps imbued his newspapers with and their steadfast support of progressive causes. In 1914 the Scripps newspapers were as powerful editorially as they ever would be. Progressive causes, exemplified in President Woodrow Wilson's "New Freedom" initiatives, were on center stage nationally. It was inevitable that the Scripps newspapers and Wilson would gravitate to each other. The attraction began before the first guns in Europe were fired in August 1914 but would become a firm bond by 1916. The Scripps-Wilson alliance, based on mutual support of progressive causes, was the single largest influence on how and why the Scripps newspapers covered the war, especially after 1917, and must be examined in detail.

The book is organized chronologically; as the discussion proceeds, it examines the connections among these three aspects of the story, showing how they changed and influenced each other over time.

A Case Study in War Coverage

Historian Loren Thompson in 1991 described the "inherent tension between the aims of journalists and the aims of soldiers in wartime." Journalists have an important role—to criticize the military if necessary to protect the public good—but, he wrote, that must be balanced with the military's need to restrict journalists at times.[5]

Journalists in World War I have earned little praise for their efforts to maintain that balance. Soon after it was realized that World War I would not bring a lasting peace, historians Michael Emery, Edwin Emery, and Nancy L. Roberts noted in 2000, postwar writers began criticizing the way journalists allowed themselves to be fooled by propaganda: "British propagandists, American munitions makers, and cynical politicians had led gullible Americans to an unnecessary slaughter, the theme ran, carrying with it the implication that American newspapers were duped by foreign propagandists and by war-mongering capitalists, and thereby misled their readers."[6]

As Emery and his colleagues wrote, besides the influence of overt propaganda, many other cultural, political, and economic reasons motivated the United States to join the war on the side of the British and French, but nonetheless the propaganda reason—with its portrayal of most journalists as gullible coconspirators—endures in historical analyses of the World War I era. In 2003, historian Thomas Fleming said that British propaganda that was carried in the U.S. media, full of German atrocity stories, created "the aggressive, often angry pro-war sentiment of the apparent American majority" in 1917.[7] Stewart Halsey Ross, in his 1996 book *Propaganda for War: How the United States Was Conditioned to Fight the Great War of 1914-1918*, mentioned that "the war was packaged, promoted, and sold to a gullible nation as a holy crusade against evil."[8]

Probably the book that best fully examined this theme is H. C. Peterson's 1939 book *Propaganda for War: The Campaign against American Neutrality, 1914–1917*—still continually cited by historians. The book says the largest factor in convincing the United States to join the war in 1917 was American public opinion, which was "the product of British propaganda," distributed mostly in U.S. newspapers.[9] Similarly, Phillip Knightley's book *The First Casualty* echoes Peterson with scathing criticism of British propagandists and their influence on American public opinion, crediting them with creating a "blind hatred of everything German" that pushed people to support the war.[10]

The series of events backing the analyses in these books seems convincing. The British controlled most communication channels coming out of Europe soon after war was declared. They censored unfavorable reports while promoting anti-German propaganda in America. After the United States joined the war, President Wilson created the Committee on Public Information (CPI), which whipped domestic public opinion to an even higher pitch with more propaganda.[11] In addition, federal laws against sedition were passed, and prosecutions against war critics were aggressively pursued.[12]

These historical studies also emphasize the censorship war correspondents experienced, supporting the idea that the American public was largely kept from knowing the truth about the war because journalists who knew the truth could not tell it to them. These analyses rely primarily on anecdotes from various reporters culled from postwar memoirs.[13]

But this analysis of propaganda, the threats of sedition, and the effects of censorship on war reporting is incomplete. Kevin O'Keefe and Ralph Otto Nafziger have looked systematically at large amounts of the content of American newspapers to see how they covered the war before 1917 but did not study available correspondence to see why newspapers covered the war as they did.[14] Just as Americans joined the war for many reasons, American journalists covered it the way they did for many reasons. They were not simply motivated by blind patriotism, censored into silence, or deceived by British propaganda. At any rate, the public's appetite for war coverage had to be fed somehow, censorship or not.

Fortunately, the surviving archival evidence for the NEA, UP, and individual Scripps newspapers is large and readily accessible to researchers who want insight from unpublished letters written at the time. Hundreds of hours were spent searching through each file of letters in the Scripps archives at Ohio University from 1912 to 1920. Likewise, for this study every edition of the *Cleveland Press*, the flagship Scripps newspaper, was read in order to find trends in news coverage—trends often supported and sometimes contradicted by letters in the archives. Spot checks of coverage of other Scripps newspapers helped verify the archival correspondence and the trends seen in the *Cleveland Press*. For example, all five Ohio newspapers published in 1916 were read to judge their consistency of voice during the presidential election, and all of the 1917 editions of the *Los Angeles Record* and *Evansville Press*, newspapers that were part of different ownership groups within the Concern, were read to judge their editorial consistency during America's divisive entry into the war. For the most part, the NEA monitored the coverage of the Scripps newspapers for consistency on national issues, so a solid indication of Scripps content can be found in the *Press*.

The first global war imposed huge financial and editorial demands, and a study such as this reveals the complex situation major news organizations faced. The Concern faced increased demand for news for its newspapers, as well as from its NEA and UP clients, but it encountered stringent controls on what it could report and increasing costs for supplies it needed to print its newspapers. Radical changes had to be made. During the war, the Scripps newspapers had to raise the penny price of its newspapers to two cents, and this study will show that it upgraded its war news to justify the higher price.

The war also created new markets for the content that was generated, and so the NEA and UP grew in staff size and client base. In particular, the Concern discovered that its syndicated news service became more attractive as the war progressed, and all newspapers needed high-quality features at low prices, such as those generated by the NEA. United Press, too, stepped up its attempts to grow globally while facing the pirating of its news coverage by rivals, and cutthroat competition from William Randolph Hearst's International News Service and the much larger Associated Press (AP).

Moreover, the NEA—the central editorial and feature service of the Scripps newspapers—made a concerted effort to gain non-Scripps clients in 1914 so as to increase profits and gain influence. The independent progressive voice of the Scripps Concern was now available for hire. Historian Alfred McLung Lee wrote that NEA management "tended to tone down its policies" after clients outnumbered Scripps members, something that had taken place by 1915.[15] This study will show that the transformation did not take place until the war was nearly finished, and it was change driven by concerns that the Scripps newspapers were too focused on advocacy and opinion-shaping.

The activities of the CPI, the United States' mouthpiece after it entered the war (an organization that the Concern grew to despise), have been written about extensively.[16] Previous studies assume that Committee on Public Information (CPI) content was used by the media and do not seek to link the CPI handouts to actual content. This study uses archives from the CPI and Scripps newspapers to try to show that the CPI's actual influence is uncertain and was partly unsuccessful. The Scripps newspapers struggled to get on the CPI's mailing lists, for example—a distribution problem other historians have not reported.

This study shows many influences on content. Sometimes Scripps directly influenced newspaper content on the basis of his personal opinions. Sometimes it was influenced by an economic concern, a technological limitation, the Concern's reputation for progressivism, the whim of a military censor, or the need to use longer war-related features to fill space. These findings give unprecedented insight into the workings of a major news organization during one of the biggest news stories of the twentieth century, and shed light on the experiences of the journalists who worked during this era.

Family War

Much of the family history portion of this book is unique to the Scripps Concern, of course, but it does shed light on the pitfalls of a private corporation controlled by family members. Most media critics lament the demise of family-owned newspapers and the current trend of ownership by a few major public corporations, but family ownership or management is not always ideal.[17]

The Bingham family battles that led to the sale of the *Louisville Times* in 1986, the Hoiles family squabbles over control of the Freedom Communications newspaper company in 2003,[18] and Rupert Murdoch's 2005 conflicts with his son, Lachlan, over control of News Corporation[19] all show how family ties can lead to bad blood in the media business. Beginning in 1917, intrafamilial disputes escalated into irreconcilable differences between Scripps and his oldest son Jim and an eventual split in the chain.

The board of directors of a publicly owned corporation probably would not have tolerated the nepotism and family machinations that affected the key management of the Scripps newspapers during the war years. The most serious part of the family dispute began when it became clear that Scripps's two sons might be forced to join the military. Afraid his sons would be drafted and killed in Europe, Scripps considered challenging the draft law in court, but then decided instead to do what he could to get his sons exempted or deferred—even though they wanted to serve in the army. What became very public maneuvers in front of draft boards made the Scripps newspapers seem hypocritical because they were otherwise vehement supporters of the draft—something competing newspapers were quick to point out.

In 1917 a desperate Scripps insisted—over objections from his oldest son, Jim—that his youngest son, Bob, be made editor-in-chief of the Concern's war coverage. Scripps hoped that with such an important job, Bob surely would be exempted from military service. But Jim knew that Bob was not qualified for such a job.

The situation was further complicated because Scripps was convinced that only someone with his blood could best understand the progressive ideals needed to run his newspapers effectively, but he was not sure which son was best suited. He wanted his newspapers run with an eye to serve the public, not simply to make profits. The draft problem made his sons seem mortal, and he wanted to protect his heirs. Business decisions were made on the basis of family concerns. With no board of directors or public stockholders to check him, Scripps's peculiar views led to dissension and frustration among Concern employees and weakened editorial leadership as the Concern struggled with what to do with Bob in 1917–18. Fallout from the draft maneuvers and other meddling by Scripps led directly to a corporate split of the Concern between 1920 and 1922. While others have studied the events of the split, this study is the first to examine in detail the origins of this major disagreement between father and sons.[20]

Inside a Progressive Force

This book provides an intricate view of how the thinking of a progressive-minded organization, founded by a progressive idealist, dealt with the war and was changed by it. Historian John Thompson argued in 1987 that much can be learned about progressivism by studying its leading writers and journalists: "Since such writers have to deal more directly and extensively with ideas than do inarticulate voters or even politicians, it is also an appropriate point from which to consider how the First World War, in its various aspects and phases, affected the thinking of American reformers."[21]

By 1914 the Scripps Concern was a powerful enough media organization to position itself as a champion of progressive politics on the national stage. In 1916 Louis Brandeis, a progressive economist and lawyer, called the Scripps newspapers "a leading progressive force in America."[22] Still, the Scripps chain had been subtle in how it exerted its influence—at least nationally. "The quiet power of these Scripps newspapers is little understood in the United States," press critic Will Irwin said in 1914.[23]

Wilson's early success with progressive causes as president helped remove any reluctance the Scripps newspapers had about taking a more prominent national role in progressive politics. The Scripps Concern rose to aggressively champion Wilson's causes and even volunteered to work directly with him. Scripps offered Wilson his top editor to be what Scripps termed a "Secretary of the People,"—a press secretary—in 1914. Although the idea was never implemented, the Concern supported Wilson vigorously during his 1916 reelection campaign (many said the Scripps newspapers won the election for him) and backed him without reservation after the United States entered the war. The findings of this study are in contrast to what some historians studying the origins of objectivity in journalism have found. Historian Richard Kaplan argued in 2002 that American newspapers adopted a standard of objectivity for various reasons in the early 1900s.[24] Michael McGerr argued in 1986 that newspapers grew more independent and less partisan in the period from 1870 to 1920.[25] David Mindich argued in 1998 that objectivity was established by the 1890s.[26]

As this study shows, Scripps's support of Wilson during the war period and during the election of 1916 was hardly "objective," but the war experience began to change minds within the Concern. These findings reflect what journalism historian Michael Schudson observed in 1978—the post–World War I era was a turning point for how journalists viewed their role in society. Schudson argued that standards of objectivity in news reporting and journalism ethics were born in the 1920s. All of this can be traced to skepticism about public opinion–shapers from the war years. The war and the propaganda machinery that fueled the war effort showed that "facts" were subject to opinion; they were not inherently indisputable, as was believed before the war.[27]

Money, too, changed the Concern's political views, even in the mind of the elder Scripps. "Once I was a poor man and hated the capitalists, and now I am a capitalist and I see the other side of the question," Scripps wrote in 1921.[28] A newspaper chain that had made its reputation railing against government controlled by major business interests was now itself a large company fattened by war profits.

Previous in-depth research on Scripps has only partially told the role of the Scripps news organs in shaping public opinion during the war years. In 1992 Vance Trimble provided the most complete account of Scripps's life, but as a breezy biography, it focused primarily on the elder Scripps and his family; little was said about how or why his newspapers covered certain events or supported certain causes.[29] Other biographies consist of memoirs by colleagues or edited collections of Scripps's writings.[30] They, too, are useful, but often show an incomplete picture. Gerald Baldasty's excellent 1999 book on the Scripps news chain focuses on its business practices and ends its analysis with Scripps's retirement for health reasons in 1908—stopping short of the period under scrutiny here.[31] This book seeks to reveal more about the heart and soul of Scripps as a progressive champion of the common laborer and how this cause manifested itself in his newspapers. This book will examine Scripps's major progressive crusade for publicity of income tax returns to generate more government revenue, his championing of Wilson's reelection in 1916, and his political disillusionment after the war.

Although Scripps aptly called himself "the spirit of the Concern," focusing on him (he retired—on paper at least—from daily business operations in 1908 and editorial operations in 1911) tells only part of the story.[32] The vast amount of Scripps correspondence that was opened to researchers at Ohio University in 1990 includes numerous letters and business documents relating to the Concern's daily business and editorial decision making. A great deal about the men who worked for Scripps can be learned from these documents. Thus, this book is not a "great man" history of journalism and progressive politics focusing solely on Scripps; it studies one major media organization in depth, not just isolated journalists, and considers many reasons for the shift in political philosophy and editorial content within that conglomerate.

Most of the correspondence in the Ohio University collection centers on the NEA, which is helpful because the NEA was the part of the Concern that coordinated news coverage among the various Scripps newspapers. Meanwhile, the Roy Howard Papers at Indiana University and the Library of Congress give insight into UP's experiences in the war years, although these papers are not nearly as complete as the NEA correspondence in the Scripps collection. Joe Alex Morris's *Deadline Every Minute* (1957) gave a useful snapshot of UP operations during the war and was based largely on reminiscences of staffers who were still alive when the book was written.[33] A more recent and expanded book about the history of United Press International, Richard Harnett and Billy Ferguson's *Unipress: Covering the Twentieth Century*, adds little new insight to the time period under study here.[34] Contemporary articles in *Editor and Publisher*, the leading trade magazine of the day (which shared an office building with UP and was extremely sympathetic to it), help fill some gaps. Finally, four books by or about World War I–era UP correspondents have been useful.[35]

Transformed by War

This book argues that the Great War had a great impact on the later development of the Scripps Concern. First of all, the Concern made a lot of money from a public and from other newspapers hungry for its war news. Excellent war coverage especially cemented the reputation of the fledgling UP and proved it could compete and thrive.

The war, however, also taught Scripps editors that they needed to separate facts from opinions in NEA news content sold to non-Scripps newspapers. The Scripps newspapers would continue to fight for progressive reforms to help the working classes after the war, but in a muted manner and with no attempt to market these reforms to other newspapers. Never before or after was the Scripps chain the partisan, national force in national politics it was during Wilson's 1916 reelection campaign. That national attention also made it an inviting target for critics, and the experience made the Concern retreat to a lower political profile after the war and vow never to align itself so closely with a national politician again.

This is a critical time in understanding the Scripps family and its management of the chain as well. The war broke out when Scripps was aged and worried about how his sons would run his newspapers after his death. The issue seemed doubly important because many of his most trusted lieutenants were also nearing retirement and were being pushed aside by a generation of editors more concerned about profits than political causes. Concerned that his sons would be drafted and killed in the military, the elder Scripps forced too many decisions on his sons and his newspapers, creating a backlash that led to the postwar split in his chain.

The Scripps newspapers and the Scripps family were very different in 1919 from the confident days of prewar 1914. This book explains what happened.

1   The Concern:
June 27, 1914

To understand a typical newspaper owned by Edward Willis Scripps before the war, one need only look at the June 27, 1914, edition of his chain's greatest newspaper, the *Cleveland Press*.[1] More than half of the front page was filled with sports, tragic accidents, and lighthearted anecdotes. The rest was devoted to a front-page editorial on political advertising and reports of local battles with the Cleveland establishment. The Scripps newspapers were designed to draw readers—in particular the working class—with a sugar coating of entertainment while administering a dose of medicine: progressive ideals of government reform and social justice.[2]

Probably three-fourths of the newspaper's news content consisted of copy from UP and the NEA syndicated service, both Scripps-owned and established to secure unique features and spot news. The name "NEA" never appeared, though, on the page. The NEA wanted its newspaper clients to use any copy as if it were produced locally because syndicated features had a bad reputation among readers.[3] By sharing costs and content of UP and the NEA, Scripps editors could ensure a steady stream of low-cost, high-quality news.[4] A 1999 study of Scripps newspaper content in the early 1900s found that Scripps papers ran less local news than their competitors.[5]

Local news was not completely absent, though. Two notable stories showed the propensity of Scripps papers to attack big business and special interests. "Threatened to Enjoin West-Side Gas Hunt" told of Cleveland homeowners trying to stop developers from drilling for gas in their area. "Defends Home Rule Bill for Schools Here" reported how conservatives were attacking a state plan to give local school districts more control.

Scripps's editors knew, though, that readers would only stand so much preaching. "We are not conducting either a church or a school," Scripps attorney and stockholder J. C. Harper wrote to the NEA in 1912, asking for more features.[6] Harper was a dedicated fighter for progressive causes but said there was "a disposition . . . to get behind too many propositions and thus scatter our fire."[7]

The largest story in the June 24 *Cleveland Press* was devoted to UP reporter William Philip Simms's column-length story from Paris, with graphics, on the upcoming heavyweight boxing match between former champion Jack Johnson and Frank Moran.[8] Many short articles had a good share of the page. One local entertaining minutia, "Girl Teaches Masher Lesson," told in thirteen sentences how a local woman induced two friends to beat up a "masher" (a man making unwanted sexual advances). A five-sentence story, "Court Shouts to Reach Boilermaker," told whimsically how a deafened Cleveland boilermaker asked a judge to speak louder so he could hear the proceedings.

Hard, sensational news pieces were kept short, too. "Lake Steamer Hits Stone Pier" told of a shipping accident in Wisconsin in four sentences. "Corpses Are Sought in Ashes of Salem" described a fire in Massachusetts in fifteen sentences. But it was not all hard news. "We need less seriousness and more humor and laughs and generally interesting and informative knowledge," Jim Scripps, the head of the Concern, said in 1912.[9] The Scripps recipe for a newspaper always included a good share of jokes, short fiction, and sports and leisure articles. As one historian noted, "content was crafted to reach working-class readers."[10] Indeed, these lurid or entertaining stories made it easier for the newsboys to sell the one-cent *Press* on street corners to weary streetcar riders on their way home. It was the easy-to-read articles about society and progressive politics, however, that gave the Scripps newspapers their heart and soul.

A Scripps newspaper was designed for what Scripps and his editors termed the "ninety-five percent"—the average working man and woman. "I am one of the few newspapermen who happen to know that this country is populated by ninety-five percent of plain people, and the patronage of even plain and poor people is worth more to a newspaper owner than the patronage of the wealthy five percent."[11] Because of catering to the ninety-five percent, circulation and advertising followed. By fighting for the underdogs and controlling publishing costs, Scripps could make his newspapers profitable even if he alienated a few advertisers; retailers would come back eventually to reach his readers. "You may say that the prime object of a Scripps newspaper is to fight for the people. Yes, but it has to get circulation to fight effectively," *Toledo News-Bee* editor Neg Cochran said in 1913.[12]

The Scripps editors, especially those with newer newspapers, could not be reckless in picking their fights because they had to make a profit. Longtime Scripps editor and editorial writer Robert Paine noted in 1913 that there were "two editorial camps" in the Concern. "One is commercialized. The other is controlled by E.W.'s peculiar principles and peculiar views of things."[13] The older men in the Concern tended to empathize with E.W.; the younger men tended to fall into the commercialized camp.

"Our Independence"

The issue of making money versus championing societal reforms arose sharply in the spring of 1913, after Paine (of the "peculiar-view" camp) sent out a series of editorials that NEA president Harry Rickey thought alienated advertisers. Paine sent them from San Diego directly to Scripps editors to prevent unnecessary delay, instead of following the usual practice of sending them to NEA headquarters in Chicago for editing and distribution by mail. Rickey explained his concerns before a conference of top editors and stockholders: "We cannot altogether disregard [current] conditions and adopt a policy which we might agree as ideal and say it ought to be put into effect regardless of consequences. While our papers should be in advance of all other papers as to Progressisveism [sic], it was just as bad for us to be too far in advance of public sentiment as to be too far behind."[14] Rickey assured the editors that Scripps newspapers "would never, under any circumstances, kow-tow to a man because he advertised." On the other hand, he said it was not worthwhile to attack advertisers "simply to show our independence."

The discussion finally erupted into a clash between Rickey and Harper, who was one of the old-school Scripps colleagues:

> Rickey: "The cardinal principle of the Scripps Papers is to make a profit. We talk much about disinterestedness; but, as a matter of fact, we are in the newspaper business to make a living for ourselves and families. When we can't do that, we will get out."
> Harper: "Some lawyers are content to make less money than others, because they will not resort to the same methods as those others."
> Rickey: "*So are we*. We make less money than we could probably if we followed some of the methods of our competitors."[15]

Progressivism and the Penny Press

As Gerald Baldasty wrote in 1999, targeting working-class readers made solid business sense for Scripps. Largely ignored by other newspapers, the working class was an underserved market the Scripps newspapers could exploit for profit.[16] While money surely motivated him, E. W. Scripps was a man of principle, too. His desire to improve conditions for the underclasses was a continual theme in his writings, public and private, throughout his life. Born to a large, poor family in 1854, he lived through a time of great economic and political promise and restlessness.

The year 1914 was close to the end of the first wave of progressive reform in government and society. "Progressivism," as historian Richard Hofstadter has pointed out, was a broad "impulse toward criticism and change that was everywhere . . . conspicuous after 1900." Historians Arthur S. Link and Richard McCormick wrote in 1983 that the men and women who called themselves "Progressives" were "varied" and "contradictory," but shared a general vision that something had to be done to improve democracy and social justice: "Certainly there was no unified movement, but, like most students of the period, we consider progressivism to have been a real, vital and significant phenomenon, one which contemporaries recognized and talked and fought about," they wrote.[17]

Progressivism coopted, extended, and replaced the Populist political movement forged by discontented farmers and businessmen in the late 1800s, which had focused on state and local government affairs. Both broad movements were in many ways reactions to the country's perceived problems with urbanization and industrialization, and the rise of large corporations. Progressives, Hofstadter noted, wanted to restore economic individualism and political democracy, which they believed had been destroyed "by the great corporation and the corrupt political machine; and with that restoration to bring back a kind of morality and civic purity that was also believed to have been lost."[18] Scripps newspapers, devoted to serving working-class leaders, would inevitably, it seemed, gravitate to progressive causes during this era.

"Progressivism," according to historian Eric Goldman, meant primarily "the ending of governmental interventions that benefited large-scale capital and a rapid increase in the interventions that favored men of little or no capital." Goldman noted that, in general, progressives backed the direct election of United States senators, popular primaries, the recall of elected officials, the initiative and the referendum, antitrust actions, federal income tax, trade unions, social welfare, women's right to vote, worker's compensation laws, minimum wage legislation, and an eight-hour work day. Progressive reform was concerned with labor, including small businessmen and white-collar workers.[19] Historian Sean Dennis Chapman described the typical progressive as "urbane and middle class, including the most articulate, literate, and expert members" of emerging new classes of professions:

> Their leaders were usually white Anglo-Saxon Protestants from affluent backgrounds and with a college education, as well as occupying a professional and commercial position, allowing them a certain economic and social status. . . . [T]hey were particularly sensitive to exposures of mismanagement, corruption and accounts of economic and social distress. They were also equipped with the necessary eloquence and with leisure time to engage in serious and considered protest.[20]

Link and McCormick wrote that progressivism spread into national politics in 1905, during the second term of Theodore Roosevelt, because many realized that only "the federal government was capable of solving the problems of a continental nation."[21]

Journalists, especially those called "muckrakers," played an important part in this reform movement by exposing—in magazines—misdeeds and injustices, allowing the public to learn about them and to do something about them.[22] As Hofstadter noted, the journalists of this era "brought to the journalistic life some of the ideals, the larger interests, and the sense of public responsibility of men of culture."[23] The muckraking style of publicizing societal and governmental wrongdoing had begun in the penny newspaper press, where it was often linked with "yellow journalism." The Scripps newspapers were among the early pioneers of this style of writing. "Yellow journalism was able only to stimulate local protest, since it depended for effect on quick reading and looked to quick results. It was for that reason a good school for the muckrakers . . . who . . . had to know how to present facts pungently to the popular mind," historian Louis Filler wrote in 1939.

Born in Rushville, Illinois, Scripps knew the reading public well. He saw firsthand the magnificent growth in population and industry that dominated the country after the Civil War. He also saw, however, the disadvantages that many laborers had in relation to those few who controlled capital and the government. Filler called Scripps "a strange, complex man who frankly thought that labor was entitled to all it could get. Although he became very wealthy, he remained democratic in an almost superstitious, American sense."[24]

Scripps said his older brother, James E. Scripps, got the idea of printing concise, small, and cheap newspapers for the masses when E.W. was a young boy. The epiphany took place as James watched ten-year-old E.W. read a volume of *Peter Parley's Tales,* a condensed volume of crime stories written in easy-to-read English. Nearly a decade later, though, E.W. would join James E. to start the *Detroit News* in 1872. It was a small newspaper—four pages and six columns wide—but it sold cheaply at two cents.[25]

Scripps took his brother's recipe for a cheap newspaper one step farther in Cleveland in 1878. The *Press* he created was smaller and sold for a penny. With Paine as editor, the *Press* championed the causes of the average working man and woman. The *Press*'s success would be repeated in other growing commercial centers along the West Coast and in the South. The Scripps empire had begun.

Politically, the Scripps newspapers remained independent—aligning themselves instead with the progressive ideal, a torch carried by a growing core of members in both the Democrat and Republican parties. Newspapers of the late 1800s tended to be more independent, relying more on advertising than on political support.[26] Scripps newspapers supported progressives from both parties.

Scripps resisted suggestions that his millions tempered his progressive radicalism. "I was a millionaire before I was thirty-five years old, but my radicalism persisted long years after this," he wrote. "I believe that all men, or practically all men, are born equal. But after birth all men have been differentiated purely as a result of environment."[27]

By 1914, the Scripps papers had been a powerful voice for economic and political reform in Ohio—where its most powerful newspapers were located—for more than two decades. One historian called the Ohio Group of Scripps newspapers a "potent journalistic force in stimulating the moral revival in Ohio politics." By targeting the working classes, Scripps papers were tuned to an audience the Ohio progressives traditionally had difficulty reaching.[28] Cochran noted in 1913: "Out of the Ohio group have grown all the progressive ventures we have made. Many of them were only possible because of the existence of the strong Ohio papers."[29]

The *Cincinnati Post* and the *Toledo News-Bee* had based their owner's reputation on crusades against corrupt local political bosses and machines.[30] As Baldasty wrote, the notion of "press as watchdog" was one way newspapers in the late 1800s exerted political power while not taking sides with a political party.[31] The *Post* became nationally famous for these battles, in particular for its successful campaign to defeat Republican boss George Cox in 1905.[32] In 1912, another Cox, this one a progressive Democrat—future governor James Cox—said the Scripps Concern was Ohio's "father of Progressivism."[33]

The editorial on the front page of the June 27 *Press* gives evidence of this: it announced that the *Press* would now accept political advertising in state and local elections.[34] Scripps newspapers previously had refused to carry political ads to reaffirm their independence. But times were changing, largely due to the progressive reforms urged by the Scripps newspapers. Candidates now would be selected in primaries, not smoke-filled rooms; U.S. senators would be elected by the people, too, not legislatures. "This year, for the first time, the people of Ohio will make their nominations for all offices at the polls, instead of permitting politicians in convention to do it for them. This is as it should be," the editorial said. The primary system, though, meant that candidates needed to communicate directly to voters. The *Press* could fill that need by accepting advertisements under certain restrictions.[35]

When the Scripps chain expanded west, it continued to build credibility among reformers. For example, the five Scripps newspapers in California ardently backed reform-minded Governor Hiram Johnson throughout his seven years as governor, beginning in 1911.[36] Buoyed by the overthrow of Boss Cox in Cincinnati, the Concern established the *Denver Express* in 1906 to publicize progressive reforms there.[37] Baldasty's study of pre-1908 Scripps newspapers found them battling against impure food, unfair wages and streetcar fares, corrupt monopolies, private ownership of utilities, and unsafe working conditions.[38] Even UP had the reputation of being much more liberal than AP. Journalism critic Will Irwin in 1914 called UP "our most powerful liberal and radical force" and boldly credited it with helping the rise of a third political party, the Progressive Party, in 1912.[39]

Consisting of twenty-one newspapers, the adless *Day Book* in Chicago, UP (with about 515 clients),[40] and the NEA (with sixty-four clients),[41] the Scripps Concern was poised to play a key part in national politics by 1914. Acting as a unit, the Scripps newspapers now had the ability to effect reforms at the national level, not just the local or state levels.

United Press

The Scripps organ with the widest reach was the United Press Associations (better known as United Press or UP). In 1907 Scripps had pulled UP together from two hodgepodge, regional press associations he operated and one he bought to compete with AP.[42] Initially barely able to survive, by 1914 UP was on a steady upswing under the direction of its thirty-one-year-old president, Roy Howard.

United Press survived by being different. While AP guaranteed its members an exclusive franchise of its wire service in their cities, UP offered its service to any newspaper. This gave many newspapers a fighting chance to compete in the area of worldwide news coverage. United Press, too, was an afternoon and Sunday morning news service (all of the Scripps newspapers were afternoons); Scripps always felt that AP favored the largest morning papers.

In 1909 a third American press association entered the competition. Upset by his lack of control in AP matters, William Randolph Hearst began his International News Service (INS) to compete with UP and AP in the morning and afternoon fields. Smaller than UP or AP, the INS was said to have had about four hundred clients by 1914. Historian Robert Desmond said the INS, though, was not up to par with the others. "Its own news coverage beyond the boundaries of the United States did not become effective until after 1916."[43] Press critic Will Irwin was even blunter in 1914. He said the INS was "mostly of use to Hearst alone. The opinion of news held by the Hearst-trained men is peculiar; their product does not suit the purposes of many editors."[44] With Hearst's deep pockets, though, competition from the INS was a continual concern for the UP.

Hearst helped teach UP a lesson, however. The public linkage of INS to Hearst's politics helped convince Scripps and Howard that UP should distance itself—in public—from the Scripps name as much as possible. As a for-profit company, the UP needed to act as an independent news gatherer as much as possible to satisfy the varied newspapers it served.[45] United Press worked quietly when it came to advancing the progressive policies of the Concern. "Howard has shown marked ability, amounting almost to genius, in co-operation with NEA in the handling of features and problems under the direction of the national policy of our papers," *San Diego Sun* editor W. H. Porterfield observed in 1912.[46]

While the AP was a nonprofit cooperative operated by its members, UP began as a for-profit corporation worth $300,000, with Scripps holding 60 percent of the stock and the rest split three ways among the principal managers.[47] Later, when Howard was promoted from news manager to president and chairman of the board, he controlled 33 percent of the stock, and Scripps's share shrank to 51 percent.

The new UP had fewer than three hundred clients when it formed, but within two years it was able to eliminate the $100,000 in total losses the regional news services suffered before they were combined into UP.[48] United Press made its first profit of $1,200 in 1909 and by that time had grown to serve nearly four hundred clients.[49] According to Howard in

1915, UP had seen profits "steadily and conservatively" improve in the past three years.⁵⁰

Management techniques and news philosophy learned from Scripps were keys to UP's success. To help make a profit, UP tended to pay lower wages than the other news associations. Expense accounts were tightly managed.⁵¹ To help control the cost of the telegraph, which was already handling ten to twelve thousand words per day in UP's early years,⁵² UP initiated a unique mail service called the "Red Letter," which furnished sidebars for upcoming news events to supplement the terse wire reports. Undated new features also were distributed to clients this way.

United Press also used a telephone-based "pony" service, which was used by smaller papers (including most of the Harper Group of the Scripps chain). It was a discount-priced summary of the day's top stories, usually wired to the city and distributed by delivery boy. When possible, UP delivered the pony report by telephone. A report of one to two thousand words could be distributed to ten newspapers in fifteen minutes this way.⁵³ United Press's Indianapolis bureau manager, Kent Cooper, devised the system and duplicated it later for AP.⁵⁴

Full-service clients leased dot-and-dash wires piped to their offices with a Western Union operator stationed in the building. The teleprinter machine, although available in 1912,⁵⁵ was not widely used by UP until 1916.⁵⁶ By the end of 1912, UP operated twenty bureaus in the United States and a total news budget of $165,000.⁵⁷ It had offices in London, Berlin, and Paris, but its overseas coverage was relatively weak compared to that of AP, which received world news under a cartel agreement with the major European news agencies. Each member of the cartel shared news from its exclusive territory with the others.

In 1912 Reuters approached Howard to see if UP would be willing to replace AP under a ten-year contract. The new arrangement would have given UP unparalleled international coverage. A Chicago meeting of Scripps's top men ultimately rejected it. The new arrangement would cost about $35,000 more in cable tolls, and the contract seemed too long. Moreover, dealing with quasi-government agencies such as Reuters in England, Wolff in Germany, and Havas in France invited concerns about censorship.⁵⁸ The cartel was a monopoly, too, which Scripps (who was not at the meeting) despised as a matter of principle.⁵⁹ Because UP would continue to build an international news-gathering network on its own, it would have an advantage during the early portion of the upcoming war years.⁶⁰

Besides keeping budgets at a bare minimum, Howard had his reporters adopt the Scripps news philosophy—write concisely, but make it interesting. Not able to compete story-for-story with AP, Howard instead asked his reporters to concentrate on memorable news features and worry only about the biggest spot news events. "We've got to do things that have never been done before," Howard is quoted as having said. "Get interviews with people in the news. People are usually more interesting than the thing they are doing. Dramatize them."[61]

The conservative AP had adopted a stiff, officious style to prevent members from complaining of bias. United Press decided to play off that by urging reporters to inject their own personalities into their reports. At a newspaper conference at the University of Wisconsin in 1913, Howard explained the UP philosophy in relation to AP's style. Press critic Irwin reported that Howard said, in effect, "I'm sorry, but we haven't succeeded in keeping our bureau colorless and unbiased. We're only human beings, and most of us have pretty strong individualities. We couldn't keep our individualities out of the news, no matter how hard we tried. . . . We make every allowance we can for the other side, and we don't lie or suppress, but there still remains the point of view. Our method is the only way to be honest with the public and ourselves."[62]

It should be noted that Howard's definition of "unbiased" was a bit unclear. It might simply mean a tendency to write in a more feature-oriented style, rather than to push Scripps's policies, which UP recognized would be business suicide. United Press reporters often used the first-person "I" in their reports, adopting a style that today's journalists would associate with column writing.

Like Scripps, Howard hired young men who were eager to prove themselves. Just a high school graduate, Howard was an early supporter of college journalism education and liked to pick the best and brightest from colleges for his ranks. He sent all of the journalism departments in the country copies of the *Hell-Box,* UP's in-house newsletter, to help educate them about UP. "We take a little bit of what we hope is our pardonable pride in the fact that the United Press was the first of the press associations to make a point of seeking out the most promising students in the various colleges of journalism and enlisting them in our ranks," he wrote a professor at the University of Montana in 1915.[63]

As new graduates, the men were motivated, intelligent self-starters who required less salary. Howard never apologized about salaries because he felt working for UP was valuable enough—a young reporter could advance his career faster in UP. For example, UP never hired experienced, high-salaried men for its executive positions but instead promoted from within. It gave its reporters bylines on their stories (something AP would not do) because "United Press has never hesitated to allow one of its men to make himself famous through doing good work for the organization," Howard said.[64]

Howard was making himself famous for the way he ran this upstart press association. Just thirty-one years old in 1914, he represented just how far a young, motivated man could go in the Scripps Concern. He had started as a newspaper reporter in Indianapolis, where he was raised, eventually working for Joseph Pulitzer and the *St. Louis Post-Dispatch*. Howard then worked for Scripps's *Cincinnati Post* and soon was managing the news for the Publisher's Press Association in New York City before it merged into UP.

Armed with confidence and a wonderful charm, Howard was a solid journalist and born salesman when UP needed both. He made numerous friendships with fellow journalists and powerful sources, and was never afraid to act.[65] Even the skeptical Scripps was impressed when he first met Howard in 1908: "He was a striking individual, very small of stature, a large head and speaking countenance, and eyes that appeared to be windows of a rather unusual intellect. His manner was forceful.... There was ambition, self-respect, and forcefulness oozing out of every pore of his body."[66]

Although no book-length biography has been done on Howard, most accounts agree he was a skilled motivator—knowing when to heap scorn or praise on an employee to get the best result. "Candid with others, Howard is no less candid with and about himself," the *Saturday Evening Post* wrote in 1938.[67] With Howard at the helm, UP grew rapidly.

The Newspaper Enterprise Association

The NEA was growing in influence by 1914 as well. In 1902 the NEA was established to provide unique features primarily to Scripps-owned newspapers and the Cloverleaf papers, a midwestern chain of weeklies and small dailies to which Scripps had loaned money.[68] Funded largely by set percentages assessed against newspapers' circulations, the NEA did not begin a concerted marketing campaign to add outside clients (who did not compete with NEA customers) until 1914.[69] To bolster its reach further, NEA in 1915 began offering a condensed version of its service. This version of a "pony service" was described as "one page of news and feature cuts each day, and the price of this service was fixed at $2.50 a week, payable in advance." That price generated a small profit for NEA.[70]

The NEA's main office moved to Cleveland from Chicago in 1915. Cartoons, editorials, sports, photographs, women's page features, and news analyses were its mainstays, all delivered by mail (NEA's product tended to be less time-sensitive because of this). As the opinion-editorial side of the Concern on national affairs, it was a centralized editorial voice for hire and for the Scripps papers. The amount of space devoted to pushing Scripps's progressive "policy"—as it was called—usually was minimized. NEA president Harry Rickey described it this way in 1913: "Out of every 100 minutes N.E.A. will give five minutes to policy matter, and 95 minutes to circulation-making copy for our newspapers."[71]

The NEA collected copies of each Scripps newspaper, and routinely critiqued how editors handled its content, especially major stories.[72] This was a constant source of frustration in the NEA. "In many of the papers our important stuff is mishandled . . . and indicates in many cases, that the editor himself pays very little or no attention to the N.E.A.," Rickey said in 1913, as he was about to turn control over to Byron H. Canfield, one of the West Coast editors.[73]

The debate led Rickey and especially his successor, Canfield, to continually push for "Must Copy" power so the NEA could direct news coverage. With "Must Copy" authority, the NEA, as dictator, could require each Scripps editor to run a particular editorial or news story. No consensus was reached in the prewar years, and this sore spot remained. "There is one thing we should guard against and that is any tendency along the big boss idea that will tend to suppress the individuality of our editors . . . either through 'must' editorials or through the editors in chief," Cochran said at an NEA trustees meeting in January 1913.[74] In form and function, the NEA was the editorial coordinator of the Scripps newspapers. It helped Scripps newspapers troubleshoot weak spots and served as a clearinghouse for ideas used successfully at other Scripps papers.

It is difficult to generalize about the news content the NEA generated; it changed regularly. Serialized features and cartoons provided predictable content for clients. The NEA had a small staff at its headquarters and at its San Francisco and Washington, DC, branches, but it utilized a long list of freelance contributors as needed. The *Cleveland Press* of June 27, 1914, for example, featured a signed opinion-editorial piece by Louis D. Brandeis about the "curse of bigness" in business.[75] Unsigned editorials were written by the general manager, Paine, or by an irregular rotation of other editors and executives in the Concern.

The NEA's management of news content worked. Scripps boasted to secretary of state Franklin Lane in November 1915 that his newspapers had a circulation of a million readers daily. With the non-Scripps NEA clients added in, that circulation reached three million. Finally, Scripps, claimed, UP had a circulation that reached one-fourth to one-third of all the people in the country.[76]

"Young Men of Force"

In 1914 Scripps was entering his twilight years. He claimed he retired in 1908 and retreated to his sprawling ranch in Miramar, California. But he maintained close contact on major editorial decisions. He hired like-minded men, who hired other like-minded men, and he still had trusted lieutenants on the job who had worked for him for years. The most important men influencing overall news content included, in addition to Rickey, who was a Scripps employee for twenty years, a former editor of the *Cleveland Press*, a former president and general manager of the NEA, and in 1914 a roving consultant asked to plug editorial holes in the Concern. Paine, whose namesake was Scripps's youngest son, Robert, was semiretired in San Diego, but still writing many of the NEA's editorials. Neg Cochran, editor of Scripps's experimental newspaper—the adless *Day Book* in Chicago—as well as the *Toledo News-Bee*, helped Scripps troubleshoot news problems inside the NEA and the newspapers. Canfield, who had cut his teeth editing the Concern's northwestern papers and had become a favorite of Scripps's son Jim, was now the president and general manager of the NEA—the de facto top editorial job in the Concern. Canfield was among the top leaders of a younger group of editors and executives who had strong allegiance to Jim, in particular, as the next generation of management in the Concern.

Finding the true source of power in the Concern can be confusing, however. If one equates power with stockholdings, it is relatively easy. Scripps's typical strategy to start a newspaper was to finance 51 percent himself and leave the remainder to other relatives (such as his sister Ellen Browning Scripps, who was the second largest stockholder) or other business associates (such as the Concern's longtime general counsel, Harper) or the newspaper's editor (to give him a stake in the newspaper's success). Scripps made millions for his associates this way. With Scripps's backing, Harper, for example, was able to become a large minority holder in what became known as the "Harper Group," a group of six newspapers in Texas, Indiana, Tennessee, and Colorado. Thus, although various people held large sums of stocks in the Concern, Scripps kept control either through stockholdings or loans.

An aging E.W., however, could not manage daily editorial decisions for so many newspapers. Besides the influence of centralized content through the NEA, the Scripps Concern was managed through a series of experienced "editors-in-chief" who supervised the editors of several newspapers in a group. Coordination among the stockholders and the editors-in-chief came through annual "editorial conferences," where general policies about editorial coverage were voted up or down by roll call. For example, Alfred Andersson (*Dallas Dispatch, Houston Press, Denver Express,* and *Memphis Press*), and F. R. Peters (*Terre Haute Post* and *Evansville Press*) were editors-in-chief of the Harper Group in 1914, while Harper and Scripps controlled the money behind this group of newspapers.

By 1914, the Scripps Concern consisted of three general groups, as one historian noted, defined by each group's stockholders.[77] The Scripps-McRae Group included the *Cleveland Press, Cincinnati Post, Akron Press, Toledo News-Bee, Columbus Citizen, Des Moines News,* and *Oklahoma News.* The West Coast Group consisted of the *San Diego Sun, Los Angeles Record, San Francisco News, Sacramento Star, Spokane Press, Tacoma Times, Portland News,* and *Seattle Star.* The Harper Group was the *Evansville Press, Terre Haute Post, Denver Express, Dallas Dispatch, Memphis Press,* and *Houston Press.*

The Scripps Concern, of course, was more than just its top management and stockholders. From the beginning, Scripps liked to hire young, largely untested, mostly inexperienced young men to edit his newspapers and write his news stories. "I have been more or less successful as a character reader," he wrote to friend Max Eastman in 1915. "I have sought to find young men of force, good health, and industry . . . and then left the job to make the man."[78]

Always wary of men who could not think practically, Scripps encouraged his editors to avoid college-trained men and to hire instead those from the lower classes because they understood the Scripps reader better and could be hired cheaply. He also doubted the usefulness of formal journalism training. "It is absolutely impossible for one writer to teach another writer how to be a writer," he wrote.[79]

Increasingly, however, college-trained men were being hired throughout the Concern. Andersson said the job of a reporter was becoming too complicated for someone with a "slight education." Andersson believed the typical reporter from a midwestern university was "not a snob nor an aristocrat, but a humble being willing to start at the low pay suitable to a beginner knowing that eventually his education will advance him rapidly."[80]

The size of the Concern meant that each editor-in-chief, in particular, had considerable daily control over whom he hired and fired, and how his newspapers covered the day's news. Much of the content of a Scripps newspaper was supplied by a centralized force (the NEA and UP), but it was up to each newspaper's editor—under the watchful eye of the editor-in-chief—to decide where each story was played or if it was used at all. For example, in 1916 E. W. Scripps asked the NEA to send him copies of income tax publicity articles he could not see because Porterfield, the editor of the *San Diego Sun* (the closest Scripps paper to Scripps's home) was not running each installment. As this study will show, these income tax stories had been written under an edict from Scripps, but Porterfield still had enough freedom to select what he ran in the *Sun*.[81] Whether it was a matter of individual tastes of editors, varying sizes of Scripps's newspapers, or the editor's reaction to local conditions, the Scripps newspapers differed on how they displayed and edited the day's news. It was demanded, however, that from a policy standpoint, each remain consistent with the Concern's overall policies, usually hammered out at editorial conferences. If a local editor did not agree with a Scripps policy or thought it was suicide to support it in his community, the conventional wisdom was to avoid the issue in his newspaper or remain neutral, but never to contradict.[82]

By June 1914 E.W. believed only his sons could be trusted to carry forward his legacy of social justice; they needed to run the chain after his death. For ten years he had been struggling to find the best way to divide the responsibility of managing the Concern among his three young sons[83]—James "Jim" George, John Paul, and Robert "Bob" Paine. John P., twenty-five, who had been editor-in-chief of the Ohio Group of newspapers and was being groomed for a new job of overall editorial chief, died after an extended illness in April 1914. With John's death, ultimate editorial control fell squarely to Jim—Scripps's oldest son—because Scripps had signed the power of attorney over the Concern's affairs to him. Jim, twenty-seven years old in 1914, had started in the Concern's business office and had taken responsibility for financial operations in 1908 after E.W. retired. To his father's disappointment, however, Jim seemed more interested in making profits than fighting any progressive battles to reform society.

Eighteen-year-old Bob was the enigma of the family. He preferred to write poetry rather than editorials and was not sure what place he wanted. Although it is difficult to document, some surviving correspondence suggests that Bob suffered from a drinking problem; at least, his father expressed concern about how much Bob drank at times.[84] How much this may have affected his performance or willingness to take on the stresses of his father's business is uncertain. He worked briefly for various Scripps newspapers, but in 1914 was adrift in life and inexperienced in the newspaper business. He moved around in California in various odd jobs trying to find his life's direction.[85] By 1916 he was in Hawaii and Australia doing some writing in and out of journalism. Both of Scripps's surviving sons would play key roles in coming years and would be the source of family tension that would force a corporate split in the Concern in the early 1920s.

Wilson, the Icicle

"Youth, in its period of struggle, is radical and near to the people; maturity and age are conservative and apart from the people." That is how press critic Irwin described UP in relation to AP in 1914.[86] The same could be said about the entire Scripps Concern. By 1912 the Concern was hoping to make its mark on the national stage, and no one was more eager than Scripps himself.

After he retired in 1908, Scripps's attention turned increasingly to national politics, perhaps as a way to keep busy and to help ensure his legacy. During his first few months in retirement he worked with muckraker Lincoln Steffens to try to set up at his ranch a "Cave of Abdullam"—a summit made up of the finest minds in progressivism. The summit's proposals would be championed in the Scripps newspapers. Unable to get it arranged, Scripps settled for private meetings with many top progressives over the ensuing years.[87]

The time seemed right for political and economic change at a national level, and the Concern seemed poised for a role in shaping it. Many progressive ideas could become reality if the federal government became more involved, it was believed. The UP was growing in clients and respect. The NEA, under the management of Canfield, was looking to expand its reach beyond Scripps-controlled newspapers. The Concern was one of the first news organizations with a national reach.

By 1914 the country's mindset was increasingly accepting of national progressive reforms long extolled by Scripps and his newspapers at the state and local level. Woodrow Wilson, a progressive Democrat, was president and had shown great promise during his first year in office; he had won over hopeful progressives with his "New Freedom" initiatives. By the end of 1913 he had won approval of the Underwood Bill, which lowered tariffs for the first time since the Civil War and implemented the first graduated income tax. Banking reform was achieved with the passage of the Federal Reserve bill in December 1913. He signed into law antitrust reform—exemplified in the Clayton Anti-trust Act—in 1914. It exempted unions from antitrust actions, a victory for labor. The Federal

Trade Commission (FTC), intended to regulate unfair business practices was approved in September 1914.[88]

The Concern's support for Wilson took time to build. He was no higher than second choice for most of the Scripps editors during the 1912 election.[89] Venturing into national politics was still relatively new for the Concern. Before the 1912 election it had avoided supporting any presidential candidate too vigorously. Harper wrote that the Scripps strategy in the four previous presidential elections was to "print the news, give the arguments on both sides and especially to report the attitude of the candidates and their backers and the developments of the campaign bearing upon our policies, *but not to become the partisan advocate of any candidate.*"[90] The 1912 election provided the first real debate over what role the growing Concern should take in national politics.

Wisconsin progressive Robert LaFollette had been the first choice of E.W. and his editors in 1912. Scripps even sent his chief political writer, Gardner, to help LaFollette get his campaign organized as a third party movement. An apparent emotional breakdown ruined LaFollette's chances, however, and allowed Theodore Roosevelt to become the candidate for the Progressive or "Bull Moose" Party.

Roosevelt was an object of love and hate for the Concern. His public style and personality made great newspaper copy, but he also was seen as a political opportunist. Since he had left the presidency in 1909, Roosevelt had tried to reach out to conservatives of the Republican Party to regain that party's nomination and also had refused to condemn conservative William H. Taft, who succeeded him. In most of the Concern's eyes, Roosevelt was not a true progressive: he was just trying to get elected by playing both political ends against the middle. "You will see our cause betrayed by Roosevelt as it has been every time the pinch came on Roosevelt," Paine predicted.[91]

On July 6, the NEA trustees unanimously decided to support Wilson in the election, but that support would not come until September 1.[92] Many of the Scripps Concern's editors thought Wilson was too aloof and too academic to lead a national reform movement. John Scripps called Wilson "pretty much of an icicle to cuddle up to."[93] E.W. just wanted a man to run a true democracy. "The man I want to support as a candidate for the presidency, is someone . . . who wants to be led by, and ruled by, the people."[94]

At the July conference, the NEA trustees decided to treat the third party movement favorably in state and local races. When the national Bull Moose platform was finished a month later and reflected many of the

Scripps ideals, it proved too much for some editors to ignore. "It seems that the Scripps Newspapers will have to recognize the Progressive Party . . . and get back of it to continue their policies and propaganda," editor W. C. Mayborn wrote to his boss, Harper, in August.[95] Harper then ordered his editors-in-chief to print the Progressive Party platform in full in the Harper newspapers.[96]

The July decision to back Wilson stood, however, because the Roosevelt-led Progressive Party still made the Concern's top men nervous. "Personally, I think Wilson is just as good a man today as he was when we supported him for the nomination," NEA president and general manager Rickey wrote August 30, "and in view of all the circumstances surrounding the Bull Moose movement, I can see no good reason why we should change fronts and support Roosevelt." Rickey said he would deal with the disagreement by deemphasizing politics in the NEA during the campaign. "I believe that the NEA can best serve the Scripps papers . . . by giving them a lot of interesting human interest stuff, humor, etc., with such politics as is interesting for other reasons than that it is political."

The end result was a confused, uncoordinated effort by the Scripps newspapers in 1912. Years later, E.W. would say Wilson could not have won in 1912 if the Concern had not supported him, but the claim was based more on wishful thinking than reality.

Crossroads

In June 1914, the Scripps Concern was entering a critical period in the development of its business operations and its political ideals. It was growing to a point where it would soon be considered both a part of the establishment and a critic of it. Scripps longed for his newspapers to do their part in supporting the national progressive agenda. The NEA and UP were adding non-Scripps clients, and any reforms they wanted to push would have to be sold to other editors.

The elder Scripps had long advocated public service over profits, but his immediate heir, Jim, was more interested in earning profits than reforming society. He delegated most of the editorial decisions to the head of the NEA and the editors-in-chief, who in many cases agreed with him. E.W.'s other surviving son, Bob, a poet, showed more concern for people than numbers and was more malleable to his father's wishes, but he seemed to lack the dedication and focus the job required. Jim, too, already was boss of both the editorial and business sides of the Concern, so what was left for Bob remained dubious.

In 1914 the Scripps Concern supported Wilson's presidency, but the president's long-term commitment to progressive ideas was still unproven. E. W. Scripps felt his Concern was ready to take its place on the national political stage, and on June 27, 1914, the opportunity to make a national impact was ripening as never before. Basic ideals the Concern had espoused for years—tolerating no special privileges for the wealthy, advocating democratic decision making, and using government intervention to control business activities—were about to become national and international issues. The Concern was ready to play its part.

2 Seeds Get Planted: June 1914 to May 1915

E. W. Scripps often used a metaphor of planting seeds to describe the impact his newspapers had on shaping public opinion. Public acceptance of new ideas takes time, he explained in a 1914 letter: "When I have planted a dollar's worth of effort to my newspapers, with a view of gathering the harvest from 10 to 20 years thereafter, I have gotten a yield of one-hundred fold. When I have planted a dollar's worth . . . with a view of plucking the harvest in a few months, I have seldom gained more than a bare twenty-five percent."[1]

In June 1914 Scripps was about to plant his biggest seed of all—offering President Woodrow Wilson the help of his newspaper chain. Scripps hoped a harvest of societal reforms would result from such an alliance. He had never been so willing to tie his newspapers to one national politician, but Wilson was proving himself to be a good progressive, and this looked like an excellent opportunity for the Scripps chain to exert influence nationally.

Scripps could not know that a world war would soon emerge to consume any chance of the bountiful harvest he hoped for. The seed of national progressive reform that Scripps intended to plant would become entangled with the unprecedented demands for covering the war. Of all the main factors that shaped the Concern during the years of the Great War, virtually all emerged quickly—before mid-1915: the Scripps Concern's allegiance to Wilson, its use of the war to build its reputation, its dealings with censors, its promotion of high-profile correspondents, its commitment to neutrality in how it presented the war, its internal battles over centralized control of editorial policy, its concerns with costs and competition, and its use of editorial campaigns to advocate its policies. These were seeds that would reshape the Concern itself. The metaphorical harvest to be reaped would have more effect on the Concern than on progressive reform.

A New Seed in an Old Haunt

Scripps was in Washington, D.C., when Serbian nationalist Gavrilo Princip killed Archduke Franz Ferdinand, heir to the Austro-Hungarian throne, and his wife, the former Countess Sophie Chotek, during the royal couple's visit to Sarajevo. Austria had officially annexed Bosnia and Herzegovina, of which Sarajevo was the principal city, in 1908, angering neighboring Serbia.[2] The assassination was the product of long-simmering hate in the Balkans.

It was June 28, 1914. While the greatest war in world history—one that would eventually topple or seriously weaken several European empires—was about to start, Scripps was on his first trip to Ohio and Washington, D.C., in ten years. The Balkans seemed far away; the popularity of the Democratic president was at the top of Scripps's agenda.[3] He intended to use this trip to solidify his own empire with the help of President Woodrow Wilson.

Scripps was particularly interested in talking with William Jennings Bryan, an old acquaintance and an occasional visitor to Miramar. "The Commoner" personified the populist spirit Scripps believed in and now, as secretary of state, held a prominent position in the Wilson administration. Scripps visited Bryan in Washington on June 27. "I had told him that it was bad for the administration, and hence bad for the country at large, that the great mass of the people (whose interests required that they should thoroughly understand the President) were kept in entire ignorance of the human and humane side of the President," Scripps wrote to his half-sister Ellen later.

Bryan agreed that Wilson needed help in publicizing his personality and achievements, and asked Scripps for suggestions. Scripps wrote to Ellen, "I immediately replied that to the present Cabinet should be added a secretary of the people—a skillful journalist who, being entirely in the confidence of not only the President, but of his Cabinet, would have imposed upon him the duty and the right to stand between the administration and the press, and who could make use of both the journalistic enemies and the journalistic friends of the administration."[4]

Bryan asked Scripps if the two could discuss the matter further later, and the two parted. "With Bryan, I finished up the business of seeing all the men I wanted to see while in Washington," Scripps said later. Ever a solitary, introspective man, Scripps was content to let the secretary of the people proposal rest for now; he had done his part to plant the seed of an idea. Gilson Gardner, the NEA's chief political writer and one of Scripps's inner circle of advisors, had other plans, however. On June 30, Gardner asked former NEA staff writer Oliver Newman to meet with Scripps. Newman had covered Wilson during the 1912 election, and Wilson later appointed Newman a commissioner to the District of Columbia. "I told [Newman] that I had nothing to say to the President that he or any one else could not say for me," Scripps said.[5]

Scripps was not the first journalist to urge Wilson to overhaul his public image and aloof attitude. Charles Thompson of the *New York Times*, Don Martin of the *New York Herald*, and James Doyle of the *New York Press* had met with Wilson during the 1912 campaign to help him understand the importance of better relations with the newspapers. Wilson declined their advice because he said he could not remake himself into something he was not.[6]

Wilson understood the news media's role in shaping public opinion and was the first president to institute regular news conferences.[7] A Jeffersonian, Wilson knew open government was important, but he could not tolerate trivial questions by reporters who did not seem to be particularly bright.[8]

In June 1914, however, Gardner refused to allow Scripps to abandon the publicity idea. He arranged for Scripps to meet Franklin Lane, secretary of the interior.[9] For an hour and a half, Gardner, Lane, and Scripps discussed the role the Scripps newspapers could play. "We were all engaged on this subject of publicity department by which, of course, we meant the use of the Scripps Institution by the administration for the purpose of publicity," Scripps told Ellen.[10] Initially timid about meeting the president, Scripps finally agreed after he got a personal call on July 1 from Joseph Tumulty, Wilson's personal secretary.

Gardner drove Scripps to the White House, where he was shown to the president's office. "For the first time in my life, I believe, I was stumped and embarrassed, and sat like a ninny for a moment or two until the President started to talk; but we were only a minute getting to the subject that I knew he wanted to talk to me about [the secretary of the people]." Wilson said he was handicapped because the public distrusted his background as a college president and was, according to Scripps, "quite enthusiastic on the subject of a journalistic representative."[11]

Why Wilson was more willing to listen to Scripps than the three New York reporters in 1912 is open to interpretation. Perhaps the power of Scripps's Concern gave Wilson hope he could reach the people and have to deal with only one powerful, trustworthy press ally. According to historians John Tebbel and Sarah Miles Watts, who have used neurologist Edwin Weinstein's medical and psychological study of Wilson, he apparently had personality changes and had up-and-down relationships with the press during his two terms.[12]

Wilson looked fine to Scripps on that summer day in the White House. "Physically he seems to be well set up and almost stocky. His hand is full and warm, and his hand pressure, if not vigorous, is at least strong enough." Scripps told Wilson that his administration was so superior to the previous one that the people ought to know more about him, even his frailties, so they would "perhaps love him." "I went a little further even and, perhaps carried by an enthusiasm born only of 'the presence,' I said 'probably no more worthy man since Lincoln has been in your seat. Perhaps Lincoln's greatest good fortune was that those around him were successful in making him known to the public more as the human being than as a superman.' On this occasion also, the President grinned delightedly."[13] Tumulty wrote Roy Howard on July 7 that the president had enjoyed the meeting.[14]

Scripps and his wife, Nackie, soon left Washington, traveled to Cleveland, and vacationed briefly at Niagara Falls, New York. Meanwhile, vacation was the last thing on the minds of the men of the Scripps Concern in the summer of 1914. They had an international incident to cover.

The Challenge of Covering a War

The war presented the Concern with the opportunity to prove to readers that it was among the elite worldwide news organization. News of the Saturday assassination of Archduke Ferdinand and his wife first reached the pages of Scripps's newspapers on Monday, June 29. The difference in time zones, the lack of full Sunday service by UP, and the lack of Scripps newspapers printing Sunday editions ensured that.

The surviving records of the Concern, and UP in particular, reveal nothing about how this event that would trigger the Great War was covered logistically. The front-page coverage in the *Cleveland Press*, the Concern's flagship newspaper, carried a Vienna dateline, did not have reporters' bylines, and was attributed generally to "The United Press." United Press made a good journalistic showing; the coverage was comprehensive and used the Scripps human-interest writing style to good effect. First, a collage of pictures showed members of the Austrian Royal Family, and a small drawing re-created the assassination. The artwork was accompanied by four lengthy stories. One put the Archduke's role in context, calling him "the real big man of the Austrian Empire."[15] Another story predicted "the map of Europe may be altered," and "the Austro-Hungarian empire today faces danger of dissolution. Possibility of a war by Austria upon Servia [sic], that would make the whole Balkan region red with carnage, is looming strong."

A third front-page sidebar story described the death scene in detail, milking the tragic drama of a royal couple dying together: "Immediately [the assassin's] second shot lodged in the archduke's throat, severing the jugular vein. Herself almost unconscious, the duchess by superhuman endeavor, raised the dying body of her royal husband in her arms."[16]

The oddity and irony of the assassination was reported in the fourth front-page article; this story recounted the assassination as the eighth tragedy during the reign of the Austro-Hungarian emperor Franz Josef I. It suggested a possible reason for the string of bad luck: a curse by a mother whose son was executed after a failed revolt in 1848.[17]

Curse or no curse, the Scripps editors at this time saw the assassination as a major event, but one confined to one region of the world. The diplomatic storm brewing in the Balkans was not UP's kind of international story. It tended to cover international stories that had broader human-interest appeal—not economic and political news stories from distant countries.[18]

Old penny press biases in favor of sensational stories seemed to cloud the Concern's judgment early on. In the days after the assassination, UP's domestic coverage concentrated on the mysterious fatal shooting of a wealthy woman in the office of Dr. Edwin Carman in a New York suburb.[19] Foreign coverage was focused on the murder trial dubbed "Paris'[s] most dramatic trial in years," in which Madame Henriette Caillaux, the wife of a former French premier, was being tried for shooting a Paris newspaper editor who printed some of her love letters.[20]

Stories about the archduke's assassination faded fast. The *Cleveland Press*, for example, on July 1 carried only a page 2 UP story about riots in Sarajevo after the assassination.[21] The next story, on the front page, appeared three weeks later when Austria issued Serbia an ultimatum.[22]

Throughout July, UP's bureau chief in Paris, William Philip Simms, repeatedly tried to warn his colleagues about the series of diplomatic breakdowns that was escalating into a major war. In late July, however, a telegram from cable editor Fred S. Ferguson ordered Simms not to worry about the war and to concentrate on the Caillaux trial.[23]

By July 27, as the European nations began to get ready to mobilize their armies, Ferguson and the rest of UP had changed their point of view, and the war was seen as a great story. The *Cleveland Press*, in a short front-page article titled "The United Press and the War," announced its pledge to cover the conflict in Europe extensively: "The developments of the great war now looming in Europe will be covered day to day and hour to hour by the United Press, whose telegraph and cable dispatches are printed in Cleveland exclusively by *The Press*. . . . Last Friday the United Press told of the terrible conflict that threatened in Europe, when other press services were carrying inspired denials."[24]

The UP historian Joe Alex Morris called the first months of World War I "of great importance to the development of the United Press."[25] Less than a decade old, UP was still an experiment in many respects; many were unsure if any organization could profitably compete with the AP. According to Morris, early success in scooping the behemoth AP on key war stories cemented UP pride and convinced staffers they could beat AP on a worldwide, developing story. Success also gave UP a needed financial boost by increasing the ranks of UP client newspapers, adding 103 clients in 1914 alone.[26]

Associated Press was weakened in the early weeks of European war because it was part of an international cartel for world news that broke down when the war began. United Press had always relied on independent arrangements to get news out of Vienna and Berlin, and was well positioned to get timely news out of those capitals, in particular, when the shooting began.

Even when news releases were given to all wire services at the same time, UP was faster than AP or the INS. On August 5, UP could boast that it had beaten its competition by six and half hours on word of the declaration of war between France and Germany, by two hours and fifty minutes on the declaration of war between Germany and Belgium, and one hour and fourteen minutes on the declaration of war between England and Germany.[27]

Censorship

United Press credited its European general manager, forty-four-year old Ed Keen, with the scoops. Based in UP's London office, Keen was adept at getting information quickly to his colleagues in New York City. Like his competitors at AP and INS, however, Keen usually was only as fast as the British would allow him to be, particularly for news out of Austria and Germany. The British had cut Germany's five transatlantic cables on

August 5, its first act of war against the invader of Belgium; thus Keen had to relay any news dispatches from Berlin or Vienna through London.[28]

Keen used neutral Holland as his base for getting news out of the European continent to London. A UP bureau was set up in The Hague, where news from Germany and Austria could be sent to him for relay to New York. By the end of September, however, as Howard reported in the trade magazine *Editor and Publisher and Journalist*, the British were opening mail coming to London from Holland. "Some of the censored letters are delivered and some are not," Howard said about the British censors. "In consequence, despite the best efforts and most ingenious schemes of American newspaper men, the cable news reaching America is filtered through anti-German channels." Howard said the only way to get German news untouched by British censors was to use the "limited wireless dispatches" and "courier by the Holland-America ships."[29] Still, with Guglielmo Marconi's wireless unreliable and oceangoing mail service slow, the United Press and the rest of the American press had to rely on the British telegraph monopoly and British military censors to get their dispatches to newspapers in the United States.[30]

United Press dispatches, like all cabled newspaper reports, faced government censorship at least twice: by the country in which the story originated, and then by the British. In October the *Editor and Publisher and Journalist* said that American newspapers and press agencies "had found it impossible to get through the London censorship any German news. The suppression of German news was not confined to news of military activities, but covered every sort of news bearing in any way on German conditions."[31] In August, on Howard's behalf, secretary of state Bryan asked the German government to give UP greater freedom.[32]

Complaints about censorship reached a boiling point in October. *New York World* publisher Joseph Pulitzer II filed a protest with the British about the arbitrary censorship, and Howard met with British premier Herbert Asquith to complain.[33] For a short time, censorship restrictions relaxed, and UP was the first to benefit. The British censors allowed a story written by Berlin bureau chief Karl Von Wiegand about German-Russian fighting in Poland to be transmitted to America with no changes. The first-person report, written "in the glare of a screened auto headlight, several hundred yards back from the German trenches," was front-page news and a huge scoop for the young UP:

> Today I saw a wave of Russian flesh and blood dash against a wall of German steel. The wall stood. The wave broke—was shattered and hurled back. . . .

Tonight I know why correspondents are not wanted on any of the battle lines. Descriptions of battles fought in the year of our Lord 1914 don't make nice reading.[34]

The *Editor and Publisher and Journalist* said "Von Wiegand's story is the first by an American newspaper man to carry any details of man to man fighting between opposing infantry divisions."

Writers and Style

From the beginning, the journalists of the Concern wrote about the war in such a way as to make it interesting and easy to understand. Reporters were given bylines for the bigger stories to personalize the reporting even more. Because of Howard's foresight and a bit of luck, UP had the staff needed to respond to the war raging in the Balkans, Belgium, France, and Poland. By sheer coincidence, he had been in Europe before the war and had finalized plans for how to respond to emergencies. Keen had the immediate ability to hire extra staff for the London, Paris, and Berlin bureaus as he saw fit.[35] Under Howard's plan, UP had agreements with reporters in Europe to work when needed. Thus, within two weeks, experienced foreign correspondents such as Warrington Dawson joined the Paris bureau, and William Slater joined the London staff. C. Bryk took charge of covering Vienna, and W. F. Harper covered St. Petersburg. Percy J. Sarl of the London bureau covered the British Navy.[36]

United Press's speed in relaying war news got the attention of American editors, and—with tragedy and drama unfolding in Europe—the Scripps type of story with human-interest appeal was particularly sought after. In addition, the European war each day was filled with complicated military and diplomatic developments. News reports contained many familiar and unfamiliar foreign names and places. The Scripps-trained writers explained the situation as simply as possible and related the war to everyday Americans. While UP's European bureaus scrambled to relay spot news stories, former UP European general manager J. W. T. Mason, now in New York, wrote a regular column in which he summarized the week's war news and put developments in perspective.[37] Mason was uniquely qualified because he had led UP's European coverage for five years.[38]

In the public's eyes, however, the "stars" of the early months of war for UP were foreign correspondents Von Wiegand, the Berlin bureau chief; William Philip Simms, the Paris bureau chief; and William Shepherd, UP's globetrotting reporter, who had arrived in London from Mexico shortly after war was declared. All three became prominent because UP distributed its stories with the reporters' bylines and photographs to run alongside UP dispatches.

Simms

Simms reported that his stories from France were stifled by "the curtain of complete censorship." Caveats in his stories, such as "It is believed certain here" and "It is acknowledged that," reveal how tentative and uncertain he was of the information he had.[39] He was more confident and dramatic in reporting what he could see in Paris: "Joy at the war was overshadowed today by the tragedies of farewells as women saw their loved ones depart for the front," he reported on August 3. "Not an auto bus remains in service. All have been transformed into army supply wagons. Paris, therefore, walks—but cheerfully."[40]

In September, Simms and *New York Times* correspondent Wythe Williams were given a military pass and a car to go the scene of what would become known as the First Battle of the Marne. Simms's reporting of the battle scene, under the yoke of French censorship, was obviously pro-French. "There is no doubt that the Kaiser's offense is broken," he reported on September 14. "I can state that the French army organization is working everywhere with almost incredible smoothness." He complimented the French commissary as "simply wonderful" and said the French army was much more unified than the German soldiers.[41]

Simms's praise of the French military did not get him any special favors, however. He and Williams were accused of spying because German artillery seemed unusually accurate when the two reporters were around; the French assumed the two were signaling the Germans. They were arrested in Soissons, sent back to Paris, and released.[42] The French did not allow any reporters from neutral countries to go to the front again until late in the fall. All was forgotten, however, when Simms was named by the French government in November as the pool representative of all American newspapers at the front.[43] Historian Morris credited Simms with convincing the French to allow front-line press visits again by showing them the positive newspaper coverage being given to the other belligerents.[44]

Von Wiegand

Indeed, Von Wiegand, behind German lines, was showing how a neutral reporter could create some positive publicity, if the reporter got some access. A journalist for fourteen years, he had worked for William Randolph Hearst and AP in California before joining UP.[45] Born in Phoenix, Arizona, the thirty-eight-year old Von Wiegand, who had lived in Berlin since 1911, as the *Editor and Publisher and Journalist* explained, was "not a native of Germany, as one might conclude from his name." Described as "tactful and diplomatic," he was fluent in German, which put him at a distinct advantage over reporters who relied on translators or their own language skills.[46] Accompanied by three German officers, Von Wiegand left Berlin soon after war was declared and visited the Western and Eastern Fronts, trying to convince the Germans to allow him to release details to the UP bureau in The Hague. His stories sometimes were sent via ship or wireless from Holland to avoid British censorship.

In his first big scoop behind German lines, Von Wiegand filed a story from Aix-la-Chappelle about the German offensive. The story was sent from Rotterdam via ship to New York.[47] He wrote the story on August 29, but it did not appear in the *Cleveland Press* until September 8. "It [the German army] is moving with relentless swiftness, hammering, hammering at every point. It is driving the Allied armies south and west toward Paris," he wrote in a vivid account.

Von Wiegand then went to Holland, filing over the British cable what UP promoted as the first complete report about conditions inside Germany. United Press noted in its coverage that British censors held the report for two days.[48] "Germany is meeting the problems of the war quietly and with determination," he wrote, and called many stories regarding Germany "absolutely false." For example, Von Wiegand wrote that, contrary to rumors, German socialists were not demonstrating against the war, and the American ambassador was not celebrating German victories. He did note he had been arrested after being mistaken for a British spy during an anti-British demonstration in Berlin, but had soon been released.

From The Hague, Von Wiegand again moved closer to the fighting. In early September he visited Belgian forts at Liege after they were taken. His story, again delayed by the British, painted a grim picture: "Part of the broken bodies of the gallant defenders were recovered and buried, but others cannot be reached and lie, decomposing, pinned down by the twisted steel and broken concrete blocks."[49]

United Press did what it could to get Von Wiegand's reports from behind the German lines. On September 19 he reported that the Berlin war office was claiming that Beaumont, near Alsace-Lorraine, had fallen to the Germans. To bypass the British, his story was sent via Marconi wireless.[50] Mail by ship remained the most practical way to bypass the

British, though. A personal column by Von Wiegand, in which he reflected on the death scene at Liege, was shipped to New York from Rotterdam. "It was here that these men went down like grass before the scythe," he wrote. "The Germans had come on—nothing could stop them—they seemed to go to their death gladly, as one Belgian remarked to me."[51]

Von Wiegand's stories were among the firsthand reports reaching the United States without British interference. United Press was doing what it could to provide balanced coverage of the war. "Until the present British censorship is altered, it will be impossible for Americans to form an unbiased opinion or judge fairly from cable reports of the day-by-day developments in the present war," Howard said in a UP story on September 25. "The press censorship in London is at variance with all British ideas of fair play."[52]

United Press and Von Wiegand did benefit from the censorship in England, however, because it kept other news services from matching any reports they could get past it. As historian Alex Morris wrote, "almost overnight, Von Wiegand had made a world-wide reputation as a war correspondent."[53]

Shepherd

William G. Shepherd was the most well-known UP correspondent before the war, and he was the first correspondent Howard sent overseas to augment the European bureaus.[54] He first made his mark as a journalist when he wrote an eyewitness description of the Triangle Waist Company fire for UP in New York in March 1911. He then made his mark in foreign reporting, covering the Mexican revolution in 1911 and various stories in Europe after the 1912 Olympics.[55]

Howard sent him to London in August. He soon became acquainted with the first lord of the admiralty, Winston Churchill. "During the many visits I paid to the dusty and historic old Admiralty Building and the several conferences I had with Churchill in his private office, I began to feel at home in Admiralty surroundings," Shepherd recounted later in his 1917 memoir of the early war years.[56] Churchill eventually allowed Shepherd to interview him on the record—the first time, according to UP, that Churchill had been interviewed since he entered the British cabinet in 1910.[57] The Churchill interview was front-page news worldwide.

A former war correspondent, Churchill understood that newspaper coverage could help to get sympathy from the neutral United States. "We are at grips with Prussian militarism," Churchill was quoted, comparing the situation in Germany to the militarism of Napoleon. "If Germany wins, it will not be a victory of the quiet, sober commercial elements in Germany, nor of the common people of Germany, with all their virtues, but the victory of the blood and iron military school whose doctrines and principles will then have received a supreme and terrible vindication," Churchill said in Shepherd's scoop.[58]

Before the British would allow the story to be cabled to New York, Shepherd had to show it to Churchill for his approval. The delay helped UP. In the time it took Shepherd to write the story, Churchill had learned about the burning of Louvain, a medieval city known for its university and library of books from the Middle Ages.[59] He gave the information to Shepherd, another huge exclusive that ran the same day as the Churchill interview. "The destruction of this ancient city was an unpardonable act of barbarism and vandalism," a separate UP sidebar story quoted Asquith as saying. "It was a deliberate act in complete violation of the law of nations."[60]

World opinion saw the burning of Louvain as "the gesture of a barbarian," according to historian Barbara Tuchman.[61] The incident helped turn world opinion against the Germans.

Shepherd also filed human-interest articles written in the simple, direct, and dramatic Scripps writing style. These less time-sensitive feature stories often were mailed to avoid expensive cable charges. "English coolness does not fool you. I'm writing this just one hour after the news has come to England that 2,000 of her soldiers have fallen today. . . . The horror of war is on hand, and it falls on you and almost overwhelms you," he wrote August 25.[62]

Shepherd served for the next year and a half in Europe as UP's roving correspondent. From Ostend, Belgium, Shepherd wrote for the first time about "the Zeppelin chill" and how the Germans were using airships to bomb enemy targets. "Little children and mothers will say their prayers in Ostend tonight and then be awake, for Ostend lies this night helpless."[63]

Shepherd admitted in his 1917 memoir that his stories favored the Allies: "The censor's big blue pencil will, in time, bring every war reporter to repentance. If he doesn't, then his career as a war reporter is irrevocably ended and he'll probably go back home. You can't be a war reporter . . . and not be 'good.'"[64]

Independent news gathering and independent transmission of news stories to America were virtually impossible on all war fronts. United Press reporters like Shepherd, therefore, competed with reporters from other news services by writing in a more readable writing style and by trying to get scoops—as long as those scoops were positive stories about the nations they were covering and could get past the censors.

The stories by Simms, Von Wiegand, and Shepherd were not the only ones the United Press carried regarding the war, of course. Scripps newspapers such as the *Cleveland Press* carried thousands of reports about war developments, most of them bylined simply "by United Press," throughout the war. Those stories, however, were usually straightforward rewrites of official releases from the capitals of the belligerents and shorter than a dozen paragraphs. Because of cable censorship, most of this news was datelined Paris or London. The scoops from Simms, Von Wiegand, Shepherd, and others, however, were what distinguished the UP service from its rivals, and gave Scripps newspapers something to market to readers wanting something unique and interesting about the war.

As Howard explained in December 1914 to a college professor in Kansas:

> The day of the old time war correspondent having passed, and the changed conditions making his feats impossible and unnecessary today, the United Press has evolved a new method and a new stile [sic] entirely. I believe that our effort is more distinctive and more revolutionary than that of any of our contemporaries. Boiled down, it simply means that we have accepted the inevitable, and have reconciled ourselves to taking the details of actual military developments from the official communiqués and official announcements by the opposing General Staffs. Then we are using our men, the 1914 Model of war correspondent, to get out behind the opposing armies, and get the details and the picture of war as it affects the women and children and just plain folks—the people who are not in uniform, but who are quite as much the heroes or the victims of the war as the fellows carrying guns.[65]

Neutrality?

From the beginning of the war and until 1917, the Concern decided it was best to be as neutral as it could. As UP struggled with censors and rapidly changing war fronts, the editors of the Scripps newspapers made most of the decisions about how to present the war each day. The NEA, the editorial and feature voice of the Scripps newspapers, supplemented UP coverage and helped guide editors through the piecemeal information flowing from Europe. During the first week of the war, NEA devoted all of its space to war features, except its serialized features, sports, and women's page.[66]

One of the early considerations was over how much to devote to war coverage. On August 3, a major stockholder, J. C. Harper, wrote Scripps, asking for advice. "You have done more reading and thinking than any other man in the concern."[67] Scripps answered by saying that he agreed "in every particular" with the view of Robert Paine's August 4 memorandum suggesting how to cover war. Thus, Scripps circulated the Paine memo to all editors. Paine, the chief editorial writer for the NEA and the first editor of the NEA, was one of Scripps's most trusted advisors.

In his memo, Paine suggested devoting 75 percent of a newspaper's news space to the war and said he would "run little or no editorial comment. . . . I would be very careful, in my headings and editing, not to 'take sides' in any respect."[68]

Other Scripps editors agreed. Alfred Andersson, an editor-in-chief in the Harper Group, reminded his colleagues that "a German is going to buy the paper in which he can find some solace in the present crisis." With Germans making up nearly 19 percent of foreign-born Americans, Andersson urged editors to at least write headlines "from the German standpoint." He mentioned a recent example of how a headline was adjusted to mollify German readers: Instead of writing "Tiny Belgium Repels German Invaders" the headline should have been written "Undaunted Germans Renew Assault upon Liege."[69]

B. H. Canfield, head of the NEA, agreed that editors should not "roast the Kaiser" because it "isn't businesslike journalism, at present." He added: "The war news should not be changed to salve anyone's feelings, but it should be handled in such a fashion that the paper cannot by any stretch of imagination be accused of taking sides."[70] This expressed support for balanced coverage by the largest newspaper chain of its day is in marked contrast to the popular view among historians that the American press, as one, immediately and vehemently supported the Allies and printed stories of German atrocities without question.[71]

A review of the pages of the Concern's first and largest newspaper, the *Cleveland Press*, shows how much effort was made not to blame one side during the first year of the war. First, on the basis of Paine's advice, little editorializing was done on the war. The NEA editorials tended to blame the war on general conditions in Europe. On August 1, an NEA editorial blamed the war on two trends: a fight over scarce territory and resources in Europe, as well as racial antagonism between the Slavic and German peoples.[72] The *Cleveland Press* warned its readers about the lack of news coming from Germany and Austria. For example, it reprinted, on its front page, an editorial from Cleveland's German-language newspaper *Waechter und Anzeiger* saying that many of the accounts from Germany were unreliable because they had to go through the British telegraph cable.[73]

The *Cleveland Press* pledged to its readers on August 11 that it would do what it could "to give our readers the straight goods." It continued, "the *Press* will, in every case so far as is possible, publish in connection with each item of war news, the source of the information. We will publish the best information we can get at its face value and the reader must judge for himself as to how much value to give to reports and rumors. . . . Blame the newspaper that takes advantage of your interest in the war to foist fakes upon you."[74]

On August 27, an NEA editorial urged readers "to be slow to believe a tenth part of the charges and counterspeeches that have been or will be made of atrocities in the war's wake." With sarcasm, the editorial said German atrocity stories had proven not to be true. "So now, when we read tales of alleged German brutalism in the wake of the army's march, we accept them—NOT."[75]

The most anti-German stories to reach the pages of Scripps newspapers were written by Mary Boyle O'Reilly, an NEA staff writer and the only female reporter in the Concern to get bylined stories consistently (other than female columnists on the Scripps women's page). O'Reilly, forty-one, was the daughter of John Boyle O'Reilly, publisher of the *Boston Pilot*.[76] She had been sent to Belgium to write about the human side of the war, and with access only to the Allied side of the lines, her stories at best were antiwar and at their worst were anti-German. In one of her most pointed stories in September, O'Reilly described how she tried to help Red Cross nurses convince the Germans to allow milk farmers to deliver milk to the besieged Belgium capital. "Today a hundred babes lie dead in Brussels," the story ended.

O'Reilly's "daring adventure in Belgium," as it was dubbed by the *Cleveland Press*, was too good to quash, however, even if some might consider it biased reporting.[77] She was the first American journalist to see the destruction of Louvain, beating other reporters by two days.[78] "It was a city in flames, an imperishable monument to the horror of war," she wrote. Walking around Belgium disguised as a refugee, a *Cleveland Press* story said, "she passed through a great German army, lived all the while on black bread and water, and wrote her notes on the white silk lining of her blouse." O'Reilly eventually was arrested by the Germans for spying but released because, she said, "I was so densely ignorant and careless of military movements."[79] Finally reaching Holland, she wrote and sent her stories.

O'Reilly was equally sympathetic to the British during the zeppelin bombings of London in January 1915. "The German air raid has come and with it panic among the millions of poor and the war widows of London," one story began.[80] About this time, a byline belonging to "H. J. Phillips" began appearing in the NEA service. Equally supportive of the British, Phillips wrote on January 18 about the pluck and determination of the British soldiers.[81] Phillips joined O'Reilly in writing stories about war-ravaged Belgium; two stories appeared jointly on the *Cleveland Press*'s front page on February 9. "The conqueror is house-wrecking Belgium and moving the debris back to Germany," O'Reilly wrote, while Phillips added: "Belgium is dying. The death rattle is in a nation's throat."[82]

O'Reilly's blatantly anti-German reporting did not play well with all Scripps editors. Howard, for example, in January said that the stories of German atrocities were "generally regarded as terrible exaggerations."[83] Bias remained a concern. "I was accused, during the early days of the war, of kow-towing to the Germans," NEA president B. H. Canfield wrote on April 24. "The Ohio management made this criticism. Later, the Mary Boyle O'Reilly articles, from Belgium, came along. That made me anti-German, almost overnight!" The Ohio newspapers were killing many of O'Reilly's stories because the reporting was too anti-German, but Canfield urged the Ohio editor-in-chief to run the stories without her byline.[84] Later that year, the Ohio editors suspected O'Reilly was using "H. J. Phillips" as a pseudonym. Canfield wrote to Martin on October 2, "I don't know anything about Phillips, and don't care a cuss who or what he is, provided he isn't a burglar, or whether Mary Boyle writes the stuff and signs it 'H. J. Phillips,' or whether the NEA janitor writes it from the *London Graphic*. The point is whether it is good stuff and whether the source of information is reasonably reliable."[85]

O'Reilly's stories began appearing when Scripps's editors were judging that their readers were growing weary of war news. Harper wrote NEA general manager Canfield on September 18, telling him he had talked to Scripps and "he thought interest in the war was petering out; that no press associations or newspapers were getting real news, but a lot of dope, and that the people understood it and interest was flagging."[86] That month Canfield told Scripps editors he was reducing the amount of war coverage: "The European men of the U.P. have done nobly, not all but most of Mary Boyle O'Reilly's matter has been fine and exclusive, and Mason's regular explanations are not only a most satisfying and exclusive novelty but really a work of genius. Next to the positive, irrefutable facts, I think Mason's stuff is the very best war matter we are publishing.... I would reduce the space given to war matter but not the display of what I did publish about the war."[87]

Disputes over Centralized Control

Paine's and Canfield's advice about how to edit the war was just that: advice. The NEA's main office did control much of what Scripps newspapers could and would print because they relied on the service to fill their news pages, but Scripps editors still had considerable freedom to choose which NEA stories and opinion pieces to use and how to display them. By the fall of 1914, with the crisis in Europe escalating, however, the leaders of the NEA were beginning to reconsider that freedom. Calls for NEA to have "Must Copy" power were renewed.

By mid-October, support for a larger army and navy was growing in the Congress, and the NEA political writer Gilson Gardner told readers that increased military spending was "the greatest topic at the coming session of Congress."[88] Public opinion, however, seemed to support President Wilson's position that the armed forces, especially the National Guard, were sufficient.[89] The NEA's editors had long believed that readers and, in turn, government would respond if they were told about needs such as that for a greater army and navy.

To build toward a populist editorial campaign on the military spending issue, the NEA launched a mail-in survey in November to survey readers on the issue. The NEA said it had eighty-five newspapers participating in the survey, in which two questions were asked on a preprinted ballot: should the U.S. navy be increased and should the U.S. army be increased?[90] "You, Mr. Man and Mrs. Woman, are the people who must pay the bills for the United States army and navy. Therefore . . . that of increasing the army and navy, should be put up to YOU first of all."[91]

At the same time, the NEA began running small editorials and quotations from advocates and opponents of preparedness. The NEA was careful to present a balanced range of opinions. Opponents such as Samuel Gompers of the American Federation of Labor were noted, as were proponents such as Admiral George Dewey.[92]

The NEA straw poll results were announced on December 10. Only 39 percent of readers returning ballots supported a larger army; 41 percent favored a larger navy. Fewer than seventy-five thousand readers sent in ballots.[93] The results surprised NEA general manager Canfield, who had predicted two weeks earlier that the public would vote the opposite way. Canfield had hoped the poll would serve as the pretense for the NEA to launch its own editorial campaign in support of increased military spending.[94] But no reader groundswell existed.

The brains of the NEA, Canfield and Paine, however, did not want to give up on preparedness. Paine said the poll was not surprising because—with the November election just completed—"the folks are tired of voting." He predicted that a larger navy would gain support. "A larger standing army is certainly objectionable to many who really favor unlimited naval preparation for defense."[95]

Other Scripps editors were unconvinced. Harper, living in Denver, for example, said the oceans were enough protection for a country "thousand of miles away from any great power." He said increased military spending would only "awaken suspicion and hostility" among the European countries and weaken chances of the United States mediating peace.[96] "What about the Philippines, Hawaii and Alaska?" Paine, in San Diego, retorted. "And President Wilson is going to stop the war by using moral suasion on the parties who are burning churches, bombing women and shelling school boys!"[97] Paine and Canfield, however, would not have the evidence to convince the Scripps editors to support increased military spending until February 1915. The lack of consensus within the Concern on certain national issues, exacerbated by different geographic views and varying sizes and profit margins of newspapers, had been exposed.

The Business Side

As was revealed through the Scripps empire's determination not to offend German readers, finances were an immediate concern. In the first few months of the war, the U.S. economy slowed with the disruption of trade with Europe. "It is a mistaken idea that the Allied Government came swarming into the American market in the fall of 1914 and gave us sudden and wonderful prosperity," historian C. Hartley Grattan wrote in 1929. Grattan noted that it was not until the second half of 1915 that American exports actually improved because of the war.[98]

Scripps believed his Concern would do well in the war. "You know that bad times are only very, very bad for bad business men. They are tolerably good times to the mediocre, and they are harvest times for the men who have money and know how to use it," he wrote to Howard on October 3.[99]

The Concern's business manager, Charles F. Mosher, noted that profits for the *Cincinnati Post* went from 15 percent in the prewar year of 1897 to 6 percent during the Spanish-American War in 1898. Likewise, the *Cleveland Press* profits shrank from 17 percent in 1897 to 6 percent in 1898. Circulation rose for both newspapers, but so did expenses. Advertising was stagnant as businesses became cautious. "Expenses are the key to the whole situation and, as to profits, it seems to me the difficulty is that there is a very large increase in circulation which [our newspapers] are absolutely unable to cash in."[100]

United Press was doing well through August 15, 1914, however. Profits stood at $466.84 per week, with clients numbering six hundred, the highest ever.[101] "The strictest orders have been issued to all bureaus and correspondents to keep expenditures ... at the lowest possible point," UP vice president C. D. Lee explained. Even cable tolls from Europe were averaging only $80 per day. "Despite [the toll cost] the United Press is receiving compliments from every quarter for the thoroughness and excellency of its war service."

Lee explained that censorship and restrictions on access to the fronts were keeping news-gathering costs down. "Practically all of the news of the war so far has been gathered in the important centers where we are already represented, namely, London, Paris, Rome, Berlin and a few outside points."[102]

On October 5, however, Howard sent a letter to all full-service UP clients informing them that, because of the "most expensive news story of all times," he was increasing rates to them by 15 percent, as allowed under the second clause of their UP contracts, effective on October 19.[103] The rates for the pony service would increase 10 percent. "Already, however, our extraordinary expense for cables, couriers, staff correspondents and tripled European staffs has amounted to thousands of dollars, all borne by us."[104]

Howard said AP, "judging from the manner in which they have been spending money in Europe and in cable tolls," would probably exceed a 25 percent increase in rates. He said he had hoped to increase rates only 10 percent, "but when we came to make our calculations we found that such an increase would not get us out with a whole skin."[105] In a later letter marked "confidential" to the editor-in-chief of the Ohio Group, Howard said UP would finish the year with a 7 percent profit because of the rate increase; its average monthly profits before the war had ranged from 6 to 7 percent.[106]

Howard later would report that "a very large majority" of UP clients accepted the rate hike,[107] and the Scripps newspapers paid higher rates for the UP service, too, but only after some wrangling.[108] The Scripps editors were not convinced they could afford to pay an extra expense that one of the Concern's own entities was charging. Production costs had increased with increased demand, creating a shortage of newsprint and other needed items.[109] By October, newspapers in New York were increasing their subscription prices,[110] and there was talk of two-cent newspapers in Pennsylvania.[111]

The early months of the war had been good to the Scripps Concern, especially to UP. But that success also inspired greed and thievery among its competitors.

Stealing

United Press's war scoops were important to its profits. They were major publicity splashes that showed nonclient newspapers that the UP service was at least a valuable supplement to AP. Howard used it as a constant pitch to nonsubscribers. "A number of the more aggressive and enterprising editors of the country have realized that, with all the due respect for the efficiency of the AP report, they cannot afford to be without the United Press report at this time," he wrote Alden Blethen, editor-in-chief of the *Seattle Times*, an AP member, in August 1914.[112] Blethen acknowledged that UP scooped AP on occasion, but "at a cost of $15,000 per annum" for UP, "I beg to say that we feel fairly well satisfied with the Associated Press."[113]

Stealing was free, however, at least among journalists in 1914. Most news organizations did not have the time or money to copyright every major story by filing the proper paperwork with the federal government. As we will see in the next chapter, the law was unclear about how news was protected under copyright law, and the U.S. Supreme Court did not clarify the issue until 1918. In the meantime, major scoops were often too tempting for non-UP clients to pass up. In November, Howard wrote the Xenia, Ohio, *Daily Republican* to scold it for its "scarcely ethical" practice of stealing UP stories from Dayton newspapers and reprinting them in Xenia.[114] Even UP's copyrighted stories were stolen; UP's interview with British publisher Lord Northcliffe was pilfered by the *Washington Post* in December.[115]

The first major theft of UP stories took place after Von Wiegand secured the biggest story of the war from behind German lines—an interview with Crown Prince Frederick Wilhelm in November. "Undoubtedly this is the most stupid, senseless and unnecessary war of modern times. It is a war not wanted by Germany, I can assure you, but it was forced on us," the crown prince was quoted as saying in the story.

Using the scoop to get more clients, UP reproduced the November 30 front page of Joseph Pulitzer's *New York World*, which featured Von Wiegand's copyrighted interview, as a one-page advertisement in *Editor and Publisher and Journalist.*[116] Meanwhile, several non-UP newspapers had copied parts of the interview, including the *St. Louis Post-Dispatch*—ironically, a Pulitzer newspaper. The *Post-Dispatch* lifted key quotations from the crown prince without permission and summarized the rest of the article. United Press's primary attorney for business affairs, J. W. Curts, was frustrated. Copyright applied to authorship, but how could UP claim authorship for quotations from the crown Prince? "Neither Von Wiegand nor UP were the authors of what the crown prince said (unless the interview was in fact written by Von Wiegand from his imagination, in which case I doubt if we would want to publicly claim authorship of what the Prince said)," he wrote to Howard.[117] Curts told Howard to quit trying to copyright stories such as Von Wiegand's interview-based story.

Charges of the theft of war news were flying from many directions in the fall of 1914. Hearst's INS, woefully underprepared to cover a world war, was accused of faking bylines attached to stories it had pilfered from other news services, especially the AP.[118] Associated Press also accused UP of stealing stories, something Howard vehemently denied.[119]

Von Wiegand continued to gather his exclusive interviews with German leaders. Because the British were less open, Howard told an English friend in January he was "having a devil of a sweet time keeping the United Press report from speaking with a German accent."[120] Howard was concerned that Von Wiegand's stories had "taken a great deal of the curse off of the German activities" and was frustrated with British unwillingness to give big interviews to counterbalance the German exclusives.[121] Howard did manage to get British publisher Lord Northcliffe to write an exclusive piece for UP, something Howard said made progress "toward evening things up."[122] In the article, Northcliffe said the German's willingness to talk to Von Wiegand was "a sign of anxiety and weakness" by the Germans.[123]

Before Christmas, Von Wiegand's interview with German grand admiral Alfred Von Tirpitz, called the admiral's first with an American reporter, was printed. "England wants to starve us," Tirpitz was quoted as saying. "We can play the same game. We can bottle her up and torpedo every English or allies' ship which nears any harbor in Great Britain."[124] Despite Curts's suggestion, the story—most of it consisting of quotations from the admiral—was copyrighted.

Von Wiegand continued on a roll. In January the Germans granted him access to all parts of the battle line. "This is the first departure from the original order, which was that foreign correspondents would be permitted to visit the front only in accordance with previously arranged plans," UP reported.[125]

In another copyrighted scoop in February, he landed a two-part interview with Count Ferdinand von Zeppelin, builder of Germany's airship bombers. In the interviews, "the only ones ever granted by him to any newspaper reporter," Zeppelin revealed that he was sorry that women and children were being killed by his airships. "They have no intention to kill woman and children . . . so far as lies in their power to avoid," Zeppelin explained.[126]

A week later, Von Wiegand landed an exclusive interview with Crown Princess Cecilie of Germany, who said that women were the ultimate victims of the war. "The men fight; the women minister and work. With the Red Cross they console and help widows, care for the wounded, work in the gardens and in the field, and anywhere a pair of hands are needed," she said.[127]

The crown princess edited Von Wiegand's story before he was allowed to send it. She "crossed out considerable [text] in my original copy," he wrote later. He found that copies of his articles cut from American newspapers, especially New York or Washington newspapers, worked best in convincing the Germans his stories were getting good play, and that encouraged them to continue to talk to him.[128]

Von Wiegand was burning out physically. He was the only UP man in Berlin against five reporters from the AP. In early January he wrote Howard that he "suffered severely under depression and was much worried about the condition of my heart action."[129] United Press's golden boy was about to quit.

The road to Von Wiegand's departure began six weeks earlier in St. Louis. The stealing by Pulitzer's *Post-Dispatch* of stories written by Von Wiegand and other UP reporters was making the *St. Louis Times*, a UP client, angry, and it was pressuring UP to do something. By late February, UP was preparing a copyright violation lawsuit against the *Post-Dispatch* for its theft of Von Wiegand's interview with the crown princess. The *Post-Dispatch* had "lifted the meat out" of the interview, Curts explained. Harper, Scripps's attorney and a major stockholder, said he believed the lawsuit would succeed because the report of an interview constituted authorship. Curts now agreed, but said the strongest part of the case was "unfair appropriation of the result of our work and expense," as well as the UP's assertion that copyright law did apply to newspaper articles.[130]

The *New York World*, Pulitzer's flagship newspaper, however, had one more trick up its sleeve. It offered Von Wiegand $200 a week to report from Berlin on its behalf. After several weeks of consideration, he accepted. United Press dropped the lawsuit because it was suing a newspaper company that had already hired away the reporter who had written the stories central to the suit. "We would be in a rather ridiculous position suing the Pulitzer outfit over his [Von Wiegand's] stuff," UP vice president William W. Hawkins wrote on March 9. Hawkins said UP had had "the finest possible copyright suit" and would "never get a better one." However, "other editors would say the Pulitzer outfit put it over us at every stage of the game—they stole our stuff and they then stole our man and left us nothing but a long, mournful yelp."[131] Andersson added his own caveat to the loss of Von Wiegand: "The fact that the United Press now is losing its crack correspondent, whose name it has made nationally famous, is another demonstration of the danger from a management standpoint of boosting a man's individuality in the papers."[132]

Promoting the President, Part Two

In early 1915, Scripps again renewed his commitment to boosting the president with his secretary of the people idea. He began writing letters to Wilson partisans to gain their support and to get them to approach Wilson about the idea. Scripps was disappointed that the president had not followed up on the proposal he had made in June.[133] He wrote industrialist Charles Crane, who had been a supporter and fundraiser for Wilson during the 1912 election, to tell him of his plans to provide Wilson with a veteran journalist for the secretary of the people.[134] Scripps proposed either Neg Cochran, age fifty-two, editor of the *Toledo News-Bee* and the adless *Day Book* in Chicago, or Harry N. Rickey, age forty-two, former editor-in-chief of the Ohio newspapers and now a roving editorial advisor to the NEA and the Ohio Group.[135] Scripps also wrote a letter to Secretary of State Bryan about the secretary of the people idea in February. He told him that he was concerned because if Wilson failed, a conservative reactionary would probably be elected instead of a progressive in 1916.[136]

Secretary of the interior Franklin Lane, however, would give Scripps's proposal the greatest push. Lane, from California, was a well-known "Roosevelt Democrat" who had served on the Interstate Commerce Commission in the Roosevelt and Taft presidencies before Wilson asked him to head the Interior Department.[137] He met with Scripps at Miramar on March 26 and suggested that Scripps go to Washington to see the publicity venture through.[138]

But Scripps had two more vigorous men in mind. Rickey turned down the idea, but Cochran was willing. Scripps proposed that Cochran go to Washington for up to three months for "intimate conversation with the President, carefully studying the situation to see if it were worth our while ('our' referring to the Scripps Institution) to make an effort, not so much to elect Wilson, as to prevent the election of a reactionary."[139] Scripps said Wilson was too willing to take "a cowardly, straddling, temporizing course" but could be a "name great in history."[140]

In April Scripps told Cochran to go to Washington "ostensibly and sufficiently notorious to study the Washington field for the publication of another adless paper" but then "introduce yourself to the President as having come by my request, and probably, incidentally, Crane's request."[141] Scripps asked Crane to tell Wilson of the plan and said Cochran would be in Washington in May. "I think the success of my plan will depend almost entirely upon whether or not Mr. Wilson will find Mr. Cochran a congenial personality," Scripps wrote Crane on April 22.[142]

Scripps advised Cochran to be discreet. "The President can say anything he wants to [you] and you will always consider it a professional secret between you two; that Mr. Scripps has no right to inquire or be informed on any subject."[143] So Cochran made plans in early May to have subordinates take over the daily management of the *Toledo News-Bee* and the *Day Book*. He was going to Washington to work with Wilson. Fate, however, would intervene.

Advocacy

Though pledged to be neutral about how it covered the fighting in Europe, the Scripps Concern made its first attempt at public advocacy on a war-related issue in early 1915 after the fighting drew closer to America. Germany announced on February 4 that it would sink all merchant vessels in waters around Great Britain. The Germans asked Secretary of State Bryan to warn Americans about traveling on belligerent ships and asked that U.S. ships stay out of British waters.[144] The Wilson administration, in turn, sent notes to Germany protesting the submarine campaign and to Britain protesting its sanctioning the misuse of neutral flags on its ships. "Two great powers, Germany and England, at war on land and sea, are trying to starve each other to death," European manager Ed Keen wrote in a February 18 story.[145]

The NEA, meanwhile, continued to write stories about the limits of the U.S. navy. "Our navy is mostly in the future tense. There are some excellent plans being considered, but we cannot fight with plans," Gardner wrote on February 20.

Even with December's negative straw poll, Canfield decided that the NEA's clients were ready for it to begin an editorial assault. With Paine's input, he had been writing two editorials for the NEA that would serve as the opening salvo for a new policy campaign. The first to appear, "The Nation of Peace," was given to the Ohio Group's editor-in-chief Earle E. Martin for his reaction before the piece was sent. Martin read the editorial at a meeting of Ohio editors, who approved it.

Canfield telephoned Martin to ask if he thought the editorials should be sent out as "Must Copy" pieces; Martin replied that he thought the Scripps editors would resent that. "I agreed with you that, because of the effects on editors of such an order, it would be well not to do it, provided the policy would be supported without it," Canfield wrote Martin, recalling their earlier conversation.[146]

"The Nation of Peace" was a call for the country to remain calm despite the encroaching war. "You and I—your neighbor and mine—every citizen, must check all hasty impulses and be guided by a higher idea."[147] The editorial said that if the United States entered the war "it would mean a veritable holocaust of carnage and death. . . . It is the holy duty of the United States—pre-eminent among the world's powers—apostle of a world's peace—exemplifying the spirit of peace on earth, good will toward men, to stand fast to those principles."

The second editorial, titled "The Greatest Navy in the World," appeared a week later. Again, it said the United States did not want war, but did need the world's largest navy "for peace insurance." The editorial embodied Canfield's and Paine's beliefs, first expressed in the previous fall:

> A navy that is second or third or fourth is very largely a waste of men, money and energy. It would produce nothing in the time of trial except, perhaps, to delay, temporarily, the march of events.
>
> The United States must be prepared to fight for its position as a pacific nation. It doesn't want to fight. It hopes not to fight. But, if attacked it will have to fight.[148]

The editorial said enlarging the navy would take years, and thus "there could be no accusation that the great navy in the world was being built for the purpose of being 'ready' to get into the present war." Relying on a large navy for defense also would "prevent conscription and the saddling of a great standing army upon the people." Finally, the editorial closed with the statement that the government should build the extra ships itself because there could be "no pocket-picking by parasites who hope to fatten off the political contracts."

The NEA followed with a statement from former president Theodore Roosevelt, in which he supported doubling the size of the navy. "To economize in this matter is precisely like a city attempting to economize by shutting down on its fire department."[149] Another NEA editorial noted that the United States had $150 billion in property, nearly twice that of Britain. "What insurance have our tens of millions of women and children that they won't be the victims of the hordes who, lured to the attack by our riches, bring war to our shores?"[150]

On March 6 Gardner wrote an article based on an assertion by Congressman Clyde Tavenner of Illinois that the U.S. government should build its own weapons. "On an average 35 cents out of every dollar spent by the government on contracts for war materials of all kinds goes in private profits to private monopolies," Tavenner was quoted as saying.[151] The proposal for the government to make weapons to save money was not new. Gardner had earlier written stories about how armor plate manufacturers price-gouged the navy, and how the federal government was already making some weapons at half the cost of private industry.[152]

Important seeds had germinated in the spring of 1915. The "Greatest Navy" campaign gave the NEA its first chance to try to shape national public opinion about how American should respond to the dangers of the war in Europe. But it also revealed the challenge the NEA faced to get the diverse group of Scripps editors to agree with and follow a major editorial policy. The editors agreed that the actual fighting in Europe should be reported in a neutral and interesting way, but they disliked being told what to print and what opinions to advocate.

E. W. Scripps was focused on his newspapers supporting President Wilson, whom he saw as a great progressive champion, and he offered a top editor to handle publicity for the president.

The war gave the Concern a great opportunity to prove itself, and it made the most of it. United Press aggressively earned early scoops, despite choking censorship, and outshined AP in the early months of the war. United Press was so successful that competitors pirated many of its biggest stories, and one rival even hired away UP's productive German correspondent.

The first nine months of war had given a tremendous boost to the profits and reputation of UP in particular and the Concern in general. But the seeds planted so far, those good and bad, would get a new spurt of growth in May 1915 from the waters off the coast of Ireland.

3 Harsh Realities: May to November 1915

On May 7, 1915, just as the German submarine *U-20* sank the British liner *Lusitania* off Ireland's Old Head of Kinsale, some in the Scripps Concern were floating a plan for an early push for the reelection of Woodrow Wilson. A proposal to use the NEA to coordinate news coverage designed to reelect Wilson came in mid-April from Alfred Andersson, an editor-in-chief for a portion of the Harper Group of Scripps newspapers. "My idea about a newspaper's influence politically is not that it is . . . in the work that it does preliminary to the campaign in giving its readers pen pictures of the candidates," he wrote to B. H. Canfield, head of the NEA.[1]

Canfield agreed that Wilson's conduct so far was "reasonably satisfactory to the American public," but he warned that the Concern should not take an early, strong stand for Wilson because "almost anything may happen in these times. What if he makes a big, unpopular mistake after we announce a flat, definite policy in his favor?"[2] The *Lusitania* incident confirmed Canfield's fears that the war in Europe made throwing support this early to Wilson too risky. E. W. Scripps's maneuverings to help Wilson establish a secretary of the people were not mentioned in the letter exchange; it is doubtful that the idea was well known yet even among the top editors.

Still, Canfield knew he was editorial head in a democracy, not a dictatorship. So he asked the Concern's trustees and editors-in-chief to write him about their views on the subject on May 10.[3] The Concern's leaders strongly supported his take-it-slow-publicly approach.[4] Attorney J. W. Curts suggested that the Concern's ability to influence opinion in the election would be greater if it appeared politically independent. "I think we will have a far greater influence if we come out for him [in the summer of 1916] instead of having our readers feel that we have been so far committed as to require our support no matter what our real opinion of him and his administration is."[5] LeRoy Sanders, an editor-in-chief for Scripps's Northwest newspapers, suggested the most popular view. Readers did not care, Sanders wrote Canfield on May 18, because "exciting international complications have arisen, which have, it appears to me, completely pushed presidential politics off the stage."[6]

Thus, while some of the Concern's editors wanted to push progressive policies through Wilson aggressively, others were a bit reluctant. The idealism of progressive reform had to be tempered by harsh reality, and the first big dose of that came in the six months after the sinking of the *Lusitania*. No longer could the Concern avoid dealing with issues of central control over editorial policy; vital global events were creeping too close to America. The Concern would have to take a stronger stand on military preparedness and America's reaction to the sinking. Would such a policy be centralized and mandated? Meanwhile, these new developments in the war boosted demand for news nationally and internationally, and so pressures on the business and logistical sides of covering the war presented their own harsh realities during this period. United Press no longer enjoyed some of the advantages it had had over its competitors in the first six months of the war. Its scoop-filled newsgathering honeymoon was over, and flashes of it would only reoccur occasionally during the rest of the war. United Press would have to slug it out on equal ground with its competitors. The NEA would have to define its role in covering the war, too.

This period after the sinking of the *Lusitania* was important for the battle over the soul of the Scripps news organization as well. The Concern, built on a reputation for fighting for working people and being free of special interests, began to lose its political independence during this period, as it aligned itself so strongly in support of one politician and his policies. Granted, that support was subtle, but little doubt remained by 1915 that Wilson had strong support among all levels of the Concern's management. This quiet allegiance to Wilson undoubtedly would have to shape the Concern's policies on America's response to the war in Europe and perhaps put its policy at odds with its previous stands and allegiances.

Torpedoed

The sinking of the *Lusitania* in May 1915 was not a complete surprise. German submarines had already sunk about ninety ships of various sizes since the submarine danger zone around the British Isles had been enforced, beginning on February 18.[7] German ambassador Count Johann Von Bernstorff had warned Americans in the shipping notices of New York newspapers about the dangers of traveling on British ships. The warning did not mention any specific ships, but the notices did appear on the day *Lusitania* launched for England. Bernstorff, in his memoirs after the war, said the timing was "one of those fatal coincidences beloved of history."[8] Wilbur Forrest, a UP correspondent in London, wrote after the war that the Bernstorff warnings "caused newspaper correspondents to keep their ears close to the ground during . . . early May in Fleet Street, London."[9]

The *Lusitania* sinking did not catch the NEA unawares either. Canfield had predicted to Ohio editor-in-chief Earle Martin that the *Lusitania* would be attacked. "I guess you think we are some sort of clairvoyants up here," he wrote Martin May 17, after his prediction became reality.[10] Canfield had the NEA put out "big pictures and stuff about the *Lusitania*" days before the attack, along with a note warning NEA clients, saying "it was quite probable the Germans would torpedo this ship."[11] Scripps newspapers, therefore, were stocked with photographs and background information to supplement UP's reports.

New NEA staff member Charles Edward Russell, the renowned socialist and ex–presidential candidate, had traveled on the *Lusitania* in early April on a voyage from New York to Great Britain. His story appeared in the *Cleveland Press* on April 30, the day before the *Lusitania* sailed on its last voyage. "Passengers are told if they got to bed that night, to have the life preserver and warm clothing handy," Russell wrote. "Open boats at night are colder than Greenland's icy."[12]

United Press again accounted for itself very well, despite the remote location of the sinking. "It is difficult to imagine a more unlikely place from which a big news story might break than the Atlantic Ocean outside of Queenstown harbor," the *Editor and Publisher and Journalist* reported on May 15.[13] United Press's Wilbur Forrest was the first American wire service reporter to arrive at Queenstown after the sinking.[14] He found the British helpful to reporters. "It was the greatest piece of anti-German propaganda the war has yet known," Forrest wrote in 1934. "British censorship . . . dealing with the Lusitania was abandoned."[15]

Finding a "fountainhead of grief" in Queenstown, Forrest focused initially on the nationally known Americans on the *Lusitania*.[16] His biggest scoop came in the confirmation of the death of Charles Frohman, a prominent New York theatrical producer.[17] Forrest found the body in one of the three morgues and identified Frohman by removing the dead man's card case from his coat.[18]

For the Scripps news organs, the sinking was a scene of tragedy and heroism, not war or terrorism. The manmade incident was reported as if it were a natural disaster. Any blame was spread among the British as well as the Germans. One UP story reported that the *Lusitania* had slowed down in the submarine danger zone and all were "united in statements criticizing the inadequacy of the emergency preparations."[19] On May 8 the *Cleveland Press* carried two stories in which local German Americans contended that the Lusitania had carried munitions and was using American passengers as shields.[20]

Forrest's stories relied heavily on quotations from survivors. Other early information came directly from the British Admiralty Office and the Cunard Company, the liner's owner. With no typewriter, Forrest handprinted his stories on telegraph slips. Forrest said he got about fifteen hundred words telegraphed before the reporters from AP and the INS even arrived. He determined that he had sent seven thousand words from Queenstown, generating less than $1,000 in cable tolls. "Perhaps also those words contributed something to a growing sentiment in the United States which eventually brought us into the European War," he wrote in 1934.[21]

"The One Man to Speak for America"

If the flagship Scripps newspaper, the *Cleveland Press*, is an indication, however, Forrest's stories of human tragedy quickly fell off the pages of the Scripps newspapers. Few of Forrest's stories were published for Cleveland readers. *Lusitania* stories only dominated the pages of the May 8 and 10 editions (May 9 was a Sunday) of the *Cleveland Press*. The weekly review of the war column, published on May 10, downplayed the incident. The column did call it "the most vital happening of the war from the American standpoint" but added blandly: "What will be its consequences cannot be foretold."[22] The Scripps Concern was cautiously trying not to stir feelings for war, perhaps more so than other American newspapers. Historian John Milton Cooper wrote that "nearly every editor and public figure denounced the sinking as a crime or an outrage."[23] The NEA, on May 15, however, called the *Lusitania* "not a neutral, but an enemy ship. It was a carrier of war munitions to the enemies of Germany."[24] While the editorial admitted it was a "brutal crime and nations have gone to war for less," it wanted a peaceful response.

The NEA first outlined its position on the crisis on May 11. Canfield wrote an editorial he wired (NEA editorials were usually mailed) to all clients. The editorial urged readers not to let the sunken *Lusitania* sweep them into in a war spirit. "We are not yet hardened on this side to the sight of thousands dying in the whiff of smoke from a manmade blast," he wrote. The editorial continued:

> If peace can be maintained with honor, President Wilson can do it. That is what he has worked for since the European conflagration started. That is what he is still working for in this crisis.
>
> The time may come when honor may demand something fraught with such consequences that nothing like it has occurred in the history of this nation. But if that time can be averted, President Wilson will do it.[25]

Alfred Andersson, editor-in-chief of the *Dallas Dispatch,* said the editorial was a "fine effort" but left him dissatisfied; and the *Dispatch* did not use it.[26] "It strikes me that the editorial struck a popular chord because almost everybody is willing to leave a hard job to the other fellow," Andersson wrote.[27] Even the Ohio Group of newspapers removed a paragraph that said that any war America got involved in would be a vicious affair. Canfield said later that a top Ohio Group editor called the paragraph "a little too much like 'war talk.'"[28]

Canfield explained that he simply was calling for united support of Wilson "in whatever policy he might finally decide to adopt." Canfield said the people had confidence in Wilson and the editorial would have been different "if we had a quibbling, or weak-kneed president."[29] The Canfield editorial reflected statements made by President Wilson in two speeches in April in which he asked the country to "resist excitement, [and] to think calmly."[30] Canfield wrote Andersson that the editorial was also a way to get the Scripps newspapers into "concerted action on this subject.... If there ever was a time when the big circulation N.E.A. now has both inside and outside the Concern should be used for united action this is it."

Recent events, Canfield reasoned, had proven the NEA's "Greatest Navy" policy was correct. The predicted attack on the *Lusitania* also showed that the NEA was in "pretty close touch with probable events."[31] Canfield was exhibiting a paternalistic, "N.E.A.-knows-best" attitude that continually drove a wedge between the NEA and individual Scripps editors on matters of national policy.

"Immediate and Concerted Editorial Action"

For years the NEA had served as a clearinghouse for content for the Scripps newspapers, but it also watched over the Scripps newspapers, analyzing coverage to see, as Canfield put it, if it was meeting with "approval or disapproval." As he explained to Andersson in criticizing the *Memphis Press*'s failure to use a picture of the *Lusitania* that the NEA supplied to it: "Whenever we note an unusual or strikingly different mode of handling we sometimes write to the editor, whether he is a Scripps editor, or a client. But, whether we write or not, the event is noted and placed with our office files about the papers so that we may be able at any time to have the paper's history of their [sic] handling of N.E.A.— both clients and members—for our future information in any possible talks we may have with them about the service."[32] In his newspaper's defense, Andersson, who was editor-in-chief of the *Memphis Press* as well, explained that the NEA had been mailed the first edition, which was the only edition that did not contain the ship picture that day.[33]

The incident added to Canfield's increasing frustration with how the client newspapers handled NEA matter on important stories. He had reason to believe he was in a strong position to lead editorial policy for the Concern. Not only was he head of the Concern's chief editorial arm, the NEA, but he had the complete confidence of Jim Scripps, who the year before called him one of the three strongest editorial men in the Concern.[34] Jim, based in San Diego, knew Canfield well from his days as editor-in-chief for the West Coast newspapers and had recommended Canfield for that job.[35] While no dictator, Canfield subtly managed the coverage of the newspapers taking the NEA service. For example, he collected editorials from various sources within the Concern, but killed many not consistent "in a *general* way on the biggest subjects."[36]

Now that war was closer to home in mid-May 1915, Canfield wanted centralized editorial control within the NEA. He announced he wanted the Scripps newspapers to agree to allow the NEA to direct "immediate and concerted editorial action by the concern."[37] This concept was not entirely new; the NEA trustees in January 1911 had agreed in principle that the general manager should have some "Must Copy" authority to tell the various editors-in-chief what policies to support in their newspapers,[38] but this authority had never been used.[39]

Canfield circulated a rewritten version of the 1911 policy for approval in June. The Canfield policy said that certain "Must Copy" had to be "published in good faith, as to display and handling, at the earliest possible moment after its receipt." The policy stated that an editor or editor-in-chief who objected to any "Must Copy" should "immediately wire the General Manager of N.E.A., stating his reasons . . . and requesting that he be permitted to cancel its publication in his paper or papers." Any violator would "have the burden laid upon him to show good and sufficient cause for his failure. . . . and unless he can make an absolutely good case for his position so taken, his failure to publish shall be looked upon as inexcusable."[40]

The editors of the Concern immediately objected. J. C. Harper sarcastically called it "revolutionary" and added: "Frankly, I do not believe that it was the sort of letter you would have wanted to receive." Harper especially disliked that editors had to answer directly to the NEA and not just to their editor-in-chief—a change from the original 1911 memo. Harper said only officers or stockholders of each newspaper should dictate its policy.[41]

Others objected for different reasons. Neg Cochran said a "czar as editorial head" would micromanage and stifle the development of young editors.[42] Eugene MacLean of the *San Francisco Daily News* said policy was not needed because editors already have been "embued with the Scripps ideals."[43] F. R. Peters, an editor-in-chief for a portion of the Harper Group, said concerted action was desirable but should not be compelled. "It seems reasonable to believe that if half of our papers followed a policy they were convinced by argument was the proper one to pursue, the sum total effect would be greater than if all complied . . . because they had orders to."[44]

Even Harry Rickey, who had wanted to use "Must Copy" authority when he directed the NEA, advised Canfield to back down. Like Harper, Rickey said "Must Copy" should go through the editors-in-chief. He noted that the issue needed to be decided now because E. W. Scripps was no longer actively running the Concern: "The tendency of our concern during the period E. W. Scripps had personal control of the business was toward unification and centralization. . . . I am quite sure that James G. Scripps, who is now the controlling stockholder . . . does not believe in centralization of authority, at least to the extent that E. W. Scripps did."[45]

No record of Jim Scripps's reaction to this debate survives in the Scripps archives. The issue over "Must Copy" apparently would not be mentioned again by anyone until April 1917, so the younger Scripps probably agreed that the NEA should advocate, not dictate, policy, as Peters said. He also probably agreed with Harper that the issues of the day were not important enough, at least not yet, to require "Must Copy" authority anyway.[46]

Isolationists

Despite the tussle over centralized control, the Scripps Concern, through the NEA, had staked itself to a weak, isolationist position by mid-1915. Harper summarized NEA policy on June 22 as "(1) supporting Wilson, (2) insisting upon a stronger navy, and (3) opposing the jingoes who would rush us into war, and insisting that sufficient time be given to get the sober second thought of the American people."[47]

As historian John Milton Cooper has explained, isolationism was a legitimate intellectual position during this time. Isolationism "was not simply a welling up of popular desires, but was formed as the result of mass interests being combined with independently formulated doctrines."[48] The Scripps Concern leaned toward what Cooper called an "idealistic isolationist" position. In its purest form, this doctrine said that the United States should reform humanity and its tendency to fight by acting as a righteous example to the world.[49] "While Europe is war-torn, hosts of human beings clashing on bloody battlefields, America is at peace with her neighbors," an NEA editorial boasted on June 12.[50]

The Concern's support for preparedness, by itself, was not unique. Most popular magazines and large metropolitan daily newspapers supported a larger army and navy by 1915. Historian John Patrick Finnegan wrote: "Sentiment for defense among the press was especially strong on both coasts; opinion was more evenly divided in the Mississippi Valley region, where the editorial opponents of army and navy increases seemed, for a change, to be more vehement than supporters."

Finnegan said support for preparedness gradually moved east to west, and drew support mostly from the middle class, the wealthy, and progressives. "Preparedness was an urban movement in a still rural America," Finnegan wrote.[51] Former president William Howard Taft claimed that support for preparedness was most dominant in "the clubs and smart set" of New York and Chicago.[52]

Thus, while the Scripps newspapers had earned their reputation fighting for labor and the underdog—the have-nots—it found itself supporting a cause linked primarily with haves—the rich and middle classes. Finnegan wrote that labor unions, socialists, German Americans, and farmers were the groups most opposed to preparedness.[53] The German American element was a particular concern to the Scripps newspapers, many of which were established in cities that were growing because of immigration of middle European. One NEA editorial appealed to the reason of this immigrant class by praising them: "No better citizens has this country ever acquired, and they have found in this opportunity to attain their ideals. ... A man may love his fatherland, but he fights for his home."[54]

Meanwhile, William Jennings Bryan, the leading idealistic isolationist, was denouncing preparedness and its associated weapons buildup as militarism and imperialism.[55] It was not surprising when the NEA chose to chide Bryan when he resigned in June because he felt Wilson's second diplomatic protest to Germany regarding the *Lusitania* was too warlike. One NEA editorial said the secretary of state's resignation was "unimportant internationally." A UP story claimed that Bryan had long wanted to quit for various reasons and "the psychological moment may have dovetailed splendidly with his final stand for his peace principles."[56] These and other missives angered Harper. "I have been sorry to see you hammering Bryan," he wrote Robert Paine, chief editorial writer for the NEA, on June 24. "Bryan is still an asset to the United States.... Our concern contributed largely to building up both Roosevelt and Bryan."[57]

Ironically, the Concern was backing one of Theodore Roosevelt's pet issues of the day, preparedness, and one of Bryan's, isolationism. That inconsistency in the NEA's policy was not lost on a Concern business manager, C. F. Mosher, who wrote Canfield on June 10 that the Concern's isolationist "peace at any price" stand begged him to ask "What's the use of a navy or any army?"[58] Canfield answered with what he had said in earlier editorials: additional defense spending was needed for "peace insurance," not for war.[59]

The Concern publicly continued its support of President Wilson, even though he did not support preparedness measures until after the *Lusitania*'s sinking.[60] The NEA had been working closely with the Army and Navy Leagues since early 1915, allowing these organizations to reprint the NEA's pronavy cartoons in their newsletters. The Navy and Army Leagues, in turn, had helped NEA a great deal by providing research for NEA's stories about the navy's needs.[61] These civilian defense societies were, according to Finnegan, "the real spearhead of the preparedness movement."[62] One example of the League's influence was reporter Harry Burton's story on April 2 that played up the inadequacies of America's dreadnoughts. "The master brick of defense building is the mighty dreadnaught [sic]," Burton wrote. He added later: "Third today, but fourth tomorrow—so our navy stands in the ranking of naval powers."[63]

Lack of consensus among Scripps newspapers had blocked the NEA from making preparedness a major push, but the *Lusitania* changed that. Wilson's change of heart on preparedness in the summer of 1915 coincided with the disappearance of dissent on the issue within the Concern. By early June Canfield was getting suggestions from inside the Concern on how to promote preparedness. The Concern's libel attorney, Dana Sleeth, suggested the NEA fund a feature film illustrating the lack of defenses on the West and East coasts.[64] Canfield ultimately suggested that Sleeth take the film idea to the Army and Navy Leagues.

To "Humanize" Wilson

Although the Scripps editors were not willing to go on record editorially in April and May of 1915 as supporting the president's reelection, they were openly sympathetic to him and the progressive causes he championed. Still, Harper suggested that the NEA adopt at least a stronger line of publicity on behalf of Wilson in its news stories and features. "I know E. W. Scripps has felt for a year past that Wilson and his administration need greater publicity than it had been getting. He did not mean boosting; he meant merely to help the American people get acquainted with Wilson and his administration—to humanize him," Harper wrote Canfield on May 25. Harper said the stories he and Scripps were suggesting were not "in any sense political propaganda. It should be and can be human interest stories of A-1 grade."[65]

On June 1, Canfield compiled all of the stories the NEA had written about Wilson. In the first five months of 1915, the NEA had sent out forty-four columns about the Democrat—an average of about one story every one and a half days. "I certainly approve the general idea you advance as to this sort of material and we plan to go to it even stronger than we have," Canfield wrote to Harper.[66]

The NEA had just released a personal feature on Wilson written by someone identified only as "a Member of the United States Cabinet." It was not explained to readers why the narrative was written anonymously, and the Scripps archives give no clue who it might be. The feature cast Wilson as an intellectual superhuman. "The assumption . . . [that] the president is nonpractical, theoretical, school teacherish, is dispelled by even short acquaintance," the feature assured readers.[67] In July, the NEA's Harry Burton traveled to Cornish, New Hampshire, to report on Wilson's vacation at his summer home and to find more about "Wilson the man." Burton reported that the president read detective stories and poetry for pleasure because he was not "an 'intellectualist' by temperament at all, but instead an incurable 'romanticist!'"[68]

Widower Wilson's impending marriage to Edith Galt in the fall of 1915 gave the NEA another feature opportunity. Idah McGlone Gibson, the NEA's popular women's page columnist, wrote the story: "No boy in the flush of his first love is happier than is the man described many times as a cold-blooded individual who had in some way made [his] great brain supply ... a warm heart."[69] The story ran in the *Cleveland Press* with a picture of a bouquet Wilson gave his fiancée. The NEA editorially supported Wilson's choice to remarry. "It is not good for a man to be alone, particularly if that man be carrying the burdens of a whole people."[70]

The End of the Secretary of the People

In May 1915 Wilson was not alone when it came to shaping public opinion. Neg Cochran, editor of the adless *Day Book* in Chicago and the *Toledo News-Bee,* was in Washington to meet with Wilson to help him as his secretary of the people. The *Lusitania* incident, however, had torpedoed the idea. As Scripps wrote to interior secretary Franklin Lane on May 23, "recent developments have been such that it appears that destiny has stepped in, and, brushing our feeble schemes aside, has chosen to direct events."[71] Cochran met with Lane, who called the editor "the right type,"[72] but he never saw Wilson. "In the present state of public opinion," Cochran wrote a Wilson supporter who helped arrange a meeting, "President Wilson will not feel any need for us. But when the sensation caused by the German controversy dies out, the agents of the reactionaries will get busy again." Returning to Chicago, Cochran vowed to stay alert to future attacks on Wilson.[73]

Thus the secretary of the people idea sank in 1915 along with the *Lusitania.* A plan to rebuild the Progressive Party as a diversion was equally short-lived. Wilson was in no mood to cooperate, and no one could blame him. "The poor man has been so worried by the great responsibilities put upon him that he has not had time to think or deal with matters of internal concern," Lane explained to Scripps on June 1.[74]

"Long Live the UP!"

In 1915 the man in the Scripps newspapers with the greatest concerns was Roy Howard, who was faced with covering a war that, with the *Lusitania* sinking, seemed to be spreading more globally. The year began with Howard's loss of his top correspondent, Karl Von Wiegand, to Joseph Pulitzer's *New York World.* Von Wiegand said he was sad to leave, admitting that UP "offers the opportunity for individualized dash and enterprise in the news-getting field and is quite willing to share the credit and glory with the men who do their part. That itself is a strong incentive to work." He said, however, that the stress of UP's demands was making his hair fall out, and he also needed the pay raise Pulitzer was giving him to report from Berlin. "Long live the UP! May it continue to prosper and grow," he wrote Howard as he resigned.[75]

Howard was losing his star correspondent at a critical time. Associated Press, which had been hamstrung in the first months of the war because of its reliance on foreign wire services, was now beginning to surpass the UP. Howard warned UP stockholder Ham Clark on February 1: "The A.P. is really getting busy. . . . They have caught their stride at last, and it is going to be up to us to get a move on if we don't want the good work of the last six months undone. . . . Our bunch have apparently all fallen dead or have gone asleep. Same old story of a little too much success and a little too much prosperity."[76]

Howard sailed to Europe in February on a whirlwind tour of London, The Hague, Berlin, Brussels, Paris, and Rome.[77] Privately, Howard said he was going over to "kick hell out of the gang over there."[78] Publicly, in the *Editor and Publisher and Journalist,* he said, "Certain phases and certain features of the [war] subject have been practically exhausted for news purposes" and his trip to Europe would "find out if it is not possible to open some new news leads."[79]

Howard had reason to worry about his competitive position. Associated Press had massive resources and funds to draw on. Its annual report to its board of directors, released in the spring of 1915, exuded confidence. Despite significant increases in its news division to meet war demands, AP showed a profit of nearly $167,000 for 1914, only about $11,000 less than 1913. At the close of 1914, AP membership stood at 909 papers—340 morning, 523 evening, and 46 Sunday—up 14 from the previous year.[80]

Associated Press was not only bigger; it was older and drew more attention from government leaders. While the world was waiting for President Wilson's first note of protest to the Germans, Howard pleaded with the president's administration to release the note for the afternoon newspapers. Howard even wired Scripps at Miramar to ask if he, too, would telegram Wilson and Secretary of State Bryan to convince them of that strategy, "in view [of] greater circulation [of] greater range and reach of news published by [the] afternoon papers."[81] When the note was released to the advantage of the morning newspapers, Howard fired off complaints to the secretaries of the interior, navy, and treasury. "Sight is lost . . . of the fact that whereas a story given to morning papers gets but a brief mention in evening papers," he explained to Interior Secretary Franklin Lane, "a story of any magnitude which first appears in evening papers is almost invariably covered in full in morning papers of the following day."[82] Navy Secretary Josephus Daniels noted that he referred the letter to the president's personal secretary, Joseph Tumulty.[83]

That did little to satisfy Howard, who continually blamed Tumulty for stonewalling UP, while favoring AP. Howard hopelessly attempted to secure a private interview with Wilson soon after the *Lusitania* sank. He contacted everyone he knew to get to Wilson, including assistant agriculture secretary Carl Vroonan. Howard had Vroonan talk to Secretary of State Bryan about helping arrange a meeting between UP and Wilson. "I feel thoroughly convinced that Mr. Bryan is very sympathetic to you and that if you can come down here and see him he will do everything in his power to put you on the right footing with the President," Vroonan assured Howard on May 8.[84]

On the other end of the *Lusitania* diplomatic tightrope, Howard had a relatively green correspondent in Berlin, the key news center for the Central Powers. Carl Ackerman, former manager of UP in Albany, New York, had already been on his way to Berlin to assist Von Wiegand when the premier Berlin correspondent had abruptly quit. Howard was confident he would do well. "He has a good sense of humor which I believe is going to be his best defense against a fatal conceit," Howard said in a letter to Ackerman's father in Richmond, Indiana.[85]

Ackerman was a prototypical UP correspondent. Young, bright, and ambitious, he sacrificed his honeymoon plans for UP and traveled with his wife to his new job in Europe. He had graduated from Earlham College and from the first class of the Columbia School of Journalism in New York.[86] He needed all of this education and experience to replace Von Wiegand's productivity.

Von Wiegand helped UP's new Berlin bureau chief during his first days on the job, but Ackerman was careful to make sure German officials knew that "the medium through which his [Von Wiegand's] articles were given such wide publicity is still open to them through me."[87] A series of factors seemingly stacked the odds against him, however. In the relatively calm weeks before the *Lusitania* incident, Von Wiegand traveled behind German lines for long stretches, leaving Ackerman to fend for himself. Then, as the diplomatic tension following the sinking of the *Lusitania* increased, cutthroat competition emerged. The Indiana native did not know German well and relied on local boys to translate for him, putting him at an inherent disadvantage. In addition, Allied ships were confiscating mail bound for Germany during this time, cutting off any feedback and newspaper clippings he was getting from the United States. The problem eventually was avoided when mail was routed through Holland, but valuable time was lost.[88] The clippings were especially helpful to Ackerman because he continually needed to reassure the Germans that he, like Von Wiegand, was giving them good publicity in America.[89]

Perry Arnold, acting news manager for UP in New York, sent 150 pages "torn from various newspapers" to Arnold in late April for that purpose. Arnold said Ackerman's stories were getting "splendid play." He noted that news from Germany was "at a premium here" compared with news from the Allies, and he urged Ackerman to continue sending stories in the mail. "It is the terse, straightforward story that makes a hit," Arnold advised.[90]

Ackerman was more worried about striking out than getting a hit in late May 1915. An interview he set up with German foreign minister Gottlieb Von Jagow to discuss the *Lusitania* situation was cancelled; Ackerman said Von Wiegand admitted he had advised Jagow not to talk.[91] Furthermore, what Ackerman could get out was butchered by German censors. Ackerman later revealed that from May 15 to June 3, five stories he wanted to telegraph were stopped completely; four others were edited heavily. Overall, 574 words were censored.[92] "Several of my messages were compromises, and, although as they were passed they did not represent what I sought to send, I felt that whatever I could get out would be better than nothing," he told UP European manager Ed Keen later.[93] When Germany replied to Wilson's first note, Ackerman managed to win a major victory over his competitors by getting the story to America first. He used the American ambassador in Berlin to intervene with the German Foreign Office so UP could get the note as soon as possible. The German undersecretary of the foreign office, Arthur Zimmerman, agreed to release the note to Ackerman on May 30. Ackerman also convinced the American ambassador to give him the English version of the note at the American embassy at noon, so Ackerman would not need to translate it. By 12:45 P.M. Ackerman was able to wire the contents of the note to The Hague for transmission to England and New York. Later that day, Ackerman also interviewed foreign minister Von Jagow and sent that story as a follow-up. The rest of the American correspondents in Berlin were surprised by Ackerman's initiative. Associated Press did not get its story sent until five that afternoon.[94]

The New York UP office was ecstatic. The *Chicago Tribune* and *Philadelphia Ledger*, both AP clients, purchased the rights to Ackerman's copy. Ackerman's wire began arriving at 6:40 P.M. in New York, Arnold reported later, and "the opposition was skinned."[95]

Associated Press would do the skinning after Germany's reply to the second note of protest from the United States. Associated Press's Berlin bureau chief, S. B. Conger, was given a copy of the note, apparently by the Germans, before the rest of the correspondents. This gave Conger time to write his story and send it minutes after the permitted time of release. While other correspondents were translating the note and writing their stories, Conger was allowed to wire his story immediately. Ackerman's was delayed thirty minutes in the telegraph office. In addition, the German Wolff news agency got the note eight hours early, even though it was supposed to be treated the same as the neutral news services.[96] Furious, Ackerman filed an official complaint with the press office of the Foreign Ministry: "There are 650 American newspapers depending upon me every day to send them information from Berlin. Thirty million readers of those newspapers undoubtedly use my information in some way to form their opinion of Germany. I need not point out what effect it would have if I cabled them that their correspondent was being discriminated against."[97]

Howard also complained to the German ambassador to the United States, Bernstorff, about the favoritism. Howard said the AP story of the note reached The Hague ten minutes before Ackerman's note began to arrive. Howard demanded "equal consideration with the Associated Press" and reminded Bernstorff that the "United Press is spending a tremendous amount of money and energy in its efforts to present adequately and fairly the German side of the pending international controversy."[98] Bernstorff relayed Howard's complaint to Berlin.

Meanwhile, UP was not the only press agency upset with AP's preferential treatment. Cyril Brown, Berlin correspondent of the *New York Times*, filed his own protest, complaining that Conger had blank telegraph sheets already signed by a censor. Ackerman reported he was "backed in my protest by every correspondent in Berlin outside of the Associated Press."[99] Ackerman, though, was getting pressure from the German press agents, who, he said, told him *"they 'feared'* it would be difficult for me to work in Berlin as a result of this incident."[100]

By August Ackerman was careful which censor he was working with, because some were leaking information to Conger and Von Wiegand,[101] and Von Wiegand was spreading unkind rumors about him. Ackerman said he had been invited to only two of eight trips made to the front and to industrial areas inside Germany since he had been there. The situation had deteriorated so much that Howard contemplated closing the Berlin bureau, but Ackerman pleaded to stay "because I feel that we have a good chance of winning the fight."[102]

The situation was finally defused on September 1 when Bernstorff announced Berlin's reply to his July 13 inquiry prompted by Howard. AP's Conger did not have preapproved telegraph sheets: "The affair was just a 'practical joke,'" Bernstorff explained to Howard. He confirmed that Conger somehow managed to get the German's second reply note in advance, but that the "Associated Press does not enjoy any privileges with regard to the censoring or dispatching of his telegrams."[103] Bernstorff assured Howard that changes would be made in the press office to prevent any future problems. Satisfied, Howard wrote Bernstorff "there will be no further cause for complaint on the part of our Berlin representative."[104]

UP Expands Globally

By the end of 1915, United Press was doing well, helped by international frustrations over the shortage of war news created by the world news cartel and military censorship. Howard had hoped to make New York what the *Editor and Publisher* called the "news clearing house" of the world, and by the fall of 1916 it looked like UP was leading the way.[105] Howard had successfully expanded his wire service's reach to South America by the signing of a ten-year contract with the Buenos Aires newspaper *La Nacion*. He also personally negotiated contracts with *O Pais* and *O Imparcial*, two Rio de Janeiro newspapers. These newspapers got a world report from UP's New York office and war news directly from UP in London. The South American newspapers had been dependent on the French news agency Havas, part of the world news cartel, which refused to send official German war communiqués. Frustrated, major South American newspapers looked to UP as an alternative, and Howard was ready to deliver.[106] He publicly linked this new business venture to the progressive ideal of world cooperation. "Such news service, it is believed by students of the Pan-American situation, will prove to be the most important factor in drawing together the peoples of the two continents."[107] Charles Stewart, a former European general manager for UP, ran the new Buenos Aires bureau. The service did well in its "first big tryout" sending returns for the American presidential election in the fall of 1916.[108]

In 1916 Howard also arranged or approved combinations with the French newspapers *Le Matin* and *Le Journal [of] Paris*. Under the arrangement, these two major French newspapers could print UP stories; in exchange, UP got the rights to distribute stories from them.[109] Ackerman had arranged a similar deal in June 1915 with the German newspaper *Lokal Anzeiger* because it wanted access to UP reports from Berlin and Constantinople.[110] The *Lokal Anzeiger* was paying Ackerman the equivalent of about $16 for some UP stories in August 1915.[111] The access and relative editorial freedom granted to neutral reporters was something native journalists did not have.

Copyright and a "Kiss"

As interest in the war grew after the *Lusitania* sinking in the United States, UP continued to struggle with the problems of competitors or nonclients stealing its news reports. The Concern's chief financial attorney, J. W. Curts, was frustrated. "The general rule is, that when news matter is published it becomes free to all the world. There is a limitation to this condition, however, arising from the importance of the element of time in publishing news matter," he wrote in April 1915. Curts cited a federal case in Chicago in which Western Union successfully stopped a rival ticker service from retransmitting information an hour after it had been sent by Western Union. But Curts was not convinced it was in UP's best interest to insist that strict standards be put on wire service matter because UP wanted the freedom to use stories from rivals, too. "Suppose, for instance, this [Western Union case] rule should be adopted and enforced in our business in New York City. This is a question which ought to be carefully considered by . . . UP before we really go into the matter."[112]

While Curts was cautious about setting a legal precedent that might backfire, Howard was enraged by the continual pirating of key UP exclusives. In July the *New York Evening Journal* reprinted a copyrighted UP story by Lord Northcliffe that had appeared in the *New York Sun*, a UP client. "Their action was a bare-faced, cold-blooded, indefensible threat," he wrote Curts.[113] The *New York Evening Journal* and the *New York American* also stole a UP story from Bulgaria.[114]

Curts carefully examined the Northcliffe theft and determined that "exactly twenty-five percent" of the UP story was stolen. "I have heard old newspaper men say that you could use a third of a copyrighted magazine article without being liable for infringement. I do not believe that there is any foundation for this belief." Still, Curts insisted that the law required "substantial appropriation" for it to be a copyright violation, and he was not convinced this incident could meet that standard. "Please do not ask me what would be a substantial appropriation, because I cannot answer," Curts explained.[115] He felt the thefts of Bulgarian stories were not even a "technical infringement" of the copyright law.[116]

Howard got Curts's answers just as he was about to send another example of Pulitzer's *St. Louis Post-Dispatch* stealing a copyrighted story. "From your letter, I take it that our only alternative is to kiss them on the other cheek. Frankly, Jay, I don't get you, but I suppose it's alright [*sic*]," Howard wrote on August 19.

United Press continued to struggle with piracy of UP stories in St. Louis, in particular, throughout the fall of 1915. The *St. Louis Times*, a UP client, suffered thefts by the *Globe-Democrat* and the *Post-Dispatch*.[117] Curts remained dubious about UP's chances of winning a lawsuit, especially when the stolen passages came from quotations gathered in interviews with key leaders: "You see, if this copyright was established, it would tie up the utterances of public men on public questions so that nobody would be able to use them for twenty-one years. . . . There's is a very real demand for the free circulation through the newspapers of all information, and I doubt if the opinions of public men upon questions of great public interest can be locked up by one man for twenty-one years upon a copyright claimed in an interview."[118]

Fixated on the ability to copyright quotations, Curts was reluctant to sue. He did not think the UP could make a convincing case that piracy was unfair competition, even though he said that was UP's most viable legal claim.[119] Meanwhile, AP was suing Hearst's INS over similar claims of stealing. Deciding to wait until that much larger lawsuit was settled, UP did not file any major lawsuits over copyright questions during the war. The AP lawsuit against the INS eventually reached the U.S. Supreme Court, which ruled in 1918 that copyright does not protect facts, only the words that expressed those facts. The high court ruled against the INS, however, on "misappropriation" grounds because it was competing unfairly by distributing AP content as its own. Curts was correct that unfair competition, now considered a corollary to copyright law, was the strongest case to make against the news pirates.[120]

"The British Censor Has Greatly Improved His Conduct"

The brunt of Howard's efforts to fight piracy and to increase foreign distribution of the UP report came as the British loosened their tight censorship restrictions. A more liberal policy was first seen in early 1916. Keen, the European general manager, wrote in the *Editor and Publisher* on March 18, 1916, that to "give the devil his due. . . . it must be said that the British censor has greatly improved his conduct in recent months. . . . With experience he has acquired a finer sense of justice; and he is less suspicious than he used to be."

Keen said the United States got "not a little information" from Germany that often was banned from England's newspapers, and he said American reporters in London could report on Parliament "with practically the same freedom that British correspondents in Washington handle similar rows in Congress."[121] Howard added in an article in November: "Practically the only thing the British press censors are holding up today is military news likely to be of interest to the enemy."[122] He said Germany and France now had the most onerous censorship. "The great difference between the British and German censors is that it is possible to send from London anything printed in the British Press. But if either the French or German newspaper say anything in criticism of their own people or Government that is objectionable to the censors its transmission to other countries is forbidden."[123]

Military censorship and hordes of news competitors prevented UP in 1915–16 from repeating the types of notable scoops it got during the first six months of the war. As the *Editor and Publisher and Journalist* editorialized in August 1915:

> Newspaper beats are becoming less and less frequent in these modern days of newspaper making, for the reason that there are so many enterprising news associations and correspondents, so many thousands of miles of cable, telegraph and telephone wires covering the earth, and available for the transmission of news, that it is almost impossible for anything of general interest and importance to happen anywhere without becoming known to many newspapers at the same time. There is no monopoly of the news or of the mediums of communication.[124]

Keen admitted months later in the same publication (now named *Editor and Publisher*) that UP got many of its scoops only because the British censor approved the UP story first. He said UP's competitors often took stories to the censor's office at the same time. "Whether the censor selected by lot the first one to go, or whether immediately after he had passed the United Press bulletin and before he had the opportunity of tackling the others the tea tray arrived, there is no telling."[125]

Censorship effectively killed stories of any type in some countries. Henry Wood told Howard and Keen in July 1915 that Greek censors in Athens were only on the job from 11 A.M. to 12:30 P.M. each day and from 7 P.M. to 8 P.M. at night. "During the rest of the day press dispatches cannot be sent. You will see at a balance I think the hopelessness of the situation."[126] Wood said Greek censors also required that "in all news relating to Greece the correspondent must give the paper or other source of information from which it came so that no one will get the impression that the factors or opinions contained therein are official."[127]

The NEA: "The Heart of Human Interest"

The NEA also struggled to find new angles to cover the war. Its most notable stunt hit the pages of its client newspapers in the summer of 1915, when it hired photographer W. H. Durborough to take pictures inside Germany. He wrote short articles to accompany some pictures. "It [Durborough's stunt] is the best thing in this country, thus far, in covering the war with pictures," Canfield boasted to Rickey on June 25. "The War—well, it has stumped us all. It has paralyzed our brains as it were. I feel we have gone through almost a year of it and hardly scratched the heart of human interest."[128] Durborough's pictures of German women planting gardens to raise food, German soldiers in the field about to attack, and German weaponry appeared over several months of late summer.[129] A photograph of a Red Cross rescue dog standing over a fallen German soldier got Harper's attention in particular.[130] "I have not seen a finer war picture; and the story is as good as the picture. It will appeal to children and women as much, maybe even more, than to men."[131]

Using pictures to describe the war seemed to be a natural way to reduce a concern among the NEA and the Scripps newspapers that editors were drowning in information and were passing it along to readers in wordy and complicated stories. Since spring 1915 Canfield had noticed that readers "are glancing at headlines and reading the bulletins" of war news. "Personally I very much doubt if the great mass or readers care for technical stories, in detail, of present battles." Canfield felt only "actual news and pictures of the war" maintained any degree of interest with readers.[132] Rickey, too, thought editors were "befuddled as to what to use and what not to use" because of the sheer volume of NEA editorials and features being distributed after the *Lusitania* sinking.[133]

The vocabulary of the war worried some in the Scripps Concern as the war dragged on. In July 1915, C. F. Mosher in the Cincinnati business office was concerned that "when we get our vocabulary so high up that the majority or a large percentage of the public don't understand the words without looking them up in the dictionary, it seems to me it is certain to affect [newspaper] circulation."[134]

The Scripps newspapers were serious about the dangers of war jargon. The *Editor and Publisher and Journalist* reported in October that the *Cleveland Press* was banning words such as "communiqué," "sector," "salient," "Anglo-French," "simultaneously," "approximately," "commence," and "diametrically opposed."[135] The trade magazine quoted *Cleveland Press* editor Victor Morgan: "Our aim will be to reduce all reading matter to the simplest terms. There is a tendency to use too many words of Latin origin. What we want to do is to stick to English."

The Tactics of Preparedness

Meanwhile, by the late summer and early fall of 1915, with Wilson and his cabinet supporting preparedness, the NEA put its collective pen to the preparedness issue in force, in a way much bolder than it had dared that spring. In April 1915 the NEA was candy-coating the medicinal message of preparedness. For example, it commissioned two fiction articles by "famous artist and navy expert" Henry Reuterdahl, in which he described an enemy invasion of New York City. The second article began: "Pandemonium! Terror stricken people fled up the Hudson to the hills. Refugees lined the roads, the rich in their limousines passing the trundling poor."[136] The NEA reprinted a history of the U.S. navy in April as well. The fifth installment described the subpar navy the United States operated in the War of 1812, in which parts of Washington, D.C., were burned by the British. "The British had seven times the armament of the whole American navy," the article said.[137] The moral of these historical lessons was always implied.

After Navy Secretary Daniels challenged the Naval War College to look for new weapons,[138] the NEA supported the immediate building of a fleet of submarines. "A battleship building program upon a large scale undoubtedly would take years to complete, and the dreadnaught [sic] by then would possibly be superseded by some newly devised naval war engine," it said, reversing its earlier support for bigger ships.[139]

Throughout the rest of 1915, preparedness remained a key issue for the NEA. Of particular interest was a proposal for the United States to build an army patterned after Switzerland's citizen militia system, in which every male citizen was required to serve. The NEA quoted Lieutenant Colonel George Bell, who said that this sort of militia was better than a regular army, because regular army troops "do not possess the endurance, education, and wonderful patriotism which would endure anything."[140]

The Swiss army model of universal military training fit nicely into the NEA's values of sacrifice and responsibility. "War means you," an editorial said on July 30. "The ordinary view of warfare is that is [sic] means the other fellow." The NEA's view was a simple reminder that if and when war came, it would be fought by many Americans and funded by those remaining behind. "Conscription—or a 'draft' as it was called in the civil war—can be made to take care of one class; national expenses will take care of the others."[141]

Historian John Patrick Finnegan noted that many Americans remained unconvinced about forms of compulsory military service such as universal military training well into 1917. "Universal military training, like preparedness in general, made its strongest appeal to business circles and the urban upper-middle class, and these were not the whole nation," he wrote in 1974.[142]

Scientific wonders and oddities had long been a staple of the penny press, and so-called defense experts had a new batch of ideas for this modern war. The NEA reported on August 3 about inventor Gus Gathmann's plan to put triple hulls on battleships: "A battleship that no torpedo can sink," the story thundered.[143] Eleven days later the NEA editorialized that the United States should train military aviators by letting them fly planes for the postal service.[144]

After President Wilson outlined his plan for preparedness in August, the NEA used one of its favorite publicity tactics—commissioning a recognized expert to write a series of columns. In this case, Franklin D. Roosevelt, undersecretary of the navy, wrote six articles outlining the needs of the navy. The first, printed in the *Cleveland Press* on September 24, ended with a reproduction of Roosevelt's signature. In one of the articles Roosevelt contradicted the NEA's position and said submarines were too unreliable and ineffective to form the backbone of a navy spending program. "We need to have about 160 of the coast defense type [of surface ship]."[145] In other articles, Roosevelt called for more support ships to act as scouts for larger ships. He also called for more destroyers to protect the ten battleships he said were needed.[146]

Throughout the NEA's call for increased military spending, it always insisted that Uncle Sam make the armaments. "We are not advocating military preparation to feed the hungry maw of a war trust that is taking from 20 to 60 percent profits out of evey [sic] dollar expended in government contracts for arms, ammunition, armor plate and battleships!"[147] Congressman Clyde Tavenner of Illinois, who was arguing the same point, wrote a column for the NEA in October attacking the "war trust" whose "control is in the hands of the same group of money kings that rule . . . the telegraph companies, the railroads, the steamship lines, the money trust, and the great insurance companies and industrial trusts."[148]

Although the federal government already operated some munitions plants, the idea proved to be grossly impractical. The Ordnance Bureau eventually estimated that 750,000 men would have to be hired to operate the new federal defense plants; the needs of the country's defenses were too large to be handled by the government munitions plants alone.[149]

The sinking of the *Lusitania* influenced the Scripps Concern in several ways. It forced a stronger consensus on editorial policy on preparedness, even while the issue of mandated "Must Copy" authority through the NEA remained unresolved. Ironically, preparedness was consuming the minds of Scripps editors so much that they were beginning to support policies divergent with those of labor unions and the working class—the traditional Scripps readership.

The *Lusitania* incident helped make the European war a hot news product again as well, providing new opportunities and new pressures. Although censorship killed the potential for big exclusives from UP, the Concern used the NEA and its easy-to-digest writing style to make the war news it did generate as attractive to readers as possible.

Most notably, the *Lusitania* incident did not change the Concern's determination to cover the war in a balanced way, and also encouraged it to hang onto its political independence a bit longer by not supporting Wilson's reelection—at least not yet.

As 1916 approached, another major factor was about to emerge that would shape the Concern and its coverage of Wilson and the war. E. W. Scripps himself was to hurl a new torpedo: his plan to publicize income tax returns in newspapers so as to stop income tax evasion. The additional tax revenue that would result was to help pay for military preparedness and various social justice programs. Coming from the top man, it was an idea Scripps editors could not ignore, and it was the only issue that could possibly change the Concern's mind about supporting Wilson.

4 "Genuine Enthusiastic Support": November 1915 to November 1916

Two issues dominated the pages of the Scripps newspapers in the year preceding the 1916 election—the presidential campaign and publicity of income tax returns. To readers the issues probably seemed unrelated, but to E. W. Scripps they were linked so tightly that he threatened to withhold his newspapers' support for Wilson unless he supported the publicity issue.

Coverage of the war, while vital to the Concern's reputation and profits, became increasingly routine as the *Lusitania* sinking slipped farther into the past. Censorship prevented major scoops, and the German threat seemed to lessen. The country and the Concern turned their attention to the 1916 election, and E. W. Scripps turned his newspapers' attention to his income tax idea. Progressive reform was on the front burner again.

Any political independence the Concern had exhibited would be lost during this period as the Scripps Concern publicly and privately became one of Woodrow Wilson's biggest journalistic supporters and was credited for helping him win reelection. But the Concern's transformation into a political mouthpiece did not take place before some behind-the-scenes negotiations played out with the Wilson administration regarding Scripps's idea for publicizing tax returns. The issue became a way for Scripps to test Wilson's commitment to the progressive cause, but it also showed how the publisher's stubborn idealism often was not based on political reality and how he still meddled actively in the editorial policies of his newspapers. One cannot understand the Scripps newspapers' relationship with Wilson without closely studying this period.

The publicity issue also created an important logistical precedent for how the leaders of the Concern, through a central editor at the NEA, could work together on big issues without invoking "Must Copy" authority and diluting the freedom of local editors. By working together for Wilson's reelection, the Concern showed itself how powerful it could be if the newspapers and the NEA worked in concert. This pattern of channeling and focusing content on a big issue in way that was designed to persuade readers was duplicated in national editorial crusades launched after the election. The issue also served as a precursor to additional meddling by the "retired" Scripps in the editorial policies of his newspaper chain.

A History of Taxing Incomes

From the beginning of the war until late 1915, the elder Scripps had mostly refrained from seriously interfering in news policy decisions. The income tax was the cornerstone of the reforms that he and other progressives believed would help restore social justice in America, however, and so on this issue he could not stay silent. The income tax would ensure the rich would pay for programs to benefit the less advantaged and to protect the country's interests from the effects of the war in Europe. But Scripps believed the rich were evading the tax, which was still relatively new at the time. A reincarnated federal income tax had been collected only since March 1, 1913. The United States had collected an income tax during the Civil War, but the unpopular tax had been repealed in 1872 because it was seen as no longer needed.[1]

Still, the income tax had been a major plank in the platform of populist organizations in the late 1800s as a way to get the rich to pay for most government costs.[2] Finally, in 1908, when Teddy Roosevelt endorsed the idea, conservative Republicans supported a 1 percent corporate tax on profits exceeding $5,000. In early 1913, enough states had ratified the Sixteenth Amendment to allow an income tax on personal incomes as well,[3] and in October of that year, Congress enacted it.[4]

The Income Tax as a Way to Show Scripps's Power

The Democratic Party and the Scripps Concern, too, had long advocated a federal income tax, and the impending war made the issue seem even more important.[5] On May 16, 1916, a "Declaration of Principles" printed on the front page of Scripps newspapers called for "complete collection of the income tax" as a "matter of justice" to pay for increases in spending for the navy and army that were needed for a strong defense to stand against the warring nations in Europe.

The Concern's support for preparedness and for taxing the rich to pay for it through the income tax came from both sides of the military spending debate in 1915–16. Antimilitarists hoped that threats of increased taxes would dampen support among the wealthy for preparedness.[6] The Scripps plan for income tax publicity would not raise taxes but would ensure taxes already owed would be paid. That rationale at least appealed to an honest person of wealth.

Meanwhile, the lure of national power to shape public opinion was growing stronger for Scripps's top men as the Concern's operations grew in size because of the European war. The growing UP was, by far, the leading competitor to AP. More important, the NEA was being sold to newspapers in markets not competing with Scripps-owned newspapers by 1916. As the NEA grew, it broadened the Scripps men's ability to shape public policy on a national scale, despite the fact that some editors worried that Scripps's often radical ideals would suffer if they had to be toned down to make them more palatable to a larger share of the country.[7]

In June 1914, NEA president B. H. Canfield began a push to get the NEA service into more newspapers. In December 1914, K. J. Murdoch was hired to run a new sales department.[8] Aided by interest in the NEA's war features, within one year, Murdoch doubled its non-Scripps-controlled clients to ninety-four taking the full service and fifty-three taking the more slimmed-down "Pony" service.[9] All told, the NEA had clients in all but ten states in January 1916.[10]

Scripps boasted to secretary of the interior Franklin Lane in November 1915 that his newspapers alone had a circulation of a million readers daily, but NEA clients added another two million readers. Counting UP clients, Scripps said his news empire had the power to reach one-fourth to one-third of all the people in the country.[11] The war had made the Concern one of the most powerful media organizations in the country—if not the single most powerful—in terms of size and geographic spread.

Scripps long had hoped that his newspaper empire would one day flex national muscle and gain the credit it deserved as a leader in forming public opinion. Thus, the income tax issue offered something for everyone within the Concern. It was an opportunity to possibly increase the NEA's clientele (presumably, new clients would become interested in the NEA when they saw its influence in shaping public opinion). In addition, with war coverage stagnating because of censorship and competition, the income tax publicity idea would provide unique copy and a progressive cause to champion.

"No More Effective Check"

The income tax publicity measure started as a formal "campaign" for the NEA during a meeting between NEA president Canfield and E. W. Scripps at Scripps's home in Miramar in August 1915.[12] Scripps was convinced that thousands of people, most of them very wealthy, were evading the tax.[13] Scripps said he had paid $10,000 on a personal income that was $342,498 in 1915.[14]

Scripps knew he could easily evade income taxes, too.[15] He reasoned that at least eight thousand more people with incomes "no greater and no less than mine" existed and if they all paid $10,000 in taxes, they alone would account for the $80 million (the amount collected in income taxes in 1914).[16] Scripps surmised that the Treasury Department was "thoroughly unequipped.... I believe that no more effective check could be adopted by the Treasury Department than by publicity."[17]

Scripps reasoned that potential deadbeats could be shamed into paying by publishing their incomes and taxes paid. In addition, the government should keep a card index of evidence accumulated from third parties to paint a circumstantial picture of everyone's wealth so as to help build cases against tax dodgers.

Scripps had contacted philanthropist Charles Crane, who knew treasury secretary William McAdoo from the 1912 campaign. Scripps said that "wholesale frauds" were being committed, and that only about 10 percent of what should be collected in income tax was being collected. Scripps wanted Crane to approach McAdoo: "I know something of the experiences of . . . my own family with large incomes, and something of the experiences of my . . . business associates. All of us made out income tax returns, or failed to make any returns, and not one of us has been submitted to any personal inquiry or investigation. I am convinced that, had I offered one-tenth of the amount of income tax that I paid, it would have been accepted and no questions asked."[18]

Meanwhile, Gilson Gardner, the NEA's top political writer, met with Treasury officials on August 25 about Scripps's suggestions. McAdoo and the commissioner of the Internal Revenue Service (IRS) were on vacation, but Gardner met with the deputy IRS commissioner, Robert Gates, and the head of the personal income tax collection division. "My impression after the interview was over seemed to work out in an expression 'let it drop,' to the effect that they were collecting 'a maximum of revenue with a minimum of friction,'" Gardner reported to Scripps the next day. Gardner said he had been told it was difficult for the IRS to obtain the evidence to sustain a conviction of tax evasion, even if it were willing. "I do not think I do the Administration an injustice when I say that I feel that the Secretary of the Treasury has not wished to antagonize the powerful interests that would be necessarily antagonized if a more rigid enforcement of the income law were insisted upon." Gardner said that the IRS was already working on a system of compiling independent information about tax filers that was close to what Scripps had suggested.[19]

Determined that he was assessing the situation correctly, Scripps now wrote Canfield at NEA headquarters in Chicago, urging him to launch a newspaper campaign. "I will not vouch for the value of this kind of copy; but of one thing I am certain," he wrote the NEA chief, "and that is, that you have it in your power to start a movement going that will, within five years, at least quadruple the receipts of the government from the income tax." Scripps called the issue the "most amazing state of immorality on the part of the governing classes that has ever been revealed in any country during any period of history."[20]

"A Weapon of Publicity"

In mid-September, Canfield wrote Scripps acknowledging that the NEA would take up the publicity issue as a cause. The goal: within five years to quadruple the receipts from the tax.[21] In the same letter he gauged his chances of success. He noted that 150 newspapers were getting the NEA service in some form: "Under the present plan of increasing the number of clients we will add to our list of papers approximately 50 a year. At the end of five years we should have in the neighborhood of 400 newspapers. With this large and rapidly growing circulation, even though we landed a feature of this sort in only half of the papers (which is a low estimate based on recent experiments) we will have a weapon of publicity that will insure the success of this movement."[22]

Within two weeks, Canfield had hired economist Basil Manly for the job of "digging up the facts for the income tax dodging campaign." Manly would head up a division of the NEA called the News Economic Bureau; he would start with the income tax but would eventually write other economic stories. Canfield said he hoped to force a congressional investigation. "The committee reports doesn't [concern us as] much as the fact that the matter will get before the country in such shape that publicity of income tax payments will be demanded," Canfield wrote.[23]

"As Good a Man"

Manly, twenty-nine, fit the Scripps mold as a bright, energetic, principled young man. "[His] facts and figures should be so deadly accurate that there will never be any questions raised about that feature of the matter," Canfield wrote about his new hire.[24] Manly had just finished working for the Committee on Industrial Relations, which Congress had set up in 1912 to study labor unrest.[25] Manly had written what was supposed to be the final report of the committee (dubbed the Manly Report), but it was eventually rejected because nonlabor members claimed it was too radical. The Manly Report said that the working classes did not get a fair share of the country's wealth, they saw the economic system as unjust, and unrest took place because workers were not being allowed to organize.[26]

A 1906 graduate of William and Lee University, Manly had worked for the Bureau of Labor Statistics and had been a fellow in political science at the University of Chicago, where his interest in progressive reform had grown.[27] Gardner called Manly a "fine investigator and a real radical."[28]

The Scripps men continued to try to change the law without having to take the administration to task publicly. Gardner went back to the Treasury Department in October to see McAdoo, but found the secretary unaware of the publicity issue, because it "had not got past the people below."[29] Gardner reported to Scripps that McAdoo said collections were doing well—for such a new law. Gardner said McAdoo "perhaps can be persuaded that it would be good politics to recommend changes in the law along the lines you have in mind." Still, Gardner said he doubted the Wilson administration, which had been trying to attract business support, would find the publicity issue "timely" or "wise."[30]

McAdoo did cooperate with Manly's investigation. Manly found he had access to all IRS information "without restrictions"—which meant everything except the details regarding individuals. Manly was already finding plenty of what he called "dope" for news stories: "I find that I will able to identify the exact amount of the income of several millionaires, who happen to be the only ones in a given district or state who pay a tax on more than $500,000 a year. For example, the richest man in California has an income in 1913 of $1,171,294. We ought to be able to name him without any trouble and to get a good story on whether that is all he has."[31] Manly promised he would "milk the Internal Revenue office dry. They are all very nice and polite and I will have to go slow to keep from scaring them, but by the time the Secretary gets back, I will have everything we can get."[32]

"Follow and Assist"

By late October, Scripps was still hoping that McAdoo or Wilson himself would speak in favor of income tax publicity, so the Scripps papers "could follow and assist." Scripps did not want to hurt the man he assumed would be the most progressive-minded candidate in 1916. "All that is necessary for the President to do is to cause McAdoo to include in his annual report to Congress a strong expression on the subject, or for the President himself, in his own message, to read the riot act to the rich rascals among his constituents," Scripps wrote Gardner.[33] A week later, Gardner met with Interior Secretary Franklin Lane, who was a friend of Scripps, and asked him to talk to talk with McAdoo, but Gardner remained pessimistic.[34]

Scripps, wanting to send his own warning shot to the administration, wrote Interior Secretary Lane on November 4. He recounted the size of the Scripps Concern—three million readers in the NEA alone—but said, "I hope . . . you will not think I am boasting or trying to exercise any undue influence." He wrote his friend the progressive leader Amos Pinchot later about the letter to Lane: "I have reason to believe that both Wilson and Lane have but small conception of the relative importance of mediums of publicity. They treat me very nicely, but, still, I know that they think I am only one of the little fellows—very earnest, very sincere, perhaps a loyal friend of the proletariat, but still not quite respectable."[35]

"Dope" on "Who Owns America"

Meanwhile, Manly was in his third week of digging around in the IRS files and was getting ready to write at least sixteen articles. "I have a lot of good dope," he wrote NEA editor S. T. Hughes on October 29. Manly had found information on dodgers he could use as anecdotal evidence. "I feel sure now that I can prove my contention that not more than one half of the tax is being collected, and that I know very definitely what the trouble is and what must be done about it." Manly admitted the IRS was already making reforms that were expected to increase collections by 25 percent, "so that with the noise that we will make, I am willing to bet that the tax for 1915 will be 60 percent greater than in either of the preceding years." The big push, Manly suggested, must be for publicity of returns, both to raise collections and "because the information that comes in through the income tax is worth untold millions in telling us the truth about 'Who Owns America.'"[36]

That point interested Scripps, even as he worried about Manly's writing style. Scripps wrote on November 9 that he was worried that Manly was going to concentrate on "a lot of good newspaper stuff" about individual stories of tax dodgers. Scripps hoped Manly's articles would focus more on the point that there was a "tremendous reservoir of money applicable . . . which the government is restrained from getting by reason of inefficient officials and dishonest officials." Scripps said a "discontented democracy" could be satisfied "at an expense to the wealthiest that would be insignificant if it were considered as an insurance against the spirit of revolt that is abroad in the country." In Scripps's way of thinking, the rich would be "those who gained the most" if their incomes were taxed to fund programs to benefit the lower classes. "I and hundreds and even thousands of other men of this country could easily pay twenty or twenty-five percent of our incomes . . . without any personal discomfort and without in any way diminishing the extent of our enterprises."[37] The goal, he said, was "to obtain more justice in this country."[38]

One Last Meeting

Scripps's subtle threats to Lane paid off. Lane sent the letters to McAdoo, who wrote to Scripps on November 15. McAdoo said he wanted to clear up "some serious misapprehensions and misinformation upon which your conclusions are based."[39] McAdoo said he was meeting with staff from the NEA the next week. Lane also replied, assuring Scripps that McAdoo "appreciates fully the interest that you take in the income tax matter."[40]

Gardner later wrote that McAdoo admitted that a "large percentage" of the tax was not being collected, but he was asking Congress for more staff.[41] "He was not prepared to recommend the publicity remedy. Postmaster General [Alfred] Burleson happened in toward the close of the interview and he expressed actual horror at the suggestion of making public the amounts paid." Gardner said McAdoo suggested keeping the threat of publishing the names of all income tax payers "without giving the amounts they pay" as a trump card to compel Congress to grant his requests for more auditors and law changes. Gardner said McAdoo might still change his recommendations in his annual report, but "he intimated that he would like to talk with others (meaning the president) before finally deciding just what he would ask Congress to do." Gardner felt McAdoo's "general attitude" freed the Concern to run with Manly's articles, "with a general showing up of the fact that the income tax is evaded, but that the administration is anxious to correct the defects." Still, Gardner was cynical. He said it would be a "long time" before the government would be collecting what it should through the income tax.[42]

E.W.'s Criticism

Manly now faced a daunting task in writing the articles. Not only did he have to synthesize a great deal of technical information, but he had to present it in a readable way. His toughest critic was Scripps. In mid-November Manly typed up a summary of his findings and sent it to NEA editor-in-chief S. T. Hughes, who sent it to Scripps. The old publisher was not impressed. "It seems to me you are attacking this subject for [sic] the wrong end," he wrote to Manly. Scripps wanted Manly to estimate the national income of the country, and then extrapolate how much income tax should be collected. Instead, Manly was "tackling the subject along the line adopted by the Muckrakers of a few years ago—that is to say, you are proposing to expose some particular cases of income tax evasion," Scripps wrote. "I did not think of appointing a sleuth to hunt down a few big and many little rascals, wealthy thieves and incompetent officials." Manly was making the same mistake as the government—going after individuals from whom to collect taxes—instead of making a "survey of the whole field." Scripps felt Manly's figures were wrong, too. For example, Scripps could not believe Manly was saying that national income was $36.5 billion in 1915. "From what source could you have obtained this figure? This figure is at least $14,500,000,000 too small." The well-read Scripps quoted Census Bureau statistics that showed Manly's estimation "must be recognized as absurd by any student of economics."[43] It should be noted that when Manly's articles began running in the NEA five months later, the national income benchmark used was $46 billion in 1914—Scripps had been correct.[44]

Scripps's concerns forced Canfield to reconsider the NEA's strategy for launching the income tax campaign. The president of the NEA told Scripps on December 14 that he was now going to tell Manly to take more time to prepare, and not publish anything until Congress gets "down to business on the matter of revenue." Canfield said he asked Manly to concentrate on anecdotal evidence of evasion. "However, it was not because this was an instinctive action [to go after good newspaper copy—but] . . . that the figures were so enormous that I believed they must be exaggerated." Canfield said he had thought it would be better for Manly to understate the amount of tax evasion, so it was more believable.

> I have good reason to believe that we could get the articles printed in nearly all the N.E.A. client newspapers. I also made up a list of a number of other newspapers and magazines to whom we intended offering the articles either for publication or reference, in the hope that they would attract some comment. I also gained the consent of the U.P. to pick up

parts of the articles and to carry their own stories on later developments. The entire plan of attempting, in this way, to get an immense amount of publicity for the matter may have been wrong, but I was quite sure from the correspondence I had with different publishers and others interested that the publicity was not to be obtained in any quarters outside of the Scripps papers unless the matter was put in a way they could easily comprehend.[45]

Canfield said he planned to start a news clipping bureau to track how many of Manly's articles got mention in "all avenues of publicity in addition to our own papers." The anecdotal cases of evasion would be reported, but they would be "merely incidental to the general line of investigation."[46] Canfield said Manly now would worry less about understating, even if the stories got less play in non-Scripps papers. Scripps quickly wrote Canfield that his concerns were "intended purely as suggestions," but he also did not object to the changes suggested.[47] The NEA's strategy was now decided: Manly would pull no punches, and those punches would be thrown when the tax revenue issue was at the top of the nation's agenda.

"On Notice"

In December, President Wilson called for a tax on fuel, a tax on internal combustion engines, a one-cent stamp tax on bank checks, and a higher tax on iron and steel. Wilson also called for changes in the income tax, such as lowering the personal exemption and the threshold for the surtax on higher incomes.[48] Support for the president's revenue plan was divided, even within the Democratic Party. Pacifists did not support the preparedness program; other Democrats and Republicans thought the preparedness program did not go far enough. Still others wanted to get a grasp on expenditures first.[49] The Scripps Concern held the Manly articles during this early debate. Treasury Secretary McAdoo had hoped that his report to Congress for the fiscal year ended 1915 (distributed in early 1916) would appease Scripps's concerns. "I feel sure that we are making real progress ... in the administration of the law," McAdoo wrote to Scripps in mid-December, and promised to send Scripps a copy of his annual report.[50]

In the report, McAdoo admitted to "wholesale evasions" of the income tax law.[51] "The remedy for this is to clarify and strengthen the law where needed and to provide a larger and more effective field force for the investigation and checking up of income-tax returns and for the discovery of those who are liable for the tax and have failed to make returns,"

McAdoo told Congress. McAdoo said it would take his 274 auditors three and a half years to complete personal and corporate income tax audits for 1915 alone. McAdoo said because the law was new, the IRS had been administering the law "courteously, but firmly."[52] McAdoo's report did not mention publicity but focused on the need for more auditors.[53]

"The First Exhaustive Investigation"

The NEA launched Manly's series on Monday, April 24, 1916.[54] The first article primarily introduced Manly (a sidebar, with picture, described his career and highlighted his work on the Manly Report) and the issue. Manly asserted that the income tax should be generating $400 million instead of the $80 million it did in 1915. "If the penalties . . . due upon the $320,000,000 evasions of last year are collected, the nation will have at its disposal $500,000,000 to spend as it chooses for national preparedness and social welfare."[55] The Manly series continued in the *Cleveland Press* for ten consecutive days. The first five articles were put on the front page. Beginning on April 29, the series began to appear either on inside pages or on the front page. Thirteen articles appeared during the campaign's first month.

Manly charged that the "treasury department was not inefficient, measured by government standards, and there was not a bit of evidence to indicate that corruption was responsible."[56] But Manly said McAdoo and the president should be exercising what Manly called their ability to make the tax forms public through executive order. Manly was referring to a clause from the corporation excise tax law of 1909 that had been carried forward into the current income tax law. Tax returns were public records and open to inspection, but they were only to be made public on the basis of rules and regulations set up by the secretary of the Treasury and the president.[57] The initial interpretation by President Taft's secretary of the Treasury was to keep details of individual returns closed, because it was anticipated that publicity would cause more outrage than it was worth.[58] With this sort of precedent set, it was probably doubly difficult for McAdoo to change that interpretation six years later.

On April 26 a long and complex analysis of national income done by Manly was printed; it was easily the longest and most number-filled article of the series. it is difficult to imagine the average reader plodding through the details and following Manly's many conclusions and extrapolations.[59] This article, however, was probably Manly's answer to Scripps's concerns that an accurate determination of national income be advanced, and it also helped show doubtful NEA clients that Manly had some facts to back up his assertions. He explained many flaws in the law that McAdoo had already outlined in his annual report to Congress, although Manly did not mention that. For example, Manly said anyone making more than $3,000 *gross* income each year should be required to file a return, instead of those earning $3,000 *net* income (required under current law). That recommendation became a central recommendation of McAdoo's annual reports in 1915 and 1914.[60]

Manly laid out his main arguments in the first five articles: the law had many loopholes, the IRS could not enforce it, and thousands were not filing returns. The answer: publicity. Manly discounted claims that more agents would solve the problem, because only publicity would ensure against bribery, which was sure to occur with a secret system. "The treasury department needs the publication of the returns to keep its . . . agents free from any suspicion of graft. The other inevitable result is the creation of a bureaucratic spy system of enormous proportions. . . . The thief fears the light of day and the rich man fears the newspapers."[61]

In the second group of five articles, Manly began giving anecdotal evidence of rich people and corporations avoiding the tax. His best evidence: L. V. Harkness, a Standard Oil magnate, showed wealth of more than $100 million, but he paid only $58,035 in income tax.[62]

The NEA also distributed editorials and cartoons to echo Manly's assertions. Eight editorials ran in the *Cleveland Press* during the campaign's first month. The strongest, "Publicity or Espionage," directly engaged McAdoo's efforts to add more auditors and set aside the publicity issue:

> Congress may choose to create in the treasury department a new secret service force, which will create a system of espionage over the entire field of business and private life, sufficient to detect every attempt at tax evasion. Such is the system in use in Prussia. There an army of inspectors and examiners collect the tax with true German thoroness [sic]. Will congress choose to transplant this system to the United States, where because of our enormous territory and great population the force of inspectors must be increased tenfold? If so, it is certain that a bureaucratic Frankenstein will have been created which sooner or later will prove a menace to our liberty and to the very spirit of our government.[63]

Impact

It is difficult to assess the impact of the Manly's campaign, which continued throughout the summer. Only two major magazines picked up the cause to any degree; *Everybody's,* for example, cited Manly's work.[64] The

New Republic also echoed Manly's assertions and called for publicity, but then fell silent on the issue.[65] The *New York Times* supported the idea in an editorial: "Certainly, publish everything. All privacy is scandalous," an editorial said. The *New York Times* had mentioned the issue once earlier in 1916—to report that Treasury Secretary McAdoo was on the defensive because of Manly's charge that national income was $46 million. McAdoo is quoted in the article as saying that Manly's articles made assumptions he could not support. McAdoo claimed national income was more like $20 million. The *Times* would mention the issue only once again that year.[66]

How much NEA's client newspapers used Manly's articles is difficult to assess. Records of the NEA's clipping service do not survive. Canfield, at the NEA's annual meeting that year, said nothing done before had attracted "anything like the national attention which this income tax feature had secured."[67]

Thirty-one articles or editorials were printed on the income tax publicity issue in the *Cleveland Press* alone from June through September 1916.[68] The idea gained support from radical progressives, especially those in the Senate. When McAdoo announced that income tax collections for 1915 would be nearly $125 million more than the previous year, the NEA took credit through the compliments of congressman Alfred Allen of Cincinnati. An NEA editorial quoted Allen: "It has come almost entirely as a result of the income tax expose of the [NEA] affiliated newspapers, which also made a campaign for publicity of returns. . . . Even if Congress should take no action as the result of this nation-wide campaign to put an end to income tax evasions, the enormous publicity has already resulted in bringing many million of dollars of income taxes in the federal treasury. This is the common talk of the members of the ways and means committee."

Ultimately, an amendment to open personal income tax returns was rejected in the Senate Finance Committee, because the majority of the committee thought a man's personal affairs should remain private and doubted publicity would increase collections.[69] Still, the NEA's campaign for income tax publicity would become a major determinant in the Concern's support Wilson in 1916.

The Scripps Papers Pick a President

The 1916 election was one of the closest in U.S. history, and the Scripps Concern was credited with playing a major part in deciding who won.[70] President Woodrow Wilson was reelected by fewer than six hundred thousand votes among the more than seventeen million cast; the electoral college was even closer, with 277 for Wilson and 254 for Republican candidate Charles Evans Hughes.[71] The final election results were not certain for three days, and the Democratic *New York World* even declared Hughes the winner at one point.[72] Ohio, with its twenty-four electoral votes, was the only major northeastern state to support Wilson.[73] In fact, New Hampshire, with its four electoral votes, was the only other state east of the Mississippi and north of the Potomac and Ohio rivers to support him.

The Concern had readers in many important states in the 1916 election and has been given credit for winning these states for Wilson. One historian noted that the Concern's role in California, and Scripps's staffers claimed their syndicated news service helped win votes in Minnesota, Washington, and North Dakota.[74]

Nowhere, however, did the Concern's newspapers have a more powerful position to influence a state than in Ohio. The Concern had five powerful evening newspapers in four of the five largest cities there (Dayton was the exception) in 1916: the *Cleveland Press, Cincinnati Post, Akron Press, Toledo News-Bee* and *Columbus Citizen*.[75] Republican Hughes's domination of the heavily populated Northeast meant Wilson would have lost if he had not won Ohio.[76] But to win Ohio, Wilson needed progressive-minded voters, especially the disgruntled Republican progressives. The Scripps Concern could help deliver those key votes because of its established credibility with Ohio progressives and the working class.

Although the Concern's support for Wilson would prove decisive in the election, it did not make its final decision to support Wilson's reelection publicly until after the party conventions in the summer of 1916. The Concern's allegiance to Wilson had cooled over the past year. The administration's stubbornness on income tax publicity and preparedness were only the latest issues to disappoint Scripps and the Concern. They had become frustrated and cautious with Wilson's failure to fulfill the promise he had shown as a progressive through his legislative efforts in 1913 and early 1914. His wife's death, the European war, and bandit attacks from Mexico seemed to sidetrack Wilson's progressive agenda. Many progressives were disappointed because they had hoped Wilson would do more.[77]

Although Wilson introduced a plan into the Democratic Congress for stronger armed forces in October 1915, it was a skeletonized proposal done for political expediency. As one historian noted, Wilson had "lofty ideas on international policy" but never grasped the importance of a strong military in achieving those ideas.[78] Meanwhile, pacifist Democrats led by William Jennings Bryan severely hampered any preparedness plans Wilson had. A weakened armed forces bill was passed in the spring of 1916. The preparedness tussle angered Scripps, who wrote Democratic Congressman William Kettner on March 11:

> I am beginning to think it may be a good thing for the country if the democrats [sic], as a party, are turned down.
>
> While I have not lost faith in Mr. Wilson, I am beginning to think that his great party . . . is turning out disastrously because the . . . Democratic [Party] in Congress, as a whole, [is] not proving up to standard.[79]

Scripps said the president's naval program was "disappointedly modest. . . . If President Wilson had the enthusiastic support of Congress, my own enthusiasm in his behalf would be far greater than it has become."[80]

On the same day, Scripps sent secretary of the interior Franklin Lane a copy of the Kettner letter to show Lane "recent developments in my own attitude." Scripps again repeated his opinion that "the Democratic Party, as a party, is being tested in these days, and, for one, I will say that the results are unsatisfactory."[81]

Wilson Woos Progressives

In 1916 Wilson knew he and his party might be unsatisfactory to radical, independent progressives such as Scripps, and he needed progressive support to win in a country still considered Republican. Although the Democrats controlled Congress, the Republicans had made substantial gains in the 1914 congressional elections, including Ohio.[82] Both parties had problems in 1916, however. Republicans were still divided by the Roosevelt-led Progressive Party split in 1912; Democrats were divided between pacifists and those who championed preparedness.

In early 1916 the president began a series of moves to earn progressive support. He appointed progressive lawyer Louis Brandeis to the U.S. Supreme Court in January 1916, a move that Scripps said "gratified me greatly."[83] He then supported a rural credit bill that backed loans for farmers, a plan he had blocked the year before.[84] Wilson also strongly supported a model workmen's compensation bill for federal employees, a child labor bill, and a bill giving greater independence to the Philippines.[85] Income tax rates were also increased on higher incomes.[86] Historian Arthur S. Link said this "metamorphosis" in Democratic policies during the summer of 1916 was obvious to everyone. Even if it might have been for political expediency, the Democrats had enacted almost every important part of the Progressive Party's 1912 platform.[87]

Republicans and Progressives "Unify" behind Hughes

The Progressive Party, still viable after Roosevelt's defeat in 1912, held its June nominating convention in Chicago at the same time as the Republican convention. Roosevelt told progressives he was willing to run on their ticket again, but he was quietly using progressive support to coerce the nomination from the Republicans. The conservative "Old Guard" Republicans, however, wanted nothing to do with the man who had ruined their chances of winning in 1912.

Scripps still hoped Roosevelt would get a more serious look because he was, after all, more progressive-minded than the Old Guard Republicans. Scripps had turned down a request to be on Roosevelt's executive campaign committee in April; at the time, he told Roosevelt's campaign manager that he did not want Wilson to be defeated, but if Wilson was to lose, "I hope Roosevelt will be his successor. In other words, I hope that Mr. Roosevelt will be the nominee of the Republican Party."[88] During two raucous conventions in Chicago, the Republicans nominated Hughes—considered a reformer—and the Progressives nominated Roosevelt, who promptly turned the nomination down. He eventually supported Hughes, alienating many of his Progressive brethren. Hughes, a Supreme Court justice, resigned from the court to try to become the compromise candidate in an uneasy alliance of conservative Republican and more moderate Progressive voters. Democrats, meeting in St. Louis, nominated Wilson, making him a focused, well-organized competitor against the reunified Republicans. The Progressive Party disbanded, but some of its leaders later met in Indianapolis to support Wilson.[89]

"Not . . . to Lie Down on the Job"

With Roosevelt's decision to back Hughes, the Concern's support for Wilson seemed assured. Only the timing had to be decided. The Concern wanted to appear to be open-minded to all candidates. In early July editorial chief Robert F. Paine advised Jim Scripps to wait to endorse Wilson until Hughes "had made public his attitude toward public measures and men." Paine said Hughes "is very acceptable to all the Republican bosses and those elements in both parties that are looters of the public domain and reactionary to the backbone." Paine also noted that the mind of candidate Hughes was "evidently that of one who, by training and environment, is convinced that riches and poverty are wholly the Lord's work; that property and courts are sacred; that all progressivism is vicious and that all revolt against the status quo is criminal."[90] Paine advised Jim that "our whole institution ought to declare itself frankly and boldly for Wilson" if Hughes took his anticipated campaign stands.[91] But Paine predicted Hughes would not take strong stands:

> If he [Hughes] does merely play politics, we should smoke him out and take such [an] attitude in the campaign as his revelations warrant. . . . He is very likely not to frankly declare himself on any subject in words that will cut any cloth. I hope otherwise, for this is a time when the country needs to know where every would-be leader intends to lead. But, summing up all the appearances, I think that our papers would do well to prepare to support Wilson, since I take it that [it] is not the intention to have them lie down on the job of promoting national and human progress.[92]

Hughes failed to satisfy the top men in the Concern from the beginning. Gilson Gardner, the NEA's chief political writer, wrote Scripps from the convention in Chicago that he was not happy with either candidate, but: "I am not convinced he [Hughes] can embody the Roosevelt-made issues, and he himself is only a respectable reactionary. . . . Wilson has responded to Progressive stimuli, and I doubt if there would be such moments in the case of Hughes."[93]

A "Quid-Pro-Quo"

For E.W. it was apparent that the Scripps organization should use its power to convince Wilson to support the income tax publicity proposal. Tax publicity was the only issue on which the Scripps papers would criticize the Wilson administration during the 1916 campaign. Under the headline "Get Busy, McAdoo," the *Columbus Citizen* chastised the treasury secretary in a July 24 editorial:

> Basil Manly's articles on the income tax frauds have shown where three hundred million dollars a year is leaking away from the federal treasury, and yet the secretary of the treasury and his horde of helpers, instead of exerting their power to stop the leak are sitting up nights trying to show the income tax frauds are not as large as Manly charges. (Suppose they aren't! Suppose they are only ONE-THIRD as great! That is one dollar for every MAN, WOMAN, AND CHILD IN THE UNITED STATES AND FIVE DOLLARS FOR EVERY FAMILY).[94]

It took a July 16 telegram from Congressman William Kent, chairman of the Wilson Independent League—a campaign organization designed to attract independent voters—to give Scripps a vehicle with which to approach Wilson with his scheme. Kent wired Scripps: "If not obtrusive, would like to know stand of your papers in matter of Presidency." Kent offered the Scripps newspapers political advertising because the "Wilson Committee naturally desires to patronize friends."[95]

Scripps fired back a telegram immediately:

> I don't want patronage of any sort. Must support Wilson because there's nothing else to do. But am not enthusiastic.
>
> However, I would . . . work for him if he would order complete publicity in all income tax matters. In fact, I want the public to know the name of every income tax paper and the exact amount each pays.[96]

Scripps later asked Kent to present the proposition to the president: "Do you or do you not think it would be decent politics for me to put squarely up to the administration a quid-pro-quo proposition?" Scripps later added, "I am not in a position to estimate the political value of the other side. For myself, I can say I speak as a propagandist to some 5 or 6 million voters in the United States every day, and that as a news purveyor I speak to five or six times as many more."[97]

Scripps then wrote Canfield, president of the NEA. He said he doubted Congressman Kent would do anything, so he wanted Canfield to intervene. Meanwhile, Scripps was assuming that Wilson would get "more or less perfunctorily supported by our papers."[98] Scripps said Wilson had been a "good enough president as presidents go," but he was not necessarily entitled to the "enthusiastic support of the men running the Scripps papers." The publisher added: "Perhaps some of your Washington men might talk with Wilson and McAdoo and let him know that Wilson has it in his power to turn our luke-warm favorable consideration of him into genuine enthusiastic support."[99]

"The Best Fight I Know"

E.W.'s quid pro quo probably surprised his editors. The cagey publisher's fickleness with Wilson prompted a flurry of activity at the NEA. Scripps's fixation with the publicity issue was well known, but it had not been linked to support for Wilson. Canfield had already selected one of Scripps's top men, Rickey, former editor of the *Cleveland Press* and one-time candidate for Wilson's "secretary of the people," to run the newspaper campaign to reelect Wilson.[100] Putting an editorial czar in charge of coordinating all coverage gave NEA the control Canfield wanted and concentrated the Concern's fire. It was the type of control Canfield had wanted for other major policy issues, but had been thwarted by concerns over central control. The general consensus among Scripps editors that Wilson was the best candidate meant Rickey's appointment raised no such concerns.

Canfield dispatched Rickey to meet with Wilson during the first week in August about the tax issue. Rickey reported to Scripps later that the president "had given little, if any, thought to the subject" because he did not know about it.[101] But he was interested in the $320 million Manly's articles claimed was being lost (Rickey later mailed Wilson copies of the NEA files on the income tax issue). Rickey stated that he did not think Wilson could interject a publicity measure this late in the congressional session: "Canfield has shown me correspondence with you in which you suggest that the enthusiasm with which we support Wilson ought to depend upon his attitude on this subject. In view of all the circumstances. . . . I do not believe that we should be less enthusiastic in our support of the president because he has not done as we would have wished in this matter."[102] Rickey said he would put forth the "best fight" he knew for Wilson's reelection."[103]

Five days later, Rickey sent Scripps a copy of a White House thank-you letter of August 10 from Wilson. Wilson said he had talked to the Treasury about the tax collection numbers, but was worried he would throw "a monkey wrench in the whole machinery of this session's legislation" if he tried to change the law now.[104] Rickey told Scripps he had expected this. "I do not agree with the suggestion that the character of our support of Wilson should depend upon this proposition," Rickey wrote. "I should be very glad indeed to have your argument on the other side if you care to send it to me."[105]

Instead, Scripps mailed the two Rickey letters to Paine for his comment. When Paine agreed with Rickey, Scripps dropped the "quid-pro-quo." "Not because of Wilson," Paine reasoned with Scripps, "but for the sake of the principles for which the Scripps concern has been pulling for years, I believe that our papers should pull the throttle wide open for Wilson, and Rickey's 'best fight he knows how' ought to prove well worth watching."[106]

A "Throttle Wide Open"

With Scripps's concerns about income tax publicity somewhat satisfied, Rickey began to oversee the campaign to re-elect Wilson from the NEA office in Cleveland. It should be noted that Rickey waged the newspaper campaign for Wilson is an era of no ethical codes for journalists; the modern-day journalistic standard of "objectivity" was not widespread in 1916.[107] Rickey ensured that the Ohio papers in particular published a steady diet of editorials, cartoons, and newspaper articles about the campaign. The campaign was not "Must Copy" material, but Scripps editors supported Wilson and did so willingly. Still, because most editorial and feature matter came to Scripps newspapers via the NEA, whoever managed that content wielded great power.

Even without "Must Copy" power, Rickey rode editors hard to hype the election. A September 26 warning letter to all of the Ohio editors, the editor of the *Oklahoma News*, and the editor of the *Des Moines News* said: "We are not getting the action on editorials that we ought to be getting. . . . In one of our papers recently, I saw two political editorials that had been in the office of the paper—three days—before they were used."[108] Rickey said at least one or two editorials should be in every issue; as for editorials appearing in the *Cleveland Press*, they should be used immediately because "as I am running the campaign, we will have to assume they are alright [sic]."[109] On the day before Rickey's letter, the *Columbus Citizen* had failed to run a presidential editorial for a second consecutive day. Rickey said that "this stuff should not be looked upon as a necessary evil, but as stuff which is of first importance from the standpoint . . . of the paper as well as . . . the country."[110]

Rickey knew how to sell Wilson's record in Ohio, in particular. The president's preparedness program and strong admonitions to Germany after its submarine attacks had made Wilson appear pro-British to many German Americans—the largest ethnic group in Ohio. Census figures show 673,795 German Americans (defined as people born in Germany or having at least one parent born in Germany) were living in Ohio in 1910. The state had a population of 4,767,121 people, of which 34 percent—or 1,621, 638—were foreign-born or had at least one parent who was born in another country. Irish Americans—another ethnic group that tended, though to a much lesser extent then the German Americans, to resent Wilson's perceived pro-British stands—made up the second largest ethnic group in Ohio, with 10.3 percent of the foreign- born population.[111]

"Hyphenism" (the perceived loyalty of some ethnic groups to their home country) became an important issue in America's melting pot in 1916. Hughes wooed the die-hard German American vote by calling for "strict neutrality" instead of the overt favoritism Wilson was showing the British. The German American Alliance, which claimed to have two million members, endorsed Hughes after the Republican convention. Roosevelt's vehement attacks on hyphenism hurt Hughes, though. He campaigned for Hughes in the late summer, denouncing "hyphenates" as disloyal and potential traitors.[112]

Hyphenism created special problems for Rickey. Although most German Americans voted Republican anyway, many German Americans in Ohio were Democrats.[113] Cincinnati was the Democrat's greatest concern because immigrants from Germany and Ireland made up a larger percentage of the residents than in any other Ohio city served by Scripps newspaper.[114] Rickey asked the head of the Democratic National Committee, Robert Wooley, for translations of the forty German dailies and nearly three hundred German weeklies operating in the United States at the time, urging him to get translators to go through them with a "fine tooth comb . . . for the purpose of picking out the most venomous stuff."[115]

Rickey hoped to rally Democratic support among non-Germans by showing them the anti-Wilson articles the German newspapers were writing. He said he wanted to reprint the German articles, without comment, because "I'm sure that for every German vote Hughes gets, Wilson will get five anti-German votes." Rickey's request went unmet; translations from the German press appeared rarely in the Ohio Group newspapers.[116]

Rickey tried to undermine Hughes's support among German Americans and Irish Americans by repeating Roosevelt's claims that some hyphenates were unpatriotic. A Roosevelt speech in Lewiston, Maine, in late August gave Rickey his best ammunition. "I condemn those professional German Americans who in our politics act as servants and allies of Germany, not as Americans interested solely in the honor and welfare of America," Roosevelt was quoted as saying, in a front-page UP story about the speech in the *Cleveland Press*.[117] Later, when Roosevelt visited Ohio, headlines from the Ohio Group papers reveal their treatment of him. "B-r-r-! Yes. T.R. Went thru City" screamed a front-page *Cincinnati Post* story. Roosevelt had been in Ohio only about twenty minutes to switch trains, but the *Post* used the innocuous visit to rehash Roosevelt's support of Hughes and his stand against hyphenates.[118] The Ohio Group of Scripps newspapers printed only one editorial that solely addressed this potentially volatile issue. It concluded: "It is unthinkable that the voters of this nation who put the interests of Germany, or any other foreign country, ahead of the interests of America, are in the majority."[119]

Some Scripps newspapers had to be subtler. Instead of a blizzard of editorials on the issue, the *Cincinnati Post* reprinted short letters to the editor almost daily in October and November to show grassroots support for Wilson from German Americans. The name of the author of the letter was not printed on many occasions; the author was usually only identified as "a reader" or a "German American." The message in these letters was always the same: Loyal German Americans support Wilson.

"The indorsement [sic] of Charles E. Hughes for president by the German-American Alliance should not be given serious consideration by any man who is a German-American," reader Adolph Schlenning wrote.[120] A "Reader of the *Post*, Arlinger, [sic] Virginia," wrote: "I am a German American, both my father and mother having come from Prussia. But I am an American first, last and all the time. I shall vote for Woodrow Wilson because I believe he has been the ablest president since Lincoln."[121] In another letter, "Another German-American Voter," who was a member of the German-American Alliance, said: "There are thousands who will use their own judgment and vote for Wilson."[122]

Besides hyphenism, another major issue Rickey stressed was each candidate's commitment to progressive ideas. He printed a series of columns and news stories from prominent progressives and Republicans, to show support for bipartisan Wilson.[123] J. P. Griffin, president of the Chicago Board of Trade, was quoted in an October 31 article as saying, "The present situation is one which requires that the voter bury party prejudice and cast his vote for the man most suitable to serve the best interests of the people as a whole."[124] Inventor Thomas Edison joined the bandwagon for Wilson in November, saying "men have got to vote as Americans, and not as Democrats or Republicans."[125] Jane Addams, a social reformer, said on the front page of the *Cleveland Press*: "The present administration comes before the country with a social program that carries assurance because of a record of pledges fulfilled and a series of legislative achievements not equaled by any other administration."[126]

Rickey used editorials to support the view that electing Hughes meant a return to the "standpat" days of bosses and big business running government. A November editorial in all Ohio Group newspapers asked: "Shall we have our government in this country for the 95 per cent who constitute the mass, or for the five per cent who are the super-wealthy class?"[127]

Wilson's intervention in a potential nationwide railroad strike in August cemented his progressive commitment for labor groups in Ohio. He unsuccessfully tried to mediate the dispute, and then got Congress to pass the Adamson Act, which mandated an eight-hour day for railroad workers for the same wages previously earned for ten hours of work. Wilson's swift action on behalf of the railroad union was popular in Ohio because all major railroads served the state—a growing industrial center.[128] From 1880 to 1910 the average number of workers in iron and steel companies rose from 300 to 849, in glass from 109 to 249, and in rubber from 94 to 663.[129] Labor membership and population increased accordingly.[130] Rickey seized on the eight-hour-day issue, especially when Hughes claimed it was a private labor dispute that should have been settled through arbitration. Hughes had supported the eight-hour day while he was governor of New York, but not now.[131]

Rickey knew he could poke holes in Hughes's vision of the role of government. "Every victory of a body of laboring men in their fight for either shorter hours or higher wages makes the fight of the next labor body that much easier," an *Akron Press* editorial explained.[132] "Whatever the president did or did not do in this matter was bound to meet with Hughes' severe disapproval," another editorial rationalized.[133] When automaker Henry Ford, who had implemented a eight-hour day in his factories in 1913, backed Wilson and the Adamson Act, an NEA editorial observed: "He ought to know something about the effect of [the eight-hour workday] on his business."[134]

Hughes got a cool reception during campaign stops in the state, particularly when he continued to criticize the Adamson Act despite warnings from Ohio Republicans that he should avoid the issue in the state.[135] The *News-Bee* reported a Hughes's speech at the Willys-Overland automobile plant, the nation's second largest, in Toledo: "Once Hughes had fairly enunciated his attitude on the Adamson eight-hour bill, the interruptions began. There were continuous calls and cheers for Wilson from men in the crowd."[136] Audiences in Ohio and California would rebuff Hughes more than in any other states he visited during the campaign.[137]

The war issue, however, was Rickey's most prevalent theme. War news was featured prominently on the front pages of Scripps's Ohio newspapers during the summer and fall of 1916, often adjacent to stories about the campaign. For example, all five Ohio newspapers during the week before the election ran a front-page analysis piece filled with grisly details by the NEA's Charles Edward Russell. He wrote, "Because of the marvelous ingenuity of modern war machinery, men are shattered with 50 wounds instead of one, or torn into bleeding fragments by the jagged pieces of an exploding shell."[138] United Press president Roy Howard, in a front-page piece in the *Cleveland Press*, predicted the war would last another five years.[139]

While Roosevelt criticized Wilson for being soft on Germany for its submarine attacks and pushed for greater preparedness, Rickey made sure the Scripps newspapers painted the Republicans as war hawks. "President Wilson has kept this country out of the European war and declares that the Republicans will get us into it. Roosevelt, speaking for Hughes and the Republicans, verifies the president's statement," an NEA editorial stated in October.[140] "Wilson has kept the boys of America—your boys and my boys—out of the European slaughterhouse, where already upwards of 15,000,000 boys, just like yours and mine, have been killed, maimed or are suffering the horrors of prison camps," according to an *Akron Press* editorial.[141] The headline on a *Columbus Citizen* editorial on the day of the election was straightforward: "Would You Die to Save Europe?"[142] By October 26, all five Scripps newspapers in Ohio carried the same masthead on their editorial pages for the duration of the campaign. It said: "HUGHES—WAR, WIDOWS, WASTAGE. WILSON—PEACE, PROSPERITY, PROGRESS."

"Our Level Best"

After the election, the editorial pages of Scripps's Ohio newspapers remained silent about its results for one week. Then all five Ohio papers ran the same editorial headlined "Hail To Ohio and the West." The editorial boasted of new power in determining presidential elections: "Ohio and the West are progressive and their hearts are not calloused [sic] by prejudice or privilege. They are truly and honestly American. It was a fine fight. We all did our level best."[143]

In a close vote, Wilson won four out of the five counties the Ohio Scripps newspapers served. With 1,165,086 votes cast statewide, Wilson beat Hughes by only 89,408 votes.[144] In Cleveland's Cuyahoga County, Wilson finished with 71,533 votes, 20,246 more than Hughes. In Columbus's Franklin County, Wilson finished with 34,103 votes, 9,996 more than Hughes. In Toledo's Lucas County, Wilson garnered 30,779 votes, 14,068 more than Hughes. Akron's Summit County gave 19,343 votes to Wilson, 7,750 more than Hughes. Cincinnati's Hamilton County, however, supported Hughes. In Hamilton County, 64,030 people voted for Hughes, 12,040 more than Wilson.[145] The five counties served by Scripps newspapers delivered a net of 40,020 more votes to the Wilson column; how much of that Rickey and his printing presses could take credit for is difficult to assess.

The *New York Times* on November 12 said Cincinnati went to Hughes because the "German-Americans did obey their leaders" in the German American Alliance. The *Times* said Cincinnati was one of the few places in the country where German Americans voted solidly for Hughes. The *Times* insisted that the labor vote did not carry Ohio or any other part of the country for Wilson." The *Times* credited former rank-and-file Bull Moose progressives with Wilson's victory, as well as the slogan "He Kept Us Out of War."[146] Hughes blamed the war. "I . . . should have been elected had it not been for the effectiveness, particularly in the Middle West, of the Democratic slogan, 'he kept us out of war.'"[147]

One historian has postulated that Wilson won in Ohio because farmers and laborers were earning more money as a result of increased foreign demand for American farm products and goods during the European war.[148] Divided Ohio Republicans also weakened their November campaign at all levels with infighting, but strong newspaper support made the Democrats' campaign that much easier.[149]

Making a President

After the election, Rickey resisted overtures to join Wilson's administration, possibly as ambassador to Great Britain. He told Scripps he declined because "it is a damn sight more satisfying to MAKE presidents than to WORK for them."[150]

Rickey had helped make a president, but it had taken Wilson's renewed commitment to progressive causes for Scripps's newspapermen to support him vigorously. Wilson balked at implementing income tax publicity, Scripps's pet issue, but was still the best progressive available in 1916. The war issue emerged as the major weapon Rickey used to convince voters to support Wilson. (Scripps would apologize to Wilson the next summer for his newspapers' heavy use of the theme "He kept us out of war." Scripps realized the claim made it more difficult for Wilson to support war against Germany.)[151]

The election of Wilson and the credit the Concern got for it publicly aligned the Scripps newspapers with Wilson. A chain that had long celebrated its political and editorial independence as a champion for working people battling the special interests was now publicly committed to one politician. The Concern felt responsible for electing him and felt forced to support him. True to its convictions, the Concern would not criticize him during the rest of his time in office.

The Scripps Concern had never flexed more national political muscle before, and it had never gone out on such a limb for one national candidate. While the income tax publicity campaign did not gain as much national attention as hoped, the efforts of the Scripps newspapers to reelect Wilson did earn them national recognition and seemed to enhance the Concern's prestige. Scripps, however, downplayed talk that Wilson was in the Concern's debt. "Further, by so much as Wilson, himself, might feel that we had any such right [to expect any favors], my respect for the President would be decreased."[152]

A little more than two weeks after he said this, problems were to come that would make him contemplate reconsidering those words.

5 Democracy versus Autocracy: December 1916 to July 1917

On December 6, 1916, E. W. Scripps asked longtime employee and friend Gilson Gardner to send him a list of houses near Washington that he might be able to buy or lease. "For several reasons, I would not want it to be known that I am making inquiries," he wrote Gardner.[1] Scripps wanted a simple but comfortable home within a car ride of the capitol. "Just what I don't want is a show place, or a place that a chauffeur would point out to a visiting stranger as being the Scripps' Home."[2] He would not tell Gardner, but the Concern's powerful role in Wilson's election was tempting him to move closer to the seat of power so he could exert more influence through his newspapers.

E.W. also was eager to exert influence within his own family. He wanted to take his youngest son, Bob, now living with him at Miramar, under his wing and get him interested in the newspaper business. It would be easier to do that if both were closer to the action at the nation's capital.

With E.W.'s move east, issues of who controlled the Concern would dominate the next seven months. Which family member was going to be the top boss? With the United States about to enter the fight, the Great War had become a symbolic struggle between the New World of Democracy and the Old World of autocratic kings and dictators. Likewise, in the Scripps Concern, a struggle over content control was about to erupt between young editors, led by Jim Scripps, and the aging autocratic publisher E. W. Scripps. How much discretion would editors have in covering the war? Would content be mandated through the NEA?

And who controlled the guiding spirit behind the Concern's editorial policies? The Concern had tied itself so closely to the president with its public support of his reelection that it now appeared to have painted itself into an editorial corner. The Concern's top editors felt they were responsible for reelecting Wilson and therefore had to defend him. They no longer could be independent in their judgments about Wilson or his policies. The Scripps newspapers also had used bloody imagery of the war to show Wilson's wisdom and adeptness in keeping America out of it and now had to explain to readers why the United States now needed to fight.

In reality, the Concern's policy on American intervention in the war, shaped by the NEA's top men, was much more hawkish than that of the president, yet it was reluctant to criticize him because it felt responsible for his reelection. The Concern wanted to remain true to the working-class and progressive principles that had built the reputation of the Scripps chain, but it also felt obligated to support one man, albeit a progressive, and his beliefs. The Concern was conflicted at its core—should it stay a blind follower of Wilson or reassert itself as independent leader on national policy, especially with war at hand?

Mixed among these tough editorial entanglements was Scripps's desire to control the careers of his sons, especially his youngest son, Bob. E.W. was convinced this was Bob's time now. According to Scripps biographer and longtime employee Gardner, it was E.W.'s "always-declared purpose to start his sons in the business when they were twenty one."[3] Bob now had reached that age and was struggling to find his place in a family business already controlled on paper by his older brother Jim and, in spirit, by his father. Although he enjoyed writing, Bob was unsure that he wanted to be a journalist. Since age twelve he had longed to become a poet, but E.W. would have nothing of that.[4] Bob had done some writing in Hawaii and Australia in 1916, but E.W. said Bob "didn't do much good" overseas;[5] after "many intimate talks" with him, E.W. was convinced "he can have a very useful and very effective career."[6] E.W. believed that Bob just needed to be inspired.

E.W. planned to send Bob east to do some "preparatory literary work" and perhaps to do some work for the NEA or UP.[7] E.W. sensed his son was not as conservative as his brother Jim and had the liberal, progressive spirit that E.W. had embodied in his newspapers. E.W. long had worried that the privileged environment his sons grew up in might dampen their zeal to protect the welfare of the common person.

"Theoretically, I think Bob is a good Socialist," E.W. wrote Max Eastman, publisher of the socialist magazine *The Masses*. "But practically,

Bob requires much more to make his life endurable than would ever be allowed to him by the most generous and most liberal-minded members of a Socialist state." Still, Bob showed great potential to become a good penny press newspaperman like his father, perhaps because he tended to acquiesce to his father's wishes, while his older brother, Jim, seemed best suited to be a major corporate businessman, and tended to challenge his father's decisions.

The war accelerated the process of getting Bob involved. E.W. would go to Washington, and Bob would abandon plans to be a poet. The coming year would bring America's entry into the war, challenge the public opinion machine called the Scripps Concern, and spark an intrafamilial war that eventually would split the Scripps empire. A year of tension and agony for the Scripps family was ahead, as Jim and E.W., especially, locked horns over who was in charge of the Concern and what should be done with Bob. It was impossible to separate Scripps family business from the Scripps newspaper business in 1917.

Peace Moves

Few in the Concern were impressed with President Wilson's attempts after his reelection to end the European war peacefully. Wilson hoped to mediate a peace settlement when he responded to Germany's call for a peace conference in mid-December.[8] Privately, UP President Roy Howard believed Wilson was acting prematurely and playing into the hands of the Germans. Howard wrote Wilson's personal advisor, Colonel E. M. House, that a peace initiative would "injure and perhaps destroy [Wilson's] great potential power for good, a power that will be measured by the timeliness of its application."[9]

As the globetrotting head of the Concern's international news machine, Howard was well respected for his opinion on world affairs. He told one of the Concern's business managers, C. F. Mosher, that he believed Germany's interest in peace was only a "diplomatic manoeuvre" to show the German people "the Kaiser is not a war lord, but a sincere peace lover." Howard was convinced Germany was still strong militarily—but so were the Allies. "It is equally certain that Germany is by no means a victor today," he wrote Mosher on December 14. "It is true that she holds most of the blue chips and that she would like to cash in and go home."[10]

Any doubts the Concern had in December about the timing of Wilson's peace moves were expressed quietly on the pages of the Scripps newspapers. United Press printed a copyrighted story from noted British publisher Lord Northcliffe on December 14 that said German interest in peace could be traced to "grave internal dissensions" and "greatly strained" relations between Germany and its allies.[11]

The NEA initially issued an editorial whose message typified its positions on every war crisis up to this time: Stand by the president. "The best way we can help [Wilson] to decide to decide wisely whether or not this is the time to sound a note of peace is to let him alone," a December 15 editorial said. When the Concern could not agree with the president editorially on an issue, it simply fell silent. For example, the *Cleveland Press* printed in December and January only eight editorials related to the peace initiatives, none of them overtly critical of the president, despite the significance of Wilson's diplomatic effort and the Concern's doubts about its timing. One editorial suggested that it was "not outside the probabilities that the real purpose of German's peace proposal was to STAMPEDE THE UNITED STATES into making a move for peace which would be considered unfriendly by Great Britain and her allies. . . . We do not say that this is so; it may be so."[12]

Wilson stood firm. On December 20 the president asked the warring nations of Europe to state their positions on ending the war. Wilson's appeal noted that all had shown interest in a league of nations to enforce world peace, and the United States also was "as vitally and directly interested" in the idea.[13] The NEA withheld judgment, but a December 22 editorial ended with a note of cynicism: "Let us hope that in this instance [Wilson's] judgment has been based upon knowledge of the European situation which the rest of us have not the means of obtaining, and that what he has done will justify itself by pointing the way to peace on the basis of justice and righteousness. Certainly a patched up peace based upon cowardly compromise . . . with nations always ready to fly at each other's throats, would not be such justification."[14]

Instead of criticizing Wilson themselves, the Scripps newspapers reprinted negative British reaction to the president's peace initiative. United Press European manager Ed Keen reported on December 22 that the more England "digests President Wilson's peace note, the more bitter it feels." Keen quoted British newspaper editorials such as one in the *Globe* that said, "We sincerely hope President Wilson is not ill, but we have grave doubts of his physical well-being."[15]

Abandoning Isolationism

The few NEA editorials concerning the peace initiatives marked the NEA's first public recognition that the United States could no longer isolate itself from world affairs. The isolationist tenor of the "He kept us out of war" campaign waged on Wilson's behalf during 1916 now changed in recognition of the possibility of U.S. intervention. A December 26 editorial stated that Britain and France surely would not sign a peace treaty with Germany without "the United States guaranteeing the good faith of the central powers."[16] An editorial four days later noted, "The future of our country will be bound up with the future of every other country" and the United States "cannot evade its responsibility" to make sure that "the peace will be permanent."[17]

Editorials about the peace initiatives also contained the NEA's first overt criticism of Germany for starting the European war. Because the NEA believed, like many of Wilson's critics, that peace now would only help Germany, the NEA mildly endorsed congressional opposition to Wilson's peace initiatives in early January. Again, the NEA opined that Wilson was acting prematurely. "WE ARE NO LESS ANXIOUS FOR PEACE than the most ultra peace-at-any-price pacifist. But it is our sincere conviction that it is far better for the world for the war to be fought to a finish than that there be a patched up peace, forced upon the warring nations by the pressure of neutral nations," a January 8 editorial said.

In the NEA's most serious war talk to date, the editorial said the "love of democracy and spirit of justice" should prevent any premature peace efforts. "Outraged, devastated Belgium; violated, bleeding France; every soul-sickening incident in the campaign of 'frightfulness,' with which the might-makes-right, divine-right Prussians have scourged the earth, the sea and the air, all are counts in the indictment of humanity against the military autocracy of which they are the fruits."[18] When the Allies rejected Wilson's peace initiative a few days later, the NEA further condemned "Prussian militarism." The editorial managed to compliment Wilson's peace proposal by saying it did "much to clarify the whole [war] situation. . . . Those of us who were so ignorant of the facts that we thought peace could be had for the mere asking, have had our illusions shattered."[19]

When Wilson delivered his "peace without victory" speech to Congress on January 22, in which he outlined his terms for world peace, much of which would become his Fourteen Points, the NEA must have been further frustrated into silence. Wilson said that a fight to the finish would breed future wars—a direct contradiction of the reasoning behind the NEA's editorials of the previous weeks. "Victory would mean . . . a victor's terms imposed upon the vanquished," Wilson said. "It would be accepted in humiliation, under duress, at an intolerable sacrifice, and would leave a sting, a resentment."[20]

A circumspect editorial about Wilson's peace league on January 23 praised Wilson for his "idealism and courage" but said that his vision of a world federation "leaves much to be desired." The editorial echoed continued blind faith in Wilson: "One thing is certain. The president has let it be known that . . . he will not lend his aid to the establishment of peace and its preservation, unless it is based upon justice to the long-suffering common people of the fighting nations."[21]

Wilson's peace terms drew sharp criticism. Isolationists feared future entanglements in European power politics, while interventionists felt a new world power structure would require the United States to abdicate its position as the mightiest nation.[22] Much of the opposition to Wilson's initiatives was political, too. The Republicans had never lost two consecutive presidential elections before, and they needed to differentiate themselves from Wilson. As one historian has noted, the Democrats played politics, too, because they nearly unanimously supported Wilson, despite their tradition of antiimperialism and antimilitarism. But most of Congress took no position on Wilson's peace proposal, and few news organizations spoke for or against it either.[23] The NEA's relative silence on the peace initiatives was not unusual. War still seemed far away.

Progressives for Peace

War drew much closer on January 31, 1917, however, when the Germans announced they would resume unrestricted submarine warfare against all Allied and neutral ships. Wilson reluctantly broke diplomatic relations with Germany on February 3, a move the NEA had said two days earlier was the "one answer which America can make."[24] On the day of the diplomatic break, the *Cleveland Press* printed a front-page picture of a bald eagle standing on an American flag with the phrase "STAND BY THE PRESIDENT." An accompanying editorial concluded, "Germany must understand—and every other nation in the world must understand—that the voice of the president is the voice of the United States of America; and that the whole hundred million of us STAND BY THE PRESIDENT."[25]

Isolationists, however—many of whom were progressives, such as William Jennings Bryan and Senator Robert M. LaFollette—rallied to keep the United States out of the European war. LaFollette worried that conservatives wanted war to divert attention from domestic reforms and rapidly rising food prices. Bryan wanted the government to warn Americans to stay off ships in the war zone and to hold a national referendum before war could be declared.[26]

The Concern's support for Wilson put it at odds with these progressives, who had been close allies on other social justice issues. The Concern's inconsistency was obvious to some Cincinnati isolationists. When the *Cincinnati Post* refused to run an advertisement reprinting Bryan's speech condemning the war, the antiwar group led by Cincinnati judge Alfred Nippert wrote to the Concern's top men. On February 11 he asked one of the Concern's large shareholders, J. C. Harper, to "back up your editorials of the past with actual deeds of today." Nippert observed: "You have been the pioneer among the American newspapers advocating the referendum. Why should the American people today be denied this great democratic prerogative on the all important question of war or peace?"[27] Daniel Kiefer, another Cincinnati isolationist, telegrammed E. W. Scripps, urging him to "at least open [the *Post*'s] columns to an expression of the anti-war sentiment of this community." He noted that the *Post* usually was the only progressive-minded newspaper in Cincinnati; now it "refuses to print what we will pay for."[28]

Scripps replied in a telegram that the "present situation has saddened me beyond description.... War is necessary and inevitable and while I respect [your] opinion.... I know it would be treason for me to do anything to embarrass the people and the people's president." He said Wilson had the "almost unanimous support" of the people, and closed the letter: "Your motives are good but your actions I believe will only encourage the enemy and cost many American lives."[29]

The NEA's chief editorial writer, Bob Paine, wrote Scripps that he did not agree with the *Post*'s decision to reject the advertisements. "I cannot see why the *Post* refused to let Kiefer, Nippert and other wild Cincinnati Dutchmen have a reasonable say in its columns and it simply horrifies me to learn that any of our Ohio papers have gone to refusing Bryan's good advertising money," he wrote.[30]

"Hasten The End"

The Concern, particularly in Ohio, had committed itself to supporting Wilson, even though he was not yet willing to enter the war. The newspapers were advocating a much stronger military policy against Germany than Wilson was ready to endorse. Despite the break with Germany, Wilson remained hopeful that war with Germany could be avoided, and he did not support a congressional move to arm merchant ships—referred to as "armed neutrality"—which was seen as a way for the United States to avoid full-fledged war by becoming a strong neutral power. Wilson believed it would promote war and did not endorse it until late February.[31]

The NEA, a supporter of preparedness and a strong navy since the *Lusitania* was sunk in May 1915, held no reservations about entering the war because "as we value peace, we value our national honor and self-respect more." The brazen resumption of submarine warfare meant "we are justified in acting on the assumption that there will be war," a February 5 editorial read.[32]

The NEA argued that war would be brief if the United States entered the fighting with its overwhelming might, perhaps because it knew it had used imagery of war's savage bloodletting to help secure Wilson's reelection the previous November. Charles Edward Russell, a former Socialist Party presidential candidate, reported on February 7 that although war was deplorable, Germany would quit within ninety days if the United States entered.[33] NEA president Canfield called Russell's column "one of the strongest things I have ever read about the war." He snidely told his chief editor Sam Hughes, "Guess we weren't right . . . on our policy of jumping in on preparedness long before we could even get concerted support for it!"[34]

The moral righteousness of entering the war also was exploited. By February 8 the NEA was beating the war drum and keeping a tally of German sinkings. Sixty-one vessels were sunk in the first eight days, it reported, "proof of the absolute ruthlessness of the Kaiser's new submarine war."[35] The NEA also sent Mary Boyle O'Reilly—"who bravely accepted the risk"—on the American liner *New York* to report on the tension of a trip through the submarine zone.[36]

"Wilson Knows What He Is Doing"

In late February, Neg Cochran was in Washington, meeting briefly with President Wilson but spending most of his time sizing up the war situation with interior secretary Franklin Lane, agriculture secretary David Houston, and Cochran's secretary of the people liaison, millionaire Charles Crane. Cochran had complained that most of the Concern's writers were only guessing about the war situation, and he wanted to see what he could find. Cochran reported to Canfield that war with Germany was inevitable. Moreover, "I think the country will be amazed to find out how well prepared [militarily and logistically] we are," he wrote. "My judgment is there is only one thing for us to do and that is to stand by the president and let him work this situation out without embarrassment from us,"[37] Later, Cochran would tell E. W. Scripps: "I have told our boys that we can't do any good by nagging—that the thing is too far along for editorials to change anything."[38]

Cochran remained intensely loyal and confident in Wilson, despite the president's reluctance to adopt a policy—at least publicly—regarding preparedness that was similar to what NEA wanted. "My impression is that Wilson knows what he is doing.... I have taken as a key to Wilson's policy the fact that he is a historian, and knowing that he must take part in the making of history, has been setting the scenery before pulling up the curtain on his part of the show," Cochran told Scripps.

Zimmermann Telegram

Wilson had been committed publicly to the idea of "armed neutrality" for less than a week when the Wilson administration gave AP what historian Barbara Tuchman would call the "the biggest scoop of the war": German foreign secretary Arthur Zimmermann had telegraphed his country's embassy in the United States in January trying to coax Mexico into any future war with the United States. The cable, intercepted by the British and given to the Wilson administration, offered Mexico the opportunity to recover Texas, New Mexico, and Arizona. Secretary of State Robert Lansing leaked the Zimmermann telegram, as it came to be known, to AP's E. M. Hood; Hood was told he must not reveal where he got the information.[39]

Breaking in March 1 morning newspapers, the AP scoop of the Zimmermann telegram must have left UP exasperated, although no evidence in the Concern archives reveals its reaction. As an afternoon service, nonetheless, UP was able to get stories about the German telegram to its clients on March 1. The UP stories contained various confirmations of the story, as pacifist senators clamored to find out how the telegram was discovered and if it had been planted by one of the warring countries hoping to lure the United States into the fight. "Doubt as to the authenticity of the Zimmermann letter, voiced in the Senate early today, because of its text having first come public thru the press was quickly dispelled," the main UP story said.[40]

When Germany admitted several days later that it had authorized the Zimmermann telegram, the UP reported the announcement "appears to have removed the last vestige of opposition in the Senate to the 'armed neutrality' bill."[41] The telegram also gave the NEA an opportunity to paint the Germans as coldhearted opportunists who had no regard for treaties they signed. "As for us, no manifestation of dishonesty, brutality, immorality or depravity by the present German government... will surprise us in the least," a March 3 editorial said.[42]

No longer were the Scripps newspapers neutral about the war. A new theme emerged: The Germans must be stopped.

"Spit in the Prussian Warhound's Face"

United Press began reporting German atrocities, which were once downplayed on the pages of Scripps newspapers but now were given front-page treatment. William Simms, with the British in France and subject to heavy censorship, used all of his literary might on March 27 to indict the evil Germans:

> One day spent in the territory just wrenched from German domination by French-British arms would make the most timid, human pacifist jackrabbit . . . spit in the Prussian warhound's face.
>
> If American voters could spend an hour among the pinched faces of babies, could hear the stories of wronged women, could see [the] devastated countryside—then any Washington politician refusing to help resist the kaiser's decision to treat Americans in the same way, would find himself suddenly snatched from his chair by the nape of the neck.[43]

Simms also reported that German troops had "swept [part of France] clear of its womanhood," forcing French women to work inside Germany.[44] United Press correspondent Henry Wood, with the French army, reported on March 26 that he had found three hundred "women, children and aged men" who had died because of "the brutality, the starvation which the Germans imposed upon the French civil population."[45]

The NEA, meanwhile, attacked American pacifists trying to block discussion of conscription, or universal military training as it was called, as unpatriotic German sympathizers. "The organization and direction of pacifist propaganda in this country is part of the German government's plan to dupe public sentiment," the NEA opined on March 24.[46]

In March the NEA also began printing reports of German spies lurking in the shadows of American government and industry.[47] Although government officials produced no spies, the Scripps newspapermen believed administration reports that activity was rampant. Harry Hunt, the main Scripps reporter in Washington for the NEA, reported privately in memorandums what he was being told, thus influencing NEA editorial policy. For example, in early April he wrote Martin that he had been told that six or seven spies had been found in the navy. "What has come of them or what has been done with them is kept a dark secret. In fact, no admission is made officially that any were found."[48] Relying on government contacts for information, with little opportunity to corroborate what it was being told, the Scripps Concern accepted its role as a mouthpiece for the Wilson administration.

"War Seems Just Ahead"

The news pages of the Scripps Concern, particularly those of March 1917, still represented a much more prointerventionist position than Wilson espoused. Even as he was pushing for the armed shipping bill, and denouncing eleven Progressive Republicans and Bryanite Democrats who filibustered the bill in the Senate as a "little group of willful men representing no opinion but their own," Wilson hoped to avoid war.[49] He repeatedly quelled preparedness campaigns designed to mobilize a spirit for war, hoping that the United States could have the greatest impact on a lasting peace if it were neutral.

After cabinet members urged the reluctant president to support a war with Germany in response to shipping losses, Wilson armed merchant ships by executive order and called Congress to a special session for April 2. He gave no public indication he was ready for war.[50] In the story announcing the special session, United Press was not sure what Wilson would do. "War seems just ahead," the March 21 story said. "If the president does not ask for a war declaration, congress may demand one."[51]

Thus, in part because the Scripps men had more access to Wilson's cabinet, which tended to support intervention, than to Wilson, who was reluctant to fight, a gap—probably the widest ever on any issue—had emerged between Scripps editorial policy and what Wilson supported. In fact, the NEA on March 23 had called for a declaration of war. "It seems perfectly clear that both our duty and our self interest point unerringly toward a hard and fast alliance with the [allied] nations to make war against Germany with them and not to make peace until it can be made upon a basis which so far as human foresight can determine will make impossible a recurrence of the cataclysm which for nearly three years has wracked the earth."[52]

The war Wilson would request, and would be granted by Congress on April 6, provided its own cataclysm for the Scripps newspaper empire. Again, the battle would be joined over centralized control of editorial policy.

"The Man Who Is Spending All of His Time on the One Subject"

By late March the Scripps Concern was relying on Harry Rickey, fresh from 1916 election coverage, to coordinate the early war coverage. The NEA's top managers in the East had allowed Rickey to take this authority from local editors. At first, he concentrated on writing many of the editorials regarding the international situation—one of several NEA staffers writing about the war. By late March, the NEA's Canfield wanted to put one person in charge of overseeing all war coverage, "the same as we did with our presidential election policy."

In Canfield's opinion, Rickey was the best suited. He was a skilled, veteran writer who was assigned no other regular duties within the Concern. He would not write everything, but he would edit and read everything going out to ensure that the policy line was consistent. Wary because of earlier battles over centralized control, Canfield again tried to justify the arrangement to the Scripps local editors:

> If we run independent editorials . . . [from other prominent NEA reporters] doubtless they will be good editorials . . . but they may differ in some detail, or in some apparently unimportant . . . opinion, from what has gone before, or what is coming next, and the man best qualified for keeping tab on all these angles is the man who is spending all his time on the one subject.[53]

Rickey thus had become the de facto chief of war policy.

In late March, Canfield also asked NEA staffers to scrutinize Scripps papers for how much war policy news, editorials, and cartoons they had been printing so far. The report said, "The papers that are doing least seem to be the *San Francisco News*, the *Dallas Dispatch* and the *San Diego Sun*. Then comes the *Sacramento Star*. Papers in the half way class are the *Evansville Press* and the *Houston Press*. Papers that are really going to the stuff are the Ohio papers, northwest papers, the *Denver Express* and the *Terre Haute Post*."[54]

Eugene MacLean, the editor of one of those war editorial policy slackers, the *San Francisco News*, later explained that he had judged the NEA output a bit too hawkish for his readers. Up to and through March, the *News* had downplayed some NEA material because "the average man in San Francisco (and I mean the average man outside the Germans and the Sinn Fein Irish, who are powerful here) was dead against the war. Pictures of the kaiser and Paul von Hindenburg were cheered in the movies. The flag was not applauded." MacLean said that the *News* would have been the most vocal proponent of war among its competitors; "if we had printed the editorials demanding that an army go to Europe, that we give a billion [dollars] to France, or any of the proposals of that sort, we would have been giving that kind of journalistic leadership that consists in going off in the woods by ones [sic] self."[55]

Indeed, California had always been an independent hotbed for the progressive movement, which tended to favor alternative measures for solving international disputes. Antiwar sentiment ran high in the West in the early days of the war. Some leaders of the radical labor union the International Workers of the World encouraged strikes and other disruptions against war-related work in western mines and lumberyards.[56] MacLean said San Francisco's reluctance to fight could be blamed on "the anti-militaristic propaganda of the trades [sic] unions."[57]

Although Wilson's declaration of war was approved, many congressmen and their constituents were unsure what this war would really mean. Fifty congressmen in the House voted against the war, part of what one historian has called the most opposed war declaration—before or since—in United States history. Many thought the war would be confined to the seas and the sending of supplies. Few envisioned a mass involvement of American infantry units on the front lines.[58]

MacLean worried that his paper was out of step with many readers. "It will sound funny to a man who is in Ohio, or almost any place outside our fair city, but the *Daily News* is regarded here as a jingo organ." Still, MacLean reported that the president was gaining support, and the *Daily News*'s backing of Wilson was paying off—paid circulation had risen 9.2 percent from January 1 to April 1.[59]

"Action!"

The NEA staff members with closest access to the men shaping Washington's war policy—NEA editor-in-chief Sam Hughes, Canfield, Cochran, and Martin—were worried that the American public, especially in the Midwest, which had been seduced by the "He kept us out of war" campaign slogan just six months before, did not appreciate the tremendous challenge the war was presenting. The war would have to be financed, and more food would have to be produced. "I have been hoping that a German submarine would shell one of our undefended coast cities," Rickey wrote in mid-April to Harper. "That would bring the fact of war home to us."[60]

Meanwhile, editor-in-chief Hughes warned J. W. T. Mason of UP in New York that there was a need to "stir the population between the Alleghenies and the Rockies to their very marrow." America needed to go to war in some way soon. "Action! Hot, fierce, enthusiastic war is what will wake them up. And they have got to see it. The papers must be full of it. Victories and losses have got to appear. Action!"[61] Hughes fired off another letter to UP a few days later. "We must alarm them; anything to end the slumber in this great territory. . . . You . . . of the U.P., living and writing in the east, did not understand the situation out here."[62]

Hughes's haranguing angered R. F. Paine in San Diego, one of Scripps's chief lieutenants and a primary editorial writer. "Editor Hughes is simply and frankly blood-thirsty," Paine wrote to Canfield on April 16. "From this and long telegrams from Rickey, I begin to fear that you heads of N.E.A. at Cleveland, being obsessed with the idea that the East knows it all, has it all and does it all, have got a rather prescribed [sic] view point and are likely to have that and nothing else."

What particularly angered Paine and others was the new arrangement that all editorials and war stories again had to be routed through the NEA's Cleveland office before distribution to newspapers. He had fought to keep autonomy over his editorials, and he complained about the NEA's veteran political writer Gilson Gardner being suppressed because he was a pacifist. "In these policies I think you are headed toward an autocracy that would make old Von Hindenberg [sic] burst with envy," he told Canfield.[63] In his 1932 biography of E. W. Scripps, Gardner said he was censored by the NEA. "My signed column, which had for years been a feature of the Scripps service, was discontinued, but the waste basket was faithfully fed."[64] The southern papers' editor-in-chief, A. O. Andersson, complained to Canfield: "Your censorship has taken the pep out of Gardner to a considerable extent."[65] Andersson called the Gardner situation a "humiliation" for a trusted writer whom all had considered "able, loyal, as effective as ever" before the NEA's centralization of coverage. Canfield admitted that the NEA was uneasy about Gardner's attitude. "On occasion he is liable to put out editorial matter contradictory to the editorial policies of N.E.A." Nevertheless, Canfield said, all but two articles had appeared exactly as he wrote them, and those discarded had been "entirely contrary to N.E.A. policy."[66]

Paine stubbornly threatened to quit writing editorials.[67] Harper wrote to Canfield that Wilson's role as president would be stronger if his policies could be allowed to persevere despite public criticism. "Because it [the president's draft bill] comes, *after debate and argument,* its value is greatly enhanced."[68] Harper's angry attacks, and his tendency to circulate copies of his complaints to other members of the Concern, infuriated Canfield. "I did not object to your attack upon N.E.A. policy, but to your action in sending such criticism of N.E.A. policy to the men upon whom N.E.A. must rely to make effective that policy," he said in early May.[69] Harper roared back: "Strong men are not developed by having somebody else do their thinking for them."[70]

Not all editors were uneasy about the war or the NEA's position on it. LeRoy Sanders, editor-in-chief of the Northwest Group of newspapers, saw dollar signs. He wrote his editors in May that these "are great days in which to be an editor." Sanders urged his editors to use war news well. "There is war news of every type, 'heavy,' 'light' 'human interest' and even 'humorous.' The wise editor will give his readers a balanced ration." From the beginning, Sanders predicted that war coverage would kill some newspapers and help others. "All papers are going to be patriotic. . . . We can gain no honors merely by standing in the ranks by them. We must do the exceptional and the different thing."[71]

Jim Scripps, chairman of the Concern's board of directors, had remained silent so far on the dispute. He asked his younger brother Bob to go east to get involved in the war coverage, something Bob had already told Jim he wanted to do as a way to get involved in the newspaper business.[72] E.W. encouraged Bob as well. "Assume that your father and brother are soon to die, and . . . you have got to assume all the burdens that they have carried. Close the book of dreams for the time being; stop philosophizing."[73]

Bob telegrammed on April 21 that a two-day conference with Rickey and Martin had concluded that the Concern had one option: "Back Wilson absolutely." He added, "West not particularly apathetic, east not 'war mad.'"[74] His assessment reflected the reluctance and anxiety of most Americans about going to war. As historian John Milton Cooper wrote: "Not that the bulk of Congressman were strongly opposed to the war, but, like the president and probably like most Americans, they found themselves torn between repugnant alternatives. It is almost certain that Wilson could have carried majorities in Congress and among the public with him in virtually every direction he chose."[75]

The top editorial men of the Scripps Concern were not circumspect about war in the spring of 1917. The Scripps newspapers, at least those in Ohio, were some of the most prointerventionist newspapers in the country at the time.

The "Restorer of Imperiled Democracy"

To the *Cleveland Press,* it was obvious that the Scripps flagship newspaper would completely support Wilson. "That this newspaper approves of President Wilson's war message even to the last sentence and word hardly needs to be said to those of our readers who have done us the honor of reading our editorials during the past several months," an editorial said on April 3; any American who refused to sacrifice to win the war was "unworthy to enjoy the liberty so dearly purchased by the revolutionary fathers. . . . No nation ever went to war with a less selfish purpose, for a more noble cause."[76]

Another editorial on April urged Congress to pay for the bulk of the war by taxing the rich, not by issuing bonds. Because most of the fighting would be done "by those who neither are rich or well-to-do," such a taxation scheme seemed reasonable. "We rather like the suggestion that an income tax so large as practically to confiscate all incomes over a certain figure ought to be levied by the government. For example, let the government say that all incomes over $100,000 or even as low as $50,000, shall be taken for war purposes," the editorial read.[77]

Editorials and opinion columns in April and May continued to elaborate on America's need to fight. To NEA writers, the war was a patriotic crusade to save democracy and defeat the barbarians of autocracy. "The United States, the savior of the world, the restorer of imperiled democracy" is how the NEA's Russell began a column that outlined America's opportunity to rescue democracy.[78] One of the most prominent figures of the American left, he was also one of the few prowar socialists. The American Socialist Party by 1916 was adamantly opposed to joining the war, while intellectuals such as Russell hoped to use it to further the socialist cause.[79] As one scholar has noted, "no doubt, the administration did see some advantage in associating well-known reformers and radicals with a war effort to which significant opposition came only from the left."[80]

For the NEA, Western civilization was now at stake. "The issue before our civilization is one of reversion to barbarism, which in process of time means the fate of those old dead and buried civilizations," one editorial said.[81] The NEA writers said the United States was being forced into the war by German aggression, and it must fight to defend its honor. "America's 'state of war' with Germany results directly from Germany's claim of the right to kill Americans found within any area of the high seas marked off by Germany," a news analysis piece said.[82]

One scholar has argued that Wilson's war declaration speech was never intended to launch an "idealistic crusade" for democracy. Although in his speech he stated emphatically that "the world must be made safe for democracy," the overall tone of the speech was not a patriotic challenge for glory; it was somber and tragic. The country would pursue a good end—peace in the world—by evil means (joining the war).[83] For Wilson, America's continued neutrality and potential role as mediator no longer was a promising method to end the war. In the end, such rationalizations did not matter to the NEA. "In the main our opinions coincide with . . . [those of] the president, as expressed in his masterly address to congress when he asked that war be declared," an editorial in the *Cleveland Press* said on April 20. "But whether we agree or disagree, we conceive it our patriotic duty just as it is the patriotic duty of every other American ... to 'stand by the president.'"[84]

Skulkers and Bushwhackers

Efforts to derail Wilson's proposal to draft two million men gave the Scripps newspapers their first opportunity to stand by the president after war was declared. Wilson was endorsing universal military training, something the Concern had advocated since 1915. Opposition to the draft in Congress was strong. Conscription was seen as undemocratic, and many remembered the draft riots of the Civil War. "So violent was the opposition that for several weeks the success of the [draft] measure hung in the balance," one scholar has noted.[85]

Newspaper Enterprise Association editorials called universal military training the "keystone of the arch of military preparedness" and said "if congress had passed such a law two years ago, which it should have done, we would now have an army of a million trained and equipped men."[86] Congress did not adopt Wilson's plan for raising an army until May 18 and only after a savage fight.

The fight over the draft showed the intolerance the NEA, under the direction of Rickey, harbored toward opponents to its war policy. Wilson's opponents were portrayed as borderline traitors. "The country will be perfectly justified in assuming that those congressmen who fail to give whole-hearted and enthusiastic support to the president and his advisers, are inspired by unpatriotic motives," an April 10 editorial read.[87] The next day an editorial said: "It makes no difference whether the members of congress who are opposing the president's war plans are animated by sincere or sinister motives. They are all in the same boat. IT IS A GERMAN BOAT AND THE KAISER IS ITS CAPTAIN."[88]

The NEA again used Russell as its primary bylined spokesman for its war policy. He blasted the "skulkers" and "bushwhackers" in the House and Senate who were undermining Wilson's war plans. "We have in the national legislature men who know nothing about their country's danger.... Men that can take into their minds no thought except their own interests; their own re-election and their own miserable little political fortunes," he wrote on April 12.[89]

Conscripting Wealth

The financing of war was consuming Scripps at Miramar. On the day Wilson asked Congress to declare war, Scripps telegrammed the president urging him to pay for it with sharp increases in income and inheritance taxes. "All incomes of over one hundred thousand dollars a year should be conscripted.... Such legislation would cost me much more than half of my present income," Scripps said.[90] Although Scripps's telegram mirrored the NEA's editorial policy on war financing, no evidence exists that Scripps ordered or even influenced the NEA's decision to take that viewpoint. The president's assistant, Joseph Tumulty, replied with a letter thanking Scripps for his patriotism.[91]

Scripps sent the telegram after he was contacted by Amos Pinchot, a progressive leader with whom Scripps frequently exchanged letters, and who was leading the American Committee on War Finance, a congressional lobbying group. This group, formed in March, was originally organized to discourage America's entry into the war but now claimed it wanted to promote fairness in financing the war.[92] Scripps agreed to allow his name and quotations from his telegram to Wilson to be used in the lobbying group's advertisements, which angered Rickey at the NEA headquarters in Washington. "They are using your telegram trying to bulldoze us into stirring up a big fight in Congress at this critical time when Congress should be standing by the president," Rickey said in a telegram to Scripps on April 10.

Scripps was not a pacifist, but he agreed with Pinchot that the wealthy needed to pay for the war if the poor had to fight it.[93] Scripps supported "pay as you go"—using income taxes to pay for all or most of the war—but he was not nearly as opposed to using bonds to finance the war as Pinchot's group was. Scripps knew it would be difficult to convince Congress to sharply increase income taxes. In a lengthy letter to Pinchot on April 9, Scripps explained that war bonds had to be sold to the public to raise money for the first year of war. "It must be understood that a period of consideration of many months [regarding income taxes] might be reckoned as prompt action on the part of a great Democracy.... If after this first large debt [of bonds] has been made, the Government shall elect to pay as they go the remainder of the expense of the War, the Government can properly continue after the close of the war to levy high taxes to pay off the debt incurred during this first year."[94]

Rickey was upset that Scripps was associating with Pinchot because it made the NEA look inconsistent. He sent Scripps an April 12 editorial from the *New York Evening Sun* that said Pinchot's group was a pacifist organization acting in bad faith in the war finance debate because it was seeking "to accomplish its purposes by misdirection." The *Sun* editorial listed Scripps's name as among those associated with the group.[95] "The fact remains that [Pinchot's] activities prior to the war declaration

... were so unpatriotic and so absolutely contrary to what you and the Scripps concern stand for that the use of your name in connection with his is certain to be misunderstood," Rickey wrote Scripps. He then gave his boss a stern lecture, telling him it was a mistake to lobby outside "the medium of the Scripps institution. The policies of the institution are being formulated here. These policies must be reasonably consistent, if we hope to make them effective."[96]

The publicity Scripps's name received was noticed in Congress as well. The chairman of the House Ways and Means Committee, populist Claude Kitchin of North Carolina, was a strong advocate for steep taxes on the rich. Through Basil Manly, Kitchin asked Scripps to come to Washington to testify on behalf of higher taxes.[97] Fresh from criticism by Rickey, Scripps seemed reluctant to go and claimed he had the flu.[98]

The opportunity to get involved in the national policy debate proved too tempting, however. Bob Scripps wired his father on April 24 to ask if he could testify.[99] An appearance by a Scripps would allow the Concern to clear up the misunderstandings created by E.W.'s association with Pinchot. The elder Scripps agreed. "Don't let anybody buffalo you and speak for yourself and for me without regards to anybody's advice."[100] The NEA sent Gardner to cover the committee hearing, at which Pinchot testified as well. Both Bob Scripps and Pinchot asked for graduated increases in the income tax and for the government to take over all incomes over $100,000.[101] On the next day Gardner wrote privately to E.W. that Bob's appearance "went off every well."[102]

Throughout 1917, however, proposals to raise large amounts of money through taxes on income generated by the war never met the expectations of many progressives who hoped to raise at least half of the war costs from taxes. As one historian has noted, efforts for higher income taxes were hamstrung because their leading proponents in Congress had voted against the war; they were easy to discredit. Costs spiraled beyond expectation, too; ultimately less than a fifth of the cost of the war in 1917 came from taxes.[103]

E.W. Goes East

The fight over war financing made Scripps antsy. He was too far from the action in Washington. His men were criticizing him for meddling with their policies, while the Concern he founded was being asked by congressional leaders to get more involved. Representative Edward Keating of Colorado wrote E.W. in mid-April asking him to come east. "[In]

Washington you could accomplish ten times as much as you could by long distance," the telegram said.[104]

Finally, during the first week of May, Scripps decided to go. He wrote Gardner, "I have no plan, or any particular purpose in view. Later, when I have been in Washington for awhile, I may get interested in some things."[105] After his retirement of nearly ten years, Scripps coming east was big news that he tried to downplay. He wrote Rickey, Canfield, and Martin at Cleveland's NEA office that he wanted to "forestall any possible surmises on your part . . . that I may intend some sort of intervention." Still, Scripps said he intended to spend several months in the East, and he wanted the NEA brain trust to "give some consideration to my personal attitude, face to face, with [regard to] the present situation of war conditions."[106] He went on to explain that he welcomed the opportunity for the United States to become a world military power. He warned, however, that soldiers must be well paid and the rich must be well taxed to finance the war, so as not to foster any military revolutions after the war, a clear reference to the March revolution in czarist Russia.[107]

Not all of Scripps's motives for coming east are entirely clear. Certainly, his longstanding desire to get his youngest son, Bob, into the business played a part, and Bob's move east pushed E.W. to follow so as to nurture his son, who already had acted as his father's surrogate in Congress. "He is very anxious for a real job or some sort of orders or directions from me," Scripps wrote from Washington to his confidante, his sister Ellen in San Diego.[108] The war emergency provided an excellent opportunity to convince Bob he had an important job to inherit. "I have told you several times that you needed waking up," he wrote Bob. "You haven't gone to sleep. You've never been awake."[109] Scripps, too, saw Bob as a vehicle for imposing his will on the Concern's policies, perhaps without usurping the authority of his older son Jim in San Diego. "I think I can do better by keeping my own personality out of sight, and working through more enthusiastic, younger, and more active men. In this matter, I may try some experiments with Bob," Scripps wrote Ellen.[110]

The debates in Congress over the draft bill and war finances also certainly influenced Scripps's move east. He later listed three reasons he went to Washington: to make sure the country was as strong militarily as it was economically, to make sure the wealthy paid the bulk of taxes, and to see that only volunteer soldiers were sent to France and all conscripts were used only for home defense.[111]

"A Fizzle"

Canfield was feeling good about the NEA's coverage of the war so far. In a June 1 letter to Bob Scripps, he took responsibility for any policy stands, saying his opinion ruled when a consensus with Rickey and Martin could not be reached. "I honestly believe the N.E.A. has had more to do with putting this country into an attitude . . . favorable—or at least not too openly antagonistic—to a program of military preparedness, than any other institution."[112] Still, NEA leaders were struggling to assess the public's true feelings about war. Paine, who again was writing editorials and sending them to Cleveland for approval, said in late May that the public was either "quietly, seriously patriotic, or they are decidedly apathetic."[113]

For the Pacific Coast newspapers of the Scripps Concern, those under the direct purview of chairman of the board Jim Scripps, the situation was clear: the American public was not convinced the war was necessary or that Wilson should be blindly supported. The *Los Angeles Record* would become the testing ground for Jim and his editors to see if the public would tolerate criticism of the president.

The *Record*'s motto, part of its masthead, was "The Only Paper in Los Angeles That Dares." The *Record* had to dare to get noticed. Like all of the Scripps newspapers, the *Record* had built its reputation on fighting for the average working person and claimed it was the first penny newspaper west of the Mississippi. It was by far the smallest of the four dailies in Los Angeles in 1917; its share of the market only represented about 13 percent of the newspapers sold in the city, and its closest competitor outsold it nearly two to one.[114]

Through April, The Paper That Dares quietly stood by the president. In late March, for example, it printed one of Russell's more philosophical columns, in which he proclaimed that the end of kings and autocracy would ensure everlasting peace for the world.[115] The *Record* also embraced the NEA's policy of financing the war by taxing the wealthy directly, and printed NEA stories asking women to follow Wilson's request to avoid wasting food and other goods.[116] Still, the NEA articles and editorials that were used in the *Los Angeles Record* were not nearly as patriotic as those appearing daily in the Ohio newspapers. The *Record* stopped short of advocating American intervention and only called for its readers to do their patriotic duty to fight the war now that it had been joined.

This appeal to duty could be seen in mid-April, when a reader wrote a letter to the editor criticizing the *Record* for "a needless war . . . almost unanimously opposed by the people of our country and which if submitted to a referendum would have been overwhelmingly voted against." Dana Sleeth, the newspaper's editor, responded, "The time for theory and argument has passed; right or wrong we are in." At the same time, he made it clear that the *Record* "from the start of the world war to the present minute has never editorially advocated war."[117]

"Short and Important"

By late May, the *Record* was ready to bolt from the NEA's patriotic fold, and Jim Scripps would play a large part in the shift of opinion. The public debate about the draft and the financing of the war—the two biggest issues Congress had faced so far—certainly played a part in convincing most of the West Coast editors that Wilson's war machinery was mechanically unsound. Poor wheat crops in 1916 and 1917, coupled with the actions of greedy food speculators, generated, as one historian has noted, "a tremendous groundwave of popular discontent, especially in the cities." Conservatives blamed Wilson's food control board, although in reality the food board had little legal authority to correct the situation.[118]

However, a furious fight in Congress in May over a White House proposal to censor newspapers during the war apparently was the major contributor to the *Record*'s change of heart. Wilson insisted that his administration needed broad powers to prevent treasonous writings, and Republicans seized on the issue as a way of painting Wilson as an out-of-control dictator.[119] Although a formal newspaper censorship bill was ultimately defeated after a series of votes in late May, the Espionage Act, restricting freedom of expression, was enacted June 15. The new law made it illegal to convey false reports that interfered with the military; to willfully cause or attempt to cause "insubordination, disloyalty, mutiny or refusal of duty" in the military; or to willfully obstruct military recruiting or enlistment.[120] The law allowed postmaster general Albert Burleson to ban from the mails any material that he judged fell under it, and to revoke a media organization's second-class mailing privileges—critical to periodicals that depended on the mail for their distribution.[121]

Wilson's attempts to control dissent and the creation of the Committee on Public Information to spread official propaganda were too much for the *Record* to accept.

On May 29, the *Record* printed an editorial titled "Short and Important":

> We gave as much patriotism as the next fellow, and mayhap [sic] a bit more. BUT until some heavy handed governmental gink arrives with a

stop order this paper is going to give its readers the free opportunity to say what they think about the conduct of this war; about enlistment, liberty bonds, conscription and other issues. . . . Better sedition—so called—than a bottled, burning sense of outrage that makes free men into anarchists. Let's have a safety valve at one place in this nation.[122]

Two days later, the *Record* unleashed a full attack. A page 1 editorial, under the byline of John Perry—the Concern's libel attorney—blasted Wilson:

> The plain truth is that neither East nor West, North or South, are people clamoring to go to war. The fact is, as far as public sentiment for this war is concerned, it's a fizzle. . . . President Wilson has committed one colossal blunder in this—that HE FIRST LULLED INTO SILENT SLUMBER THE MILITANT WAR SPIRIT OF AMERICA—THEN HE DECLARED WAR. As a result, the people are . . . responding . . . very coldly.
>
> President Wilson is asking . . . for more power than was every entrusted to any English king, . . . any German emperor. . . . [H]e demands a press gag that can effectively choke to death any honest effort to curtail the abuses or misuses of this lordly power. . . . [Press censorship] MURDERS THE TRUTH, PUTS A PREMIUM ON LIES, BURIES DEMOCRACY AND MAKES SLAVES AND SERFS OF FREE MEN.[123]

Although he supported the *Record*'s stand, Jim dutifully had major parts of the editorial wired to E.W. in Washington on the next day.[124] E.W. was most concerned about the lack of unity the Concern was showing. "Perry is altogether too nearly right in what he gave the *Record*, but Cochran and I think that that utterance was premature, and that something not quite like it should have been formulated for all of our papers, the Newspaper Enterprise Association and even Howard's association [UP]," Scripps wrote Jim.[125]

San Diego Sun editor W. H. Porterfield, one of the few West Coast editors who thought the *Record* went too far, called the Perry piece "mildly treasonable" and "too radical and in poor taste just before we were attempting the greatest experiment in the history of Democracy."[126] Perry wired Scripps on June 7 that since his article had been published, circulation of the *Record* had jumped five thousand: "If we avail ourselves [of] this psychological opportunity, we can very greatly increase [the] Concern's power, prestige and property, because we can obtain the ear and hearts of many millions more readers in this crisis and largely help mould [sic] future policy of America. I am not making these statements from impulse, nor mere enthusiasm, but based upon careful tabulation results of my editorial."[127]

E.W. wrote Jim that he and his editors were out of touch. "War conditions, and our situation in the war, are far worse than you think it is, and far worse than I had thought it was before coming." Jim had expected a rebuke from his father, but what particularly angered and surprised him was a meeting that took place in Washington on June 6, after which he was told that Rickey, who was moving to Washington, had been formally installed as "chief on the spot" by a "grand conference" of E.W., Cochran, Bob Scripps, Martin, Rickey, and Howard. "Conclusion: N.E.A., U.P., and all papers must take more definite stand on war policy. Object: wake country up to real fact of serious situation," said Bob's telegram to Jim about the meeting.[128]

Jim wanted to make Canfield, a man he trusted and knew well from his work with the Scripps Northwest newspapers, the editor-in-chief for all of the Concern, but E.W. balked. Canfield traveled to California to meet with Jim. E.W. wanted Canfield to concentrate on the NEA. Scripps also said that Rickey's position was "temporary," doubting Rickey's physical health.[129] E.W. insisted to partner Milt McRae that he was not usurping Jim's authority: "While I say that I am not going to run the Concern, and while I am determined not to do so, and while the most that I dare to do is to suggest, I can say that there is a strong inclination on the part of others to consider me as though I am not only the head of the Concern, but actively at the head. I can protest until I am black in the face, but that does no good."[130] Scripps still was not satisfied that the Concern was doing enough, but it certainly was doing more since he came to Washington. He said he had convinced "our boys" that they had to wake the country up, "whether it makes or breaks the Scripps Concern as an institution." Scripps asked Paine, an early critic of the NEA's war policy, to "just be a 'good soldier,' and do all that you can, in your writing, to throw the fear, if not of the Lord, then at least the fear of the German Kaiser, into the heart of every one of our readers."[131]

"You and Others Will Be Inclined to Give Some Weight"

Scripps could not resist reinstating himself as the general of his soldiers. In mid-June, Scripps fired a telegram to Jim containing the word "urge"—a favorite verb used by the elder Scripps to speak his mind without blatantly usurping Jim: "I urge you to wire your papers west of Mississippi . . . directing them they must print United Press and Newspaper Enterprise Association war matter, especially that produced by our combined Washington bureaus under Rickey's direction."[132] The telegram was referring to editorials and features that were designed, for the most part, "with the idea of arousing the people to the dangers" of the war.

On the same day Scripps telegrammed a "request" to his oldest son that he personally wire his editors, ordering them to publish a piece written by California senator Hiram Johnson. "I have agreed that it shall appear in full in every one of our paper's front page," the elder Scripps told his son, who controlled the editorial side of the business. "Answer when you have complied with my request."[133]

At a loss for what to do, Jim asked Harper for help. Harper asked Paine to draft the message to the editors. "It seems to both of us," Paine wrote about his discussions with Jim, "that it will not be an easy matter to formulate." Not only were "Must Copy" articles hard to swallow for editors accustomed to local control, but the primary problem was space; most of the papers only had about six pages for copy, and the NEA and UP were generating a great deal of war news.[134]

E.W. just was getting started. He sensed the resistance to central control and wanted to clear the air. On June 16 he sent a letter, using individually signed copies so that it would not look like a circular letter, to all editors and top administrators in the Concern that placed on the record the formal action of the "grand conference" more than a week before. E.W. again reaffirmed that a person had to be in Washington to fully appreciate the war dangers. Still denying that he was taking control of the Concern, he could not resist the urge to "urge":

> Perhaps because of my age and long experience, you and others in authority will be inclined to give some weight to my expressed opinions.
>
> I have urged on the powers that be in this Concern that some one man of great ability and experience in our Concern should locate himself here in Washington permanently, during the period of the war, and that he be empowered to direct the editorial policy of all of our institutions, and coordinate the effort of all in one direct line, the purpose of which will be that we should be of public service to this country in a period of stress.
>
> I have further urged that this man have both the authority and responsibility to direct, not only what shall *not* be published, but particularly what *shall* be published.
>
> You may instantly recognize what a great departure this course is from my life-long practice of securing absolute, local self-government.... For the time being, I would like to see every Editor and, in fact, every man, no matter how humble his position in our Concern, forget circulation, personal ambition, fame, and profit: so that every energy may be bent to one end: the country's final victory in war.[135]

Response to the spirit of this letter was positive and perhaps a matter of relief, at least among the editors who responded directly to E.W. The *Cleveland Press*'s Victor Morgan said centralization was an "unpleasant" choice but was "the only one whereby the collective punch can be delivered."[136] G. B. Parker of the *Oklahoma News* said this would greatly help editors "in administering the vital public mission."[137] Ralph Millett of the *Memphis Press* said the plan "can do much to awaken the nation."[138] The *Evansville Press*'s editor wrote that the war situation "makes a conscientious editor halt and think before advocating or denouncing a national undertaking about which he lacks fullest information."[139] The *Portland News*'s Fred Boalt said, "I do not know what is going on in Washington; I want to know. I want to be told what do in the matter of war policy." The NEA's Hughes wrote, "My daily experience and observation from the NEA tower was long ago destroyed by faith in ABSOLUTE local self government, or ABSOLUTE group self government, as a Scripps policy. It is inefficient in vital cases."[140]

Cochran praised Rickey, saying that he had "used tact in getting the Concern's men working together." Cochran also told E.W. "your inspirational touch was needed to coordinate our forces, so that the entire Concern might function as an organization rather than dissipate its influence by scattered efforts.... No one else could have done it with so little friction."[141]

But not all of the Concern was happy. Harper in San Diego asked Scripps, "Is Washington the best place to determine what the country ought to be thinking about?... You fear revolution. Is Washington a good place to determine either the causes of possible revolution, or the remedies which out to be applied to prevent it?" But he conceded, "I am a good soldier. I am not going to start any insurrection in the Concern because I feel this way."[142]

Sleeth, the *Los Angeles Record*'s editor, who had sponsored the barrage against Wilson, objected vehemently: "As the first editor in the Concern, perhaps in the country, that tried to translate this war to the people... this subject of war control of press opinion is somewhat vital to me," he wrote E.W.

> I am strong for an immediate central control of this Concern if we can find a man who can touch the hearts and imaginations and faiths of the people, but this Concern would be wrecked in six months if we endeavor to vest such control, say in the average Washington correspondent.... We cannot drive this nation. We must lead. We must prove that we are in earnest. That we understand the problems that touch the homes of a hundred million.... Give me the man who can talk to my people ...

in their own tongue. Then that man can have "my" policies, my front page, editorial page, back page and the rest of the space without any order from anybody. But give us no formal prophet.[143]

To much of the West Coast portion of the Concern, the Washington-focused NEA was simply out of touch with public opinion in the West.

The "Most Smoke and Most Noise"

Concerned about the negative feelings the centralized policy was creating, E.W. told Harper he would ask Rickey to travel around the country occasionally to get a feel for public opinion. But E.W. insisted that Rickey be based in Washington, comparing the situation to a general directing his troops from a hilltop—"out of the smoke and noise of battle." But the best general, he reasoned, occasionally joins the smoke and noise to see what the troops are experiencing. "The nation's capital is the place where there is most smoke and most noise."[144]

Scripps also tried to make peace with Sleeth, but ultimately did not send a letter he wrote on July 3. He said he was sympathetic with Sleeth's concerns, but "just at present I am urging you and all our other men to concentrate effort."[145] It is not known why he chose not to send the letter, but he might have felt Jim would have seen it as further meddling.

Pleased with Rickey's performance so far, Scripps wrote him on July 10 outlining his "own particular and personal views of the situation." E.W. said the Concern should target its persuasion at the people, not government leaders directly. "We should present to the public all the important facts which we are ourselves cognizant of and which the law will permit us to divulge; and, further, that we shall present to this public such opinions we have and such arguments as we have to make, rather than to any member of the government: leaving it to the people to formulate and express that public opinion which our rulers should submit to."[146]

Although Scripps again claimed he was not assuming any authority over him, Rickey was now aware of what the chief stockholder wanted, and Rickey knew that E.W. wanted him in charge.[147] Scripps had a longer version of the same letter drafted five days later to send to Jim but decided not to send it.[148] Again, he probably was worried about being accused of meddling.

Not only did Jim resent his father's interference, but the Scripps men in the West were convinced that Rickey epitomized how much the NEA was out of touch. "Rickey is a strong man, but inherently he is an aristocrat; he don't [sic] know the point of view of the miner or the ditchdigger," Harper wrote to Cochran. Harper said Rickey just wants to "do the thinking for the editors."[149] An editorial Rickey wrote in late June, published in the Concern's Ohio papers, alarmed many Scripps editors and readers. Titled "Shut Up or Be Locked Up," it said that criticism of the government during wartime should not be tolerated—even from the press: "Appeals to any of our citizens to rebel against any of the laws passed by Congress to carry out the purposes of OUR war, are attacks on OUR government. The time has come for treasonable editors and orators to shut up or be locked up. . . . It's time to go right down the line and lock up others who use their liberty in free America to lend aid and comfort to the Prussian enemy of democracy and civilization."[150]

When the editorial appeared in the *Cincinnati Post* on July 5, Kiefer, one of the progressive pacifists who had tried to buy antiwar space in the *Cincinnati Post*, could not resist the urge to comment on the Concern's inconsistencies. He chided the *Post:* "If you haven't done so, you should send a copy of your 'Shut Up or Be Locked Up' to the editor of the *Los Angeles Record*. . . . If the Kaiser had sense enough to know good propaganda for his cause, he would have your editorial circulated . . . as evidence of how little the American press cares for democracy and how it really favors despotic rule."[151]

Needless to say, the Rickey editorial was never published in the *Los Angeles Record.* Jim Scripps and several of his West Coast editors had become increasingly convinced that Wilson's cabinet members were incompetent and should be criticized for slowing the war effort. Canfield, now working in Los Angeles for the NEA, said soldiers hated Newton Baker, the secretary of war, because he imposed curfews and banned cigarette smoking among the new draftees.[152] As the biographer of navy secretary Josephus Daniels noted, "protecting those young men against the evils of alcohol and vice was a task dear to Daniels' heart."[153] Venereal disease was crippling before penicillin, and Baker had set up zones around training camps that outlawed prostitution. The new rules ran opposite to the traditional view that sex and booze were necessities for a manly fighter.[154]

Now under the influence of Jim and the other Pacific Coast editors he saw regularly, Canfield felt that Rickey was not criticizing the Wilson administration enough. "I think the position of N.E.A. should be like this: We believe Wilson is the best man for the job, or at least as good as any man we know. We are for Wilson, but that doesn't mean that we are apologists or defenders for his chief clerks." Canfield asked his editor, Hughes, to control Rickey. "Until you get such an order from Mr. Scripps [E.W.] you will, of course, take your instructions from me.

As I am president of N.E.A. and you are editor, you are the fellow I hold responsible, not Rickey, who's running N.E.A.'s Washington bureau. . . . I am still directing you as to editorial policies." Canfield admitted that Hughes might be "confused" because of E.W.'s June letter about editorial policy.[155]

The Record Strikes Again

Throughout June and early July the *Los Angeles Record* cooled its criticism of the war effort. Instead, the newspaper opened its pages to dozens of letters from readers each day, asking them to comment on the war and Perry's May 31 article. Usually printed under the headline "What You Think of the War," the letters represented a wide variety of opinions. "We cannot print a tenth of the letters we receive, but we especially endeavor to print those that differ from us," a column presumably from the editor said on June 4.[156] The *Record*'s only requirement for printing the letters was that they must be signed. "Several hundred handy letter writers are flooding this office with screeds that they haven't the manhood to sign; these go into the wastebasket. If YOU dare, WE do."[157] Using the newspaper pages as a public forum cleverly prevented the Concern's Washington bureau from contending that the *Record* was instigating government criticism. By late July, however, Jim Scripps and the *Record*'s editors were poised to step to the front of the war debate again.

The *Record*'s second barrage against the war effort was launched on July 17. Under a banner headline, "Whose Flag Is This," an editorial and cartoon that covered half of the front page above the fold concisely summarized the *Record*'s concerns about the war effort. The editorial's thesis was that exploitive army contractors, food speculators, and incompetent government bureaucrats were taking control. "In this world war for democracy is this nation going to be conducted for the welfare of the people, or the profit of a plunderbund? Are we, fighting for democracy across the seas, to give up such freedom as we have left at home?" the editorial asked. "We cannot plunder the masses and beat them down with sudden terrorism. . . . Let America get right with her people."[158]

The editorial did not mention War Secretary Baker or Navy Secretary Daniels, but obvious jabs were taken at them. The oblique references to Wilson's cabinet were not lost on *San Diego Sun* editor Porterfield, who wrote in a July 18 letter that the editorial characterized Daniels and Baker as "rubber stamp patriots—walking rubber stamps and old maids" because they demanded strict disciplinary policies on soldiers.[159]

The *Record*'s editorial offensive apparently never raised the ire of postal censors, even though Postmaster General Burleson had told all postmasters on the day the Espionage Act took effect to look for newspapers that violate the letter of the new law "or otherwise embarrass[ed] or hamper[ed] the Government in conducting the war."[160] Under the broad way the federal courts interpreted the Espionage Act in some cases, the *Record*'s attacks could have been considered illegal.[161] As historians H. C. Peterson and Gilbert Fite have noted, however, the Espionage Act was never invoked against major newspapers and magazines, even the Hearst newspapers, which initially were hostile to aspects of the war. Instead, the government focused on "the little newspapers, the reform or radical publicans, along with the foreign-language press."[162]

Illegal or legal, the *Record* certainly was running opposite to official NEA central policy. The *Record*'s editorials appeared as E.W. was urging Rickey to place "Must Copy" orders on important war policy editorials, particularly "such important pieces of news matter as are the foundation of editorial policy, and such editorials as you deem to be extremely important."[163] The next day Rickey wrote to all of the Concern's editors-in-chief, telling them to publish an editorial titled "What Is America's Duty to Its Allies and to Itself in This War for Democracy?" Rickey added: "Please instruct your editors to mail to me under first class postage copy of their papers containing this editorial."[164]

Jim was furious. "Either you have got to boss this job or I have got to boss this job. I am not in sympathy with the Washington Bureau. In my opinion Rickey should be divested of all authority if not entirely laid off," he wrote his father. "Big mistakes are being made in assuming that the public will take what is handed to them."[165] E.W. was equally angry about the *Record*'s latest barrage. He called some of the statements "false" and "unscrupulous."[166] Jim retorted that he had laid out the series of articles and cartoons in the *Record*, and that most of the pieces had been written by Sleeth and edited by Canfield. Jim said the coverage had elicited no retributions from advertisers or readers. "They seem to take this stuff as quietly as society news," he explained. Jim said potential draftees were "either intensely sore or scared to death," and labor groups were worried about being exploited.[167] E.W. acquiesced. "You are and should be absolute dictator. My health and condition of mind entirely disqualifies me from doing anything but offer advice."[168]

E.W., however, did ask Jim to halt the critical policy stand until Jim could come east to discuss the matter. Then, another "Must Copy" order from Rickey slipped through on July 27. "I am opposed to Rickey's holding 'must' authority," Jim wrote. "Rickey is known to be prejudiced against western and southern papers.... Am I right?"[169] E.W. responded immediately that the order had been sent before Rickey knew the power had been taken away. E.W. said Rickey had "broken down under the strain [of the *Record*'s attacks on the administration] and I advised him to go. . . . I am unaware if there is any head to the Washington organization now." Scripps asked Jim to wait before appointing Canfield to take over.[170] Rickey stepped aside, remaining on the payroll of the NEA for the time being. With his reassignment, a cease-fire, in effect, was declared.

The War Gets Personal

On May 31, twenty-one-year-old Bob Scripps registered for the draft, as the new law required, in Washington, where he was staying with his father. He had been coached by one of the Concern's attorneys, Jay Curts, on how to describe his job with his father's newspapers. Bob, who had married in the spring, was struggling to find his place in life. He reported to Curts what happened when he registered: "I . . . explained that I was 'assistant to the chairman of the board', etc., [and then] the official who took my deposition said: 'You are, then, engaged in the newspaper business?' I said 'Yes,' and he wrote in 'newspaper-man' without more ado." Curts also told Bob to list the five Ohio newspapers as his places of employment, but because the registration form did not have enough room, "employed by the Scripps-McRae league at Washington and Cleveland, Ohio," was substituted.[171] Thus, Bob's registration form grossly exaggerated the importance of his position.

Meanwhile, Jim registered in San Diego. The truth behind his responsibilities personally and professionally did not need to be stretched. Jim had a wife and four children to support, and he was chairman of the board of a large newspaper empire. But he refused to claim exemption from the draft, which he could have done. This frustrated Harper and Concern executive C. F. Mosher, who were trying to advise him. "Jim's feeling about this matter is highly creditable; he is patriotic; he wants to do his duty," Harper reported to E.W. on June 11. Harper assured E.W. it was "inconceivable to me" that Jim would get drafted because he was married and had four children. The lists of single men, in Harper's view, would have to be exhausted first.[172]

The war in Europe was now striking close to home for E. W. Scripps, and he would do everything in his power to prevent it from harming his two sons. What he could not predict was the unintended consequences his actions on the draft issue would have for his relationship with his sons and ultimately for his newspaper chain.

6 "To Advocate a Policy and to Yourself Meet Its Requirements": July to December 1917

By the summer of 1917, the Scripps newspapers, particularly those in Ohio, were solid supporters of compulsory military service—a key component in the NEA's editorial policy on preparedness since shortly after the *Lusitania* was sunk. The NEA said in a December 1916 editorial, "You can find no legitimate excuse for opposition to the training of young men and boys in the manual of arms." Like many progressive thinkers, the NEA believed that military training was good for the soul, too, and would "give the United States a finer body of young manhood than it now possesses."[1] Forced military service was not a violation of democratic principles because "no higher right could exist in government, especially in democracy, than the right to compel its citizens to defend their own liberties as well as the liberties of their fellow-citizens."[2]

When Congress adopted and Wilson signed the Selective Service Act on May 18, the NEA was ecstatic. "There can be no higher honor than being picked from among your fellows in the crucial hour of civilization's status, in a cause that is both God's and humanity's."[3] To the NEA, the draft demonstrated the fairness inherent in a democracy fighting a war. "It knows not the rich man's son nor the poor man's son. It knows only justice."[4] The NEA had no tolerance for those trying to impede the draft. "The men in this country who are trying to delay the carrying out of the government's military program . . . : are just as much traitors to their country as was Benedict Arnold," a June 2 NEA editorial noted.[5]

Of all the issues that arose during the war, the draft had the greatest effect on the Scripps family, the management of the Concern, and its reputation as a progressive leader. No other issue would so publicly challenge the Concern's willingness to practice what it preached on an issue it had helped frame on progressive principles. On a family level, the draft and the meddling it inspired would drive a wedge between E.W. Scripps and his sons. The elder Scripps wanted to protect his sons so they could continue his chain after his death; the sons wanted, at least initially, to serve in the military and avoid public shame. In the end, the draft sparked a chain of familial disagreements that fostered the Scripps corporate split in the early 1920s.

More immediate effects on overall coverage were seen, too. The draft drove E.W. to insist that greenhorn Bob be put in the top editorial position, creating internal dissent, undermining the Concern's public reputation with accusations of slackerism, and hamstringing the Concern's war coverage. The controversy Scripps created with his efforts to get his sons exempted from the draft dogged Bob Scripps until his death; his 1938 obituary in the *New York Times* mentioned the draft issue and noted how in 1920 he had been queried about the circumstances surrounding his exemption during a Senate investigation.[6]

This was not the only issue on which the Concern had to face the realities of what it had been advocating, however. The Concern now had to pay the higher taxes it had been advocating. It was expected to buy war bonds, too. That's not easy for a corporate entity facing increasing printing and labor costs. Dissatisfaction with some of Wilson's policies still quietly festered among some Scripps editors, as they doubted some of what they were preaching to their readers.

With Americans readying for battle in Europe, war news was as hot as ever. While America's entry in the war fed the public appetite for war news, it did not add much to UP's news-gathering costs. Censorship still controlled and made somewhat routine how reporters gathered the news and what they reported.

What was not routine in the summer of 1917 was that E. W. Scripps was living in Washington, and what he would do over the next five months because of the draft would start an internal war within his family and ultimately the Concern.

"Lottery of Death"

The suddenness of Bob's selection on the first day of the draft lottery shocked the family. Bob's wife, Peggy, three months pregnant and with Bob in Washington at the time, was very upset. "I suppose that more than half of my anxiety in all this matter has been occasioned of my feeling for Mrs. Scripps and Bob's wife," E.W. wrote on July 27.[7] E.W. said Peggy nearly had a miscarriage over it,[8] and Nackie, his wife of thirty-one years, was in a state of "more or less suppressed hysteria" because she regarded the draft as a "lottery of death."[9]

For E.W., keeping Bob from serving in the army or navy was necessary to save his newspaper empire. "If I should lose both of my sons, the institution, which is an important factor in the business affairs of the country, would immediately fall into other hands and become disintegrated," he told his longtime attorney and fellow stockholder J. C. Harper on July 28.[10] This statement might seem like hyperbole, but to him the fear was legitimate. He had trained his sons to carry on his ideals, and he believed only they could implement them after his death. He needed both sons because each had his own limited abilities.

Neg Cochran, the longtime Concern editor and trusted Scripps lieutenant, wrote in his biography of E.W. that the aging publisher studied his sons "biologically as he might study any other specimens."[11] Years of observation had convinced E.W. that Jim was a conservative businessman who had "only contempt for the altruist."[12] Thus, Jim was not the best suited for running editorial policy for a chain of penny newspapers focused on serving the needs of the working class.

On the other hand, E.W. and others saw a lot of the old man's traits in Bob. "[Bob] is sensitive, sympathetic and altruistic, but has not been so much of a recluse as E.W. was," Cochran wrote in 1933. He said that E.W. had intended Jim to run the business side of the Concern, with John P., his second son, running the editorial side. With John's death in 1914, however, that role fell to Bob.[13] The problem was convincing Bob he wanted the job and convincing Jim that Bob could do it.

Bob, like Jim, was not afraid to serve in the military and refused to consider claiming exemption for himself. Although the Scripps boys surely foresaw shame if they avoided the draft, that cannot explain it all. One historian has suggested a complex web of reasons why men enthusiastically served in World War I. One was a desire for manly adventure among young men who were increasingly becoming bored in the standardized industrial economy; the war provided a chance for escape.[14]

When E.W. heard Bob's number had been drawn, he asked Jay W.

Curts, lead attorney in the Concern's Cincinnati business office, what should be done to get Bob exempted.[15] The system established by Congress required draftees to file exemption claims before a local draft board with appeals to be heard by a district board. Bob's legal home address was the family's ranch in Butler County outside of Cincinnati. Thus, he was assigned to the local draft board covering the area outside the city of Hamilton. Curts recommended that Bob's wife, Peggy, file a dependency claim on Bob's behalf, and if that did not work, E.W. could file an occupational exemption at the district board level.[16] Although Jim's draft number had not been called, Harper, in San Diego, immediately began preparing papers to get Jim exempted on occupational grounds as well. Although Jim was married with four children, Harper wrote E.W. that he agreed with Jim, who insisted that an exemption on dependency grounds was not justified because his estate was large enough to take care of his survivors.[17]

Harper, however, told E.W. that an occupational exemption for Jim should be sought because of Jim's obvious position of importance in the Concern. But Harper was not convinced a similar case could be made for Bob, who had no formal role. "I suppose it is Curts' job to work up a plausible case [for Bob's occupational exemption]; I am glad it is not my job. Maybe I am not informed as to the work that Bob has been doing since he went East with you. It would be gratifying if Bob was exempted on merit and not as a matter of favor."[18] Harper wondered aloud to E.W. what he would do if he were in his position. "It is quite different to advocate a policy and to yourself meet its requirements," he noted to E.W.[19]

"Our Fear Was That There Would Be Some Anarchists"

Meanwhile, Curts drove to Hamilton on July 22 to find out what he could about the men serving on the draft board of rural Butler County. Starting with a friend of the Scripps family, he met John Beeler of the draft board and ultimately paid the editor of a local newspaper, the *Middletown Journal*, $25 per week to report to him what he heard about Bob's draft situation.[20] "I told [Beeler] that our fear was that there would be some anarchists or Socialists on the [rural Butler County] Board who would stand up so straight against appearing to favor the rich that they would actually discriminate against persons who would otherwise be entitled to exemption." Beeler assured Curts that no such radicals were on the board.

The "Old, Elemental, Every-day Problem of Food"

Meanwhile, the Scripps newspapers' advocacy for the war effort continued. Not only did the masses need to be convinced to conform to the draft and other wartime laws but also they needed to be convinced to buy Liberty Bonds to finance a war halfway across the world and to save food and other resources to prevent shortages

President Wilson also needed public support throughout 1917 because of the intense political acrimony he faced in Congress.[21] A bill to control food prices—controversial because it gave the Wilson administration broad authority—consumed most of the debate during the early summer. The food situation was serious. The 1917 wheat crop was expected to yield only half of what was needed. Many farmers were hoarding grain, and food speculators were storing food to drive up prices. Consumers, especially those in cities, implored the government to intervene.[22] The issue usually pitted urban states, which consumed food, against rural states, which produced it.

Little doubt remained over which side the NEA, with its urban readership and record of backing Wilson, would support. The NEA writer Harry Hunt, in a *Cleveland Press* column in June, wrote that the "old, elemental, every-day problem of food" was more important to winning the war than men or munitions.[23] When consideration of the bill, first introduced in mid-April, dragged into late June, the NEA opined: "Senatorial courtesy and . . . gab are costing us too much now they cannot be permitted to cost us the war."[24] The NEA rhetoric became increasingly vitriolic—painting those opposing the bill as traitors—as the summer continued. "This [food] condition is more valuable to the German cause than to win two or three battles on the land."[25] A watered-down version of the Food Control Bill finally passed in early August.

"Shall We Pay It with Cash in Hand?"

The NEA already had a track record for the other controversial bill of the summer of 1917—increased taxation of the wealthy. The NEA felt its initiative for income tax publicity was now more viable than ever. Gilson Gardner, in an NEA column, predicted that "in all probability" income tax publicity would be part of the war revenue bill.[26] The NEA economic writer Basil Manly wrote that tax publicity could raise "vast funds justly and quickly."[27] An NEA editorial said Manly's investigations had shown that $300 million was being lost already to tax evaders, and with the drastic tax increases now being discussed "the fraud and evasion will be increased ten-fold, unless effective means (publicity) are found to prevent it."[28]

As cost estimates for the war escalated, the income tax debate became too supercharged to allow discussion of income tax publicity to become more than well-intentioned rhetoric. The real fight centered on how much of the war should be financed through bonds and how much through increased taxes. Although the Concern fervently supported the Liberty Bond drives, the Scripps newspapers, like many progressives, wanted most of the war paid immediately with higher income taxes. "Shall we pay for it with cash in hand and be thru with it, or shall we pay for it this year and next and all other years, generation after generation?" an NEA editorial asked. The answer was clear to the NEA: if the poor have to be drafted to fight the war, the rich must have their wealth drafted to pay for the war.[29] The NEA never backed down on this or the income tax publicity idea. Debate over war revenue would drag on for six months before a bill passed that dramatically raised taxes but financed the war with bonds at a four-to-one ratio over taxes.[30]

"Exerting the Last Particle . . . to Save Your Boy" with a Lawsuit

Meanwhile, E. W. Scripps was concerned about the Wilson administration's plan to send conscripts overseas to fight, and he wondered if the U.S. Constitution could stop it. He asked Cochran to begin preparing a series of articles to convince the administration to change its mind.[31]

Senator Bob LaFollette, who supported Scripps's position, heard Cochran was working on the issue and sent Hannis Taylor, an attorney, legal historian, and former ambassador to Spain, to meet with Scripps on July 24. Scripps considered Taylor "the highest authority on constitutional law" and was very interested when Taylor told him that he was about to file a lawsuit to restrain the president from sending overseas any troops other than regular army troops. Scripps said Taylor cited several cases in which the Supreme Court had unanimously held that the militia "shall only be used for the purpose of enforcing the law, putting down rebellion, and defending our country from actual invasion of its soil."[32]

Scripps volunteered to pay for Taylor's expenses and gave him $5,000. Gardner worked with LaFollette to build a mailing list of possible supporters.[33] The publisher then wrote his wife, Nackie, in Ohio to explain: "I am sending this to comfort you. I not only want you to know that I am exerting the last particle of my strength to save your boy as well as many hundreds of thousands of other boys. . . . I am not only willing to spend hundreds of thousands of dollars, if need be, in this fight, but I am quite willing to take a large amount of personal risk in opposing a governmental action that I feel to be entirely wrong."[34] Because he knew Bob would not support what he was doing, he ordered Nackie to destroy the letter and to say nothing.

Scripps did tell Jim, who at the time was directing the attacks on the government's war effort in the *Los Angeles Record.* E.W. was concerned the *Record'*s barrage and his lawsuit would make the Concern vulnerable to accusations of sedition. He said "positive danger" existed that some of Jim's West Coast papers "might be closed up." Scripps reminded his son that war gave little room for the press to criticize. "There is a big fight being raised now by the friends of a free press on account of the utterly unconstitutional and utterly unlawful suppression of a lot of Socialist papers. Neither the people nor the courts would permit such a thing at any other time than this," the father admonished his son. E.W. added: "The fact that our papers, would, at the same time [as the Scripps-Taylor lawsuit], be openly and perhaps illegally attacking the government along other lines, may or may not seriously embarrass me."[35]

Scripps then hired Clarence Darrow, a friend and prominent attorney, to look over Taylor's arguments.[36] Darrow said the case was legally sound but would still fail. Scripps said Darrow told him the "Supreme Court may and probably will render a decision based rather on public opinion than on the letter of the Constitution—a sort of 'rule of reason' decision." Now, Scripps pulled back.

On July 28, Scripps prepared a letter he ultimately did not send in which he told Taylor that he was in "full sympathy" with the lawsuit, but he could not join it because of his newspapers. "This situation [of owning a newspaper chain] limits my freedom of personal action, much to my own discomfort and exasperation. There are too many millions of persons who only know the name Scripps."[37] A revised version of the letter was not sent until August 22.[38]

At the time, Scripps was getting angry criticism from Harper: "*It is a mighty serious matter to limit the War-power of our nation.* . . . *You are in a position to exercise a great and beneficent [sic] influence in this War.* . . . *Do not impair it or throw it away,*" Harper wrote Scripps. Harper and others also were worried about being associated with LaFollette, a controversial antiwar figure.[39]

Gardner wrote at least two articles on Taylor's lawsuit in early August. The articles presented both sides of the issue; in one, Gardner paraphrased a prominent lawyer who called Taylor's lawsuit "dangerous propaganda."[40] Taylor ultimately challenged the draft law in *Cox v. Wood (1918)*, and the U.S. Supreme Court unanimously rejected his challenge.[41] Historians agree with Darrow's assertion that the Court used the wartime political climate, not a strict reading of the law, to guide its judgment in ruling against the other selective service cases.[42] In his 1932 biography of Scripps, Gardner insisted that Taylor "showed convincingly that conscription for foreign service is unconstitutional."[43]

"Patriotic and Full of Fight": NEA Stunts

Doubts about the constitutionality of overseas service had no place on the editorial pages of the Scripps newspaper. The Wilson administration could count on its willing and powerful ally, the Scripps newspapers, to make the draft, the war, and its inevitable miseries as palatable to the public as possible. Initially the NEA used the method of bringing the human-interest element alive to shape the Concern's war coverage. The NEA editorials targeted readers with rational arguments for a need to fight for democracy, while the NEA features targeted the hearts and emotions of readers with stories of daring and enjoyable challenges and opportunities that the war provided American manhood.

For example, with war looming in March, C. C. Lyon, the NEA's most famous participatory journalist, joined the navy, which needed new sailors to face the submarine threat, to write a series about living conditions and opportunities for those who volunteered to serve.[44] His stories, written in first person, told of sailors who were "patriotic and full of fight," and the series began to appear within a week after war was declared.[45] The stories, which ran primarily in the Ohio newspapers throughout April and May, reassured men that many "mighty poor specimens, physically, join the navy," but all were transformed into healthy fighting men.[46] "A spirit of competition enters into everything [the recruits do] that makes work seem like play," Lyon explained in one installment.[47]

The new weaponry available in the war also was glamorized. One stunt included a first-person report by the NEA's Mary Boyle O'Reilly, the war correspondent who had been accused of being anti-German, who took a ride in a navy warplane in May. "I was flying to learn how the old navy and the new protect our nation's coast, and to see war above the clouds," O'Reilly wrote.[48] Lyon also wrote separate articles about his service on a U.S. submarine and an American battleship.[49]

To differentiate its content from that of its rivals, the NEA made full use of one of its star correspondents, Charles Edward Russell, the former Socialist Party candidate for president, who had been on the full-time payroll since 1916. In May, Russell was selected to join a special diplomatic mission to Russia that summer to visit the provisional government that had been installed after the czar's abdication. Dubbed the Root Commission because Senator Elihu Root led it, the mission's primary purpose was to make sure the new Russian government stayed in the war against Germany. Russell volunteered to publicize the mission's message to the Russian people directly, but his efforts were mostly a failure because he could not find good translators and could not get enough American government support.[50]

Upon his return, Russell wrote at least twenty-five columns about the Russians in the war for the NEA beginning in mid-August. The NEA billed the articles as "an epoch-making series" from a "world reporter, well-known."[51] He repeated similar themes throughout. First, Russia was still willing to fight. "She will put up a strictly firstclass article of fight and she will win with it," he wrote.[52] Second, German antiwar propagandists were gaining the upper hand. "This did an immense amount of harm. They spread the flub-dub thick over all Russia, and millions there were that fell for it."[53] Third, the Russians were idealists, not conquerors. "He wouldn't shed any blood for any amount of territorial expansion or trade. But he will fight as hard as any other man in the world and perhaps a little harder, if he thinks his democracy is in danger, or the revolution, light of his soul and breath of his life, may be overthrown.... The ideal that is the real—that is Russia."[54] By late winter, Russell was working for the Committee for Public Information as a successful "Four-Minute Man" speaker to rally war support, and he was assigned to run the CPI's London bureau in May 1918.[55]

"Systematically Eliminating Everything in the Nature of a Scoop"

The NEA features dominated the war news in the Ohio newspapers, especially because the Ohio editors had become disenchanted with the awkward UP reports. Many of UP's stories arrived in New York with the paragraphs out of order, because of problems with censors and access to the transatlantic cable. Roy Howard explained in May that any cable filing had to be limited to segments or "takes" of twenty-five to fifty words—at a cost of 25 cents a word from London and 31 cents a word from Paris—making it necessary to break a story into pieces. If censors delayed some takes, they would arrive out of order in the New York office, where UP copy editors often rewrote and retransmitted the same story as unexpected takes arrived. "It is not infrequent that the main punch of a story—the take which was filed first—is received last in New York," Howard explained to the disgruntled acting editor of the *Toledo News-Bee.* "We then face the dilemma of having the story reach you wrong end first."[56]

United Press also no longer seemed to get the major scoops it had seemed to claim as a matter of routine early in the war. Howard maintained that UP had not "deteriorated, but we know the opposition has improved." He also blamed the censors. "The 'every fellow for himself' system of the early stages of the war has given place to intensive organizations even in the handling of news," he explained. "Just so far as it is possible to do so officials abroad are systematically eliminating everything in the nature of a scoop or an exclusive story."

Howard said a prime example came when UP obtained an exclusive statement by British premier Lloyd-George in 1917: "Naturally, however, we had to submit the story to the censor, who held the cable up and took the matter up with the press bureau, with the result that we were told that we could only send the story on the condition that we consent to it's [sic] being given to the Associated Press and all of the other American correspondents in London. Our own . . . enterprise went for nothing."[57]

Howard also criticized the Ohio editors for not understanding. "What's worrying me, Howard wrote Ohio editor-in-chief E. E. Martin in late May, "is that your Ohio telegraph editors haven't yet been tipped off to the fact that they should do anything with the UP report other than knock it."[58]

The "Fastidious Taste" of Censorship

The problems UP faced in sustaining the enterprise it exhibited in the early days of the war were illustrated by the experiences of one of the new UP foreign correspondents, Westbrook Pegler, who later became a notorious rightwing syndicated newspaper columnist. The twenty-one-year-old Pegler was another typical UP reporter—young and single, smart but inexperienced, eager and inexpensive.[59] He had started with UP as a boy, transmitting UP stories via telephone from the Chicago office, and worked at various UP bureaus in the Midwest.[60] He went to London during the summer of 1916 when Howard was beefing up UP in Europe. With no seniority, he worked at night, writing about twenty-four hundred words in "cablese"—the nickname for the shorthand used to save money on cable charges. He earned about $27 per week, barely enough to buy food and other necessities.[61]

Pegler got his chance to elude the dreariness of his London job with an assignment to cover the navy in Queenstown, Ireland, after the United States joined the war. But his brashness and desire to scoop AP in a slow news town soon got him into trouble with the American commander in the Atlantic, Admiral William S. Sims. Pegler got approval from the censor to cable a feature story on how the American sailors were more popular with the local women because they had more money than their British counterparts. Even though his censor had approved the story, Admiral Sims felt the story showed discontent between the two fleets. Pegler also reported, in another story he convinced Sims's censor to approve, that the American navy had sunk its first German submarine. At the time, war policy prohibited any publicity about the sinking of submarines; the U.S. navy wanted the Germans to wonder why one of its U-boats was late to return to port. Sims retaliated by accusing Pegler of "faking" the story, an accusation AP was quick to publicize. Pegler disputed that he had faked anything, but stubbornly refused to give navy officials the carbon that showed the censor's approval. Therefore, Simms had Pegler placed under what was described as "open arrest" and sent to London, where he gave the carbon to Ed Keen, head of the London UP bureau.[62] Keen sent it stateside to Howard, who approached Secretary of the Navy Daniels.

Howard asked for "nothing less than a square deal" in how UP was being treated, especially when the AP was being allowed to call Pegler's story a fake when it had been approved by the censor as true.[63] Daniels did not need much convincing; he already distrusted Sims. He ordered the admiral to reinstate Pegler.[64] The British Admiralty then objected to Pegler's return, something that infuriated Howard because he assumed Sims had solicited British help. "I trust that very shortly Admiral Sims may have something more to tax his resourcefulness than finding ways of circumventing your orders and venting his spleen on a correspondent whose literary style doesn't happen to please his fastidious taste," Howard wrote Daniels on July 21.[65]

Nonetheless, Howard decided to drop the matter. Pegler was given a raise to $45 a week and sent to the European mainland to cover the army. "The fleet base did not offer big news opportunities and we had only sent a man there through the belief that it might contribute somewhat to the efforts to stir up patriotism and enthusiasm in this country," Howard explained to Daniels on July 26.[66]

The American censors assigned to the American army in France, however, led by veteran journalist Frederick Palmer, were not much more lenient than those of the British and French. In his 1934 memoirs, Wilbur Forrest, a veteran UP correspondent who was accredited with the French army and later the American Expeditionary Forces, ranked the French censors as "by far the worst. The Americans were perhaps the most liberal. Occasionally the British censor demonstrated a flash of broadness."[67]

Forrest, however, agreed that censorship was necessary because "there was need during the four-year struggle in Europe to protect the morale of civilians in all Allied combatant countries and . . . shake the confidence of the enemy peoples."[68] In his memoirs General John J. Pershing, commander-in-chief of the American Expeditionary Forces, said the war correspondents were told much more than they were allowed to publish, but it was not difficult to get their consent.[69] Howard, too, agreed that some information must be kept from the public, but he was continually frustrated by occasional arbitrary decisions by censors to withhold even innocuous details. In September, he asked Navy Secretary Daniels to trust that the press would use their own judgment to voluntary censor themselves when necessary. He said UP desired "to cooperate with you and all other branches of government—but we do want to co-operate intelligently" by getting as much war news as possible.[70] Daniels replied he would pass Howard's wishes along.[71]

Military historian Joseph J. Mathews noted that journalists, caught up with the spirit of the time, saw the European war as a serious task on behalf of democracy, and accepted censorship as part of the sacrifice needed to win the war. Not wanting to be objective, they portrayed the enemy as negatively as possible. Those, such as Forrest, who wanted to portray the war realistically, were censored into writing bland descriptions. Although postwar critics attacked the war's reporting for being too naïve and too heavily censored, the reporting of World War I, in general, was still more realistic and less romanticized than reporting of earlier wars.[72]

Interestingly, Forrest, as a schoolboy, had become enamored of war reporting by reading the fanciful accounts of the Spanish-American war in Chicago newspapers. He did not find that his war experience matched his childhood dreams. "There was some romance in the work of a correspondent [during the European war], I found, but it was a grim romance," he wrote. Although he seldom got to tell his readers, Forrest noted that he often heard much about the grim facts of the war, he was often under enemy gunfire, and he "shared the life of a soldier." Correspondents looked the part, too. With the American Expeditionary Forces, correspondents wore a traditional American officer's uniform, with no rank insignia, and a green armband, marked boldly with a white *C*. Although Forrest loved to wear the uniform, he knew the fight had been taken out of his reporting: "The war correspondent of 1914–1918 was ... a sort of glorified disseminator of official military propaganda. I cannot recall any outstanding "beats" performed by my colleagues comparable to the recorded deeds that marked newspaper reporting during the Civil War, the Franco-Prussian struggle of 1870 ... and our own mix-up with Spain in 1898."[73] Forrest said he was allowed to write "any amount of picturesque descriptive material, narrative incidents of the war and even discuss after-the-fact strategy, on condition that such material had been denuded of facts which might give the enemy military information or afforded him 'aid and comfort.'"[74]

Young Pegler also soon collided with the limits of what was acceptable to the army's leaders. Within three months he ran afoul of General Pershing and others. Upset by the poor living conditions of the troops and believing the commanders were incompetent, he wrote Howard in early 1918 to outline his feelings about these inadequacies. He hoped Howard could find a way to bring the poor conditions to the attention of the public. Censors intercepted the letter, however. In turn, Pershing asked that Pegler's accreditation be removed, and secretary of war Newton Baker agreed, saying Pegler was "too young."[75] He went back to New York; even Roy Howard could not save him this time.

"We Have Not Claimed That the Whole Concern Will Disintegrate If Bob Is Withdrawn"

In late summer 1917, Bob Scripps and his older brother Jim were determined to serve in the army. By mid-August Jim had already spoken to a general at Camp Kearney cantonment, near Miramar in San Diego County, who thought Jim could serve as an officer and one of his aides. E.W. even warmed to the idea because a brief stint in the army would make Jim "more thoroughly interested in military matters [and] ... hence more sympathetic and efficient as a journalist thereafter."[76] Business partners Milton McRae and Harper agreed to help secure Jim's occupational exemption, if he was drafted as a private.[77] Meanwhile, the local draft board in Ohio rejected the dependency claim for exemption filed on behalf of Bob. Curts reported to E.W. that the board turned down all dependency claims "where parents were able to care for wives and children."

Curts then immediately filed an occupational claim with the district draft board, which was the next step in the appeal process. Writing to E.W., Curts predicted that a direct appeal to the president would ultimately be Bob's best bet.[78]

Curts struggled to find anyone outside of the Concern who could file an affidavit affirming Bob's role in the family newspaper business, because he had never held a high-profile position. If anything, Curts knew that any broad claims about Bob's importance would have no credibility in Ohio, where the Scripps family was well known. On August 31 he told E.W. how Bob's occupational exemption claim was handled: "We have not claimed that the whole Concern will disintegrate if Bob is withdrawn. We have not said that he is the only man who can co-ordinate and control the editorial forces of the Concern. We have not said that he is in charge of the editorial policy of the Concern. To have made any of these statements would, in my opinion, have weakened our case."[79]

The district board denied the occupational exemption request, and, barring intervention by the president, Bob was ordered to report to the Chillicothe, Ohio, cantonment. Jim's draft number remained uncalled, and at the urging of his father he traveled to Washington for eight days in mid-September to iron out their differences over the draft and the Concern's editorial policy.

"That Would Be Preferable to Wearing an Exemption Button"

"Jim seems to be dissatisfied with everything," E.W. reported to his wife within a few days after Jim's arrival. "Nearly all the time that Jim was here, his jaw was sticking out about an inch further than usual and he seemed quite willing to pick a quarrel with anybody and even rather anxious to do so."[80]

For one, Jim felt at least one Scripps son should serve in the military. "He told me that he would be quite willing to draw lots with Bob to see which should go," E.W. reported to his wife later.[81] Jim recognized, however, that his talents would be wasted as a private, so a few days before his arrival he had asked his father to try to find a suitable position in the army or government where he could be of the greatest use. E.W. then met with George Creel, head of the CPI, and later Walter Lippmann, editor of the *New Republic* and a special aide to Secretary of War Baker, about Jim's desire to serve the war effort.[82] Nothing suitable came from these inquiries. When Jim finally arrived he told his father he would rather be commissioned to work in the cantonments for a year or two and then be released to return to the newspaper business. "Jim says that he is not hankering for the rough-and-tumble and danger of the battle-field, but that that would be preferable to wearing an exemption button," E.W. said.[83]

Jim also was upset with his father because he apparently had come out of retirement to retake the responsibility he had given Jim eight years earlier. Specifically, Jim wanted to decide who would run the Concern's editorial policy regarding the war—Canfield, for example, instead of Rickey. The latter, one of his father's most trusted lieutenants, represented too much of his father's regime and was too elitist and dictatorial for Jim's taste. Jim wanted weaker national direction and more discretion for local editors to set war policy. Such a system, he believed, would develop young editors and create stronger management. "These young [editors], upon whom he was relying [to shape war policies for their newspapers], had been accustomed to exercise authority and assume responsibility," Harper explained to E.W. in a letter he wrote after meeting with Jim in August. "To go back to the old order [of more national control], putting Rickey in the saddle ... meant pulling down what it had taken [Jim] years to build."[84]

As Harper explained in another letter, Jim might have chosen this structure because—although he did not want Rickey in charge—*he* also did not want to be responsible for overseeing editorial policy: "[Jim] has felt incapable of managing the Concern as you did. He cannot jump from one subject to another and do justice to any; he cannot handle a lot of tangled threads, at least he so feels. Jim's mind is more primitive. He deals with things directly; wants propositions reduced to their simplest forms; to take up one question at a time, exhaust it, and when he has finished, to put it on the shelf and take up another."[85]

E.W., on the other hand, felt Canfield and the editors at the *Los Angeles Record,* to whom Jim was listening, were nothing but "wild 'fire eaters'" who would carelessly insult the Wilson administration. He feared Canfield and the *Record* editors were "trying to start a campaign in the west that would make every man connected with the Administration only too glad to get Jim and Bob into the army and where they could not do the government any harm."[86] E.W. fears were backed by Cochran, who felt that the *Record*'s attacks were sure to attract government reprisal. "There are indications enough that the government is going to jump on anything like treason or sedition with hob-nailed boots."[87]

The two Scrippses locked horns. Scripps wanted a trustworthy, pro-Wilson editor running the Concern's editorial policy; Jim wanted freedom to shape his own editorial policy and freedom to serve in the military. He was certain that antiwar and antidraft feelings in the country would soon blow up in Wilson's face, if the newspapers did not force him to conform to public demands.

E.W. trusted Rickey, who had led the successful NEA campaign to reelect Wilson, because he felt Rickey would do nothing to jeopardize any feelings of goodwill the president and his cabinet had for the Scripps newspapers. The Concern's patriotism was not lost on McRae, who traveled a great deal and read many newspapers. "With the single exception of the *Los Angeles Record*," he reported to E.W. in mid-August, "I have not seen a newspaper with the name of Scripps connected with it that was not doing its part in this great game of war."[88]

Jim had said nothing to Rickey about how upset he was with him, but Rickey knew his feelings and took full responsibility. "Whatever the good or bad there has been in our war policy at this end, up to this time has been mine. As I received neither order nor criticism from you or Canfield, I have done what in my judgement was for the best interest of the country and the Concern," Rickey explained to Jim in early September.[89]

Rickey was in an awkward position. Canfield had asked him to coordinate the NEA's war coverage, and E.W. seemed to confirm Rickey's role when the publisher came to Washington in June. Jim, on the other hand, was not part of the June discussions and never accepted Rickey's leadership role. Canfield, too, had become disenchanted with Rickey after Canfield went west in the spring to oversee the Pacific Coast newspapers that he still managed as editor-in-chief.

Canfield, however, kept a low profile in the battle to make him supreme head of war policy. Canfield agreed that Rickey was not handling the war news correctly. "The Washington stuff is too heavy, too academic, too propagandish, too damn serious, too press agenty in tone, and in short not the kind of stuff that *attracts* readers," Canfield said in late August. He implored his editor-in-chief, Sam Hughes, to get "more human stuff' out of Washington in spite of Rickey, although he asked Hughes to keep his request confidential.[90] No one was certain who was in charge in August and September of 1917; it was either E.W. or Jim, but everyone was careful about whom they criticized or supported.

E.W.'s September meeting in Washington with Jim and Bob accomplished little. "I feel as though I had been wrestling with a threshing machine," E.W. wrote his wife after Jim left.[91] Jim soon left for Cincinnati to decide what to do next. E.W. conceded he would not oppose Canfield's elevation to head of war editorial policy, "providing only that he . . . will diligently support the government."[92] E.W. said he needed to be "thoroughly assured" that any appointee would agree "that we must do all we can to prevent discontent and riotous, revolutionary action on the part of any class of the people."[93]

To show that the president's cabinet was competent, the elder Scripps arranged a meeting for Jim with Secretary of War Baker, and Jim emerged with more respect for him. "But Jim is obsessed with the idea that we ought to have a coalition cabinet made up of strong men of all political parties and the various social, business or economic classes," E.W. said. Jim's opinions reflected the criticisms leveled by Republicans who blamed the Wilson administration for all of the problems associated with mobilizing a democracy into a fully functioning combatant.[94] E.W. did not buy this politically inspired attack, especially in view of the Concern's strong support of Wilson in 1916. "We have got the President and can't get rid of him. The country's welfare depends upon the country's support of him," E.W. said.[95]

The draft, however, remained the most serious issue dividing father and sons. "Jim does not . . . want to appear as one of those people who got out of the war by any sort of excuse," E.W. wrote his wife.[96] E.W., on the other hand, was convinced the Concern would wither and die if both Bob and Jim were killed in combat. Jim was not bothered by this, as his father explained later: "Jim declares that I ought not feel uneasy about the business. He says it would run along very well without much work on my part for at least three years, and then I could keep it going easily enough until it was found out whether or not he or Bob (either one or both of them) would be killed, and that then I could sell it. He talks about such matters in a way that makes even my blood run cold."[97] E.W. knew his young sons were breaking free of his control. "All the members of my family are each clamoring for his or her personal rights," E.W. lamented, "and it appears to me that no one thinks of his or her duties to others."[98] After Jim left, his father continued to try to find a safe government job "big enough" to satisfy his son. He talked with Supreme Court Justice Louis Brandeis, who talked to Food Commissioner Herbert Hoover about a possible job for Jim. At E.W.'s urging, Cochran contacted Wilson's friend and confidant Edward M. House for ideas.[99] Although Jim's reaction to his father's continued efforts to find him a government job is not known, he must have been exasperated by the continued meddling, and he did nothing to encourage the inquiries being made.

"There Is a Responsibility of Decision in This Case"

The meeting in Washington convinced Bob that his only choice was to serve in the military. He and his brother agreed their futures would be tarnished forever if they did not serve. Bob, too, came away convinced his brother felt he was not needed to help run the Concern, an idea E.W. tried to dispute. "I am rather inclined to feel that Bob is not only the second most important element in the Concern, but that he is one of two equal elements of importance," E.W. wrote on October 2. Such high praise did not ring true, even for Bob, however. E.W. now regretted some of the criticisms and doubts he had leveled at Bob over the years because he knew they only reinforced Bob's belief that he was not needed. "He had learned from me in previous talks that I was not entirely satisfied with his own attitude of lack of willingness, or, rather, great desire, to enter on responsible duties."[100]

Hoping to find an ally his father would trust, Bob unburdened himself to Cochran, who agreed to act as an intermediary with E.W. He reported to E.W. that Bob did not want the Concern to seek any favors on his behalf with the president. He said Bob felt it would be "embarrassing for Wilson to make an exception in his case because of the well-known fact that the Scripps Concern was largely responsible for Wilson's election." Bob, according to Cochran, wanted to "do his bit as a private soldier in the selective service army, take his chances and then when it was all over, take his place in the Concern, not only with the respect of everybody in the Concern, but also with the public." Cochran agreed. "I think Bob is right," he wrote E.W. in late September.[101] He noted that the trade magazine *Editor and Publisher* had done two articles on Bob's draft status, so it was public. "The novel question of the importance of important newspaper executive positions [will be] put up to the President," one of the articles reported.[102]

Publicity or no publicity, E.W. had no intention of withdrawing the appeal he had made for an occupational exemption for Bob. So Bob wrote a letter to Secretary of War Baker, asking for all appeals to be waived so he could was report to the army cantonment in Chillicothe. He made an appointment with Baker on October 1 to deliver the letter. "There is a responsibility of decision in this case that must rest upon some one. Insofar as is possible it is my desire to assume that responsibility myself," the letter said.[103]

An odd series of events then took place. Thirty minutes before Bob's scheduled meeting with Secretary Baker, E.W. received a telephone call informing him that Bob's exemption had been granted by the adjutant general's office. But E.W. was unable to reach Bob. So E.W. asked Peggy, Bob's wife, for advice on what to do. "She felt that both she and Bob would rather suffer the burden and danger of actual service in the army than to suffer always the feeling of shame and humiliation," he said.[104] The two agreed not to interfere, and when Bob called his wife minutes before meeting with Baker, she said nothing about the exemption. After the meeting Bob went to Cincinnati to enter the army. No one told him the paperwork to get him dismissed was already being processed.

Curious about why Bob had been exempted, E.W. asked Tom Sidlow—an attorney for the *Cleveland Press* and a law partner of Secretary of War Baker, to inquire. Sidlow told Scripps on October 2 that he recently had dined with Baker, who had assured him that he would grant Bob's dismissal if the adjutant general did not. E.W. told Jim about his discussion with Sidlow to show his son that the Wilson administration respected the Scripps newspapers: "Baker told Sidlow that this matter of Bob Scripps has been taken up in one of the Cabinet meetings, at the President's instance, and that several of the Cabinet members were outspoken in their sentiments that there ought to be no question at all in the matter, and that Bob should be released. The President himself spoke in the same strain." [105] Sidlow, according to E.W., said Baker told him the decision was made "as a subject of large and important public policy. And that there was not the least idea in the minds of any of the authorities of paying a political debt."[106]

The surviving archival evidence and what is known of the draft at that time appears to bear this out. First, President Wilson wanted to rely on draftees because conscription disturbed the industrial and social structure of the country less. With draftees, the government could choose who served; with a volunteer system, valuable workers needed domestically might become drunk with patriotism and enlist.[107] On the other hand, the government could not give blanket exemptions to certain classes of workers because it would be a public relations nightmare. As Baker wrote Wilson in May, "it was deemed wiser, indeed seemed necessary, rather to let the draft fall where it will and make exceptions after the men are drawn, than to create classes, and the consequent class feeling, by exemptions in advance."[108] In November, after the Scripps rival the *Cleveland News* criticized Baker for exempting Bob to earn favor for Democrats, the former mayor of Cleveland wrote Sidlow that only the adjutant general's office had been involved with granting Bob's exemption:

> Fortunately, the record is perfectly clear; the exemption papers were not even filed with me, although I had expected that they would be, they went directly to [Adjutant] General [Enoch] Crowder and were acted upon in his office as all other such applications were, and his decision promulgated without my knowing what it was. The whole thing, however, shows a shockingly low moral tone in a newspaper which could suspect any such bargain and use such statements in a mere newspaper local fight.[109]

E.W. in mid-October also told his wife that he did not believe that either Wilson or Baker "officially passed on the matter."[110] Scripps had met personally with Wilson on June 27, but the meeting focused mostly on

Wilson's management of the war and publicity of income tax returns. Bob's or Jim's draft status was not discussed.[111]

"I Never Saw Bob More Cheerful and More Interested in Anything"

Bob, however, oblivious to the exemption, was headed to Camp Sherman in Chillicothe. On October 3, Curts helped Bob gather and pack supplies he would need in the army. Curts also rented a room in Chillicothe so Bob's pregnant wife could be near him. "I never saw Bob more cheerful and more interested in anything than he is over his prospective experience at the camp," Curts reported to E.W. Curts also said Bob hoped to write reports on the life of a private in an army camp. He said that comment "indicates to me very clearly that the Concern and the duties of the Concern to the public occupy a very large part of his attention."[112]

On October 7, Curts ventured to Chillicothe to see how the young recruit was doing. Bob had been assigned to the headquarters company of the 322nd Regiment of field artillery. He had been put to work as a personnel clerk, making cards "in which each private designates to whom he wants his personal effects to go in case of accident." Knowing Bob could work a typewriter, his captain told him to expect to be company clerk in a few months. Despite the desk duty, typing what amounted to each soldier's will, Curts reported Bob "seemed to be enjoying it."[113]

Bob's mother, however, was upset with the thought of her son in a military camp, apparently one step away from the trenches in France. Doubly confusing to her was the news that he had been exempted yet he was still in uniform. E.W. told Nackie he still did not want to say anything to Bob about the exemption. "So long as there is a remote possibility of a slip-up in this matter, I haven't wanted to disturb Bob's mind," E.W. wrote his wife. E.W. said if he could have his way, Bob would serve at least a couple of months because he was being heralded as proof that the draft law favored no one:

> A great deal of comment is being made on the subject of Bob's father being a wealthy man, the owner of many newspapers, and of great political influence. Bob's case is being cited as an example of how thoroughly impartial the government is in making no distinction between persons of wealth and power, and other men. If immediately following all of this publicity should come the report that, after all, Bob had been exempted, or even dismissed, there would be a great deal of comment made—perhaps some very disagreeable reflections.[114]

Peggy also agreed that since Bob was enjoying the army so much, she wanted him to have more time in the service.[115]

Bob's days as a soldier ended, however, within ten days. On October 9, AP reported that Wilson had exempted Bob. As mentioned earlier, the president probably did little more than approve of what the adjutant general's office had decided, but the story was reported in such a way that the president appeared to have been directly involved. The story mistakenly said that Bob had asked for the exemption because of his newspaper work, when it was E.W, in fact, who had filed the exemption request. "The application of the young Scripps for exemption has attracted wide attention by newspaper editors and newspaper workers owing to its nature," the article said.[116]

A few days would pass before official word got passed down to the camp commander in Chillicothe, and by the time it arrived, Bob was seriously ill with a bad cold. Only a few days into his stay at Camp Sherman, he had been weakened by an antityphoid inoculation he was given and had then caught a cold. "Bob reports that conditions in camp at Chillicothe are wretched and that about half the man have bad colds and many of them are in bed. There are not enough doctors there, either, and practically no hospital accommodations," E.W. wrote after meeting his son in Washington shortly after his discharge. The barracks also had no heat, and a cold snap had just hit. "Bob tells me that the first thing he wants to do is to get down to see Secretary of War Baker and tell him of conditions there," E.W. wrote his wife.

E.W. said Bob was not surprised he was released and "appears neither exultant nor depressed on this account." The realities of army life probably made him grateful to leave the camp. "He is rather dark under the eyes and his hoarseness makes it very painful for him to talk or for anyone to talk to him," E.W. reported.[117]

"Pretty Nearly a 'Sink or Swim' Chance"

Bob did not have to do much talking because his father had already decided his youngest son's next role. He was to be appointed chief of editorial policy regarding the war—the position Rickey had been holding. As soon as he got word on October 1 that Bob was to be exempted, E.W. had written Jim suggesting the position for Bob, as a way to convince the poet not to volunteer; E.W. was worried Bob would disregard the exemption and insist on serving. "With the feeling that [Bob] had something of great importance to do at home, his conscientious scruples [to serve in the military] would perhaps be more than offset."[118]

E.W. believed they could help ease Bob into the new job with the help of Cochran and Howard, but Jim was unconvinced. He felt Bob was too young, too unfocused, and too irresponsible. "Jim is reluctant to expose Bob in a position of very great responsibility while he is yet so young and so untried, but I have no reluctance on my own part. I entrusted Jim with just as great a place when he was Bob's age (and even much more responsible)," E.W. explained to his wife.[119]

Jim returned to Washington to discuss Bob's appointment with his father. Deep down, Jim did not trust or support Bob in such an important position. First, he wanted his younger brother to show his newspaper acumen by rejuvenating the failing *Denver Express*. But Jim ultimately had no effective counter-argument to E.W.'s assertion that Bob should be given the same chance Jim had been given. E.W. told his sister Ellen about the agreement he and Jim had made: "The plan is to throw Bob into the job with pretty nearly a 'sink or swim' chance.... [W]e will give him leeway to make some very bad mistakes and to learn by them."

E.W. also clarified his role and tried to reassure Jim that Bob would not become a rival for the control of the Concern:

> I told Jim that it was my idea not to meddle, or, rather, intervene much more in the future than I have in the past, but that there must be a clear understanding that I am the head of the family and the silent—to a very, very great extent—inactive head of the institution itself, and that my views must be considered, and that it must even be expected at times that I will enforce my wishes.
>
> I told him that I have had no idea, however, of breaking my rule of one-man power or of establishing two heads to the Concern, either during my life or afterwards, and that I expected him to succeed me, with control based upon stockholding; that nevertheless, if Bob made good, I would find my own means to enrich him without injuring the harmony and the control—single man control—of the institution.[120]

On the day after Bob was released from the army, he was officially appointed "Editor-in-Chief of all the Scripps papers, the Newspaper Enterprise Association and the United Press Associations." In the October 17 appointment letter, Jim told Bob: "You are personally responsible for the direction of the editorial policies of all our several corporations—responsible to me."[121] Bob would earn a salary of $500 a month for his new job. E.W. threw in another $500 a month for "housekeeping expenses" and paid $8,500 in annual rent for a four-story home, equipped with an electric elevator, at 2131 Massachusetts Avenue, N.W., in Washington. Despite his reassurances that he wanted single-man control, E.W. joyously told his wife that he and their sons "have constituted ourselves a triumvirate" in which the father would give advice and would be consulted, but he would not "order and direct affairs." E.W. envisioned the newly rented home as an "embassy" at which he and his sons would rule their newspaper empire. Indeed, a Bulgarian diplomat had rented the home previously; for now, a ground floor room was made into an office for Bob.[122]

Bob accepted the job. E.W. said it was because the exemption process had "convinced [Bob] of the seriousness of my purpose and of the great respect I had for his abilities." Privately, E.W. said he liked Bob's spirit and "latent spirit of militancy in dealing with sociological matters—a spirit similar to mine despite his unfortunate training and upbringing as a rich man's son." But Bob lacked self-discipline. "If he had resolution and persistence equal to his natural capacities, he would go far," E.W. wrote McRae in late October.[123]

E.W. was particularly happy now that twenty-two-year-old Bob had been given a defined role and purpose in life. "Has there not been a change in twelve months time! As you will recall," he told Nackie on October 21, "it was almost exactly a year ago when Bob came home from Australia. At that time, I was almost in desperation on account of my great anxiety for the boy." He said he planned to stay in Washington at least another year to advise Bob.[124] He asked Cochran to "coach and assist Bob," although Bob's wife said she worried he would feel too dependent on his mentors "or that we [Cochran and E.W.] were managing him."[125]

"If Bob Had Been Older and Had Been Holding a More Responsible Position"

Not everyone was pleased with Bob's exemption, however. Rival newspapers jumped at the opportunity to criticize the superpatriotic Concern. Places where Scripps had lived and was well known were particularly attentive to the hypocrisies of the situation. The *San Diego Union* said the exemption was an "absolutely unique example of vicarious patriotism—something quite new under the stars and stripes. A patriot by proxy or a patriot by inheritance is certainly a patriot *sui generis.*" McRae, in San Diego, told E.W. in mid-October that there was "a good deal of newspaper talk in this town" about Bob's exemption. "I don't think there would have been much criticism if Bob had been older and had been holding a more responsible position," he said.[126] The *Cincinnati Enquirer* snidely claimed Bob "came here to do some little work around the office and beat some of the reporters out of their jobs, and was drafted."[127]

The exemption also became an issue in the mayor's race in Cleveland, where one of Harper's former law partners, Alfred G. Allen, a Democrat and former congressman, was a candidate supported by the *Cleveland Press*. Republicans accused Allen, who held about $1,250 in bonds owed by the *Cincinnati Post,* of pulling strings in Washington to secure Bob's exemption.[128]

E.W. felt the "ill-natured notoriety" Bob's exemption was receiving in rival newspapers "was inevitable." The exemption was being misunderstood, he told McRae, sticking by his belief that only Scripps blood could lead the Concern. "It was natural that everyone should have supposed that my sole anxiety in Bob's case was based on my affection for my son. However great as was this anxiety, my anxiety for business reasons (that is to say, the claim for his exemption on occupational grounds) was extremely great." For E.W., the draft was a blessing because it "caused [Bob] to take stock of himself and his duties."[129]

E.W. was most bothered about doubts being expressed internally about the exemption. E.W. knew even his longtime associates believed he had intervened simply to save his son's life. E.W. wrote veteran editorial writer Robert Paine in late October that he knew he and others did not believe the claims E.W. made in his affidavit filed during the draft appeals. "Even those who are most friendly and who most esteem Bob only regard him as a boy—as a young man who had the good (or bad) fortune to have a wealthy, forceful and a too affectionate father." E.W. insisted Bob has "got as good or better stuff in him" than his older brothers and would prove his worth in his new role.[130]

Many Scripps editors privately grumbled when novice Bob was elevated to such an important position only because of his bloodline and his father's apparent desire to save his hide from German bullets.[131] McRae said the promotion of Bob created "considerable gossip and comment."[132] Rickey, the odd man out in the shuffle to crown Bob policy prince, was particularly upset. Another of Scripps's sons was displacing him. He had been replaced as editor-in-chief by the now-deceased John Paul just three years earlier. This time, after his successful handling of the 1916 election, the insult was multiplied. E.W. spent most of the afternoon of October 26 trying to settle him down. "Of course, I cannot tell Rickey or anyone else about reasons and necessities," E.W. wrote his sister.[133]

E.W. said he was "greatly grieved" that his longtime associate was going to take the matter so very hard. He repeatedly reminded Rickey that he had "no official sanction" for what he had been doing in the Washington bureau. "Rickey's high esteem of himself prevented him from understanding how fragile his tenure was," Scripps wrote later.

"He knew that his individuality and his views had been dominating the whole Concern in a national, political way, and especially with regard to war policy, and it was impossible for him to believe that his dominion was in danger."[134]

Rickey said he wanted to quit, which bothered E.W. a great deal. E.W. said Rickey, a thirty-year employee, was "flesh of the institution's flesh and bone of the institution's bone. All that he is and has been, has been a part of the institution."[135] E.W., however, realized that Rickey was too caught up in war fever and was ignoring other important Scripps principles along the way. "For example," E.W. wrote to his sister Ellen in early November, "he would win the war by all means, even at the expense of our democracy . . . and he would not even balk at the establishment of an absolute monarchy or autocracy. He is entirely inconsiderate of the welfare of the people."[136]

Jim said Rickey's future was up to Bob to decide, but he reminded Bob that he had promised to give Rickey a year's notice on his $14,000–per-year job before he terminated him. Jim and Rickey later agreed to waive the year notice, but Rickey would be able to stay on the payroll at least until January 1.[137]

"Just as the matter of your exemption from military service caused considerable comment, just so will Rickeys [sic] leaving the Concern cause considerable comment in the Concern," Jim advised his younger brother. He could not help but notice that a changing of the guard was near with Rickey, the youngest of their father's old editorial lieutenants and with Paine and Cochran approaching retirement age. "With Rickey gone the old crowd in the editorial department will be pretty well cleaned out," Jim told Bob.[138]

Rickey later solved the problem of what to do with him by quitting to join the CPI's Foreign Section, eventually serving as assistant general director.[139] After turning down a diplomatic position in the wake of Wilson's reelection a year earlier, he was now a government employee, and did not have to worry about being criticized as a Wilson partisan.

Only once did E.W. respond publicly to criticism about Bob's exemption. In late October, he wrote a letter to the editor of the *Cincinnati Post*. Scripps's biographer Vance Trimble called the letter "rather devious," but it said publicly what E.W. said privately. In it, he said that he did not believe that the president or secretary of war had intervened, and claims otherwise were "inspired by personal malice as well as by political motives." The letter ended: "[Bob] has been elected to a more difficult and dangerous task than that which he preferred to undertake: namely, that of a common soldier in the ranks of his country's armies."[140]

"All of That Part of My Income Which the Government Doesn't Conscript"

E.W. was relieved that his youngest son was safe from the Germans, but he was a bit distressed and tightfisted about the tough business climate that he faced now with America in the war. "Our finances are going to be straitened on account of the enormous taxes we will have to pay and on account of many other untoward happenings in the business," he wrote his wife in mid-October. Scripps was particularly concerned about the new war tax on corporate excess profits, which has just passed, retroactive to the first of the year.[141] United Press's telegraph operators also were demanding a 10 percent wage increase, estimated to cost $70,000 a year. Howard projected UP would make no money in 1917 because of the higher taxes and higher wages.[142] The cost of newsprint in 1917 also had increased to about 50 percent more than that of 1914.[143]

Scripps was feeling so broke he turned down a request in October by San Diego's Liberty Loan Committee to buy bonds to support the war effort. "It really looks as though all of that part of my income which the government doesn't conscript is to be conscripted by the manufacturers of newspaper supplies and by the trades unions," he wrote Julius Wangenheim, a banker friend who led the local drive.[144] E.W.'s senior business partners were appalled by his attitude. "We have not been slackers in words; we must not be slackers in acts," Harper wrote E.W. after he saw the letter sent to Wangenheim. "Is it possible that we are going to put our Concern and ourselves in the category of those who preach but do not practise?" Harper insisted that newspapers were not suffering any more than any other industry in the tax bill, and the UP workers deserved the salary increase because "the cost of living has gone up from 50 percent to 70 percent." According to Harper, the Concern was doing better in 1917 than most businesses: "For the first nine months of this year, the newspapers of our Concern made more than twice the profit which they made for the same period in 1913 and more than $130,000 in excess of the profit for that period in 1916. That year (1916) showed such an enormous profit that it caused you anxiety lest the Concern and your family should become fat and degenerate."[145]

The Scripps newspapers certainly were doing their part to convince their readers to buy bonds. Money and bullets were needed to defeat Germany. "We have to make the decision now as to whether . . . we will stand for Americanism as against Kaiserism. It is BONDS versus BONDAGE."[146] Other editorials argued a financial line. "You are not GIVING Uncle Sam anything. You are just LOANING him a little money at good interest. . . . And you don't have to pay taxes on it."¹⁴⁷ Other pitches played off parallels to conscription. "Enlist your money! Send it into service!. . . . SELECT YOUR MONEY FOR SERVICE."¹⁴⁸ Arguments poured on the guilt. "The point is how many of us are going to buy so heavily that we will have to economize and pinch until it hurts? Only when we have done this can we say that we have supported the government loan like good patriotic Americans."¹⁴⁹

McRae, too, could not believe it when Wangenheim told him of E.W.'s refusal to follow the urgings of his own newspapers. "You will always have more money than you want to spend or ought to spend. So why should you worry?" he wrote.¹⁵⁰ E.W. was surprised his associates were so angry and challenged Harper to prove that the Concern would continue to make money. "If the demand for money to meet excess-profit taxes, income tax, extra white paper bills and extra wages take all of our money, what sense is there in 'hollering your head off' and charging us with being inconsistent because we urge other people to buy Liberty Bonds with *their* surplus money. We would only be inconsistent if we should happen to have surplus money and did not spend it on liberty bonds."¹⁵¹

E.W. also probably was influenced by the actions Jim had already taken without consulting his father. During the first Liberty Loan drive in June, Jim authorized $225,000 of subscriptions to bonds by fifteen of the individual corporations that made up the Scripps newspaper empire. Interest from the bonds would be distributed as dividends to the stockholders. E.W.'s sister Ellen also subscribed to $50,000 worth of bonds, and Jim offered interest-free loans to any Scripps employee earning less than $50 per week who needed money to make a purchase.¹⁵²

The Concern did suffer one notable loss during the year. The *Day Book*, Scripps's adless newspaper in Chicago, folded in July. Although its editor, Cochran, was spending a great deal of time in Washington tending to the NEA's coverage of the war, one historian has noted that the decision to close the newspaper had been made the previous October; thus, Cochran's absence could not be blamed for the demise of the *Day Book*.¹⁵³ E.W. believed the war had killed the experimental newspaper. "Yes, it is too bad the *Day Book* had to go. However, that was one of the by-products of this war . . . which called for a style of journalism entirely different from what we wanted the *Day Book* to be."¹⁵⁴

The cost of newsprint also was a constant concern during the year. In mid-September, McRae killed an idea to make newspapers out of hemp after the process proved not feasible financially. For two months, McRae worked with millionaire Harry Timken, owner of the Detroit-Timken Axle factory in Canton, Ohio, on the proposed venture. Timken had hoped to use the process to make cheap clothing, but he was willing to consider Scripps's idea to use it to make paper as well. On August 3, McRae met with the maker of the "decorticating machine" used to make the pulp, George Schlichten, a German-born inventor.[155] Although the machine and process looked promising, it became evident that paper could not be produced cheaply enough for the newspaper business. McRae decided to pull the plug.[156]

Rising newsprint prices were making the Scripps papers and their penny press rivals consider a price increase, but worries persisted about how the public would react. Alfred Andersson, editor-in-chief of the *Memphis Press*, commissioned interviews with thirty-three current subscribers to find out what they would do if the price increased to two cents. Four said they were "doubtful" they would continue to subscribe, and three said they would not. Even losing 21 percent of his subscribers, the price increase would net the *Memphis Press* an extra $56 a day. That money would allow the paper to publish more pages, which would be necessary because those subscribers who stayed would expect something for the extra money. "We would necessarily have to, and be glad to, spend a good deal of added money on the reading contents of the paper," Andersson said.[157]

The Concern, however, was in good shape compared with individually owned newspapers. The three mills supplying paper to the Concern provided a constant supply at a good price. "Fortunately, the mills we are doing business with look upon our business as being as desirable as any," Ohio business manager Willis W. Thornton, president of the Ohio Group of papers, said in May.[158] Thornton also told *Editor and Publisher*, that soon "it will be impossible for daily papers to sell [any] longer at their present price."[159]

In May the Chicago dailies increased their prices to two cents, which Cochran, editor of the *Toledo News-Bee*, predicted would influence other cities in the Midwest. Cochran's paper was doing well, earning profits ahead of 1916 and projecting a profit of $200,000 for all of 1917, despite an expected 15 percent wage increase in a new contract for the typographical union. Cochran said the paper mills seemed determined to force an increase to two cents "so it will be that much easier to . . . make their future profit certain."[160] Later, a colleague told Cochran that the Chicago dailies lost 25 to 35 percent of their circulation after their price increase.[161]

The Scripps newspapers resisted the price increases during 1917, driven in part by fears that readers would not pay double for their product. The Scripps newspapers were a good buy for the average reader at one cent, but were they worth two cents during a time of runaway inflation on all goods? "Our newspapers are all small newspapers," Thornton warned in May. "They are one-cent newspapers if any newspapers are one-cent newspapers."

The FTC helped by fixing prices that summer until after the war.[162] Some of the Concern's newspapers, such as those in the West Coast group, also began conserving paper in some areas because the war news commanded so much attention. "We are now using in excess of 5,580 tons of paper per year, whereas we used less than 4,200 tons during the last year of our old contract," acting editor-in-chief LeRoy Sanders wrote in July.[163]

"There Are Going to Be Lots of Things That Will Want Criticism"

Meanwhile, Bob had his own worries. With Rickey deposed, he knew a great deal was expected of him. Harper wrote Bob soon after his appointment, challenging him. "You have ability. Seriousness of purpose, application, and adaptability are yet to be demonstrated," he said. "Has anyone else ever been put in a position of great responsibility in the Scripps Concern who was so devoid of newspaper experience as you are?" Harper also noted that the Scripps newspapers had great power to shape public opinion among working people, and the country was facing the most difficult of times. "The whole fabric of industry and society is being made over. It is a great opportunity. It ought to call out the best that is in any man. . . . The world will never again be what it was up to the summer of 1914."[164]

Bob replied that he appreciated the "criticisms and advice" and knew he was facing a "big job" made extra difficult because of the circumstances in which he got the job. "However, so far as I can see," Bob wrote Harper, "the only thing for me to do is to give the best there is in me to it; in other words, to accept those handicaps as part of the game, and go ahead and win out anyway."[165]

One of the temporary handicaps Bob had been fighting was laryngitis; he was not given clearance by his doctor to do much talking until the end of October. Still, he fired off letters to Canfield, asking for the Washington bureau's budget and for reports on how NEA and UP copy was being handled in the newspapers.

Fighting Censorship

Bob was especially concerned about censorship and government attacks on radical publications. Anxiety about assaults on the First Amendment was growing among intellectuals as the war dragged forward. Bob probably was being influenced by the attitude of his father, who said he was "stirred up a great deal" about the censorship. E.W. went so far as to accompany Max Eastman, publisher of the socialist magazine the *Masses,* to plead the magazine's case with Postmaster General Albert Burleson in late October.[166] Since the Espionage Act had been enacted in June, Burleson had broadly exercised his discretion to prohibit certain radical publications, including the *Masses,* from using the U.S. mail.[167]

By the fall of 1917 a small group of civil liberties advocates were trying to raise public awareness about free speech issues relating to the Espionage Act. The National Civil Liberties Bureau was formed in October, and it was determined to put on the national agenda the government's onerous sanctions against those who disagreed with the war effort. The group was spearheaded by Roger Nash Baldwin, who later founded the American Civil Liberties Union.[168]

Bob was concerned about the position that the NEA, under Rickey, had already taken on censorship. Specifically, Bob noted the "Shut Up or Get Locked Up" editorial Rickey had issued in June, which Bob told Canfield was "a rotten idea. This kind of copy, played heavily in Scripps papers, put us in the position of having to back up the Administration and the P.O. [Post Office] department in their censorship activities if we are going to be consistent." Bob was watching the issue closely because "there are going to be lots of things that will want criticism, or at least public discussion," and a "certain amount of freedom is desirable from any point of view, even if it's only to serve as a safety valve." His comments echoed what the *Los Angeles Record* had argued the previous summer.

Bob predicted that the biggest fights over censorship still loomed ahead, and he asked Canfield to monitor the issue with "a regular hawk's eye" and to write stories on each case of censorship.[169] Stories about those prosecuted for sedition, however, remained short and fact-based. The NEA steered clear of editorializing against censorship with Burleson's sword potentially hanging over its head and in view of its own superpatriotic stands. Fighting for radical publications was also unprofitable, no matter how righteous the First Amendment may have seemed. As historians Horace C. Peterson and Gerald Fite noted in 1957 in their study of the suppression of dissent after 1917, "In order to get economic support, editors were likely to emphasize popular issues and gave only meager consideration to dissenting ideas and views, except possibly to criticize them."[170] The Concern was not going to speak out publicly for the right of radical publications to dissent when it would not even allow its own newspapers to stray from the company's pro-Wilson editorial policy. Even Canfield, who had helped mastermind the *Los Angeles Record*'s attacks on the administration, was more conservative now. He noted in his reply to Bob: "I do not think we should be in the attitude of looking for things to criticize, but that we should be in favor of public discussion."[171]

On November 6 Bob's father reported that Bob spent a "good deal of time every day" at the NEA's Washington bureau. "He is himself making the assignments for the men, directing their work, editing their copy, and occasionally himself writing." E.W. said he was concerned only that Bob and Jim drank too much, but drew comfort in that neither drank as much as he once did.[172]

E.W. was feeling feisty. In early October he told his sister that he could stand "ten times more work and worry and shocks and jars than I could have stood any time in the last several years." His old habits from his days as an editor were returning, including the propensity to drink. "I have consumed more whiskey perhaps in five months that I would have at home in fifteen months, but so far no bad effects seem to have resulted," he wrote on October 2.[173]

E.W.'s luck with his health began to run out six weeks later, however. One day his face grew numb. Eating and smoking cigars was becoming a problem. His doctor told him that "something had gone wrong with the blood in the veins of the brain, and that he must cease all activities and have complete and absolute rest if he was to avert another stroke, which would probably be his last."[174] He was to rest and to get away from the stress of the capital for at least six months.

By December, E.W. was doing just that in Key West, Florida. With Bob only a month into his new job, the timing of E.W.'s stroke could not have been poorer. Jim was worried about his brother being able to handle the chief editor's job without their father's help. Then, just as the family was caring for its sick patriarch, Jim's number in the draft was called in California.

"There Should Be Some Representative from Each Family"

Jim's selection in San Diego County came as a surprise because it had been believed that his number was high enough to be safe at least until the spring. The rejection of an unanticipated number of men because of physical unfitness made it necessary to call more recruits, however. Still, most of the affidavits needed to secure an industrial exemption for Jim had been filed in advance in August, by McRae, who, with Harper, was handling the process for Jim. The two were confident that Jim's exemption was justified; the only worrisome point was Bob's earlier exemption. "The feeling is very general that there should be some representative from each family.... This is the chief obstacle we have to overcome in Jim's case; but I expect to overcome it," Harper wrote E.W. on November 15.[175]

Fortunately, most of the rival newspapers in Los Angeles, where the district draft board convened, and in San Diego, where the local board was located, were friendly to Scripps. Los Angeles was particularly important, for the local board abstained from industrial exemptions and bumped the matter to the district level.

Most of Scripps's competitors in southern California were friendly in the fall of 1917 because they respected the spunky *Los Angeles Record*. It dared to do what they were reluctant to do—criticize what it called the "Invisible Government" led by E. T. Earl, millionaire publisher of the *Los Angeles Tribune*. The *Record* was in the process of fighting off seven libel lawsuits filed by Earl's cronies. Of the seven lawsuits only one, filed against the *Record* by Earl's attorney, was successful, and he was awarded one dollar in damages.[176] Earl himself sued the *Record* for $150,000 after the newspaper called him a "political boss," but he lost on December 1 after a five-week jury trial.[177]

Harper said the Earl trial had made the *Los Angeles Times, Examiner*, and *Herald* "all very friendly to us." The editor of the *Herald*, a William Randolph Hearst paper, even wired his boss to get his support for Jim receiving an exemption. Hearst wired back, according to Harper, "I agree that it would be a great mistake from the point of view of the country and particularly of the administration to take so important a man away from his work."[178] In turn, Hearst's *Los Angeles Evening Herald* editorialized on November 14 that Jim Scripps headed "a string of newspapers which are doing their bit for patriotism and freedom and ought to be exempted": "He is a general of America's army of patriotic publicity and to remove him from his high position of loyal direction to place him as a single individual in the ranks, carrying only a single musket and capable of aiming only at one infinitesimal fraction of the foe's vast forces, would seem a misdirection of endeavor at a time in our country's history when it is our plain duty to obtain the highest service from every man."[179]

Harper said a similar editorial ran in Hearst's *New York American*. Hearst's willingness to help out a business rival was not surprising because the maverick publisher had been inquiring occasionally about possible opportunities to merge his INS with UP since 1915.[180]

The year was not going well for Hearst. Federal judge Learned Hand had issued an injunction in March against the INS for illegally pilfering news copy from the AP. Hand's decision worried Howard because it said that local news taken from AP client newspapers, even the facts of the story, could not be used by competing news organizations. United Press was willing to live with a prohibition against using news from the actual AP telegraph report because most of it was international or national news. This new twist worried Howard, however, because UP rewrote *local* stories from AP client newspapers routinely. "In other words, the Court holds that if a reporter on the *Cleveland News* sees a man assassinate the mayor of Cleveland and then goes into his office and writes that story for the *News*, it is illegal for Hearst or the United Press to obtain that news fact either from the reporter . . . or from the *News* itself."[181]

Harper, an attorney, also was worried about Hand's condemnation of reusing local news, but he warned about joining the Hearst lawsuit on appeal. "It seems to me a matter for grave consideration whether the U.P. should in any way identify itself with Hearst in the defense of this case," he wrote. "The Hearst service has been caught red-handed in thievery." Harper suggested the local use issue should be challenged in a separate case if necessary.[182] In the meantime, he suggested UP send out to its clients "as large a measure as possible of its own work and expense—something more than a rewrite."[183]

Although Howard remained concerned about the court case, the litigation was positive for UP, in that Hand's ruling also affirmed the copyright concept of news as property, and that legal point would prevent a recurrence of the widespread pirating of UP scoops of 1914–15.[184]

"How The Scripps Papers Have Backed Up the Government"

Hearst's support for Jim's exemption was used as evidence in the pending hearing before H. W. Wright, who handled industrial claims for the district draft board in Los Angeles. Harper and McRae had one sympathetic person on the five-member district board, Ed Fletcher, a sometimes business rival of Scripps in real estate deals. Fletcher did all he could to secure Jim's exemption. Although he was not supposed to, Fletcher told McRae that the board had received about a dozen letters in opposition to Jim's exemption. One claimed that Jim spent too much time hunting and fishing to be as important as he claimed, Fletcher reported. Others said a rich man's son should have to fight and two sons from the same family should not be exempted. McRae said Fletcher told him "it would have been a walk-away" to get an exemption for Jim had it not been for Bob's earlier exemption. Fletcher assured McRae that even if Jim were not exempted, he would demand that Jim not be inducted until the president had an opportunity to rule on an appeal.[185]

The fact-gathering hearing before Wright did not go well. McRae and Harper claimed that "newspapers ... are necessary in a military way." They also argued "Jim has not taken a vacation in year" because he was indispensable. "The nearest that I can think of would be if Hearst or [AP's head] Melville E. Stone should appear and ask for exemption," McRae told Wright.[186]

Wright was not convinced. He recommended that Jim's application for exemption be denied, and the district board unanimously agreed on November 23. Fletcher was sick the day of the vote and missed the meeting. In denying the exemption, Wright noted that Jim was no more patriotic "than ... thousands of young men who have sacrificed earnings and opportunity to give to the country their personal service." He also said that Bob and E.W. were in Washington and could direct the newspapers. Wright did note, however, that the president should determine "if a further coordinating head is necessary to the success of the above chain of newspapers."[187] Indeed, at the district board's next meeting, Fletcher requested and was granted a "stay of proceedings" motion until the president could decide Jim's fate. He then wrote to Wilson personally on November 28, asking him to exempt Jim, "believing that I know the situation better than the other members of the board."[188]

Unbeknownst to Fletcher and the others, however, the situation—at least for now—was moot. The army was in the process of rewriting the way men were selected. Industrial leaders were concerned that the draft was taking away too many skilled workers, so a new system, patterned after Great Britain's, was developed.

Under the new draft law, local draft boards used a detailed questionnaire to place the ten million men who had registered into four categories. First to be drafted were in Class I, consisting of unskilled workers or those who were in nonessential industries, were bachelors, or were deadbeat dads. Classes II and III were married men in useful employment, skilled workers, technical experts, and certain managers. Class IV included the leaders of necessary business enterprises. During the war, only Class I registrants were taken.[189]

To start clean with the new classifications system, all previous appeals for exemptions to the president, including Bob's, were rescinded.

The process for Jim, too, was back to square one. Although the arguments before the draft boards for their exemptions remained the same, new battles would now be waged over how Bob and Jim would be classified.

The end of the year 1917 left many things unresolved. Financially, the Concern was doing well, but the future was uncertain. Internally, Bob was head of war editorial policy, but his older brother did not trust him, and their sick father was unable to mediate. Editorially, the Concern remained a staunch supporter of the president it had helped to reelect. Wilson needed that support as much as ever as the war dragged into the winter of 1917–18. Complaints about his administration's mobilization efforts grew increasingly vitriolic. The Scripps newspapers knew they needed to come to the rescue again, but first they wanted a little respect.

7 Reconsidering an "Ostrich Type of Patriotism": 1918

On January 23, Neg Cochran, Bob Scripps's mentor on war policy, visited the offices of the CPI in Washington, hoping to get some attention. He carried a map, normally hanging in the NEA's bureau office, showing the locations of all of the daily newspaper clients of the syndication service. The NEA had at least one client in each of the forty-eight states, including one in the District of Columbia, four in Canada, and one in Cuba—with a combined circulation of four and a half million. Cochran pointed out that about two-thirds of the 301 clients took the NEA full service of assorted editorials, serials, stories, and special features.

Cochran wanted to see George Creel, chairman of the CPI, because he felt the Wilson administration was not using the Scripps newspapers as much as it could. "I simply came down here to help as much as I might to back up the President and get the truth to the people of the nation concerning his policies," he told Creel.[1]

Cochran was hoping to help rescue the Wilson administration from intense criticism it was receiving for its perceived incompetence in managing the war. Reports of poor conditions and disease at the army camps had surfaced the previous month. Many soldiers were still waiting for rifles and bullets. Republicans and unfriendly Democrats were directing blame at war secretary Newton Baker, who defended himself in mid-January during a three-day Senate hearing. Cochran believed the NEA could fight for him, too.

A frustrated Cochran wanted Creel to see the NEA map so the Scripps syndicated service would be better appreciated. "More importance is attached to one New York city newspaper than to the nearly 300 [NEA client papers] scattered all over the country," he wrote to Creel later. "Yet the influence on public opinion, so far as it is affected by newspaper publicity, is many times that of all New York, Philadelphia, Boston, Chicago and all New York state dailies combined."

Cochran also reminded Creel that the twenty-one newspapers under Scripps's control were concentrated in key states Wilson had won in the 1916 election with Scripps's support. "Through no magazine and no other newspaper service is it possible to reach so many people all over the country.... Here in Washington that fact doesn't seem to be understood," Cochran told Creel.

This showdown with Creel exemplified the frustration with the Wilson administration that had been building among the Concern's top management and editors since the 1916 election. Faced with a seemingly ungrateful Wilson administration and harsh public criticism on the draft issue, the Concern was beginning to rethink its unwavering allegiance to the president. Still, it was inconceivable to rebuke or criticize him—instead, the Concern began to depoliticize itself. In 1918 the Concern began to focus on selling news more as a product and less as progressive political ideology.

Cochran, a fifty-year-old champion of liberal causes, though, was not quite ready to abandon Wilson—not until he gave Creel this last chance. Creel, in effect, had taken the role of secretary of the people that E.W. had wanted Cochran to fill three years earlier, but Cochran was still willing to help, if he could only get some government cooperation. "I simply came down here to help as much as I might to back up the President. ... This had not always been an easy task, because of the difficulty of finding out just what the truth was," Cochran lamented.

Creel relented. He asked Cochran to put a reporter on the War Department's activities to, as Cochran put it, "get the truth and give it to the public." Cochran assigned Harry Hunt to the task, and he got to work on January 25. Initially, Bob Scripps said, Creel "was inclined to balk" at the idea of turning Hunt loose, but he agreed the stories should be exclusives to maximize their impact and he gave Hunt a letter telling every official in the War Department to cooperate. "I think Creel never realized before what a big thing N.E.A. really is," Bob said.[2]

The Concern's frustration with the administration was just one of several factors motivating the Scripps newspapers to change their news and editorial content in 1918. Financially, the war had been profitable, and the Concern had generated its share of accolades for its war coverage. But with higher taxes on excess profits and higher operating costs, an increase in the penny price charged for each copy of a Scripps newspaper seemed inevitable. The Scripps editors felt they had to give something back to their readers to justify such a dramatic increase. War censorship and the centralized control of government information through the CPI made it difficult for UP to differentiate its news content from that of competitors, so it fell to the NEA to generate better, more unique features. This improved NEA feature service could also help create a new market niche because other newspapers were facing the same issues as they raised their prices.

Meanwhile, continued turmoil in the Scripps family disrupted the management of the newspaper chain throughout 1918. The Concern suffered from weak leadership in the last year of the war. Jim Scripps was not happy with his younger brother Bob's role as editor-in-chief of war coverage and fought to reassign him. Their father, recovering from a stroke, was in self-imposed exile to avoid stress and could not mediate this dispute between his two sons. Both were under considerable stress. The draft status of the two remained unresolved and served as a target for public criticism.

"Mere Party Organs"

While Cochran was still trying to help the Wilson administration, the Ohio newspapers, once the most patriotic of the chain, began to lose patience with part of Wilson's war effort. Without strong central leadership to guide its overall wartime policies, the Concern's allegiance to Wilson was becoming inconsistent and lukewarm. The Ohio Group began attacking Wilson's fuel administrator, Harry Garfield, a former academic colleague of Wilson, for his handling of a winter coal shortage. It started on January 17 when Garfield ordered the shutdown of all manufacturing plants east of the Mississippi for five days and subsequently ordered a series of "coal-less Mondays." Garfield hoped the manufacturing shutdown would clear the railways of unnecessary traffic so coal could be delivered unimpeded for ships bound for Europe. One historian, calling the order "an unnecessarily radical measure," has noted that the unexpected, forced shutdown was harshly criticized by many.[3] The order hurt business and only marginally relieved congestion. This was not the first time Garfield had angered the Ohio newspapers. The previous fall he had created a coal shortage in Ohio when he diverted shipments to some ports on the Great Lakes.[4]

The editor-in-chief of the Ohio Group of newspapers, Earle Martin, felt Garfield clearly was incompetent. He wrote an editorial that ran on the front pages of the five Ohio papers, calling the order "more than a blunder—it is a calamity." He said passenger traffic should be suspended to relieve congestion, and production should be increased, not decreased, to win the war.[5] That same day the *Cleveland Press* reported that 750,000 factory workers in Ohio would be idle during the five-day shutdown, and nearly 1.1 million would be idle on ensuing coal-less Mondays.[6]

Cochran was appalled when he saw the editorial on the front page of the *Toledo News-Bee*, a paper from which he had taken a leave of absence as editor. He thought the editorial was a cheap shot, and it certainly did not conform to the pro-Wilson image he had cultivated with Creel.

Martin said the editorial offered a "constructive suggestion—the elimination of needless passenger traffic," and criticism was warranted. "Newspapers which adopted the ostrich type of patriotism [by burying their heads in the sand] and which are willing to underwrite the mistakes by the Garfields of the national administration are very apt to lose their editorial influence and become mere party organs. I yield to no one in my desire to stand by the administration but that does not mean to me either the suppression of facts or the silencing of suggestion."[7]

The criticisms that were printed in the Ohio newspapers were tame compared with those made in the *Los Angeles Record* in 1917. They showed, however, that even the patriotic Ohio Group was beginning to rethink its blind support of Wilson, and it could do so because the only central policy head ready to discipline it was Cochran, Bob's mentor. Still, the desire to be consistent kept most Scripps editors faithful to supporting the president.

By January 21, the first coal-less Monday, Ohio newspapers had adjusted their attitude; they editorialized that "happily . . . loyal obedience to the fuel closing order is universal." The familiar sacrifice-for-the-common-good theme emerged again, too. "The coal which we are denying ourselves today is thundering into the bunkers of a fleet of 130 vessels . . . for these boys whom we have put at the very foot of the altar of sacrifice." The editorial urged voluntary curtailment of pleasure travel on trains,[8] something Bob called "the only piece of really sound constructive criticism that I have seen out of the mass of purely destructive criticism that was offered [by Wilson's detractors]."[9]

"To Be Clearly Recognized by the Most Unintelligent Reader of our Stuff"

"Destructive criticism" was an apt description of the barbs others were hurling at Wilson and Baker, in particular, during late January and early February. Garfield's surprise order only encouraged more Republicans, led by Theodore Roosevelt, to charge the Wilson administration with mismanaging the war. Even Senator George Chamberlain of Oregon, a Democrat and chair of the Military Affairs Committee, complained that the War Department had failed miserably to fight the war.

Chamberlain sponsored bills to establish a munitions director as a cabinet position to unify military purchasing and an independent war council to direct all war affairs. As one historian has noted, the proposal would have made Baker and navy secretary Josephus Daniels subservient to the war council.[10] Cochran was even blunter, in a column he wrote for the NEA: "The real purpose of the Chamberlain bill is to take the conduct of the war out of the president's hands and turn it over to the profiteers of Big Business."[11]

Bob was eager for the Hunt series to refute these claims of mismanagement. Cochran and he especially remained steadfast in their support for Wilson. They believed the public would support the president if given the facts. On January 29, Bob said, Hunt found "no obstacles" in his dealings with the War Department, and Creel had assured Hunt he could tell "an authoritative story in his own way." Bob characterized the battle as a "tempest in a teapot."[12] "It is our job to support [Wilson] against this bunch of blackmailers who are obviously out of political capital when what the country needs is the concentrated and combined effort of everybody in it to the one end of winning the war. We can not go too strong along this line. . . . N.E.A.'s stand and the stand of the Scripps papers should be so definite as to be clearly recognized by the most unintelligent reader of our stuff."[13]

"Now Is the Time for the People of This Democracy to Swat the Plotters"

Unfortunately, Hunt's series on the Wilson administration's war management would not be ready until February 21. By then most of Wilson's detractors had abandoned the push for a war council and munitions director because Wilson had retooled some procedures and alleviated most criticism. Republicans remained bitter, however. Republican senator Henry Cabot Lodge said the Military Affairs Committee had revealed "enough information to defeat a dozen Administrations," but the public remained ignorant because the press was too scared to criticize Wilson and his cabinet because of the Espionage Act.[14]

Even before Hunt's series, the NEA did what it could to defend the president during late January and early February, when attacks were the most intense. The NEA accused the Republicans of playing politics. A front-page editorial in the *Cleveland Press* on January 23 condemned this "dirty political turmoil. . . . The Country will stand behind the president. It wants war business, not political vaudeville."[15] Flashes of opinion appeared even in UP's breaking news stories of the floor debate in the Senate. One UP report said "the numerous probes were merely foraging expeditions for ammunition."[16]

Cochran, likewise, wrote regular analysis pieces in which he referred to the Military Affairs Committee's investigation as "a plot" with a goal of making Roosevelt "supreme dictator of the United States. . . . This is not Russia."[17] One editorial noted that many people and publications were being prosecuted under the Espionage Act "for utterances not half as traitorous or comforting to the enemy as a United States senator is permitted to rise and spout forth whenever he pleases."[18]

When his series debuted, Hunt promised to give "actual facts, not vague generalities. . . . For this is the people's war. And no people will fight efficiently and enthusiastically in the dark!"[19] A small editorial that ran in the *Cleveland Press* on the day Hunt's series was launched asked readers to pay attention to his stories as they appeared in upcoming days. "These articles are purely informative, solely the product of many hours' digging by our reliable representative at the capital," the editorial declared. The series "is unbiased and in shape to be easily understood."[20]

Hunt unleashed at least ten lengthy stories in mid-March that contradicted the claims made by Wilson's Senate critics. In one installment devoted to small arms weapons, Hunt reported that since January 18, the army had enough rifles for every soldier and "a reserve sufficient to replace any waste or loss that would be met in service."[21] In another article, Hunt said the army already had acquired enough machine guns to equip, "on the basis of our standards of a year and ago, an army of 3,500,000 men."[22] When it came to bullets, Hunt reported in one story that "our production of ammunition is greater than that of Great Britain and much greater than that of France ever was."[23] Another story predicted huge increases in airplane production.[24] Hunt reassured readers that the army's medical corps was adequate and highly skilled.[25] The only real weakness Hunt admitted in the series was the lack of artillery pieces, but he blamed that on a "meager" amount of money appropriated by

Congress before 1917.²⁶ Another NEA Washington correspondent, Milton Bronner, did several articles on how well the navy was doing.²⁷

The Hunt series was brief by NEA standards, with only a few editorials accompanying it. This was in stark contrast to the blizzard of lengthy, detailed stories and supporting editorials of Basil Manly's 1915–16 income tax publicity drive and the 1915 push to increase navy spending. Byron Canfield, NEA president and general manager, had learned from those earlier campaigns that less was more when it came to convincing NEA clients to run stories that were part of an NEA campaign. The previous November, Canfield had called the earlier series "two first class examples of how not to put across a propaganda [campaign]—providing, of course, that we want to get as much as possible of that 4,100,000 circulation." He explained to Bob that he now believed an editorial campaign should start strong and run shorter, avoiding needless repetition: "Even if we compel or influence a certain number of them to start it, we will not get the right popular response unless the editors have their hearts in it—and they won't have unless the start arouses their curiosity, enthusiasm and pep and unless the later stuff doesn't become tiresome to them. Therefore . . . I think it would be fatal to flood them with stuff."²⁸

Thus, the NEA's defense of Wilson was brief and less blatantly opinionated than the earlier campaigns. The retreat of many of Wilson's critics before the series was ready played a part in its brevity, but the decision to change strategy played an equal or greater part. The NEA also probably wanted to continue to tone down some of its public support of the president so as to salvage some semblance of independence.

"Our Big Chance for News Differences and Distinction"

As more American troops went to Europe, the NEA's war coverage was becoming increasingly important to the Scripps newspapers, and, one can assume, its clients as well. Martin advised his editors of the Ohio Group not to overplay UP war stories, because AP and UP reports were "apt to be more or less alike covering the same topics." The attentive editor, Martin said, would find "very frequently our big chance for news differences and distinction will lie in a big NEA story." Martin warned he was seeing an "unconscious tendency" among editors to think of UP stories as more important because they came by telegraph wire, while the NEA service was mailed.²⁹

In late November 1917, Martin said his editors had agreed that "war news is the big news and at this moment pretty much the only news."

Martin said the Ohio papers had to go back to "our program of the fall and early winter of 1914–15": Give war news prominent play. That philosophy remained in full force in 1918. Martin wanted to make the Ohio Group "The War Newspapers of the State," and in a way "so obvious that the most casual readers will get it."[30]

The NEA, which historically had focused on human-interest stories and serials, now geared that expertise to find distinctive ways of covering the war. By early 1918, however, many were gone from the stable of well-known and skilled writers the NEA had relied on in previous years. Harry Rickey and Charles Edward Russell were now working for the CPI. Manly, too, was working for the government. He took a leave from the NEA in early February to join his former colleague, Francis J. Heney, to investigate meatpackers suspected of profiteering.[31]

The NEA still had some noteworthy names on its payroll, however. Idah McGlone Gibson, writer of the popular women's page feature "Confessions of a Wife," went to France on behalf of the American Red Cross and the NEA. She first sent back what was dubbed the "first exclusive interview" with General Pershing since he had arrived in France. The story focused solely on the work of the Red Cross, which Pershing called "the first great constructive contingent of the American army."[32]

Gibson's series was obviously designed to generate support for the Red Cross—which relied on public donations of money and handmade clothing—and generate good copy for her employer. Later installments talked about how American soldiers appreciated the sweaters, scarves, and socks that the Red Cross was distributing to them for free. "I wished every woman in America could realize just how much comfort these garments were bringing to those they loved," Gibson wrote.[33]

In January, February, and March the NEA ran a series of eyewitness accounts of conditions inside the borders of the major belligerents. The first was written by the *Cleveland Press* editor Victor Morgan, who wrote a dozen articles about conditions in Germany, even though he had only been able to get as far as Switzerland, "Germany's neighbor, where he had exceptional opportunities for collecting facts about Germany," an editor's note explained.[34]

Morgan did not find many positive facts about Germany, or least none he told his readers. He reported that the Germans did not deny atrocities blamed on them because they wanted them publicized. "A judiciously placed atrocity, in the German militarist's plan, does the work of a regiment of soldiers. Cow a community, inspire it with horror, and it will need little watching by soldiers."[35] He assured his readers that German soldiers were poor fighters because their morale was low.[36]

The NEA also hired George Randolph Chester, who was dubbed "the greatest reporter in the world," and his wife, Lillian, to write about conditions in France. The central theme of the series was that the French were brave, patriotic, and determined, despite nearly four years of war on their own soil. "Behind the weariness and suffering is a calm, steady fire which has no quenching, a light which is an inspiration to see."[37] Chester, who had gained fame as a fiction writer, used all of his storytelling powers to bring a slice of France back to America.

The Chesters reported that the "most inspiring" situation they encountered was the treatment given to newborns. "You see, France cannot afford to lose a single baby. She must be a miser with them, since they are the most precious of her possessions."[38]

For its series on Russia, the NEA hired Bohemian American journalist Joseph Martinek, who had just returned from a visit there. The NEA introduced him as editor of the Bohemian-language weekly *American Workingmen's News*. The editor's note accompanying the series said Martinek spoke Russian fluently and went to Russia to try to establish "a Czecho-Slovak republic, to be known as the United States of Bohemia." His series attacked the Bolsheviks, who had signed a peace treaty with Germany. He said they had "signed their own political death warrant. . . . Another revolution will follow in Russia."[39] In Martinek's eyes, the Bolsheviks were out of touch with the masses.[40]

The war permeated every page of the Scripps newspapers. Thrift was a common theme in short testimonials written by experts. "If you cannot go to the trenches yourself, send your savings as the best substitute," one economics professor urged.[41] A women's page feature showed five pictures of a woman demonstrating a "patriotic manicure"—how to file your own nails. "In these days of economy and thrift, many girls who formerly had their nails manicured by a professional, are doing this for themselves, and are investing their savings in Thrift Stamps," the accompanying explanation noted.[42]

Articles urged women especially to think about growing food to supplement family meals. Beginning in mid-February, the *Cleveland Press* printed a series of gardening "lessons" for the upcoming spring. "The garden will give you vegetables to eat, thereby cutting your food cost, and at the same time reducing the nation's transportation and distribution troubles." The source of the series was not clear; the articles were vaguely bylined "By the Press Garden Expert."[43] The NEA also chimed in with editorials, calling the job of growing enough food during a war a "superman task. . . . But it must be done—or the kaiser wins!"[44]

"More in a Fighting Mood Now": The German Offensives of 1918

In late March 1918, it looked like the kaiser indeed might be able to win the war. His Western Front armies were beginning the first of five major offensives to break the French and British lines. On March 21 a ferocious attack began at the juncture of the French and British lines, with the British forces absorbing most of the blow. Using new tactics, the Germans advanced forty miles. By April 1 the German forces had outrun their supply lines, however, and stalled. Regardless, the offensive greatly concerned the Allies.[45]

United Press, on occasion, reprinted the official statements from the British, French, and German governments about the offensives, which newspapers such as the *Cleveland Press* ran side by side. These statements were short, however; each ran about three to six sentences.[46] Most of the other articles appeared credited only to "United Press," probably because the news came in snippets from many sources, and the copy desks in London or New York assembled the stories.

These wire stories acknowledged that the German attack was strong, but Allied censors made sure no panic was shown. "British military officials are confident the drive will be stopped, but they sounded a warning today that the world's destiny may depend on the human wall against which the enemy is hurling its shock troops," the first UP story about the offensive said.[47] On that same day William P. Simms, a UP correspondent now with the British army, reported that the British were "driving them back in places, the latest reports indicate. . . . Officers and men are smiling confidently as this is cabled."[48] Still, occasional doubt seeped through. A March 28 story from UP London bureau chief Ed Keen said: "Undue optimism regarding the definite checking of the German rush must be guarded against."[49] J. W. T. Mason, UP's war analysis expert, again began a series to give meaning to the mishmash of bulletins and war communiqués coming from Europe. His stories never carried a dateline, probably because he was based in New York, not in Europe, and because his stories were not breaking news pieces.

Though far from the action, Mason synthesized the themes emerging from UP reports from Europe. Many, if not all, of his main points were taken from the heavily censored UP wire stories that often ran alongside his column. He noted that the Germans had retaken ground that they had voluntarily given up in the previous year to shore up their defenses.[50] Although American troops were not part of the action, Mason said the presence of American troops forced the Germans to hold back reserves to counter any American threat.[51] He also repeated the most recurrent theme in the UP dispatches—any German gains were "not worth the casualties. . . . Each destruction of a German division at this time is a victory for the allies, whether or not the Germans gain a small additional area of territory."[52]

The NEA editorials reassured readers not to worry. With the defeat of Russia, it was common knowledge that the German army was larger than ever on the Western Front. That the American public might lose its will to fight because of the German advances created a great deal of anxiety. An NEA editorial in late April warned about the "poisoning voices of defeat" being heard in the United States. "Every whispered utterance that weakens the will to win is a voice of defeat. . . . Talk can help to win the war when it strengthens determination. Talk it."[53]

The major German offensives in 1918 failed to reach their objectives. The theme inherent in UP's reports of these attacks remained firm: the Germans were wasting troops in a desperate offensive; the French and British were bravely holding. Indeed, the Allied line did not break, and German losses removed any hope of victory.

The German attacks ensured that the war was a daily topic of conversation, and that gave the Scripps newspapers a reference point for their public exhortations, such as the Liberty Loan drives. "The British fight with their back to the wall. . . . Uncle Sam is coming with his last dollar and his last man to help save the day for democracy,'" an editorial for more bond subscriptions urged.[54]

The attacks also seemed to unleash, or at least coincide with, a stream of sensational atrocity propaganda from France. The Scripps newspapers, which had eschewed atrocity reports before the American declaration of war, now gave them front-page prominence. The April 22 *Cleveland Press* carried a UP story in which "hitherto unrevealed German atrocities" were described from an upcoming edition of *Everybody's* magazine. The UP report said Brand Whitlock, the U.S. minister to Belgium, would reveal in the magazine "carefully organized barbarities" unleashed by the Germans in Belgium after that neutral country was invaded.[55]

Next to the article was a "photograph of a picture painted for the French government" depicting a Frenchman being burned alive in the streets by German soldiers. The large photograph appeared under the headline "The Huns Did This." The caption for the photo said it "is vouched for by President [Raymond] Poincaré and General [Joseph] Joffre" of France.[56] Another atrocity picture had appeared in the *Press* under the same "The Huns Did This" headline two days earlier. The sketch showed

French soldiers opening a closet and discovering a crucified, nude body, that of an eighteen-year-old girl, according to the caption, who had been "tortured by the soldiers of the Saxon Guard and nailed to the wall by a bayonet."[57]

Atrocity stories were so commonly employed that the Ohio Group assigned Mosher to handle what he called "atrocity stuff" for its newspapers during the bond drives. He spent five weeks planning the atrocity campaign, reading more than thirty books and timing the articles for maximum impact. "The point was to build up a logical, consistent, convincing story which would lead up to a climax before the end of the Liberty Loan Campaign," he wrote to Martin on October 5. He complained privately that most of the atrocity incidents were old. "The great atrocities are over," he wrote with disappointment. "They are a matter of history."[58]

"Creel Can Go to Hell"

The NEA's drive to get people to buy Liberty Bonds was the only concerted campaign it waged during the war after March 1918. The theme of the bond drives could be summarized, one editorial concluded, as "BUY TILL IT HURTS."[59] On other important war issues, however, the NEA—with Bob essentially a paper tiger and with Harry Rickey gone—was a heavyweight boxer bewildered as to which punches to throw editorially. Cochran was getting no further cooperation from Creel. "So far as I am concerned, Creel can go to hell," he wrote to Alfred Anderson on August 6. He was upset because months earlier Creel had made him wait while Creel talked to others in his office, "until I finally made a kick to his private secretary." He said he was refusing to meet with Creel after the incident and now sent other NEA reporters "any time I want to get anything out of him." He explained to Andersson:

> I have a hunch that too much dependence is being placed on Creel to take care of newspaper publicity [for Wilson] . . . but when it comes to editorial or news policies they are slow to take advantage of our publicity. . . . You know as well as I do that we are trying to help in any way we can, but I don't think the administration thinks to take advantage of it. Every cabinet member and every man in responsible positions is very busy of course and has a big lot to carry, but we are busy too. . . . I told President Wilson a year ago . . . in a long talk I had with him [that] what he lacked and what practically his whole administration lacked was a sense of publicity. There has been little change in that particular since.[60]

Other members of the Concern found Creel and the CPI wanting, too. The Ohio Group's main office was continually dropped from the CPI's mailing lists, and after several letters failed to fix the oversight, the NEA's Bronner was asked to go in person.[61] On August 26 Bronner said to Creel's personal secretary, "It's damn aggravating that a Concern like ours, which has and is doing so much for the government, cannot get the necessary informative documents without each time begging and pleading for them."[62]

The Ohio Group was put on the CPI's mailing lists, but then on October 1 the NEA's Martin told Bronner that the Ohio newspapers had been cut off again. "I am anxious that there should be an uninterrupted service . . . both to myself and each of the editors," he said.[63] Bronner contacted Creel directly, saying it was "about the tenth time" that Martin had complained about the CPI mailings, and Bronner had a complaint also. "I discovered today that though I have been here for over 15 months and have repeatedly asked that all matter be mailed to me, that my name is not yet on the mailing list," he wrote Creel.[64] Creel's secretary confirmed on October 7 that Martin was not on some mailing lists and that complaints about the CPI's mailing division were coming in daily from other newspapers. Creel was assured by his secretary, however, that Bronner "will be well looked after."[65] Thus, a month before the war's end, the Ohio Group finally got on all of the CPI's mailing lists.

Assessing how much the Concern used CPI news releases is extremely difficult. The *Cleveland Press*, for example, never credited any stories to the CPI in its bylines, although it routinely credited photographs to the CPI. It probably treated photographs differently because it got war pictures from various sources, including its own photographers, the syndicated picture service Underwood and Underwood, and the government.

The Scripps newspapers undoubtedly rewrote many government handouts, and Martin said he wanted copies of what was being given to the Four Minute Men—patriotic speakers who represented the government—to help him write editorials.[66] In his 1920 memoirs, Creel claimed that his Division of News "saved the newspapers thousands of dollars in time and in men by the daily delivery and equitable distribution of the official war news." He said the division also cleared the way for reporters to get firsthand information for stories they initiated.[67]

Historical studies of the CPI's news division help little in judging how newspapers used its releases. James Mock's and Cedric Larson's 1939 book said the division did a "mighty and pivotal job" for the CPI.[68] According to this positive account, it was "largely the doing of the Committee on Public Information" that "Americans stood together in the comradeship of battle in 1917 and 1918."[69] Stephen Vaughn in 1980 wrote a more balanced account of the CPI's activities, but his book also concentrated on what the news division produced and assumed that newspapers used the material.[70]

All references to the CPI in the surviving Scripps archives are negative, however, and only a couple of the dozens of letters after 1917 discussing the Concern's coverage of the war even mention the CPI. To the men of the Concern, the CPI was an impediment it resented. The Concern was looking to differentiate its news product from its competitors, and the CPI's job was to make news coverage as uniform as possible. Paine called the war information coming from Washington "a mere matter of 'canned news' and official 'handouts.' . . . Creel's organization is a joke in Washington and a eunuch everywhere else."[71]

The communication problems the Concern had with the CPI and the NEA's internal problems helped prevent it from forming any policies regarding two important issues in 1918: the need for a new tax bill and the investigation into corruption in the Wilson administration's aircraft production program. The Senate began investigating Wilson's aircraft program on March 26, and over the next ten weeks the issue would become what the *New York Times* called "the bitterest debate of the war."[72] The situation was diffused when Wilson replaced the man in charge of aircraft production and Charles Evans Hughes, Wilson's opponent in 1916, was appointed on May 16 to investigate the issue.[73] With another $8 billion needed for the war effort, the new tax bill question dominated the news of the late spring and early summer.[74]

The NEA wrote little on either issue. The *Cleveland Press* ran no editorials on the aircraft production investigation, and the tax issue, with Manly no longer part of the NEA, got little attention. Wariness about continuing to boldly support Wilson and frustration with CPI interference also probably played a part in the silence. No evidence exists that suggests that the Concern was scared into silence in 1918 because of the Sedition Act that was enacted on May 16. This amendment to the Espionage Act added new crimes to it, including the printing or publishing of "any disloyal, profane, scurrilous or abusive language" directed toward the government, the Constitution, military service, and the flag.[75]

Even with these laws in place, an increasingly vocal minority in the Concern was itching to criticize Wilson on some issues. C. F. Mosher, the Concern's business manager, complained on July 24 that after two months of congressional debate, "we still have no policy on taxation . . . and we are not doing one single thing in the way of constructive criticism. When the government itself arrests its own members for dishonesty and discharges them for incompetency, it surely could not be unpatriotic for our papers to dig up instances of dishonesty or incompetency."[76]

Mosher was still in the minority, however. Martin found in a survey of his Ohio editors in June that they wanted to stand by the president.[77] Cochran wrote E.W. July 15 that "Wilson is doing a wonderful work. He has . . . touched the human heart, which is the same the world over."[78] Compared to the rest of the Concern, the Ohio Group and the Washington bureau of the NEA continued to hold strongest to supporting Wilson unconditionally.

In 1918, however, standing by the president meant little more than that the Concern would not criticize his administration while supporting the nation's general war aims, the troops, and the Liberty Bond drives. The Concern would cover the war as news and stay out of political advocacy.

"More Valuable to the Government Than Carrying a Gun"

The Concern could not erase the record it had already established, however, on the draft issue, and it continued to pay the price for its perceived hypocrisy. On January 9 the *Cleveland News,* a Scripps rival, criticized the Wilson administration for delaying the decision on Jim Scripps's exemption claim. In a story datelined Washington, the *News* said the exemption "is being so 'juggled' here that young Scripps probably will be able to evade service in the national army." The *News* questioned why Jim had not been sent to the army cantonment while his appeal was being considered, as his brother Bob had been. It said the adjutant general's office also was refusing to let reporters see the Scripps records on file.[79]

Draft boards were about ready to use the new system of classifying men in one of four draft categories that had been adopted on November 8, 1917. The popular term "exemption" was to be replaced by "deferred classification"—essential workers were to be placed in a higher class and drafted later. As noted earlier, the efforts to get the Scripps boys exempted had to start over; as Bob himself said, "the case of every registered man whether previously exempted or appealed or not is to be considered as a fresh one."[80]

Jim's application for an exemption, which many in the Concern felt surely would be granted, in fact remained dubious. One San Diego County draft official told Milton McRae that "a great number of people" in San Diego felt Jim should not be exempted. He said Secret Service agents had "looked into the methods" of Jim's life and found "he did not seem to have much responsibility or rather did not give much evidence of it, because he was having a good time constantly.... I know I am going to get Hell for my decision if I grant this exemption."[81]

Jim had two potential claims for deferment. As a married man with dependent children, he could be placed in Class II. McRae and Harper, the two men handling the exemption claims, felt Jim was too wealthy to pursue that option. They insisted Jim be placed in Class IV as the head of a necessary industrial enterprise, but those arguments faced growing public outrage. Many remained convinced it was Jim's personal riches, not his importance to the home front, that would get him deferred. Some rival newspapers were portraying Jim as an example of a rich man promoting something he did not want to do himself. The draft board was getting enormous pressure to take a stand against favoritism.

This pressure led the San Diego County board to try to coordinate its consideration of Jim with the classification of Bob in southern Ohio. What bothered many was that both Scripps sons were to be exempted. "It does not seem right when we consider the sacrifices that many of our sons are making in this crisis, that two sons of a very wealthy man should seek to evade what most of us feel would have been our duty," R. C. Allen, chairman of the San Diego County board, wrote to the Southern Ohio board on January 30. He asked the Southern Ohio board to "work in harmony" as if both sons were before the same board. Allen noted that the facts seemed to show "no doubt . . . James is the active and efficient directed head of all these [Scripps] enterprises . . . but in regard to Robert, we find among those who have been associated with him at the Scripps enterprises, a consensus of opinion that he is not imperatively needed."[82]

The draft boards in Ohio, however, had already decided Bob's case before the letter from San Diego arrived. His claims for industrial exemption essentially were denied. He was placed in Class II on dependency grounds, however, because he was married with an infant son. McRae knew Bob was fortunate to get that much of a deferment. "It appears to me that Class Two will not be reached for a year," he wrote Bob on January 30, "and I think the war will end before then, though this is merely a guess on my part."[83] Jay Curts, still managing Bob's case, appealed to the president the denial of the industrial exemption, but it was not to be considered until Class I was exhausted.[84]

Jim's situation dragged along for several months. After writing its letter to Ohio, the San Diego County board voted unanimously to recommend to the district board that Jim be classified in Class II as a married man with children and Class IV as an important industrial manager. The district board, however, denied the industrial exemption on February

16 and brazenly asked the local board to place Jim in Class I despite his family responsibilities, which it did.

McRae again tried to appeal Jim's case to the president. Under the new draft law, however, he had to get the local draft board to consent to the appeal. The three members of the local board refused to sign off on any of Jim's appeals unless Bob withdrew his claims for exemption in Ohio. Eventually the deadlock was broken, and Jim was placed in Class IV.[85] Thus, under the new draft system, President Wilson did not have to intervene for either Scripps son.

Even though the enemies of the Scripps newspapers portrayed this as a case of a rich man's sons getting preferential treatment, Bob and Jim's cases were not treated any differently from those of other men in their situations. On the other hand, there is no doubt that their father pulled many strings to get the system to grant exemptions for his sons, and Bob's role in the Concern was grossly exaggerated. Yet ultimately E.W.'s influence was not necessary because they would not have been drafted under the 1918 system anyway. No evidence exists that Wilson personally ordered Bob to be exempted in 1917 under the old conscription system either, but it is evident that the president knew about Bob's situation and expressed his support for the younger Scripps.

Although many reporters served in the regular army during the war, newspaper work was, under the right circumstances, considered an important war industry eligible for deferment. In mid-August secretary of war Newton Baker explained this in *Editor and Publisher:* "I do not hesitate to say that the gathering of news for the public information is an indispensable industry." Baker said, however, that deferred classification should only be granted when "a newspaper would be irreparably injured without the services of the drafted employee." Baker urged draft boards to consider exempting newspaper workers on a case-by-case basis.[86]

"Strongly Opposing Me in My Efforts to Keep Bob on His Job"

Bob still struggled with where his true place was in 1918. He was being publicly accused of being a slacker while his brother and coworkers wondered about his ability to direct coverage of the war. By midsummer, E.W. was feeling better and reading more about the war.[87] He said he was disappointed because Bob was being subjected to "tremendous pressure from parties inside of the Concern. I have been led to believe that Jim himself, Harper, Paine and many if not all of the younger captains and lieutenants in the Concern are strongly opposing me in my efforts to keep Bob on his job." Scripps continued to insist that few understood his belief that the Concern could only be run by one of his sons. They had been trained to carry the torch after their father died, and without them at the helm, the Concern would have to be sold. "Perhaps the most difficult and unpleasant part of the situation [the criticism of Bob] is that my course is being condemned by others who would most heartily applaud it if they were as fully informed as I am myself," E.W. said.[88]

Bob had been placed in an impossible situation. For reasons that his father could not or would not explain to others in the Concern, he insisted that Bob be named editor-in-chief. The unhappy resignation of Rickey, who was still respected by most the Scripps editors, also was directly attributed to Bob's promotion. E.W. said he believed the many second-guessers in the Concern hurt Bob's success.[89] The war presented numerous logistical and editorial problems as well, an enormous task for someone with little journalism experience, regardless of his bloodline. In addition, Bob had been physically ill when he was promoted. It took most of October 1917 for him to recover from the cold and laryngitis he had contracted at Chillicothe, and then he caught the measles and had to be quarantined for much of January.[90] Some of the surviving correspondence also shows that E.W. and Cochran were concerned in late 1917 that Bob's drinking would affect his performance as chief editor. The elder Scripps told Cochran in December 1917 that it was "extremely important that [Bob] should be very, very temperate for the present."[91]

The "Pioneer in Slackerism"

The public and private struggle to get Bob exempted, in particular, stood in stark contrast with the Scripps newspapers' unwavering patriotism and support of the draft, and their longstanding advocacy of social equality and justice. Nowhere was this apparent hypocrisy attacked more often than in Toledo, where the *Toledo Times*, the city's smallest daily, hammered away on the issue. At the beginning of 1918 the *Times*, a morning paper, had about one-fifth of the circulation of Scripps's *Toledo News-Bee*, and a third of the *Toledo Blade*, both afternoon papers, but its scathing words cut deep.[92]

The nastiest of the *Times*'s attacks came on July 21 in a front-page editorial titled "Scripps Patriotism." The editorial reprinted an editorial in the *News-Bee*, which praised women who had had sons killed in the war. "Consider the nerve of that man Scripps" for taking such a position, the *Times* editorial observed. "It is true that Scripps, the American father, did not raise his sons to be soldiers, so he exempted them. He did not even raise his boys to be MEN. He is proud of his boys, not because they are men, but because they are exempt and safe, unwilling to do their part in the great task which Almighty God has given them."[93]

The editorial also accused Scripps of war profiteering because the *News-Bee* had recently increased to two cents and Scripps was "paying himself FORTY-ONE per cent cash dividends on his *News-Bee* stock, all . . . paid by the people of Toledo." Later *Times* editorials played with the truth by claiming that war secretary Baker had exempted Jim and Bob in an "outrageous case of political favoritism."[94]

The most sustained barrage from the *Toledo Times* came in early September. For ten consecutive days beginning on September 5, it printed front-page editorials attacking Scripps as "the pioneer in slackerism."[95] The editorials hit the same themes and usually began with a reference to a news item about slackers or the draft. "They are rounding up slackers in New York. When will they round up the Scripps herd?" one queried.[96] "No man in the country is held in more universal contempt than Scripps, and he knows it," another asserted.[97]

With one rival newspaper attacking another, the *Toledo Blade* moved to capitalize on the situation. In early August, the *News-Bee* heard rumors that the *Blade*'s "circulation canvassers" were approaching *News-Bee* subscribers and "basing their solicitation on the allegation that the *News-Bee* is a 'slacker' newspaper. This surprised Cochran because he had not thought the *Blade*'s editor, Nat C. Wright, would stoop so low. "If the report is true," Cochran wrote Wright on August 7, "I am sure you know nothing about it, for I knew you are not that kind of a fighter."[98] Wright assured Cochran that the reports of *Blade* skullduggery were untrue and said the *Blade* was willing to counter the *Times* attacks on its pages if Cochran wanted.[99]

By mid-September, however, the *News-Bee* began to hear increasing talk among advertisers, subscribers, and newsboys about the purported Scripps exemptions. The *Blade* seemed to encourage the rumors.[100] Acting *News-Bee* editor Frank M. Heller wrote to Cochran on September 16 that "the advertisers are beginning to peg it as *Blade* propaganda and are kidding about it, but at the same time [one advertising salesman] says, he has heard more talk on the street cars than formerly and rather thinks someone besides the *Times* is boosting it along." Heller said he also had heard unsubstantiated reports of various *News-Bee* boycotts.[101]

Although Wright continued to claim his newspaper was not exploiting the *Times*'s attacks, Heller insisted in late September "the *Blade* is making the most of the situation" and the *News-Bee* had lost one thousand "subscribers due directly to the slacker cry." The morale of carriers and street vendors was down, and the numbers of them willing to be associated with the *News-Bee* were "falling away." The *News-Bee*'s business manager sent an advertising salesman to talk to ten former subscribers to find out why they had stopped taking the paper. Heller said the salesman "found in each case that the subscriber had not seen the *Times* stories but had been given the information by *Blade* solicitors."[102]

The situation in Toledo became so critical that Cochran was transferred back to Toledo in early October to assume direct control of the *News-Bee*, while still maintaining some of his duties with the NEA.[103] He said he found the *News-Bee* in a "debilitated, anaemic condition. Its powers of resistance were low." Cochran gave his employees letters explaining the Scripps situation. That, he said, "put them on the offensive with the old time pep."[104]

During the previous winter the Scripps editors had agreed never to fight back against competitors who criticized them about the exemption claims.[105] The Scripps editors did not want to give any credence to the attacks, which would only escalate if they returned a volley. Not until December 7 did Cochran print an article defending E.W. Scripps and his efforts to exempt his sons. Privately, Cochran said at the time that it was difficult to tell how much circulation the *News-Bee* had lost due to this issue, because the paper had increased its price during the year.[106]

"A Solar Plexus Blow" to the Penny Press

In mid-June Scripps's Ohio newspapers were among the last in the country to abandon the penny price.[107] The last New York newspapers had gone to two cents in January, joining newspapers in other major cities, which had already moved to two cents in 1917.[108] The American Newspaper Publishers Association reported in April that only 101 English-language dailies were still at one cent and called the penny price "unwarranted under present war conditions."[109]

The Ohio Group had been doing well financially. Although operating costs had increased dramatically, increased circulation had more than covered the higher costs associated with the war. During these early years of the war, the Ohio papers did so well that they did not increase advertising rates, even though costs had gone up. "It must be remembered too that it was pretty hard to increase [advertising] rates over a period when we were making such a big profit and high rate of profit," W. W. Thornton, president of the Ohio Group, recalled on July 3.[110]

By the summer of 1918, however, Thornton said "a solar plexus blow" had been delivered. Excess profits taxes approved by Congress in the previous year and higher paper costs had taken away the comfort level. In June the Ohio Group learned that its five newspapers would have to absorb an increase of $45,000 in transportation costs alone for newsprint.

Wages, especially in the mechanical areas of the business, also were spiraling upward. In June the Ohio Group's printers were given a minimum wage of $30 per week. "We will have to meet these folk with war bonuses to keep them on the job," William. H. Dodge of the Ohio Group's business department explained.[111] An increase in the price of the daily newspaper was needed.

"A Service—Not a Syndicate."

The Scripps editors knew readers would be more discerning of a newspaper's content at the two-cent price, so NEA features had to be improved. The nationwide trend to two-cent newspapers also seemed to give quality syndicates an opportunity to grow. In a climate of cost cutting, syndicated material could help editors sell their newspapers at a higher price and save operating costs. As long as the syndicated matter was relevant and high in quality, newspapers would not have to hire as many reporters to write copy. Opinion pieces were not encouraged; the features could be unbiased so that no editor with differing views would be offended by the content. A new marketing approach was born.

The first signs of the NEA's news marketing strategy could be seen in a January 19 article in *Editor and Publisher* under the byline of Sam T. Hughes, editor-in-chief of the NEA. He asked, "Can it be doubted it is cheaper to join with scores of other newspapers in meeting the costs of 'wallop stunts' than it would be to put the same show on all by one's self?" Hughes also insisted on calling the NEA a "service," not a "syndicate," to differentiate his company from its rivals. He said the distinction was warranted because the NEA dealt in "high class features and high-class art"—something doubly needed when readers were confused by the fragmented stories from the wire services: "More and more unsatisfying becomes the spot news of the day—this from the reader's viewpoint. The events of to-day, while of an importance never before equaled in the history of this old world, are, when detailed simply as events, simply as news, puzzling to the reader."[112] In some cases, Hughes said, readers wanted to forget the war entirely, creating a need for other features.[113]

Hughes was talking publicly about what the NEA was about to launch. In May Canfield acknowledged that the NEA, as a service delivered by mail to its clients, had to overcome the stereotype that it could not be a viable news service. "We must first impress upon [editors] the idea that a large part of NEA *is* news and, in fact, has been news for a long time, and next we must make a much stronger play with news that we have made." He said he was already noticing that many editors were using NEA news features to supplement wire copy. "The wires cannot carry much except the spots news. The side lights are in the magazines and in features. A big mass of real news in-between is not touched," he observed.

Canfield wanted no opinion pieces and editorials, however, a traditional role of the NEA. "We want facts and lots of them. In other words we want a job of reporting. We wouldn't discourage them from turning in a fine piece of writing in a way of human interest, or anything else, but primarily [the reporter's job] is to *report.*" Canfield began assembling permanent bureaus in London and Paris to beef up war news for the NEA.[114]

By mid-June, Canfield had selected the reporters for what he was calling the "foreign news service." He was confident he had a good group. "With [the foreign bureau staff] on the job over there and our desk man here, who will handle nothing but the war news and international stuff ... we should put N.E.A. on the map as a real war news service as well as a 'feature service,'" he said.[115]

The new staff was introduced to newspaper editors in an advertisement in the *Editor and Publisher* on July 13. The ad featured pictures of Harold Bechtol, manager of the London bureau; Edward Thierry, manager of the Paris bureau; A. E. Geldhoff, the NEA's stateside war editor; and J. R. Grove, C. C. Lyon, and Burton Kniseley, staff writers. The ad said these men comprised "one department of a service replete with every editorial need for publishing a modern newspaper."[116] Canfield said privately he hoped to cut some of the expenses in the NEA's Washington bureau to help pay for the new foreign service.[117]

Beginning in May and running throughout the year, the NEA ran full-page advertisements in *Editor and Publisher*, every other issue, alternating with full-page ads for UP. Each ad ran with the motto "A Service—Not a Syndicate." One published in May summed up the NEA's new pitch. "N.E.A. GIVES ITS CLIENTS WAR NEWS That Can't Be Told by Dots and Dashes—And all of it is WAR NEWS THAT IS *EXCLUSIVE.*" The ad said the NEA carried war news "of human interest the battle-busy wires cannot carry." It said it would get "the biggest beats of the war from intimate, official sources which only staff correspondents not limited as to filing time, may truly cultivate."[118] Ensuing ads focused on individual writers and serials featured in the NEA.[119]

The NEA also needed to adjust the reporting style of its Washington bureau. Unfortunately, Bob did not seem to have the necessary skills. His role in the Concern would have to be clarified again before this new organization, at least the Washington part of it, could be fully implemented.

Pulling "Bob Scripps off the Washington Job"

In early June, Jim, who had been living in Cincinnati for more than a year, asked Bob to meet him there to discuss his future role in the Concern. The two brothers agreed that Bob would go to Europe in late June to see firsthand, as Jim put it, the "actual conditions" of the war and to gain some experience. The trip gave Bob a graceful exit and a way for Jim to get rid of him so the NEA in Washington could be reorganized. The brothers agreed Bob would come to Cincinnati to study together the business side of the Concern after he returned.

Jim admitted to Harper later that he doubted he and Bob could ever work well together. "With Bob working next to me, I will have the opportunity of getting his judgment on all the specific subjects I am dealing with and his reasons.... Mr. Harper, I am very doubtful that Bob and I will be able to work together in the management and conduct of this business."[120]

What sort of relationship Jim and Bob had personally is difficult to ascertain. The best discussion of the personal relationships and the interplay of personalities among E.W., Jim, and Bob is in Cochran's biography of Scripps, published in 1933. Cochran, who knew all three men well, devoted an entire chapter, titled "Father and Sons," to the subject.[121] Cochran said Bob was close in personality and outlook to that of his father, while Jim was different. Jim was a conservative businessman who made big decisions deliberately and tentatively. Jim, according to Cochran, said his father "always wants to whoop things up and get them started, and I have had more trouble through being in a rush than through any other cause." E.W. saw Jim as someone who "regards money as valuable only for the use it can be put to for the purchase of the petty comforts of life for himself and family," while E.W. believed profits should be sacrificed for public service, if need be. Jim, according to his father, had more of a "spirit of egotism" than a "virtue of altruism."[122] Cochran said a clash between Jim and E.W. was "inevitable because of temperamental differences."

Bob reminded Jim of their father, too. "In a great many ways, he resembles his father," Jim wrote on November 11, 1918.[123] But Jim resented his father's tendency to meddle. "If mistakes have been made, and in my opinion mistakes have been made in regard to Bob, my father has made them," Jim wrote on June 17. "From the start I have been more or less opposed to the way in which Bob had entered the business." He said he was opposed to renting the "embassy" house in Washington, and "starting Bob off on such an elaborate scale."[124]

Jim admitted Bob was entitled to an opportunity in the Concern, but Jim was not sure what that should be. Jim felt it would be best for Bob to get experience managing a newspaper or two. Jim insisted his entry into the family business a decade earlier had been different because the Concern was smaller then and his father had not retired yet. "And there was not a war going on which has upset everything," he added.

As Jim noted in a memorandum in October, the agreements that the two brothers made effectively "pulled Bob Scripps off the Washington job." Jim noted that their father seemed indifferent to the move.[125] Bob had been editor-in-chief for eight months, about two of which he spent sick or under medical quarantine.

Bob Goes to Europe

During the third week of June, Bob was on his way to the trenches of France—as a civilian. Along with twenty-five hundred American soldiers and about forty civilians, Bob boarded a Canadian ship bound for Great Britain out of New York. Cochran was now editor-in-chief.[126]

Bob was not headed to Europe to write for the Scripps newspapers. He was going as an editor and administrator in training, and what he was to find was not for publication. Canfield hoped Jim could talk to the men in the NEA's new bureau in London to see what they "might want to get to us but cannot write because of the censorship. . . . I do not mean by this to avoid censorship, which would be dangerous at this stage of the game, but to report for our editorial guidance."[127]

Before he left Washington, Bob said he wanted to see "how our men act when they are under fire," but he primarily wanted to see how the domestic fronts of Europe were doing. "They are the reactions of the war, which we have to experience likewise sooner or later in this country."[128] Upon his arrival Bob said he found "no visible excitement in either England or France. . . . There are no flags or parades. There are no loan speeches being made on the street loan corners and loan posters on the boardings. It has gotten to be a regular business."

Bob was gone for two months, spending two weeks in France and the rest in England. During his stay, he met with British commanding general

Sir Douglas Haig, British publisher Lord Northcliffe, and the deposed head of the Russian provisional government, Alexander Kerensky. Bob said it was apparent that "the Allies have finally got the war going their way," but he also concluded that peace would be difficult. Bob said he worried that "some sort of settlement [of the war] will be forced which will make this war only the prelude to another."[129]

"An Adequate but Compact Organization of the Best News-Getters"

Bob had left America knowing that the NEA's Washington bureau would be reorganized.[130] Some Scripps editors were unhappy with the lackluster nature of the news coming from the bureau. Mosher, who was writing occasional editorials for the Ohio Group, said the Washington staff was focused too much on routine news. Mosher acknowledged "it is very difficult to get a 'scoop'" because "there is a great deal of press agenting going on." But he noted on August 7 that "the War and Navy Departments are certainly giving out a greater volume of stuff than they did four or five months ago." Mosher said the NEA should assign a man to read this information and synthesize it into good story with a unique perspective. "The 10-grain pearl set alone does not look like much, compared with forty, fifty or sixty 8-grain pearls strung as a necklace," he explained to Martin.[131]

Likewise, Mosher and others in the Concern believed the NEA would do better if its two primary duties, news reporting and editorial writing, were split:

> As an Ex-Editor and stockholder my idea of the Washington bureau is that it ought to be a News bureau and that no one connected with it should write editorials. The reason for that is that gathering news is gathering facts; writing editorials is expressing opinions. The two things don't go together. Nor do I think that the Washington Bureau, either its head or its members, should be active in Propaganda. The peculiarity of Propaganda is that it draws one instinctively towards those who favor or say they favor a policy and arrays one in opposition to those who do not favor a policy.... It interferes with the gathering of news.[132]

Martin agreed. He said he wanted to "omit all editorials and editorial paragraphs from the Washington report, because I believe the continuance of these in the report gives the staff there the wrong idea of their job."

Martin knew the NEA had been drifting aimlessly since America had joined the war. Rickey's appointment, Bob's appointment, and Rickey's departure had left the editorial side of the NEA unfocused. Martin called for "a clearer understanding among ourselves as to just what is our editorial policy concerning the various topics connected with the war, growing out of the war, and following the war." He suggested that "some one man or group of men in the Concern should formulate an outline of policy" and distribute it among the Concern's executives."[133]

For unknown reasons, changes were not made, however, until early October. The uncertainty of Bob's position probably made Scripps executives tentative. Cochran's return to Toledo in late August to defend the *News-Bee* also was a diversion. Martin believed that Cochran, if he had stayed in Washington, could have handled all of the editorial-writing needs of the bureau. The reorganization also represented such a major philosophical change that a consensus had to be reached. The right people to fill the new roles had to be found as well.

The first changes were made in the reporting staff. The NEA's main office in Cleveland sent three additional reporters to the Washington bureau. Gilson Gardner, who had spent a great deal of time away from the capital accompanying E.W., was put in charge of the bureau because Hughes said Gardner "knows Washington like a book."[134] With Bob now officially out of the picture, Jim noted that the "Washington bureau is back in the same form it was prior to E.W.'s arrival in Washington."[135]

Hughes had high expectations. He wanted Rodgers, Johnstone, and Geldhoff to use "footwork reporting" to get a "crackerjack bunch of up-to the-minute news and features from this center of the world." He wanted them to "cut out all propaganda on policies.... Make it all bright, clever and snappy, interesting and entertaining and likewise informative. Be extra careful of fakes. Be extra careful of ALL troublesome things which include libel and the censor."[136]

The new arrangement had only mixed success. Bad blood emerged between the newcomers and the veteran staff over the use of typewriters in the office and the help of an office boy that the men had to share. Canfield managed to mediate the disputes. "The Washington atmosphere breeds more of this sort of thing and more office politics than exists anywhere else," he noted in exasperation.[137]

The quality of the product generated by the reconstituted bureau also was questioned. On October 16 Mosher said "it is a long time since the N.E.A. sheets were of as little value to the Scripps papers as they are today."[138] Martin felt the new men's stories were contradicting each other, and their articles sometimes were too anti-British. Cochran, on the other hand, felt the NEA was becoming too anti-German because it claimed the Germans were "without honor." He also felt the news service printed too much atrocity propaganda.

Canfield was frustrated. "It all reminds me of the controversy we had soon after 1914, when some claimed we were Anti-German and Pro-British, and others that we were faking stories by Mary Boyle O'Reilly, who was writing about the Germans deporting women from Louvain, and still others insisted we should give the Germans hell," he wrote on October 28.[139]

Bob's New Role

One major role of the NEA's Washington bureau—the editorial writing—remained completely unsettled in October 1918. "I am afraid to turn the machine over to Bob," Jim lamented on October 7. He knew, however, that E.W. and Bob wanted Bob to become the editorial head of the Concern. "How are we to define the responsibility and authority?" he asked himself in a memo.[140] Jim knew E.W. had to agree with Bob's role, but E.W. was being advised not to come to Cincinnati to meet with his sons because of the influenza pandemic spreading through Ohio.[141]

Instead, Harper and Mosher met in Cincinnati on E.W.'s behalf on November 5 to try to find a new role for Bob. The conferees agreed that Bob should enter the Concern through the editorial side, and that he should be groomed eventually to replace Jim. Bob, however, wanted more power right away. "I think that my authority should be, in the absence of your veto, the same as your own," Bob tried to reason with Jim. "That is to say, I should have authority to do anything that you could do in the absence of direct or general orders to the contrary."[142]

Jim was adamant, however, that Bob needed to be eased in: "Bob's entry into the Concern, his field of action, his responsibilities, his authority, etc. must be in the nature of an evolution rather than invention—By this I mean it is necessary to make a start and develop and extend Bob's field of activity.... I do not believe it is either practical, or good business, at this time to try and formulate the exact authority and responsibility and field of action that Bob shall have and occupy."[143] The three finally agreed to make Bob the head of a new Scripps Editorial Board. Harper said the board position would act as a "starter to work toward Bob's [plan to become head of all news content] as the ultimate objective."[144]

The new editorial board, consisting of Bob, Cochran, and Paine, would take over the editorial writing that the NEA Washington bureau had been doing, but would distribute that material only to Scripps newspapers. The NEA would no longer offer the Scripps editorial voice to non-Scripps clients; it would just offer them news features. Bob described the new board this way: "The function of the Scripps Editorial Board will be to produce editorial copy and to inaugurate propaganda and policies exclusively for Scripps Newspapers. It will be a Scripps service."[145] Bob's new position was formally announced on November 13.[146] Two days after the armistice in Europe, a cease-fire had been agreed on in the Scrippses' intrafamilial war as well. Bob had a new role, and so did the NEA.

"I Think We're Going to Have a Great Year"

While the NEA struggled to remake itself in 1918, UP struggled to maintain the momentum it had been riding since its glory days of 1914–15. The year began well. In mid-January, Joseph Shaplen, the UP correspondent in Petrograd, obtained an exclusive interview with Leon Trotsky, a leader of the Bolshevik revolution. Howard said he hoped it "will also serve to let the opposition know that we are [still] on earth. . . . I think we're going to have a great year." In the interview, Trotsky said Wilson's declaration of America's war aims—the Fourteen Points—did not go far enough and the Russians did not trust the Allies.[147]

Howard also was upbeat because the South American service of UP was growing. The three largest newspapers in Chile had joined UP on January 1. United Press now had three clients in Argentina and two in Brazil. Howard decided to go to South America in early February to "get a line on [the] makeup" of the Chilean editors who were now taking the service. He also hoped to obtain new client newspapers in Sao Paolo.[148]

His optimism was short-lived. He ended up staying in South America for about eight months, trying to salvage what he could of UP's business on the continent. By midsummer AP, despite its agreements with the news cartel (discussed in chapter 1), entered the South American market and was aggressively signing up newspapers. Howard's troubles had begun earlier, however, when Buenos Aires publisher Jorge Mitre, whose newspaper, *La Nacion*, had been the first to take the UP report, broke his ten-year contract and started his own news service. Mitre eventually became a member of AP. Howard wrote his mother that Mitre had broken the contract "for no other reasons in the world than Jealousy and an inherent Spanish love of treachery."[149]

The breakdown in UP business came quickly. Howard said on May 30 that UP had eight clients in Chile, Argentina, and Brazil, earning UP $88,500 a year in profit, and the next day it faced a loss of $104,000 because it had only one paper left.[150] Howard tried to recover. He found a client in Rio de Janeiro and closed a new deal in Sao Paolo. But much had been lost. One historian has said that UP was "all but cleaned out on that continent" by the time he left South America on September 14.[151]

He headed directly to Europe with his wife to visit the European front for the first time in two years.[152]

"Being a Correspondent Is as Hard Work as There Is Done in France"

Howard found his men in Europe still struggling with tight censorship and clogged cables, but UP often was beating AP reports by an hour or two, a situation that got so bad that Melville Stone of AP met with General Pershing to try figure out why. Some of the cases were easily explained: the UP sent its dispatches marked "urgent," while the AP did not. In other cases, the reason was not known. Pershing assured Stone that AP was being treated equally. Neither man knew that UP had made a secret deal with a French newspaper to use the paper's leased telegraph wire to get UP stories out of France quicker.[153]

With the strict censorship at the front, speed was the only true way for the wire services to compete in 1918. "To most of the reading public a few hours more or less in the publication of war news didn't make a great deal of difference," one historian has noted. "But to those in the business, speed was the essence of news gathering, and the difference of a few minutes meant getting an extra on the street ahead of a rival."[154]

A speed-based scoop in mid-September gave UP its most noteworthy accomplishment of the year, and Fred Ferguson, a seven-month veteran of front-line reporting, deserved all of the credit.[155] Before the United States' first major offensive of the war, at Saint-Mihiel, the army briefed the correspondents about the order of battle and the objectives to be taken. Ferguson assumed the battle would unfold as it was described, and so he wrote a dozen short takes describing each part of the battle. None of the UP telegraph stories were long. One of Ferguson's stories of the battle that appeared in the *Cleveland Press* was only nine sentences long.[156]

Unbeknownst to his newspaper rivals, Ferguson got censors to pre-approve the takes and also got the military to agree to send them as the battle unfolded. To circumvent any unexpected delays, he arranged to have one copy of each take sent on several separate cables. Ferguson then drove to the front with his fellow newspapermen, who waited to file their dispatches when they got back. Only when the reporters returned to headquarters late on the first day of battle did they discover that Ferguson already had sent his series of dispatches.[157]

Even if the average reader did not notice or care too much about scoops such as this, UP knew its newspaper colleagues would, and so it made sure to point them out. The scoop at Saint-Mihiel was the subject of two full-page advertisements in *Editor and Publisher*. Although most UP ads boasted of several scoops, Ferguson's scoop was the only one featured in two ads. A September 28 advertisement quoted the *Saint Paul Daily News:* "Ferguson got his wonderful news through to us by using THREE DIFFERENT CABLE LINES. That's typical UNITED PRESS ENTERPRISE."[158]

Thus, UP was still a legitimate challenger to the much larger AP. During his European tour, Bob marveled at the enterprise and energy displayed by Ferguson and by Frank Taylor on the French Front. Bob said Ferguson began his day at 6 A.M. in a "flash car," which Bob said were "so called because they are manned by crack drivers who are supposed to go like the devil all the time." Bob said the car usually returned about 7 P.M., and Ferguson would have an hour to write his copy before a motorcycle courier took it to Paris to be cabled.

Meanwhile, Taylor took what was called the "noon ride." Bob said the noon rider "would not attempt to cover so much ground, as his time for turning the story over to the courier would be one o'clock." He said the two would alternate these roles "seven days a week, in all kinds of weather, under all conditions!"[159]

In his 1936 memoir, UP reporter Webb Miller described how correspondents with the United States army were given great freedom of movement among the United States forces but had to submit anything they wrote to two former reporters now working for the army as censors. Miller typically started his day with a car trip to corps headquarters to find where the most newsworthy fighting was that day. He was then driven to the division headquarters directing those battles. Miller said the commanding generals were cooperative and even let him talk to officers in the front lines by telephone. Miller seldom went to the front itself because it took too long and "descriptions of the front line were old stuff." He also felt his duty as a wire service reporter was to "find out what was happening and get the news back to the telegraph wires. This left little opportunity for sight-seeing."[160]

Despite the determination of the UP reporters, their stories were not the backbone of the war coverage, even in the Scripps newspapers. The Scripps editors' preoccupation with improving the NEA service revealed how much they felt the UP wire service needed bolstering. United Press supplied the breaking news; the NEA supplied the color, analysis, human interest, and column inches. Censorship made the UP stories vague and too similar to those of AP. High cable charges and limited time for each dispatch on the transatlantic cables made sure any UP stories were short, even for the breezy style of a Scripps newspaper.[161]

"Too Much Ginger": Tangling with Censors

Any attempts in New York to fatten a skimpy UP story from Europe brought the wrath of the censor. For example, in December 1917 the military admonished UP for adding information to stories William Philip Simms, UP's veteran correspondent with the British army, wrote in November. Associated Press had prompted the military investigation when it saw Simms's stories in the *New York Sun* and *New York World* and complained to the army that the articles were fakes. Afterward, Simms urged Ed Keen, the London bureau manager, to put a rein on UP's rewrite men—"too much ginger on the part of one of whom already having done us immense damage."[162]

This was not the only noteworthy entanglement that UP had with military censors over published stories. Reporter Lowell Mellett accidentally crossed the military censors when he filed a story about a new gas mask in 1918. He learned from an American soldier that the improved mask was easier to wear longer and made it easier for him to breathe and see. Mellett wrote a story based on what the soldier told him, listing all nine gases the mask was intended to stop. Before Mellett submitted the story to censors, however, he was reassigned. In the confusion of the transfer, Miller, who replaced Mellett, mailed the story for distribution in America.

Army officials saw the story printed in American newspapers about ten days later and wanted to know where Mellett had got his information and how it had got past censors. The list of gases in the story especially concerned the military. Mellett and UP's reputation held them in good stead, and the army accepted their explanation. After all, the story contained information that would have been readily apparent to any Germans who captured a soldier with one of the masks.[163]

"To Inflame Public Opinion against the Japanese Government"

The push to expand the NEA's reach globally also got the news service into trouble with military censors. Burton Knisely, normally assigned to the NEA's San Francisco bureau, had traveled to Japan to continue the NEA pattern of writing stories about life inside the borders of the belligerents. Knisely's "Japan Today" series began appearing in mid-July. Japan and the United States, allies in the fight against the Germans, were nonetheless friends with an uneasy relationship because of Americans' fears of Japanese imperialism. The Japanese government had gone out of its way to declare war against Germany in 1914 so it could grab German concessions in China and German-controlled islands in the Pacific.[164] In the late summer of 1918, the relationship between the Wilson administration and Japan was being tested in particular. Wilson had sent American troops to Archangel and Vladivostok as part of a multinational force because he feared the Japanese would intervene in Russia. Publicly it was said the troops were guarding Allied munitions and some Czech troops who wanted to continue to fight the Germans.[165]

Knisely's articles began appearing in NEA client newspapers during this swirl of suspicion, diplomacy, and sensitive military intervention. His first features were harmless observations about Japanese lifestyle and culture.[166] In one article, however, Knisely tackled directly the issue of whether Japan represented a "yellow peril" to the United States. An optimistic Knisely said he had spent "weeks of patient search and openmined investigation" and had found "no PRESENT danger" of Japanese aggression. He said the United States had to help Japan reform its "PRESENT political, social and spiritual organization" so as to help it peacefully enter "the family of nations." He also said he did not think Japan and the United States would come to conflict "in this generation."[167]

It was a Knisely story about Japanese pottery manufacturing, however, that got him into trouble with censorship authorities in San Francisco, including the U.S. Naval Intelligence Bureau. The chairman of the postal censorship committee said the headline of the article was "particularly objectionable at this time."[168] The *San Francisco Daily News* had headlined Knisely's pottery factory story "Look Out, Mr. Laboringman, Businessman, Storekeeper, Japan's after Your Bread and Butter." In the article, Knisely wrote about a pottery factory in Nagoya. "I came here [to Nagoya] to study one particular thing, one highly interesting thing—THE TRANSFORMATION OF HANDICRAFT JAPAN INTO FACTORY JAPAN." The article concluded with Knisely asserting that American pottery makers and other manufacturers should be wary because Japan was gearing to compete with them for world markets. He said the "bread and butter" of American business was at stake if it did not pay attention to the increasing industrialization of Japan.[169]

The U.S. navy's cable censor office wrote to Creel about Knisely's articles, which it claimed were of a "nature to inflame public opinion against the Japanese Government, one of our Allies."[170] Thomas Bryan, the assistant chief cable censor, asked Creel to intervene because the article had not been cabled and was outside his jurisdiction.[171] Creel immediately asked Canfield for an explanation. Canfield answered that the two hundred clients of the NEA had already printed more than twenty of Knisely's articles on Japan and this was "the first breath of criticism heard from anywhere in the country." Canfield said that before Knisely had left for Japan, he had been told not to write anything "that would tend to hurt Japan's feelings. It was decided to make the articles informative, interesting, entertaining and up to date."[172] Canfield said military censors in San Francisco read every article before they were printed.

Canfield said he thought it was the "yellow peril" article that Knisely wrote that probably drew undeserved attention to the series. That particular article was printed in the *San Francisco Daily News* under the headline "Will Japan Fight Us? X-Ray Turned on the 'Yellow Peril?'" Canfield told Creel he thought that the catchy headline drove the censors to think that Knisely's writings were "inflammatory and dangerous," even though the censors did not read the article thoroughly. "All thru the article there were . . . a lot . . . of such reassuring statements and paragraphs, to the very end. No Japanese could have said it better." Creel agreed. He told Canfield he would write to "all the various censorship authorities" who complained. The matter was dropped.[173]

The False Armistice

During the first week of November, the end of the war in Europe seemed to be near. By November 3, Germany's allies—Bulgaria, Turkey, and Austria—had surrendered. "In every city, town, and village, in every family, in every heart, there was tension, a feeling of emotion tugging to explode," journalist Mark Sullivan wrote in 1939, describing the first week of November 1918.[174]

Howard found the same excitement and anticipation in the French port city of Brest, where he was waiting with his wife to take a troop transport back to New York. So it is plausible he felt he was the luckiest newsman in the world after he paid a courtesy call on American admiral Henry B. Wilson, commander of U.S. naval forces in France. When Howard arrived to see Wilson about 4 P.M., he found the admiral's office full of excitement. The admiral had received a telegram stating that the armistice had been signed at eleven that morning, and fighting had stopped at 2 P.M.

"I twice inquired . . . as to whether the news was official, and being fully assured, knowing the extreme conservation of all army and navy officials in such matters, asked the admiral if I might use the dispatch," Howard said later in an *Editor and Publisher* article. "'Certainly, go ahead,' replied the admiral."

Howard asked for a translator and hurried off to the office of the French newspaper *La Depeche,* which had an agreement with UP to send cables to New York. In the meantime, Admiral Wilson had the conductor of a United States marine band playing in the town square outside of his office announce the armistice to the gathered crowd, which set off a frenzy. "As I went to the office of *La Depeche* the streets were thronged with excited French men and women, hugging and kissing every American soldier or sailor they could catch," Howard recalled.[175]

Howard assumed the UP bureau in Paris had the same news, but he hurried to send his own dispatch to New York in case the telegraph cables from Paris to Brest were jammed. He was in the best position. Brest, after all, was a head-end for the transatlantic cable to New York. "My only thought was to 'back up the play,'" Howard explained later, although he undoubtedly was eager to play a part in the war's last big scoop. He cabled, in the shorthand language of the wire services:

UNIPRESS NEWYORK

URGENT ARMISTICE ALLIES GERMANY SIGNED ELEVEN SMORNING HOSTILITIES CEASED TWO SAFTERNOON SEDAN TAKEN SMORNING BY AMERICANS

HOWARD SIMMS[176]

"Simms" referred to the Paris bureau chief, who was UP's designee for cabling messages from France. Howard also sent a brief second cable describing the jubilation in the streets of Brest. That message reached the UP office in New York and seemed to confirm the first cablegram.

Howard assumed that the French censor at the Brest cable office would kill his cablegrams if the armistice story indeed were false. But he did not know that the cable office had heard of the announcement made at the band concert. No French censor would doubt Howard's cables under those circumstances. The telegraph was sent, no questions asked. Howard later lamented: "The only time . . . censorship might have functioned to the advantage of a newspaper man—it had not."[177]

Howard soon was doubting his initial telegraph. While he was eating his dinner at a local restaurant, some U.S. army officers told him the French army had said the armistice announcement was unconfirmed. He then went looking for Wilson, telling the admiral about the French army report. The admiral "was not disturbed, however, still believing the news was true," Howard said. He said the situation left him "annoyed" but "not particularly worried." He then sent a third cablegram, two hours after his first one, reporting the armistice story was "not official and was not confirmed." Howard did not know it at the time, but this third cablegram would not reach the New York bureau for nearly twenty-four hours, and by then it was too late.

"Such an Almighty Fluke!"

Howard's first cablegram arrived in New York at 11:20 A.M. on November 7 and was quickly put on all the UP wires. A navy wireless operator later said the dissemination of the news "certainly deserves being termed a marvel, first for getting a copy of that message [from the admiral] and secondly for getting it into America in such quick shape."[178] United Press clients quickly gobbled up the news. The *Cleveland Press* called the armistice story "the great beat in newspaper history" and said it got the UP report at "exactly noon" and had its "Peace Extra" edition on the streets "just one minute after the United Press flash was received. As usual, the *Press* beat all its competitors."[179]

Throughout the country, people reacted to the news with joy. Sullivan described what he saw in New York City: "Universal holiday was assumed and not questioned. Crowds stampeded out of offices and factories. No traffic could move. Confetti and ticker-tape rained from office windows.... A melting exulting, half-sobbing, half-heart-lifting mood seized upon a whole city."[180]

Associated Press accounts on the following day said the festivities in New York were "a combination of Fourth of July, election night, New Year's Eve, Thanksgiving Day and Christmas merged."[181] The *Cleveland Plain-Dealer* reported that the crowd insisted the report was true: "Extras of afternoon papers cried conflicting statements concerning peace, but emphatic denial the armistice had been signed failed to dampen the enthusiasm and joy of those who gave the peace report the full benefit of the doubt."[182]

In Chicago, the *Daily Tribune* described the premature peace celebrations as "the most madly riotous scene that Chicago has ever witnessed."[183] The *Washington Post* said the streets of the capital became a "swirling mass of hilarious humanity, especially along Pennsylvania Avenue, which was the scene of scores of impromptu parades." The celebration lasted until midnight.[184] The excitement was duplicated in city after city. The *Atlanta Constitution* said millions would not know "they were fooled until they read the morning papers."[185]

Sullivan said after about four hours of celebrating in New York, the UP story became "too damn exclusive" because no rival newspapers were following it up. War Secretary Baker and Secretary of State Robert Lansing could not confirm the story. "Little by little people looked at each other, realized their delusion. The heart went out of the excitement," Sullivan said.[186]

The heart was out of the excitement of the UP bureaus, too. Hours passed, but no additional reports came from Howard or Simms at the Paris bureau. The New York office was flooded with inquires from newspaper editors wondering why AP contended the armistice was unconfirmed. William Hawkins, the UP vice president, stood his ground. After all, the cablegram had come from Howard and Simms, two of the most respected men in the Concern. Attempts to reach Howard or Simms from New York were unsuccessful because the cables were jammed.[187]

Early the next morning Hawkins received an anonymous telephone call that he believed to be from the American naval censor's office, telling him that Howard had sent a third cablegram, which said the armistice was unconfirmed, but the American military had intercepted it. This cablegram was not delivered to UP until late in the morning of November 8.[188] The damage had been done.

By now Howard, too, knew the armistice report was false, and he had some idea of what had taken place in the United States. He said he went to the office of Admiral Wilson on the morning of November 8 "and laid my cards on the table, explaining that about the only tangible asset of a press association is its reputation for accuracy and dependability."[189] Trying to control damage to the news service, Admiral Wilson gave him a statement that led the UP's explanation printed on November 8. Wilson said UP had "acted in perfect good faith, and that the premature announcement was the result of an error, for which the agency was in no wise responsible." The UP story explained the military's delay in delivering Howard's third cablegram and reprinted Howard's messages from Brest.[190]

Many of the Concern's rivals could not resist an opportunity to pummel the upstart UP for this mistake. Joseph Pulitzer's *St. Louis Post-Dispatch,* which earlier in the war had found UP good enough to steal its copy, now called the news service the perpetrator of a hoax that was "the most colossal and impudent in the history of American journalism."[191] The *Post-Dispatch* printed a full-page advertisement saying that it was the only evening newspaper in the city that "did not falsely announce the End of the War!" The advertisement also mentioned that the *Post-Dispatch* used the "Reliable ASSOCIATED PRESS."[192]

In Toledo, the *Times* said the revelry spawned in the city "wrecked the homefront" by bringing the city to a standstill. It called the *News-Bee* a "Judas."[193] A later editorial said the armistice story "did more than all the propaganda of the German government was able to do in four years" by stopping war work in Toledo for the day.[194] Even the normally friendly

Toledo Blade called the armistice story "rotten, reprehensible newspaper work."[195]

Other newspapers resisted taking overt shots and instead boosted AP as the better alternative. The *Columbus Evening Dispatch* said AP "does not handle rumors or gossip. It deals only in the solid facts of the activities of the world."[196] The *New York Times* said the blame needed to be shared between UP's Paris bureau and the French censor who allowed the cablegram to be sent.[197] A later editorial in the *New York Times* said the public reaction to the story showed how much everyone knew the war's end was soon to come. "It was not celebrating a newspaper 'fake,' but a great historic fact"—that the war was about to end.[198]

The false armistice story was a huge embarrassment to UP and left a bitter taste in the mouths of those who had worked so hard to compete with, and often beat, AP during the war. The incident, however, soon died down and had little effect on UP business. For example, in Toledo, where the criticism was its harshest, Cochran told Bob that "public sentiment was quite generally with the *News-Bee*" despite attacks in the *Times* and *Blade*. Cochran said AP members would have made the same mistake if their president, Stone, "had been at Brest and had sent the same wire." Cochran admitted the situation in Toledo had been "mighty tense . . . for twenty-four hours" until Admiral Wilson's explanation was printed.[199]

Not everyone in the Concern was as forgiving. Paine said the armistice story "was awful" and the admiral's "assumption of the character of 'goat' was only partial relief." Paine said Howard should have known that no armistice could have been struck so quickly. "However, the damage falls largely on the United Press rather than our editors . . . regardless of what our competitors said about the matter," Paine surmised. "It cannot be denied that the U.P. service throughout the war has been perfectly fine. Too bad that its record should be impaired by such an almighty fluke!"[200]

United Press acted quickly to repair its reputation, placing an advertisement titled "Big Enough to Be Fair" in *Editor and Publisher* by the end of November. The ad reprinted two editorials from two newspapers, both of whom were "not receiving United Press Service," empathizing with UP. One from the *Topeka Capital* called the armistice story "an honest error, founded on what appeared with reason to be official advices."[201] Joe Alex Morris, in his 1975 book about UP, said "amazingly, [UP] lost only one client on the basis of the November 7 armistice story—the Burlington *News* in Vermont."[202] In 1936 Howard said the public quickly forgave UP. "The indignation and outraged feelings of the Associated Press were of slight interest to the public." Howard said he believed a German spy had planted the armistice rumor to get the public to pressure the Allies to stop the war.[203]

A week before the war officially ended on November 11, Andersson noted in a letter to the NEA's Hughes, "interest in the military end of the war is waning. . . . Get your Washington men to envision peace conditions, not war."[204] With UP's war coverage now a source of embarrassment, a change in topic surely was welcome.

1918 had ushered in many changes. A Scripps newspaper now cost two cents. Bob Scripps had been removed from management and then put back in a new position. The NEA had been transformed into an information service, and was no longer a vehicle to distribute Scripps editorial policy to other newspapers. Despite the journalistic errors made in the false armistice story, the Concern's editors had learned that it was easier to report the news than to try to shape public opinion.

Conclusion: "Harder... to Be of Public Service"

Four years of covering a world war had changed the Scripps Concern in ways its leaders could not have anticipated in 1914. Much of the war's impact was positive: profits were fatter, readership was up, and more newspapers were buying UP and NEA services. These two services, in particular, had shown they could compete in and adapt to complex, international news environments.

But the war also was a negative force. It created a split among E.W, Bob, and Jim Scripps over how the family should manage the newspaper chain. The Concern's longstanding reputation for strong, independent, progressive advocacy, something upon which E.W. had built his chain, also was tarnished. In its quest to be a national force in remaking government and society through progressive politics, the Concern had been frustrated and embarrassed. It was now more timid about its advocacy. In 1916 the Concern had given up its political independence to support President Wilson boldly, and when the United States entered the war, it had felt obligated to support how the president waged it. It did not matter that the president's actions were often politically controversial and sometimes seemingly incompetent—the Concern refused to challenge him or his administration. Progressive politics and a war, in a complicated brew, had made permanent changes in the Scripps newspaper chain.

"We Are Richer by Reason of the War"

The war certainly solidified the Concern's finances going into the 1920s. Exact financial data for the war years in the Scripps archives are spotty, but E.W. Scripps wrote in July 1919 that "the institution is in a very prosperous condition." War taxes and higher operating costs had curtailed the increases to some degree, but "it can be assumed that the expansion of our business and the appreciation of values have been permanent. . . . In other words, we are richer by reason of the war than we would have been had there been no war." Scripps said the aggregate receipts for the entire Concern in May alone were more than $1 million, and he valued the entire business at a minimum of $30 million.[1]

In 1957 historian Joe Alex Morris wrote that UP recovered quickly after its 1918 setbacks in South America, and by 1919 the wire service was "highly profitable," with 745 clients in the United States, Canada, and Latin America.[2] Indeed, Howard told Scripps in January 1920 that UP had earned a profit of $180,000 in 1919.[3] Foreign editor James Henry Furay, writing a recap of UP's war activities in the *Editor and Publisher* of May 22, 1919, said the wire service had "increased its prestige and clientele . . . throughout the world."[4] Despite the embarrassment of the false armistice story, UP was thriving.

No financial data for the NEA at war's end survives, but because it was so closely tied to the fortunes of the Scripps newspapers, one can assume it did well. One study has noted that the circulation and advertising revenue for the Scripps newspapers grew from $4,472,000 in 1908 to $17,000,000 in 1920, while advertising revenue for the entire newspaper industry during the same period increased from $148,554,000 to $521,685,000. Thus the Scripps chain did better on average over this twelve-year span.[5]

As a whole, the Scripps newspapers grew in circulation from 890,884 readers in 1914 to 932,942 in 1919, a 4.7 percent increase. That was a solid increase, considering that each issue doubled in price from one penny to two during this time, but it lags behind the growth of the competing dailies in the same markets. Overall, the direct competitors to the Scripps newspapers grew in circulation at a 9.8 percent rate from 1914 to 1919. The most unsettling figure among the circulation statistics during the war years was that circulation for the *Cincinnati Post*—the second largest Scripps newspaper—dropped 9.2 percent from 1914 to 1919, while competitors in that market saw their circulation rise overall by a modest 1 percent. No explanation (except for the price increase) is evident for the decrease, although Cincinnati was a hotbed of criticism of the Scripps draft exemptions. The impact of the draft criticism was also evident in Toledo, where the *News-Bee* took hits on the issue, too. Circulation for the *News-Bee* remained virtually the same, increasing by twenty-three readers from 1914 to 1919, but it lost its position as the highest circulation newspaper in town to the evening *Blade*, which gained nearly forty-three thousand readers.[6]

Covering History's Biggest Story

On the basis of the archival records, the respect and credibility the Scripps Concern earned for its news coverage of the war itself appear to be justified. In fact, the Scripps newspapers did a fairer job of covering World War I than some historians apparently have thought was possible for newspapers in this era. Stewart Halsey Ross, in his 1996 study of propaganda during the war, said, "Germany [at war's outbreak] almost overnight faced a generally hostile U.S. press," and every English-language newspaper in America was "editorially parroting England's propaganda line" because of its controls on the transatlantic cables and attempts to influence public opinion.[7]

The evidence about the Scripps newspaper chain, the largest in the country at the time, shows that those generalizations are too broad. The Scripps newspapers, at least until early 1917, worked to remain neutral and balanced in how they covered the war. United Press built much of its reputation on the sympathetic news it managed to get out of Germany early in the war. The Scripps newspapers, too, through the NEA, avoided blaming the Germans for the sinking of the *Lusitania* in 1915. Only when war seemed inevitable in March 1917 did the Scripps newspapers abandon any sense of fair play in their news coverage, and it was not until a year later that it began to print anti-German atrocity propaganda.

Furthermore, no evidence exists that suggests the Concern worked actively with pro-British propaganda agents who operated in the United States before 1917. The British propaganda bureau was managed by fiction writer Sir Gilbert Parker. One historian has said that British propagandists' "almost complete capture of American correspondents ensured that in American newspapers the war would be seen as if through British eyes."[8] Historian Horace C. Peterson in 1939 made a more accurate observation about British influence on the American press's impartiality when he noted that the "most noteworthy aspect of Western and Midwestern newspapers from 1914 to 1917 was the lack of attention given to the war." He said that the British were dumbfounded by the lack of interest in the war in the West and Midwest but were pleased that the war dispatches from Europe did mimic the line dictated by British censors.[9] Undoubtedly, UP, under the watchful eye of military censors by 1915, was at the mercy of the Allied governments. Censorship eliminated all independent reporting and opportunities to duplicate the notable scoops that UP had generated early in the war. Yet those same military controls saved UP money and kept it competitive by forcing it to rely on government handouts; it could concentrate its correspondents with each of the Allied armies, assured that its rivals had to do the same.

The record of cooperation with the CPI, America's chief propaganda bureau, is unclear. The Concern's top news people resented the CPI for its apparent incompetence and inefficiencies, but professional jealousy was likely to blame for some of that. George Creel was essentially the secretary of the people that Neg Cochran had hoped to be, and the CPI standardized the way newspapers obtained government information at a time when the Concern was accustomed to getting Washington news on its own. As historian Stephen Ponder said in 1998, "the flood of news releases from the CPI and the wartime agencies went far to complete the institutionalization of the 'handout' as a preferred form of communication between the government and the news media."[10] Still, the CPI's failure to correct its mailing lists and Creel's unwillingness to use fully the Scripps newspaper chain show the CPI was not always the shrewd and efficient propaganda machine that historians have generally described.

Beyond Censorship and Propaganda

Certainly, censorship and government propaganda, the major influences on World War I news cited by historians, were not the only reasons that the Scripps newspapers covered the war as they did. Competition from other news organizations also played a part, as it created an unprecedented world demand for news and a way to show which news service was best. The pressure to beat one's news rivals was exemplified in the push for scoops, the problems with news piracy, and the theft of top news correspondents, such as Karl Von Wiegand. United Press used the war to its advantage, though, expanding to South America and positioning itself as the best alternative to AP. The NEA felt the heat of competition, too. With the coming of two-cent newspapers, the NEA remade itself in 1918 to better compete with other syndicates, adding more staff to write unique features about the war and no longer producing editorials for its non-Scripps clients, who wanted more news and less opinion.

The Scripps editors did the best they could to listen to their readers, too. Audience research was limited, for the most part, to mail-in surveys, interviews with subscribers, and informal discussions with people on the street. In 1915 and 1916, war news moved back and forth from the front to the inside pages and was reduced or increased, depending on perceived public interest. Concerns about alienating German American readers led the Scripps newspapers to avoid taking sides in the war before 1917. Great care was taken to report the war in the Scripps style—explaining it simply and with an eye toward human interest.

Technology was another factor that influenced the Concern's coverage of the war a great deal. The NEA relied on the postal system to deliver its product, so its stories tended to be less time sensitive and more feature oriented. Its editorials were less time sensitive as well. Cabled stories from Europe were short, not so much because that was the Scripps style of writing as because stories were expensive to send. The cable from Europe often was jammed with messages, too. The false armistice story can be blamed on the limits of 1918 communication technology as much as anything else. During the war, the limits on news carried on the transatlantic cable, the backbone of the UP report, caused the Scripps newspapers to turn to the NEA. The NEA was already providing most of the national news stories to Scripps newspapers and to increasing numbers of non-Scripps clients, but increasingly it was asked to feed the public's desire for war news, too.

The structure of the NEA, the editorial-policy nerve center of the Concern, influenced the news it produced and the policies it advocated. Most of the NEA's news originated in its Washington bureau, which tended to rely on the news and ideas emanating from the capital.[11] Only in the fall of 1918 did the NEA make an attempt to establish news bureaus in Europe, and only after adding even more reporters to the Washington bureau. Although the NEA's focus on the capital encouraged it to write about the president and see him as the center of power, the Scripps men had little direct contact with Wilson. Instead they relied on continual access, especially before 1917, to many of his key advisors, including interior secretary Franklin Lane, navy secretary Josephus Daniels, Supreme Court justice Louis Brandeis, and war secretary Newton Baker. This apparently had some implications in the Concern's support for preparedness in 1915 and for the need to declare war on Germany in early 1917. Both of these positions were at odds with the president's, but they mirrored what his cabinet was urging him to support. The Washington bureau also worked closely with the Army and Navy Leagues in 1915 to prepare inexpensive content to promote the building of a larger navy and the establishment of universal military training.

Although the Scripps chain professed to give each local editor plenty of autonomy, the control an editor had was limited because he had to rely on the NEA and UP for virtually all of his paper's news about the war and national politics. Editors-in-chief above each local editor, in turn, watched the content of their group's newspapers. The NEA, which received copies of all Scripps newspapers, monitored the entire Concern. Thus, the local control each editor possessed on national and world news was somewhat of an illusion. Editors criticized overt attempts to dictate exactly what NEA copy should be run—"Must Copy"—but the fact remains that the NEA had great organizational power to influence the content of any Scripps newspaper. Editors could refuse to use an NEA story, delete some of its passages, or handle the graphic display differently but could do little else to produce alternative content about the war or President Wilson. Even the *Los Angeles Record*'s locally written criticism of the Wilson administration in the summer of 1917, led by Jim Scripps, was eventually quashed by internal institutional pressure applied by the Scripps Concern's power center in the East.

Jim's support of the Wilson criticism was the only editorial initiative he was active in during the war. For the most part, the Scripps sons, though they had top executive positions, had little direct impact on how the war was covered. Jim stayed on the West Coast for most of the war and trusted Canfield and the other top editors to make the decisions about how to cover the war. Bob was made chief of war policy in the fall of 1917 to justify his exemption from the draft, but it is clear from the surviving archives that he had little influence and was taken off the job before the war was over.

As Bob's mentor, Cochran was the de facto head of war policy by late 1917. Indirectly, Bob's appointment had noteworthy impact on how the Concern covered the final year of the war because the appointment caused internal dissension and caused Rickey, a seasoned editor, to resign. The need to mentor Bob also distracted Cochran, and his editorship of the *Toledo News-Bee* suffered. E.W., although retired during this period, remained the most dominant personality, pushing for a secretary of the people for Wilson, a campaign for income tax publicity, and, ultimately, support for Wilson in 1916.

Wilson and War

E.W.'s fascination with Wilson grew gradually from 1912 until reaching its zenith in the 1916 election. Wilson seemed to embody the Scripps principles of social justice when he worked an ambitious agenda of political reforms through Congress early in his first term. The attraction was sealed when he played to E.W.'s ego by entertaining suggestions that the Concern might become the president's personal publicity machine, and later left open the possibility of publicizing income tax returns to catch cheaters. If the war in Europe had not intervened, one wonders what alliances might have developed between the Concern and Wilson.

But it was the Concern's belief that it played a vital part in reelecting Wilson that finally cemented its commitment to him and made it feel responsible for his second term. To criticize the president after November 1916 would appear hypocritical, even after his administration bungled important aspects of the war mobilization. This allegiance to Wilson, coupled with determined patriotism, was an overriding influence on how the Concern covered the war and America's effort in it beginning in 1917. The Concern was not hoodwinked into supporting the war against Germany by the CPI or British propagandists; it made decisions based on its own patriotism, its realization that Germany must be stopped, and a feeling that it was responsible for Wilson and his administration.

Disillusionment

The war's biggest influence on the Concern was on its progressive spirit and on the tone of its advocacy. The changes are evident when one examines the editorial conference Jim Scripps organized in July 1919. The forces that had shaped the war news of the Scripps Concern were now shaping its organization and corporate mission.

Seventeen of the Concern's top editors, business executives, and stockholders, including Jim and Bob Scripps, gathered in San Diego on July 1 to adopt and publish a "Declaration of Principles" to guide them and to tell readers what they could expect from a postwar Scripps newspaper. Bob wrote Jim on June 28, "you stated, and I agreed, that nine-tenths of the reading matter of our newspapers is properly devoted to 'telling the people what they want to hear'—news, features, comics, etc.; and that one-tenth is properly devoted to telling them 'what we think they ought to know'—editorial and policy matter."[12]

None of the conferees disagreed on the need to change one important part of current editorial and policy—the Concern's unconditional support for President Wilson. Bob, head of the Scripps editorial board, spoke for all when he said it was time to distance the Concern from Wilson. "It seems to me that supporting an administration as such in time of war is a defensable policy; but that the same course in time of peace is not," he wrote to Jim.[13] The conferees agreed unanimously, and C. F. Mosher summarized the consensus:

> My understanding of R. P. [Bob] Scripps' attitude is briefly this: During the war we printed some things we would ordinarily not have printed, and refrained from printing some things we ordinarily would have printed. The motive governing these decisions was a desire to help win the war. Now that the war is over, Mr. Scripps believes that we should go back to the normal Scripps policy of independence, and that the policy should be the controlling motive in the conduct of our newspapers.[14]

Other questions about the direction of future editorial policy were much more controversial. Should the Concern continue to advocate aggressively for progressive causes as it had for publicity of income taxes? The Scripps newspapers had built their reputation as fighters for the working class, but Jim had assembled a conference of men who tended to see the Concern first and foremost as a business enterprise. He had not invited his father to join the conference, even though E.W. was living nearby at Miramar. The war and E.W.'s meddling had left a rift between father and son, and Jim knew he and his father would lock horns on any fundamental changes in editorial policy.

The situation frustrated E.W. He thought with Jim at the helm his chain was becoming more conservative and too profit-conscious as it grew. E.W. wrote an open letter to the editorial conference, pleading with it to keep longstanding Scripps principles in mind. "We can afford, and we should feel ourselves duty bound, more now than ever before, to do right, even if the doing right shall not be immediately profitable." Scripps reminded the conferees that the readers of Scripps newspapers had put "great confidence in us as instructors and leaders," and he urged them to conduct the Concern in a "spirit and motive" based first on public service and "only secondarily and incidentally, and necessarily, intelligently conducted as a business institution."[15]

Scripps privately doubted the sincerity of any "Declaration of Principles" that this editorial conference would produce. "The peculiar thing about this editorial conference was that it was not an editorial conference," he wrote to Gilson Gardner on July 27. "Some fifteen or twenty lawyers, business office managers and publishers assembled and along with them several—three at least, or maybe four or five—editors."[16] Indeed, the Scripps men who had gathered had different perspectives on the role of a newspaper. This group was most concerned about maintaining and building circulation, and not championing social justice no matter the cost.

Scripps felt that summer that the Scripps principles needed to be championed more than ever. The Concern needed to take chances and be a leader on issues, with the country in the middle of industrial and social upheaval. "It appears to me that as a matter of fact, this war has not only made the rich richer, but has really made the poor poorer," he noted on July 27.[17] During the year four million—a fifth of the country's workforce—would participate in thirty-six hundred strikes, most of them disputes over wages that were not keeping pace with inflation.[18] The first troops began arriving home in April 1919 and could not find jobs, straining the labor situation even more. Wilson, obsessed with the peace treaty negotiations in Paris, also had no plan to convert war industries to a peacetime basis, and this caused many workers to lose their jobs. With all this combined with a series of bombing incidents and calls from Bolsheviks and American radicals to revolt, American society in 1919 was in upheaval. One historian wrote in 1990, "during the war Americans had been admonished to think and act patriotically, and the armistice did not break the grip of this wartime psychology. In 1919 it provided the atmosphere for the explosion of a Red Scare in America."[19]

Scripps undoubtedly knew his newspapers had helped create that wartime psychology, and he felt the Concern was responsible for electing Wilson and his administration, which was responding clumsily. Wartime sedition laws were still in force in 1919 and were being used by attorney general A. Mitchell Palmer to prosecute vigorously the radicals believed to be behind the social unrest.[20] "To call the age extraordinary is putting it mildly," Tom Sidlo, a Concern attorney, said on October 1. "Perhaps you older men have seen situations in the past as jumbled as the present national panorama, but I doubt it."[21]

Since November 1918, Scripps had worked behind the scenes to try to get Wilson to grant an amnesty to all political prisoners and conscientious objectors jailed during the war.[22] He also wanted a repeal of all wartime restraints on freedom of speech and the press. "There is a vast public discontent especially amongst the working class ... because of the suppression of free speech, free assembly and free press. This policy is continuing months after the time when there was any excuse at all for it," he wrote Wilson advisor E. M. House at the Paris Peace Conference on May 16.[23] Scripps asked Sidlo to try to convince War Secretary Baker to support these proposals, and he asked Gardner to approach Navy Secretary Daniels and Justice Brandeis to talk to Wilson about them as well.[24] Although the president considered granting amnesty to all political prisoners during the summer of 1919, Palmer talked him out of it.[25]

Most of the men gathered for the editorial conference were not nearly as interested in amnesty as E.W. was. They were not interested in launching any major advocacy campaigns. The topic was on the conferees' agenda, but most were more concerned about money. "The question with me is whether adopting these resolutions about freeing political prisoners, and so on, is going to make us circulation," Jim Scripps said in the minutes. LeRoy Sanders, editor-in-chief of the Northwest Group, concurred that his editors "did not want their circulation-making programming cluttered up with a lot of propaganda." Earle Martin of the Ohio Group agreed, saying the test for every item had to be "is it interesting?" He said that test was more important now with two-cent papers.

Bob chimed in, asking Sanders, "You hold to the theory that you are running a public service institution, don't you, and that your financial success is in a large measure to do this?" Sanders, realizing he was being challenged on a Scripps principle, answered "Certainly." But he noted that his editors had "to slip over their sermon with a vaudeville show. . . . To preach dull policy or principles nowadays when people were tired of the war was to take a chance of losing their support."[26]

The exchange at the editorial conference revealed what E.W. feared. As he noted in a January 1920 letter to Gardner, "my view as you perhaps know, is that the already developed wealth of my own institution makes it harder for it to be of public service."[27] Size bred conservatism and a profit mentality. Another of Scripps's fears came to pass at the conference. Jim was convinced he could not work with his brother, and he was tired of his father's meddling. On the last day, he promoted Canfield from president of the NEA to assistant chairman of the board, responsible for managing the Scripps newspapers. It was the job as second-in-command that E.W. had wanted for Bob. Andersson replaced Canfield.[28]

Scripps had been working with Sidlo to establish a holding company that would, in Sidlo's words, "create a situation where one son will have control of the business and without interfering with the control of other son, or of yourself, of the editorial end."[29] Jim's promotion of Canfield, however, led Scripps to strip Jim of the power-of-attorney controls and give them to Bob. This familial power play between father and son escalated and resulted in the six West Coast newspapers breaking away into a separate chain. Although Jim died from an illness in January 1921 at age thirty-seven, his widow Josephine finished the battle and separated the six papers from the Concern in August 1921.

This split had broad implications for the future direction of the remaining Concern's editorial policies. Roy Howard was promoted to chairman of the Concern to help Bob in June 1920 as the relationship with Jim deteriorated.[30] Howard was much more ambitious and aggressive than any of the Scripps sons. He also was probably more politically conservative than Jim. By the late 1920s, Howard was leading the Concern's editorial policies farther from progressivism. "The chain's papers have become increasingly orthodox," press critic A. J. Liebling wrote in 1941 regarding Howard's conservative influence on the Concern, "and they no longer reveal any of the Scripps crotchets about the dangers of monopoly or the right of labor to organize."[31] While Howard's later leadership certainly played a part in the move to the right politically, the dynamics of the 1919 editorial conference show that the younger leaders of the Concern were ready to rethink much of the Scripps editorial spirit. Only after E.W. died in 1926 and Bob showed increasing deference to Howard's bolder leadership did this generation of editors and executives put the move to the right into practice.

E.W.'s actions during the war had destroyed any ability he had to work with Jim and made a split seemingly inevitable. The draft issue had caused E.W. to force Bob into a prominent role in the family business, angering Jim. E.W. also felt Bob was more committed to the principles that had built the chain, and he tended to acquiesce to his father's demands. At the editorial conference Bob insisted the Concern take a stand on one of his father's pet issues—the release of political prisoners, especially Eugene Debs, a Socialist Party presidential candidate who had been jailed for sedition. The conference rejected a resolution that called for the Scripps newspapers to "advocate" the release of the war's political prisoners, by an eleven-to-five vote on the third day of the conference.[32] Bob brought the issue back two days later with a motion that said the Concern would "favor" the release of the prisoners, and that resolution passed ten to eight. Bob, however, was only able to sway the vote by stating that Debs was doing more harm than good in jail as a martyr of government oppression.[33]

Bob also found a compromise on another contentious issue facing the conferees, the Treaty of Versailles and the League of Nations. The conferees favored the treaty, but many felt the League would entangle America too much in world matters. Jim felt the League would keep monarchies in power, but he tended to support it because the public seemed to want it. "It is probably good business for us to be for the League," he told the conference, showing again that he was focused on the bottom line.[34] The League was too unpalatable for the others, however. Bob ultimately secured support for a proposal that he already had championed through the Scripps editorial board—a call for a national referendum on the issue. A resolution to let the people decide passed, eight to seven.[35]

The conferees ultimately passed fifty-two resolutions in their Declaration of Principles. On paper, the platform made it appear the Scripps principles were alive and well. The resolutions included calls for a national conference of capital, labor, and consumers to devise a new plan for industrial relations, an eight-hour day, a prohibitive tax against child labor, a living wage for labor, collective bargaining rights, government supports for affordable housing, the abolition of West Point and Annapolis in favor of a "democratic army and navy," and taxation based on ability to pay. Interestingly, although the conferees reluctantly had agreed to favor the release of political prisoners, that resolution was not included among the fifty-two. Instead, the declaration favored "the resumption of the right of free press, free speech and free public assembly."[36]

In reality, these were issues to be supported, not necessarily aggressively advocated. The conferees sensed the public was not ready for any more publicity campaigns. As one historian has written: "Some observers have suggested that the United States in 1919 was tired—tired of Great Crusades, of reform, even of progress. . . . It was a spiritual fatigue, involving a lack of moral stamina, of faith in the principles of democracy, of wisdom, and of effective leadership, which finally brought the nation to the brink of nervous exhaustion."[37]

Scripps wholeheartedly agreed with the editorial conference on one issue: he no longer wanted to align his newspapers so closely to one political candidate. On January 10, 1920, he wrote Gardner two letters about the upcoming presidential election. Although E.W. said the country was in "need of a great leader . . . I am not desiring to try my hand again at making a President."[38] Scripps said the only potential candidate who interested him was food administrator Herbert Hoover, who he predicted would be more independent than anyone nominated by either political party. "As you know," Scripps wrote in his second letter to Gardner, "I would rather not be the supporter under any circumstances of a winning candidate. My own personal interest or desire would be to be left in a position to freely criticize a candidate like Hoover, both during and subsequent to the campaign."[39]

Despite his strong opinions in his letter to the editorial conference, the war and the upheaval of the Red Scare had shaken his ideals about reforming the world through government. His thoughts are reflected in his "Blind Leader of the Blind" disquisition of July 1921. Abandoning some of his belief in democracy, Scripps wrote, "The workingman, because he has been a workingman, is necessarily ignorant in matters political and economic. Being ignorant, he is self-confident and knows naught of . . . his power to vastly injure himself as well as all of his fellows in the nation." Still, the publisher insisted, democracy was the best government.

Scripps said any demagoguery on his part was "through ignorance and thoughtlessness.... Once I was a poor man and hated the capitalists and now I am a capitalist and I see the other side of the question."[40] Deep down, perhaps, Scripps understood all too well why the men gathered at the editorial conference were toning down the push for advocacy and reform.

Scripps maintained that the Wilson administration could have done more to ameliorate the problems that faced the country after the war. "In many ways I have been deeply grieved by Wilson's course, and all the time I have to be conscious of the fact that Wilson would not have been President the second time had I personally had the ideas concerning him that I now hold," he wrote fellow progressive Amos Pinchot in February 1920. He continued: "I only feel that everything that I was for decades before the middle of the year 1917 has passed away. I cannot feel that any of the political and other issues that absorbed me prior to that time are now living issues at all."[41] Even after Wilson left office Scripps admitted he "felt a sort of grudge against Mr. Wilson for not pardoning Debs and issuing a general amnesty."[42]

The grudge festered until friends urged Scripps to see the former president. Scripps visited Wilson for about fifteen minutes at the president's home in Washington on October 29, 1921. He was saddened by Wilson's physical appearance; he had not fully recovered from a stroke he had suffered on September 25, 1919. "Whatever little feeling of resentment that I had previously harbored against the man disappeared instantly. It was a pitiable sight. I certainly would not have recognized him had I seen him anywhere else."[43] The war's stresses had weakened and nearly killed the president. To some extent, the war had the same effect on the progressive editorial policies of the Scripps newspapers.

NOTES

Editor's Note

The Robert E. and Jean R. Mahn Center for Archives and Special Collections at Ohio University, Athens, began reorganizing many of the letters and other documents within its E. W. Scripps manuscript collection in 1998. Therefore, the box and folder numbers for Scripps correspondence cited in this book may no longer be accurate because the Scripps manuscript research for this book was done in 1994–96. Letters and other documents cited from the Scripps collection can still be found within the listed subseries by their dates and by names of the correspondents, however.

Introduction

1. E. W. Scripps to Thomas Sidlo, December 11, 1919, subseries 1.2, box 19, folder 8, E. W. Scripps Papers, Alden Library, Ohio University, Athens (hereafter EWS Papers).

2. Quoted in E. W. Scripps Company, *A Handbook of Scripps Howard* (Memphis, Tenn.: Memphis, 1948), 18.

3. In this study, this nickname will be capitalized for the sake of clarity; however, it is shown in lower case in nearly all the Scripps correspondence—perhaps because of modesty.

4. While wire services such as Associated Press could also be considered "national" media, a wire service could never mandate that any of its stories be printed or dictate how they were displayed, while the Scripps chain, a vertically integrated media company, could, with its own newspapers.

5. Loren B. Thompson, "The Media versus the Military: A Brief History of War Coverage of the United States," in *Defense Beat: The Dilemmas of Defense Coverage*, ed. Loren B. Thompson (New York: Macmillan Books, 1991), 3–5.

6. Michael Emery, Edwin Emery, and Nancy L. Roberts, *The Press and America*, 9th ed. (Boston: Allyn and Bacon, 2000), 252.

7. Thomas Fleming, *The Illusion of Victory: America in World War I* (New York: Basic Books, 2003), 43.

8. Stewart Halsey Ross, *Propaganda for War: How the United States Was Conditioned to Fight the Great War of 1914–1918* (Jefferson, N.C.: McFarland, 1996), 1.

9. H. C. Peterson, *Propaganda for War: The Campaign against American Neutrality, 1914–1917* (Norman: University of Oklahoma Press, 1939), 326.

10. Phillip Knightley, *The First Casualty: The War Correspondent as Hero and Myth-Maker from the Crimea to Kosovo*, rev. and updated with an introduction by John Pilger (London: Prion Books, 2000).

11. See Harold D. Lasswell, *Propaganda Technique in the World War* (1938; reprint, New York: Garland, 1972); Arthur Ponsonby, *Falsehood in War-Time: Containing an Assortment of Lies Circulated throughout the Nations during the Great War* (New York: Garland, 1971); James Morgan Read, *Atrocity Propaganda, 1914–1919* (New Haven: Yale University Press, 1941); Gary S. Messinger, *British Propaganda and the State in the First World War* (Manchester, England: Manchester University Press, 1972); Kathleen Burk, *Britain, America and the Sinews of War, 1914–1918* (Boston: Allen and Unwin, 1985); Cate Haste, *Keep the Home Fires Burning: Propaganda in the First World War* (London: Allen Lane, 1977); Peterson, *Propaganda for War*; and John Patrick Finnegan, *Against the Specter of a Dragon: The Campaign for American Military Preparedness, 1914–1917* (Westport, Conn.: Greenwood Press, 1974).

12. For books about the war protestors, see: Frederick C. Giffin, *Six Who Protested: Radical Opposition to the First World War* (Port Washington, N.Y.: Kennikat Press, 1977); H. C. Peterson and Gilbert C. Fite, *Opponents of War, 1917–1918* (1957; reprint, Seattle: University of Washington Press, 1968); Harry N. Scheiber, *The Wilson Administration and Civil Liberties 1917–1921* (Ithaca: Cornell University Press, 1960); and Ernest A. McKay, *Against War and Wilson, 1914–1917* (Malabar, Fla.: Krieger, 1996).

13. Joseph J. Mathews, *Reporting the Wars* (Minneapolis: University of Minnesota Press, 1957), 155–73; John Hohenberg, *Foreign Correspondence: The Great Reporters and Their Times* (Syracuse, N.Y.: Syracuse University Press, 1995), 80–118; Emmet Crozier, *American Reporters on the Western Front, 1914–1918* (Westport, Conn.: Greenwood Press, 1959); Harold Elk Straubing, ed., *The Last Magnificent War: Rare Journalistic and Eyewitness Accounts of World War I* (New York: Paragon House, 1989); M. L. Stein, *Under Fire: The Story of American War Correspondents* (New York: Julian Messner, 1968); and James R. Mock, *Censorship 1917* (Princeton: Princeton University Press, 1941).

14. Kevin O'Keefe, *A Thousand Deadlines: The New York City Press and American Neutrality, 1914–1917* (The Hague: Nijhoff, 1972). As the title suggests, O'Keefe focused on the New York City papers. Ralph Otto Nafziger, "The American Press and Public Opinion during the World War, 1914–April 1917" (Ph.D. diss., University of Wisconsin, 1936), 8–9, did not include a Scripps newspaper in his study of ten newspapers, and he did not explain his selection of newspapers, except to say that he included four New York newspapers because New York was an important receiving station. He included three Hearst papers. A few other papers were added to the group when Nafziger studied important crises during the April 1914–April 1917 period.

15. Alfred McLung Lee, *The Daily Newspaper in America* (New York: McMillan, 1947), 589.

16. See: James R. Mock and Cedric Larson, *Words That Won the War: The Story of the Committee on Public Information, 1917–1919* (Princeton: Princeton University Press, 1939); Stephen Vaughn, *Holding Fast the Inner Lines: Democracy, Nationalism, and the Committee on Public Information* (Chapel Hill: University

of North Carolina Press, 1980); and George Creel, *How We Advertised America* (1920; reprint, New York: Arno Press, 1972).

17. See Ben Bagdikian, *The Media Monopoly*, 6th ed. (Boston: Beacon Press, 2000).

18. See James Boylan, "The Bingham Saga," *Columbia Journalism Review*, July/August 1991): 96. See also John Morton, "Who's Buying," *American Journalism Review* (May 2003): 72. Morton called the Freedom sale a "classic example of what happens to a family-controlled newspaper company after three or four generations of ownership: Dissension within is resolved by selling the business."

19. Richard Siklos and Geraldine Fabrikant, "An Empire Shaken; Hands That Rocked the Cradle Now Shape a Company's Fate," *New York Times*, August 2, 2005.

20. See Edward Adams, "An Early Hostile Corporate Takeover: The Split of the Scripps Newspaper Empire, 1920–1922," paper presented at the annual meeting of the Association for Education in Journalism and Mass Communication, Chicago, July 30, 1997. See also Ed Adams, "How Corporate Ownership Facilitated a Split in the Scripps Newspaper Empire," *Journalism History* 27 (summer 2001): 56–73. Adams has focused on the actual split, but this study devotes much more time explaining the war period that set the stage for it.

21. John A. Thompson, *Reformers and War: American Progressive Publicists and the First World War* (Cambridge: Cambridge University Press, 1987), 7. Thompson's book does not include any Scripps journalists.

22. Louis Brandeis to Aaron Aaronsohn, August 13, 1916, in *Letters of Louis D. Brandeis*, vol. 3, ed. Melvin I. Urofsky and David W. Levy (Albany: State University of New York Press, 1973), 157.

23. Will Irwin, "The United Press," *Harper's Weekly*, April 25, 1914, 6.

24. Richard Kaplan, *Politics and the American Press* (Cambridge: Cambridge University Press), 2002.

25. Michael McGerr, *The Decline of Popular Politics* (New York: Oxford University Press, 1986), 107–8.

26. David Mindich, *Just the Facts: How Objectivity Came to Define American Journalism* (New York: New York University Press), 10.

27. Michael Schudson, *Discovering the News: A Social History of American Newspapers* (New York: Basic Books, 1978), 120–59.

28. E. W. Scripps, "A Blind Leader of the Blind," in *I Protest: Selected Disquisitions of E. W. Scripps*, ed. Oliver Knight (Madison: University of Wisconsin Press, 1966), 145.

29. Vance H. Trimble, *The Astonishing Mr. Scripps: The Turbulent Life of America's Penny Press Lord* (Ames: Iowa State University Press, 1992).

30. Edited writings can be found in: E. W. Scripps, *Faith in My Star*, ed. Vance Trimble (Memphis, Tenn.: Commercial Appeal, 1989); Knight, *I Protest;* and E. W. Scripps, *Damned Old Crank: A Self-Portrait of E. W. Scripps*, ed. Charles R. McCabe (New York: Harper, 1951). Two colleagues who wrote biographies of Scripps are: Negley Dakin Cochran, *E. W. Scripps* (1933; reprint, Ann Arbor, Mich.: University Microfilms, 1968); and Gilson Gardner, *Lusty Scripps: the Life of E. W. Scripps* (New York: Vanguard Press, 1932).

31. Gerald Baldasty, *E. W. Scripps and the Business of Newspapers* (Urbana:

University of Illinois Press, 1999). The circumstances of Scripps's retirement are described in: Knight, *I Protest*, 83.

32. This is how Scripps described his relationship to the Concern after retirement. See E. W. Scripps to Robert P. Scripps, April 16, 1917, subseries 3.1, box 49, folder 11, EWS Papers.

33. Joe Alex Morris, *Deadline Every Minute: The Story of the United Press* (Garden City, N.Y.: Doubleday, 1957).

34. Richard Harnett and Billy Ferguson, *Unipress: Covering the Twentieth Century* (Golden, Colo.: Fulcrum, 2003).

35. See William G. Shepherd, *Confessions of a War Correspondent* (New York: Harper, 1917); Webb Miller, *I Found No Peace* (New York: Literary Guild, 1936). Wilbur Forrest, *Behind the Front Page: Stories of Newspaper Stories in the Making* (New York: Appleton-Century, 1934), 15–217; and Oliver Pilat, *Pegler: Angry Man of the Press* (Boston: Beacon Press, 1963), 67–80. A second book about Pegler gives only brief attention to his days as a UP reporter during the war. See Finis Farr, *Fair Enough: The Life of Westbrook Pegler* (New Rochelle, N.Y.: Arlington House, 1975), 50–74.

Chapter 1: The Concern

1. The *Cleveland Press* had a circulation of 168,731 in April 1914, the largest of any afternoon or morning paper in the city. Meanwhile, that same month, the *Cincinnati Post*, Scripps's second largest paper, had a circulation of 106,924, second to the Taft family's *Time-Star* (another evening newspaper) by roughly thirty thousand. All figures from "Official Circulation Figures of Daily Newspapers," *Editor and Publisher and Journalist*, April 3, 1915, 888–89.

2. Scripps and Joseph Pulitzer tailored their newspapers in similar ways. According to historian Sidney Kobre, "both were faced with similar urban conditions and political and industrial developments which called for their type of journalism." See Sidney Kobre, *Development of American Journalism* (Dubuque, Iowa: Wm. C. Brown, 1969), 454.

3. B. H. Canfield to John Perry, October 18, 1915, subseries 3.1, box 44, folder 14, E. W. Scripps Papers, Alden Library, Ohio University, Athens (hereafter EWS Papers). The NEA philosophy, as explained by Canfield in this letter, was that syndicated features had a poor reputation among readers because a great deal of bad stuff was being produced through many syndicates. If a feature was not labeled as syndicated, the average reader would never guess it came from a syndicated service.

4. A concise description of the Scripps business philosophy and marketing tactics can be found in Gerald Baldasty and Myron K. Jordan, "Scripps' Competitive Strategy: The Art of Non-competition," *Journalism Quarterly* 70 (1993): 265–75.

5. Gerald Baldasty, *E. W. Scripps and the Business of Newspapers* (Urbana: University of Illinois Press, 1999), 33–54. Baldasty says Scripps papers had about a third as much local news as their competitors. This study looks at Scripps newspapers before 1908, when E. W. Scripps was still active in managing his chain.

6. J. C. Harper to H. N. Rickey, April 1, 1912, subseries 3.1, box 37, folder 1, EWS Papers.

7. J. C. Harper to F. R. Peters and A. O. Andersson, September 30, 1913, subseries 3.1, box 39, folder 6, EWS Papers.

8. William Philip Simms, "Big Odds on Johnson as Fight Draws Near," *Cleveland Press*, June 27, 1914.

9. James G. Scripps to H. N. Rickey, April 2, 1912, subseries 3.1, box 37, folder 1, EWS Papers.

10. Baldasty, *E. W. Scripps and the Business of Newspapers*, 145.

11. E. W. Scripps, *Damned Old Crank: A Self-Portrait of E. W. Scripps.*, ed. Charles R. McCabe (New York: Harper, 1951), 4.

12. Quoted in Minutes of Editorial Conference, Cleveland, Ohio, June 10, 1913, subseries 3.1, box 38, folder 14, EWS Papers.

13. Robert F. Paine to J. C. Harper, May 3, 1913, subseries 3.1, box 38, folder 13, EWS Papers.

14. Minutes of Editorial Conference, Cleveland, Ohio, June 10, 1913.

15. Ibid. The minutes quote the participants verbatim at key points.

16. Baldasty, *E. W. Scripps and the Business of Newspapers*, 104.

17. Richard Hofstadter, *The Age of Reform: from Bryan to F.D.R.* (New York: Vintage Books, 1955), 5. Arthur S. Link and Richard McCormick, *Progressivism* (Wheeling, Ill.: Harlan Davidson, 1983), 3.

18. Hofstadter, *The Age of Reform*, 5–6.

19. Eric Goldman, *Rendezvous with Destiny: A History of Modern American Reform* (1952; reprint, New York: Vintage Books, 1977), 59–60.

20. Sean Dennis Cashman, *America in the Age of the Titans: The Progressive Era and World War I* (New York: New York University Press, 1988), 48.

21. Link and McCormick, *Progressivism*, 34–35.

22. Hofstadter, *Age of Reform*, 186. Hofstadter lends an interesting perspective to the role of journalists/muckrakers in the Progressive Era, 184–214.

23. Ibid., 191.

24. Louis Filler, *Crusaders for American Liberalism: The Story of the Muckrakers* (1939; reprint, New York: Collier Books, 1961), 49.

25. E. W. Scripps to Robert Pollock, September 5, 1916, subseries 1.2, box 17, folder 7, EWS Papers. This letter—which is marked "not sent"—contains a concise memoir of Scripps's earlier years.

26. Gerald J. Baldasty, *The Commercialization of News in the Nineteenth Century* (Madison: University of Wisconsin Press, 1992), 7.

27. E. W. Scripps to Gilson Gardner, June 28, 1916, subseries 1.2, box 17, folder 6, EWS Papers.

28. Hoyt Landon Warner, *Progressivism in Ohio, 1897–1917* (Columbus: Ohio State University Press, 1964), 150–51.

29. Minutes of Editorial Conference, Cleveland, Ohio, June 10, 1913.

30. Warner, *Progressivism in Ohio*, 151–63.

31. Baldasty, *E. W. Scripps and the Business of Newspapers*, 105.

32. George E. Stevens, "Scripps' Cincinnati Post: Liberalism at Home," *Journalism Quarterly* 48 (1971): 231–33.

33. John Scripps to E. W. Scripps, June 6, 1912, subseries 1.1, box 33, folder 2, EWS Papers.

34. "Concerning Political Advertising," *Cleveland Press*, June 27, 1914.

35. Ibid. The editorial still laid down many restrictions on candidates placing

ads: no more than one hundred inches from any candidate; no ads in a single issue could exceed twenty inches. Furthermore, all ads were subject to *Press* censorship; a uniform rate was charged, and a time limit was to be placed on its acceptance.

36. Spencer C. Olin, Jr., *California's Prodigal Sons: Hiram Johnson and the Progressives, 1911–1917* (Berkeley: University of California Press, 1968), 32.

37. Oliver Knight, ed., *I Protest: Selected Disquisitions of E. W. Scripps* (Madison: University of Wisconsin Press, 1966), 186.

38. Baldasty, *E. W. Scripps and the Business of Newspapers*, 104–19.

39. Will Irwin, "The United Press," *Harper's Weekly*, April 25, 1914, 6.

40. Irwin, "The United Press," 8. The number of clients changed continually, but Irwin's numbers are consistent with contemporary UP claims.

41. NEA Clients and Client Fund, November 9, 1916, subseries 3.1, box 49, folder 2, EWS Papers.

42. Before the formation of UP, Scripps operated a special telegraph service called the Scripps-McRae Press Association in the Midwest and the Scripps News Association on the West Coast. Scripps originally cooperated with an Atlantic seaboard press association called the Publisher's Press Association, but then he bought it outright and united all three entities under the UP banner in June 1907. Joe Alex Morris, *Deadline Every Minute: The Story of the United Press* (Garden City, N.Y.: Doubleday, 1957), 19.

43. Robert W. Desmond, *Windows on the World: The Information Process in a Changing Society, 1900–1920* (Iowa City: University of Iowa Press, 1980), 313.

44. Irwin, "The United Press," 8.

45. The desire to stay clear of the Scripps name is mentioned in a Howard letter in which he mentions that he reconfirmed this tactic with E. W. in May 1917 when Scripps came to Washington, D.C. Roy Howard to Ham Clark, May 26, 1917, reel 2, Roy W. Howard Papers, Manuscript Division, Library of Congress, Washington, D.C. (hereafter RWH-LOC Papers).

46. W. H. Porterfield to H. N. Rickey, April 1, 1912, subseries 3.1, box 37, folder 1, EWS Papers.

47. Vance H. Trimble, *The Astonishing Mr. Scripps: The Turbulent Life of America's Penny Press Lord* (Ames: Iowa State University Press, 1992), 260.

48. Roy Howard to Louis Brandeis, December 18, 1915, reel 1, RWH-LOC Papers.

49. Morris, *Deadline Every Minute*, 36.

50. Howard to Brandeis, December 18, 1915.

51. Morris, *Deadline Every Minute*, 51.

52. Ibid., 23.

53. Ibid., 34.

54. Desmond, *Windows on the World*, 70–71. He joined AP in 1910.

55. Ibid., 71.

56. Roy Howard to Jim Scripps, June 2, 1916, reel 3, RWH-LOC Papers. The letter says the Western Union did not want to pay the salary for an operator who did very little for much of the day. Howard agreed to hire the operators himself and charge Western Union for the work they did do.

57. Desmond, *Windows on the World*, 50.

58. Trimble, *The Astonishing Mr. Scripps*, 316.

59. Ibid., 317. At the same Chicago meeting, a proposal to make UP into a cooperative was rejected.
60. Morris, *Deadline Every Minute*, 55.
61. Ibid. Quoted at 36.
62. Irwin, "The United Press," 6. Although Irwin put Howard's statement in quotes, it appears he was actually paraphrasing the essence of his speech.
63. Roy Howard to Carl Getz, October 21, 1915, reel 2, RWH-LOC Papers.
64. Roy Howard to Carl Getz, November 8, 1915, Roy W. Howard Papers, Indiana University, Bloomington, Department of Journalism (hereafter RWH-IU Papers).
65. The *Scripps-Howard Handbook* says Howard was a "complex personality, full of contradictions." Vance Trimble, ed., *Scripps-Howard Handbook*, 3d ed. (Cincinnati: E. W. Scripps, 1981), 77.
66. E. W. Scripps, "The Case of Roy Howard," in Knight, *I Protest*, 308.
67. Forrest David, "Press Lord," in *Post Biographies of Famous Journalists*, ed. John E. Drewry (Athens: University of Georgia Press, 1942), 181. This is a reprint of a *Saturday Evening Post* biography from March 12, 1938.
68. A history of the Cloverleaf newspapers is in James F. Evans, "Cloverleaf: The Good Luck Chain, 1899–1933," *Journalism Quarterly* 46 (1969): 482–91.
69. K. J. Murdoch to E. W. Scripps, December 28, 1915, subseries 1.2, box 35, folder 13, EWS Papers.
70. NEA Clients and Client Fund, November 9, 1916.
71. Minutes of Editorial Conference, Cleveland, Ohio, June 10, 1913.
72. H. N. Rickey to J. C. Harper and W. H. Porterfield, May 3, 1912, subseries 3.1, box 37, folder 5, EWS Papers. Rickey complains about handling of the *Titanic* sinking in this letter.
73. H. N. Rickey to NEA Trustees, October 3, 1913, subseries 3.1, box 39, folder 7, EWS Papers.
74. "Trustees Meeting," January 17, 1913, subseries 3.1, box 38, folder 9, EWS Papers.
75. Louis D. Brandeis, "The Inefficiency of Merely Big Business," *Cleveland Press*, June 27, 1914.
76. E. W. Scripps to Franklin Lane, November 4, 1915, subseries 1.2, box 16, folder 15, EWS Papers.
77. Edward E. Adams, "Market Subordination and Competition: A Historical Analysis of Combinations, Consolidation, and Joint Operating Agreements through an Examination of the E. W. Scripps Newspaper Chain, 1877–1993" (Ph.D. diss., Ohio University, 1993), 60. Scripps started no new newspapers during the period of this study. By 1920 the adless *Day Book* was shut down, but it was not part of any group.
78. E. W. Scripps to Max Eastman, November 2, 1915, subseries 1.2, box 16, folder 15, EWS Papers.
79. E. W. Scripps to Robert Scripps, September 10, 1915, series 2, letterbooks, box 29, EWS Papers.
80. Alfred Andersson to C. F. Mosher, September 10, 1915, subseries 3.1, box 44, folder 10, EWS Papers. The University of Kansas was Andersson's favorite.
81. E. W. Scripps to W. A. Porterfield, May 27, 1916, subseries 1.2, box 17, folder

1, EWS Papers. Scripps went out of his way to tell Porterfield he was not criticizing him for not running the Manly articles.

82. B. H. Canfield to L. Sanders, March 21, 1916, subseries 3.1, box 47, folder 11, EWS Papers. In this letter Canfield tells an editor-in-chief that it is unwise for Scripps papers in one part of the country to be advocating a national policy on Mexico that is opposed to that supported by other Scripps papers.

83. E. W. Scripps had four sons. His second youngest, Edward Willis MacLean, died in 1899 at age seven.

84. E. W. Scripps to N. D. Cochran, December 29, 1917, subseries 1.2, box 18, folder 11, EWS Papers.

85. Trimble, *Scripps-Howard Handbook*, 69–72.

86. Irwin, "The United Press," 6.

87. Trimble, *The Astonishing Mr. Scripps*, 274–76.

88. Ibid., 44–50, 66–70, 73–76.

89. The biggest complaint against Wilson was that he was from one of the traditional parties, the Democratic Party. Neg Cochran summed it up: "As the nominee of the Democratic party [Wilson] is bound to that reactionary old hulk; he is a slave to the party system." N. D. Cochran to H. N. Rickey, July 9, 1912, subseries 3.1, box 37, folder 10, EWS Papers.

90. J. C. Harper to E. W. Scripps, June 4, 1912, subseries 1.1, box 32, folder 7, EWS Papers. Harper's emphasis.

91. For a description of Gardner's activities on behalf of Scripps, see Stephen Ponder, "Partisan Reporting and Presidential Campaigning: Gilson Gardner and E.W. Scripps in the Election of 1912," *Journalism History* 17 (1990): 3–12. Ponder's article, however, ignores the fact that most of the Scripps editors felt Gardner (who operated directly under E. W. for this venture) was biased in favor of Roosevelt, and many would not run his articles. See, for example: John P. Scripps to R. F. Paine, April 5, 1912, subseries 3.1, box 37, folder 1, EWS Papers.

92. J. C. Harper to Peters, Gurley, and Andersson, July 8, 1912, subseries 1.1, box 32, folder 7, EWS Papers.

93. John P. Scripps to E. W. Scripps, March 14, 1912, subseries 1.1, box 33, folder 1, EWS Papers.

94. E. W. Scripps to R. F. Paine, March 18, 1912, subseries 1.2, box 14, folder 4, EWS Papers.

95. W. C. Mayborn to J. C. Harper, August 8, 1912, subseries 3.1, box 38, folder 1, EWS Papers.

96. J. C. Harper to Peters, Curley, and Andersson, August 8, 1912, subseries 3.1, box 38, folder 1, EWS Papers.

Chapter 2: Seeds Get Planted

1. E. W. Scripps to William Kent, October 3, 1914, subseries 1.2, box 16, folder 1, E. W. Scripps Papers, Alden Library, Ohio University, Athens (hereafter EWS Papers).

2. See James L. Stokesbury, *A Short History of World War I* (New York: Morrow, 1981), 11–36.

3. See: E. W. Scripps to Roger W. Babson, May 7, 1914, subseries 1.2, box 16,

folder 12, EWS Papers. E. W. Scripps to Julius Wangenheim, June 27, 1914, subseries 1.2, box 15, folder 14, EWS Papers.

4. E. W. Scripps to Ellen B. Scripps, July 1, 1914, subseries 1.2, box 15, folder 14, EWS Papers.

5. Ibid.

6. George Juergens, *News from the White House* (Chicago: University of Chicago Press, 1981), 128.

7. John Tebbel and Sarah Miles Watts, *The Press and the Presidency: From George Washington to Ronald Reagan* (New York: Oxford University Press, 1985), 371.

8. Ibid., 368.

9. Just two weeks later, Gardner would write a short piece for the NEA in which he suggested that Lane might run for president in 1916. The Democrats would want to hold Wilson to a single term and Bryan was done running for president, Gardner reported. "He has made a wonderful record of efficiency in his cabinet office," Gardner wrote. See Gilson Gardner, "Lane Groomed for President," *Cleveland Press*, July 13, 1914.

10. E. W. Scripps to Ellen B. Scripps, July 1, 1914.

11. Ibid. Wilson was president of Princeton University from 1902 to 1910.

12. Tebbel and Miles Watts, *The Press and the Presidency*, 365. See Edwin A. Weinstein, *Woodrow Wilson: A Medical and Psychological Biography* (Princeton: Princeton University Press, 1981).

13. E. W. Scripps to Ellen B. Scripps, July 1, 1914.

14. Joseph Tumulty to Roy Howard, July 7, 1914, reel 3, Roy W. Howard Papers, Manuscript Division, Library of Congress, Washington, D.C. (hereafter RWH-LOC Papers).

15. "Crown Prince's Aggressive Policy Dominated the Empire," *Cleveland Press*, June 29, 1914.

16. "Wounded to Death, Brave Duchess Clasps Dying Prince in Her Arms," *Cleveland Press*, June 29, 1914.

17. "Nation Believes Mother's Curse Is Being Fulfilled by Tragedies," *Cleveland Press*, June 29, 1914.

18. Joe Alex Morris, *Deadline Every Minute: The Story of the United Press* (Garden City, N.Y.: Doubleday, 1957), 61.

19. "Woman Slain, Police Track Mystery Hand," *Cleveland Press*, July 1, 1914.

20. "Tears Flow as Caillaux Trial Is On," *Cleveland Press*, July 20, 1914.

21. "More Lives Pay Toll for Death of Royal Pair," *Cleveland Press*, July 1, 1914.

22. World War over Serbia Threatened," *Cleveland Press*, July 24, 1914.

23. Morris, *Deadline Every Minute*, 61.

24. "The United Press and the War," *Cleveland Press*, July 27, 1914.

25. Morris, *Deadline Every Minute*, 70.

26. Ibid., 68. Morris also states that UP added twenty-two clients in November 1914 alone.

27. "Correspondent Ed Keen's War Scoops Set Journalism Record," *Cleveland Press*, August 5, 1914.

28. Stewart Halsey Ross, *Propaganda for War: How the United States Was*

Conditioned to Fight the Great War of 1914–1918 (Jefferson, N.C.: McFarland, 1996), 27–28. Only a Liberia-to-Brazil telegraph connection, which was inconvenient for a news wire company needing quick service, remained for anyone in Germany to use. That cable, too, was cut in 1915.

29. Quoted in "News Censorship," *Editor and Publisher and Journalist*, October 3, 1914, 298, 809.

30. The United States eventually took over Germany's two wireless receiving stations in New York and New Jersey, severely limiting Germany's ability to use them. Halsey Ross, *Propaganda for War*, 28.

31. "British Censor's New Policy," *Editor and Publisher and Journalist*, October 10, 1914, 318.

32. Roy W. Howard to William Jennings Bryan, August 3, 1914, reel 1, RWH-LOC Papers.

33. Roy W. Howard to Herbert Asquith, October 7, 1914, Roy W. Howard Papers, Indiana University, Bloomington, Department of Journalism (hereafter RWH-IU Papers).

34. Karl H. Von Wiegand, "Graphic Story of Battle Direct from Firing Line," *Cleveland Press*, October 10, 1914.

35. "British Censor's New Policy," *Editor and Publisher*, October 10, 1914, 318.

36. "Meet War Emergency," *Editor and Publisher and Journalist*, August 8, 1914, 154. This article says Dawson had been manager of the Paris bureau for six years and had accompanied Theodore Roosevelt when he went on an African safari after he left the presidency in 1909.

37. J. W. T. Mason, "Germans Seek to Crush Allies in Huge Vise," *Cleveland Press*, August 24, 1914. Although Mason's column would take many forms and would later become more standardized, this early analysis piece appears to be the first in which he tried to give the reader a general perspective on the fighting.

38. "Meet War Emergency," 154.

39. William Philips Simms, "Armies Massed by National to Fight," *Cleveland Press*, August 10, 1914.

40. William Philip Simms, "Tourists Flee France as Army Meets Germans," *Cleveland Press*, August 3, 1914.

41. William Philip Simms, "Offense of German Army Broken," *Cleveland Press*, September 14, 1914.

42. Morris, *Deadline Every Minute*, 69.

43. "W. P. Simms, Correspondent," *Editor and Publisher and Journalist*, November 21, 1914, 447.

44. Morris, *Deadline Every Minute*, 70.

45. "Getting News from German Fronts," *Editor and Publisher and Journalist*, December 30, 1916, 24.

46. "UP Scores Big Beat," *Editor and Publisher and Journalist*, December 4, 1914, 485.

47. Karl Von Wiegand, "United Press Writer Sends Account of Kaiser's Campaign," *Cleveland Press*, September 8, 1914.

48. Karl Von Wiegand, "Truth about Germany," *Cleveland Press*, August 17, 1914.

49. "Karl H. Von Wiegand, "Death Is Master in Forts of Liege," *Cleveland Press*, September 10, 1914.

50. "Karl H. Von Wiegand, "Berlin Says Beaumont Falls," *Cleveland Press*, September 19, 1914.

51. Karl H. Von Wiegand, "Just a Basketful of Tags at Liege, but Each Tag Was Death," *Cleveland Press*, September 25, 1914.

52. "British Censor Violates Fair Play Standard," *Cleveland Press*, September 25, 1914.

53. Morris, *Deadline Every Minute*, 67.

54. Ibid., 63–64.

55. "United Press Staff Man Scores First Big Scoop of Mexican War," *Cleveland Press*, April 20, 1914.

56. William G. Shepherd, *Confessions of a War Correspondent* (New York: Harper, 1917), 24–25.

57. William G. Shepherd, "Churchill Tells Britain's Story," *Cleveland Press*, August 29, 1914.

58. Ibid.

59. This is described in Morris, *Deadline Every Minute*, 65.

60. "Britain Denounces Destruction of Louvain as Act of Vandalism," *Cleveland Press*, August 29, 1914.

61. Barbara Tuchman, *The Guns of August* (New York: Ballantine Books, 1962) 321.

62. William G. Shepherd, "London Lights Shine, but Heart Is Chilled," *Cleveland Press*, September 4, 1914. Shipping usually delayed stories sent by mail at least a week.

63. William G. Shepherd, "New Terror of War Holds Ostend—'Zeppelin Chill,'" *Cleveland Press*, September 12, 1914.

64. Shepherd, *Confessions of a War Correspondent*, 14.

65. Roy W. Howard to Merle Thorpe, December 7, 1914, RWH-IU Papers.

66. B. H. Canfield to Scripps Editors, August 5, 1914, subseries 3.1, box 41, folder 4, EWS Papers,

67. J. C. Harper to E. W. Scripps, 3 August 1914, subseries 1.1, box 34, folder 10, EWS Papers.

68. E. W. Scripps to Editors, 4 August 1914, subseries 1.2, box 15, folder 15, EWS Papers. The Paine memo is attached to this letter.

69. Alfred Andersson to Editors, August 8, 1914, subseries 3.1, box 41, folder 4, EWS Papers.

70. B. H. Canfield to L. Sanders, August 10, 1914, subseries 3.1, box 41, folder 4, EWS Papers.

71. In the most recent scholarship in this area, one author claimed that "one month into the war, nearly every newspaper in English in the United States was editorially parroting England's propaganda." See Halsey Ross, *Propaganda for War*, 20.

72. "The European Crisis and What Has Caused It," *Cleveland Press*, August 1, 1914.

73. Woldemar Von Nostitz, "Censors May Warp Dispatches on War," *Cleveland Press*, August 6, 1914.

74. "The Press and the War," *Cleveland Press*, August 11, 1914.

75. "Be Slow to Believe the Ill That You Read," *Cleveland Press*, August 27, 1914.

76. Julia Edwards, *Women of the World: The Great Foreign Correspondents* (Boston: Houghton Mifflin, 1988), 25.

77. "Press Woman Has Daring Adventure in Belgium," *Cleveland Press*, September 16, 1914.

78. Edwards, *Women of the World*, 25.

79. Mary Boyle O'Reilly, "Ten Thousand Women and Tots Driven from Louvain to Unknown Fate," *Cleveland Press*, September 16, 1914.

80. Mary Boyle O'Reilly, "Millions of Britain's Poor Made Panicky by Air-Raiders," *Cleveland Press*, January 21, 1915.

81. H. J. Phillips, "English Find Joy in Advancing to Front," *Cleveland Press*, January 18, 1915.

82. These two stories appeared under the same headline but with different bylines: "Germans Work Grimly at Wiping Belgium off Map," *Cleveland Press*, February 9, 1915.

83. Roy Howard to Ham Clark, January 14, 1915, reel 2, RWH-LOC.

84. B. H. Canfield to E. E. Martin, April 24, 1915, subseries 3.1, box 43, folder 8, EWS Papers.

85. B. H. Canfield to E. E. Martin, October 2, 1915, subseries 3.1, box 44, folder 13, EWS Papers. The remaining historical record does not prove or disprove the existence of a real H. J. Phillips.

86. J. C. Harper to B. H. Canfield, September 18, 1914, subseries 3.1, box 41, folder 7, EWS Papers.

87. B. H. Canfield to Scripps Editors, September 30, 1914, subseries 3.1, box 41, folder 8, EWS Papers.

88. Gilson Gardner, "'Army and Navy' Big Topic for Congress," *Cleveland Press*, November 23, 1914.

89. Thomas Knock, *To End All Wars: Woodrow Wilson and the Quest for a New World Order* (New York: Oxford University Press, 1992), 59.

90. "Vote on Army and Navy," *Cleveland Press*, November 23, 1914.

91. "What Do *You* Think about Increasing *Your* Army and Navy?" *Cleveland Press*, November 18, 1914.

92. "Shall Uncle Sam Have a Bigger Army and Navy?" *Cleveland Press*, November 13, 1914. This type of balanced spread of views was repeated November 16.

93. "People Vote against Larger Army-Navy," *Cleveland Press*, December 10, 1914. The army question drew 71,235 ballots; the navy question drew 73,092 ballots.

94. B. H. Canfield to R. F. Paine, November 27, 1914, subseries 3.1, box 41, folder 13, EWS Papers.

95. R. F. Paine to B. H. Canfield, December 1, 1914, subseries 3.1, box 41, folder 14, EWS Papers.

96. J. C. Harper to R. F. Paine, December 14, 1914, subseries 3.1, box 41, folder 14, EWS Papers.

97. R. F. Paine to J. C. Harper, December 21, 1914, subseries 3.1, box 42, folder 1, EWS Papers.

98. C. Hartley Grattan, *Why We Fought* (New York: Vanguard Press, 1929), 131.

99. E. W. Scripps to Roy W. Howard, October 3, 1914, subseries 1.2, box 16, folder 1, EWS Papers.

100. C. F. Mosher to W. H. Dodge and E. E. Martin, August 4, 1914, subseries 3.1, box 41, folder 4, EWS Papers.
101. C. D. Lee to C. F. Mosher, August 19, 1914, subseries 3.1, box 58, folder 7, EWS Papers.
102. Ibid.
103. Roy Howard to All Leased Wire Clients, October 5, 1914, subseries 3.1, box 58, folder 7, EWS Papers.
104. Alfred Andersson to Roy Howard, October 10, 1914, subseries 3.1, box 58, folder 7, EWS Papers.
105. Roy Howard to Jim Scripps, October 5, 1914, subseries 3.1, box 58, folder 7, EWS Papers.
106. Roy Howard to Earle Martin, October 16, 1914, subseries 3.1, box 58, folder 7, EWS Papers.
107. Roy Howard to B. H. Canfield et al., October 23, 1914, subseries 3.1, box 41, folder 11, EWS Papers.
108. Andersson to Howard, October 10, 1914. Editor-in-chief Andersson led complaints against the increase. Andersson said on April 15, 1914, that UP was "utterly inconsiderate" of Scripps papers. He said the Scripps newspapers had gone from being sustaining members of the UP to just another bunch of clients for UP. See Alfred Andersson to H. L. Schmetzstdorff, April 25, 1914, subseries 3.1, box 40, folder 10, EWS Papers.
109. "Newsprint Increase," *Editor and Publisher and Journalist,* November 28, 1914, 1.
110. "Increase Subscription Price," *Editor and Publisher and Journalist,* October 31, 1914, 391.
111. "Publishers Discuss 2c. Paper," *Editor and Publisher and Journalist,* December 19, 1914, 526.
112. Roy Howard to Alden Blethen, August 13, 1914, reel 1, RWH-LOC Papers.
113. Alden Blethen to Roy Howard, August 18, 1914, reel 1, RWH-LOC Papers.
114. Roy Howard to *Daily Republican,* November 5, 1914, reel 1, RWH-LOC Papers. Problems with this newspaper continued into 1915. See series of letters attached to J. W. Curts to V. C. Gardner, April 13, 1915, subseries 3.1, box 43, folder 7, EWS Papers.
115. W. W. Hawkins to managing editor of *Washington Post,* December 31, 1914, reel 1, RWH-LOC Papers.
116. The advertisement appeared in *Editor and Publisher and Journalist,* December 5, 1914, 489.
117. J. W. Curts to Roy W. Howard, December 15, 1915, subseries 3.1, box 42, folder 1, EWS Papers.
118. Robert W. Desmond, *Windows on the World: The Information Process in a Changing Society, 1900–1920* (Iowa City: University of Iowa Press, 1980), 313.
119. Roy W. Howard to *Evening Mail,* November 28, 1914, reel 1, RWH-LOC Papers. In this letter Howard denied UP was stealing AP stories through other New York City news organizations.
120. Roy Howard to J. A. E. Malone, January 11, 1915, reel 1, RWH-LOC Papers.
121. Howard to Clark, January 14, 1915, RWH-LOC Papers.
122. Howard to Malone, January 11, 1915.

123. Lord Northcliffe, "Lord Northcliffe, Britain's Great Publisher, Sizes Up War," *Cleveland Press*, December 29, 1914.

124. Karl Von Wiegand, "Threat of Great Submarine War Made by Naval Chief of Germany," *Cleveland Press*, December 22, 1914.

125. "Germany Gives Von Wiegand Pass to All Parts of Her Battle Line," *Cleveland Press*, January 9, 1915.

126. Karl Von Wiegand, "Zeppelin Answers," *Cleveland Press*, February 8, 1915.

127. Karl Von Wiegand, "Women War's Real Victims, Crown Princess Asserts," *Cleveland Press*, February 15, 1915.

128. Karl Von Wiegand to W. W. Hawkins, January 26, 1915, reel 3, RWH-LOC.

129. Karl Von Wiegand to Roy Howard, January 23, 1915, reel 2, RWH-LOC.

130. J. W. Curts to J. C. Harper, February 19, 1915, subseries 3.1, box 42, folder 12, EWS Papers.

131. J. W. Curts to Campbell Cummings, March 18, 1915, subseries 3.1, box 43, folder 3, EWS Papers.

132. Alfred O. Andersson to B. H. Canfield, March 11, 1915, subseries 3.1, box 43, folder 1, EWS Papers.

133. E. W. Scripps to William Jennings Bryan, February 6, 1915, subseries 1.2, box 16, folder 5, EWS Papers. Scripps talked about the president's "lack of assistance" in advancing the idea.

134. John J. Boresamle, *William Gibbs McAdoo: A Passion for Change, 1863–1917* (Port Washington, N.Y.: Kennikat Press, 1973), 69.

135. E. W. Scripps to Charles R. Crane, January 6, 1915, subseries 1.2, box 16, folder 4, EWS Papers.

136. Scripps to Bryan, February 6, 1915.

137. Keith W. Olson, *Biography of a Progressive: Franklin Lane, 1864–1921* (Westport, Conn.: Greenwood Press, 1979), 4.

138. E. W. Scripps to R. F. Paine, April 2, 1915, subseries 1.2, box 16, folder 8, EWS Papers.

139. E. W. Scripps to Neg Cochran, March 28, 1915, subseries 1.2, box 16, folder 7, EWS Papers.

140. Scripps to Paine, April 2, 1915.

141. E. W. Scripps to Neg Cochran, April 21, 1915, subseries 1.2, box 16, folder 8, EWS Papers.

142. E. W. Scripps to Charles R. Crane, April 22, 1915, subseries 1.2, box 16, folder 8, EWS Papers.

143. Scripps to Cochran, April 21, 1915.

144. Patrick Devlin, *Too Proud to Fight: Woodrow Wilson's Neutrality* (New York: Oxford University Press, 1975), 200–201.

145. Ed L. Keen, "Fleets Fight Blockade," *Cleveland Press*, February 18, 1915.

146. B. H. Canfield to E. E. Martin, February 24, 1915, subseries 3.1, box 42, folder 12, EWS Papers.

147. "The Nation of Peace," *Cleveland Press*, February 22, 1915.

148. "For Peace Insurance: The Greatest Navy in the World," *Cleveland Press*, March 1, 1915.

149. Theodore Roosevelt, "Navy Our Only Insurance against War, Our Only Guarantee against Disaster," *Cleveland Press*, March 1, 1915.

150. "The Richest Nation, a Fine Lure to the Greed of the World," *Cleveland Press*, March 3, 1915.

151. Gilson Gardner, "Millions Lost by U.S. in Buying Its Armament," *Cleveland Press*, March 6, 1915.

152. Gilson Gardner, "How Armor Plate Combine Holds Up Uncle Sam," *Cleveland Press* December 12, 1914. Gilson Gardner, "United States Ought to Make Its Own Arms!" *Cleveland Press*, December 14, 1914.

Chapter 3: Harsh Realities

1. Alfred Andersson to B. H. Canfield, April 1, 1915, subseries 3.1, box 43, folder 7, E. W. Scripps Papers, Alden Library, Ohio University, Athens (hereafter EWS Papers).
2. B. H. Canfield to Alfred Andersson, April 27, 1915, subseries 3.1, box 43, folder 9, EWS Papers.
3. B. H. Canfield to Trustees and Editors-in-Chief, May 10, 1915, subseries 3.1, box 43, folder 11, EWS Papers.
4. Six letters written to Canfield survive in the EWS Papers. See J. W. Curts to B. H. Canfield, May 12, 1915, subseries 3.1, box 43, folder 11, EWS Papers; C. F. Mosher to B. H. Canfield, May 15, 1915; H. N. Rickey to B. H. Canfield, May 28, 1915; LeRoy Sanders to B. H. Canfield, May 18, 1915; R. F. Paine to B. H. Canfield, May 14, 1915; and W. H. Porterfield to B. H. Canfield, May 24, 1915, all in subseries 3.1, box 44, folder 1, EWS Papers. Canfield wrote on May 25 that the "opinions advanced by all except Andersson appear to support my argument." B. H. Canfield to H. N. Rickey, subseries 3.1, box 43, folder 14, EWS Papers.
5. See Curts to Canfield, May 12, 1915.
6. Sanders to Canfield, May 18, 1915.
7. Thomas A. Bailey and Paul B. Ryan, *The Lusitania Disaster: An Episode in Modern Warfare and Diplomacy* (New York: Free Press, 1975), 94.
8. Quoted in Johann Von Bernstorff, *My Three Years in America* (New York: Scribner's, 1920), 137–38.
9. Wilbur Forrest, *Behind the Front Page: Stories of Newspaper Stories in the Making* (New York: Appleton-Century, 1934), 25.
10. B. H. Canfield to E. E. Martin, May 17, 1915, subseries 3.1, box 43, folder 12, EWS Papers. Canfield recounted his prediction in this letter.
11. B. H. Canfield to Alfred Andersson, May 14, 1915, subseries 3.1, box 43, folder 12, EWS Papers. Again, Canfield recounted his earlier warnings about the *Lusitania* in this letter.
12. Charles Edward Russell, "How It Feels to Cross the Submarine Zone!" *Cleveland Press*, April 30, 1915.
13. "Lusitania Story," *Editor and Publisher and Journalist*, May 15, 1915, 1047.
14. Ibid. In this *Editor and Publisher and Journalist* article, Roy Howard claimed that Forrest was the first American reporter on the scene, but Forrest's memoir says that Fred Pitney of the *New York Tribune*, whom he met on the train to

Notes to Pages 60–64

Landore, accompanied him the rest of the way. Forrest, *Behind the Front Page*, 31.

15. Ibid., 27.
16. Ibid., 34–35.
17. Bailey and Ryan, *The Lusitania Disaster*, 91.
18. Ibid., 40.
19. "Lusitania Slowed Up While in Danger Zone," *Cleveland Press*, May 10, 1915.
20. See "Derberg Says Lusitania Had Big Arms Cargo," *Cleveland Press*, May 8, 1915; "Editor Defends Germany's Act," *Cleveland Press*, May 8, 1915.
21. Forrest, *Behind the Front Page*, 36–38, 44–45.
22. "Weekly Review of the War," *Cleveland Press*, May 10, 1915.
23. John Milton Cooper, Jr., *Vanity of Power: American Isolationism and the First World War, 1914–1917*, ed. Stanley I. Kutler (Westport, Conn.: Greenwood, 1969), 33.
24. "Wilson's Policy—Honor, Justice and Sound Reason," *Cleveland Press*, May 15, 1915.
25. "President Wilson and the Nation's Crisis," *Cleveland Press*, May 11, 1915.
26. B. H. Canfield to C. F. Mosher, June 1, 1915, subseries 3.1, box 44, folder 1, EWS Papers.
27. Alfred Andersson to B. H. Canfield, May 11, 1915, subseries 3.1, box 43, folder 11, EWS Papers.
28. Canfield to Mosher, June 1, 1915.
29. B. H. Canfield to A. O. Andersson, May 13, 1915, subseries 3.1 box 43, folder 12, EWS Papers.
30. Quoted in Cooper, *Vanity of Power*, 35.
31. B. H. Canfield to Alfred Andersson, May 14, 1915, subseries 3.1, box 43, folder 12, EWS Papers
32. Ibid.
33. Alfred Andersson to B. H. Canfield, May 25, 1915, subseries 3.1, box 43, folder 12, EWS Papers.
34. Milton McRae to E. W. Scripps, December 15, 1914, subseries 1.1, box 34, folder 14, EWS Papers. McRae said Jim Scripps had told him that Andersson, Howard, and Canfield were the top three editorial men.
35. Vance H. Trimble, *The Astonishing Mr. Scripps: The Turbulent Life of America's Penny Press Lord* (Ames: Iowa State University Press, 1992), 294.
36. B. H. Canfield to H. N. Rickey, May 20, 1915, subseries 3.1, box 43, folder 13, EWS Papers.
37. Canfield to Mosher, June 1, 1915.
38. The memo was signed January 16, 1911, but a copy was not found in the surviving Scripps archives. Enough of it is described in various letters to reveal its scope, however. See J. C. Harper to F. R. Peters and A. O. Andersson, June 30, 1915, and J. C. Harper to B. H. Canfield, June 30, 1915, both in subseries 3.1, box 44, folder 3, EWS Papers.
39. B. H. Canfield to J. C. Harper, June 24, 1915, subseries 3.1, box 44, folder 3, EWS Papers.
40. B. H. Canfield to H. N. Rickey, et.al., June 29, 1915, subseries 3.1, box 44, folder 3, EWS Papers.

41. Harper to Canfield, June 30, 1915.
42. Negley Cochran to B. H. Canfield, July 2, 1915, subseries 3.1, box 44, folder 4, EWS Papers.
43. Eugene MacLean to B. H. Canfield, July 2, 1915, subseries 3.1, box 44, folder 4, EWS Papers.
44. F. R. Peters to B. H. Canfield, July 13, 1915, subseries 3.1, box 44, folder 4, EWS Papers.
45. Harry N. Rickey to B. H. Canfield, July 6, 1915, subseries 3.1, box 44, folder 4, EWS Papers.
46. Harper to Canfield, June 30, 1915.
47. J. C. Harper to B. H. Canfield and R. F. Paine, June 22, 1915, subseries 3.1, box 44, folder 3, EWS Papers.
48. Cooper, *Vanity of Power*, 76–77.
49. Ibid., 4.
50. "Show Your Patriotism," *Cleveland Press*, June 12, 1915.
51. John Patrick Finnegan, *Against the Specter of a Dragon: The Campaign for American Military Preparedness, 1914–1917* (Westport, Conn.: Greenwood Press, 1974), 31–32, 92.
52. Ibid., 31–32, 92.
53. Ibid., 124.
54. "Standing by Uncle Sam," *Cleveland Press*, May 27, 1915.
55. Cooper, *Vanity of Power*, 26.
56. "Bryan Had Long Been Planning to Quit Cabinet," *Cleveland Press*, June 12, 1915.
57. J. C. Harper to R. F. Paine, June 24, 1915, subseries 3.1, box 44, folder 3, EWS Papers.
58. C. F. Mosher to B. H. Canfield, June 10, 1915, subseries 3.1, box 44, folder 2, EWS Papers.
59. B. H. Canfield to C. F. Mosher, June 11, 1915, subseries 3.1, box 44, folder 2, EWS Papers.
60. Finnegan, *Against the Specter of a Dragon*, 39. Finnegan said the United States needed some sort of deterrent during its showdown with Germany, and public opinion also made it politically helpful to support increased military spending.
61. B. H. Canfield to E. L. Mariarty, June 5, 1915, subseries 3.1, box 44, folder 1, EWS Papers.
62. Finnegan, *Against the Specter of a Dragon*, 96.
63. Harry P. Burton, "Dreadnaughts Essential for Wall of Peace," *Cleveland Press*, April 2, 1915.
64. B. H. Canfield to Dana Sleeth, June 5, 1915, subseries 3.1, box 44, folder 1, EWS Papers.
65. J. C. Harper to B. H. Canfield, May 25, 1915, subseries 3.1, box 44, folder 1, EWS Papers.
66. B. H. Canfield to J. C. Harper, June 1, 1915, subseries 3.1, box 44, folder 1, EWS Papers.
67. "Great Man in Great Crisis," *Cleveland Press*, May 17, 1915.
68. Harry P. Burton, "Here's What President Is Like on Vacation," *Cleveland Press*, July 15, 1915.

69. Idah McGlone Gibson, "How President Makes Love," *Cleveland Press,* November 2, 1915.

70. "It's Right, Woodrow," *Cleveland Press,* December 12, 1915.

71. E. W. Scripps to Franklin Lane, May 23, 1915, subseries 1.2, box 16, folder 9, EWS Papers.

72. Franklin Lane to E. W. Scripps, June 3, 1915, subseries 1.1, box 35, folder 11, EWS Papers.

73. Neg Cochran to Walter S. Rogers, June 28, 1915, subseries 3.1, box 44, folder 3, EWS Papers.

74. Franklin Lane to E. W. Scripps, June 1, 1915, subseries 1.1, box 35, folder 11, EWS Papers.

75. Karl Von Wiegand to Roy Howard, March 3, 1915, reel 3, Roy W. Howard Papers, Manuscript Division, Library of Congress, Washington, D.C. (hereafter RWH-LOC Papers).

76. Roy Howard to Ham Clark, February 1, 1915, reel 2, RWH-LOC Papers.

77. "Roy Howard Sails," *Editor and Publisher and Journalist,* February 6, 1915, 688.

78. Howard to Clark, February 1, 1915.

79. "Roy Howard Sails," 688.

80. "A.P. Directors Report," *Editor and Publisher and Journalist,* April 24, 1915, 974.

81. Roy Howard to E. W. Scripps, May 12, 1915, subseries 1.1, box 35, folder 10, EWS Papers. It is not known if Scripps did so.

82. Roy Howard to Franklin Lane, May 14, 1915, reel 1, RWH-LOC Papers.

83. Josephus Daniels to Roy Howard, May 14, 1915, reel 1, RWH-LOC Papers.

84. Carl Vroonan to Roy Howard, May 8, 1915, reel 1, RWH-LOC Papers.

85. Roy Howard to John Ackerman, July 10, 1915, container 145, Carl Ackerman Papers, Manuscript Division, Library of Congress, Washington, D.C.

86. "Family Exercises Censorship to Help Son in Getting War News," *Cincinnati Post,* July 14, 1915.

87. Carl Ackerman to Perry Arnold, March 25, 1915, reel 1, RWH-LOC Papers.

88. Carl Ackerman to Perry Arnold, April 6, 1915, reel 1, RWH-LOC Papers.

89. Perry Arnold to Carl Ackerman, April 23, 1915, reel 1, RWH-LOC Papers.

90. Perry Arnold to Carl Ackerman, April 27, 1915, reel 1, RWH-LOC Papers.

91. Carl Ackerman to Ed Keen, May 25, 1915, reel 1, RWH-LOC Papers.

92. Carl Ackerman to Perry Arnold, June 4, 1915, reel 1, RWH-LOC Papers.

93. Arnold to Ackerman, April 27, 1915.

94. Carl Ackerman to Roy Howard, May 31, 1915, reel 1, RWH-LOC Papers. Ackerman describes how he got the telegraph sent in this letter.

95. Perry Arnold to Carl Ackerman, June 7, 1915, reel 1, RWH-LOC Papers.

96. Carl Ackerman to Ed Keen, July 22, 1915, reel 2, RWH-LOC Papers.

97. Carl Ackerman to Press Abteilung, July 12, 1915, reel 2, RHW-LOC Papers.

98. Roy Howard to Johann Von Bernstorff, July 12, 1915, reel 1, RWH-LOC Papers.

99. Carl Ackerman to Roy Howard, July 15, 1915, reel 2, RWH-LOC Papers.

100. Ibid.

101. Carl Ackerman to Roy Howard, August 2, 1915, reel 2, RWH-LOC Papers.

102. Carl Ackerman to Roy Howard, August 12, 1915, reel 2, RWH-LOC Papers.

103. Johann Bernstorff to Roy W. Howard, September 1, 1915, reel 1, RWH-LOC Papers.

104. Roy Howard to Johann Bernstorff, September 10, 1915, reel 1, RWH-LOC Papers.

105. Roy Howard, "N.Y. to Be News Clearing House of World," *Editor and Publisher*, November 11, 1916, 5. Note that this magazine, which had merged with the *Journalist*, shortened its name in mid-1916.

106. Terhi Rantanen, *Mr. Howard Goes to South America: The United Press Associations and Foreign Expansion*, Roy W. Howard Monographs in Journalism and Mass Communication Research, no. 2 (Indiana University School of Journalism, May 15, 1992), 14-15.

107. Quoted in "United Press Extends News Service to Central and South American Points," *Editor and Publisher*, August 12, 1916, 8.

108. "UP System Worked Well," *Editor and Publisher*, November 11, 1916, 6.

109. "Combination Benefits UP and French Papers," *Editor and Publisher*, October 28, 1916, 10.

110. Carl Ackerman to Roy Howard, June 13, 1915, reel 1, RWH-LOC Papers.

111. Carl Ackerman to Ed Keen, August 13, 1915, reel 2, RHW-LOC Papers.

112. J. W. Curts to V. C. Gardner, April 13, 1915, subseries 3.1, box 43, folder 7, EWS Papers.

113. Roy Howard to Jay Curts, July 30, 1915, reel 2, RWH-LOC Papers.

114. Roy Howard to Jay Curts, August 11, 1915, subseries 3.1, box 44, folder 8, EWS Papers.

115. J. W. Curts to Roy Howard, August 11, 1915, subseries 3.1, box 44, folder 8, EWS Papers.

116. Jay Curts to Roy Howard, August 13, 1915, reel 2, RWH-LOC Papers.

117. See Jay Curts to Roy Howard, September 19, 1915, and J. W. Curts to Globe Printing, September 18, 1915, both in subseries 3.1, box 44, folder 11, EWS Papers; John Petry to Roy W. Howard, November 17, 1915, reel 3, RWH-LOC Papers.

118. J. W. Curts to Roy Howard, November 5, 1915, subseries 3.1, box 45, folder 2, EWS Papers.

119. Ibid.

120. *International News Service v. Associated Press*, 248, U.S. 215 (1918). For a description of the case and its ramifications, see: Wayne Overbeck, *Major Principles of Media Law* (Fort Worth, Tex.: Harcourt College, 2002), 264-65.

121. Ed. L. Keen, "Good Words for the British Censorship," *Editor and Publisher and Journalist*, March 18, 1916, 1256.

122. Howard, "N.Y. to Be News Clearing House," 5.

123. Ibid, 32.

124. "The World's Notable Beat," *Editor and Publisher and Journalist*, August 28, 1915, 280.

125. Keen, "Good Words for the British Censorship," 1246.

126. Henry Wood to Roy Howard and Ed Keen, July 24, 1915, reel 2, RWH-LOC Papers.

127. Henry Wood to Ed Keen, June 25, 1915, reel 2, RWH-LOC Papers.

128. B. H. Canfield to H. N. Rickey, June 25, 1915, subseries 3.1, box 44, folder 3, EWS Papers.

129. See "Women of Germany as War Helper! Durborough Photographs Them," *Cleveland Press*, June 28, 1915; "Press Photographer Shows How Germans Attack Enemy," *Cleveland Press*, June 23, 1915; "Wonderful Photography of German Infantry Charge," *Cleveland Press*, June 24, 1915; and "Durborough Photo Shows German Rapid Fire Machine Gun in Action," *Cleveland Press*, August 11, 1915.

130. W. H. Durborough, "German Red Cross Dogs Save Many Wounded from Death," *Cleveland Press*, June 30, 1915.

131. J. C. Harper to B. H. Canfield, June 30, 1915, subseries 3.1, box 44, folder 3, EWS Papers.

132. Byron Canfield to C. F. Mosher, April 27, 1915, subseries 3.1, box 43, folder 9, EWS Papers.

133. H. N. Rickey to B. H. Canfield, July 1, 1915, subseries 3.1, box 44, folder 4, EWS Papers.

134. C. F. Mosher to A. O. Andersson, July 19, 1915, subseries 3.1, box 44, folder 5, EWS Papers.

135. "Simple Words Favored," *Editor and Publisher and Journalist*, October 30, 1915, 536.

136. Henry Reuterdahl, "New York Captured by Enemy in Vision of Marine Writer," *Cleveland Press*, April 23, 1915.

137. John M. Oskison, "Uncle Sam's Navy," *Cleveland Press*, April 8, 1915.

138. "Make U.S. Navy Best in World, Daniels Urges," *Cleveland Press*, June 26, 1915, EWS Papers.

139. "Get Plenty of Them," *Cleveland Press*, July 9, 1915, EWS Papers.

140. "U.S. May Adopt Military Plan of Switzerland," *Cleveland Press*, June 11, 1915.

141. "What War Means," *Cleveland Press*, July 30, 1915.

142. Finnegan, *Against the Specter of a Dragon*, 181.

143. "Battleship No Torpedo Can Sink, Planned," *Cleveland Press*, August 3, 1915.

144. "Harness the Aeroplane," *Cleveland Press*, August 14, 1915.

145. Franklin D. Roosevelt, "Submarine Is Imperfect as Weapon in War," *Cleveland Press*, October 7, 1915.

146. See Franklin D. Roosevelt, "Points Out Need for Destroyers," *Cleveland Press*, October 1, 1915; Franklin D. Roosevelt, "Navy Official Says We're Shy Ten Battleships," *Cleveland Press*, October 4, 1915; and Franklin D. Roosevelt, "Our Navy Is Blind! It Lacks Scouts to Find Hostile Fleet," *Cleveland Press*, September 24, 1915.

147. "The National Defense League," *Cleveland Press*, June 14, 1915.

148. Clyde H. Tavenner, "Congress Can Shake Off War Trust's Grip; How Will Your Representatives Vote?" *Cleveland Press*, October 14, 1915.

149. Finnegan, *Against the Specter of a Dragon*, 137.

Chapter 4: "Genuine Enthusiastic Support"

1. For a discussion of the Civil War version of the income tax and its eventual repeal, see Roy G. Blakey and Gladys C. Blakey, *The Federal Income Tax* (London: Longman, Green, 1940), 1–8. Other books on the early history of the income tax include: Randolph E. Paul, *Taxation for Prosperity* (Indianapolis: Bobbs-Merrill, 1947); Sidney Ratner, *American Taxation: Its History as a Social Force in Democracy* (New York: Norton, 1942); and John D. Buenker, *The Income Tax and the Progressive Era* (New York: Greenwood Press, 1985).

2. Robert Higgs, *Crisis and Leviathan: Critical Episodes in the Growth of American Government* (New York: Oxford University Press, 1987), 97. The U.S. Supreme Court also ruled an income tax to be unconstitutional. *Pollock v. Farmers Loan and Trust Company*, 157 U.S. 429 (1895).

3. For an analysis of the politics surrounding the adoption of the amendment, see Bennet D. Baack and Edward John Ray, "Special Interests and the Adoption of the Income Tax in the United States," *Journal of Economic History* 65 (September 1985): 607–25.

4. For a concise description of the income tax fight in the early twentieth Century, see Higgs, *Crisis and Leviathan*, 112–13.

5. E. W. Scripps, "The Principles of the Scripps Idea of Journalism," in *I Protest: Selected Disquisitions of E. W. Scripps*, ed. Oliver Knight (Madison: University of Wisconsin Press, 1966), 273.

6. John Patrick Finnegan, *Against the Specter of a Dragon: The Campaign for American Military Preparedness, 1914–1917* (Westport, Conn.: Greenwood Press, 1974), 137.

7. See, for example, Robert F. Paine to J. C. Harper, May 13, 1913, subseries 3.1, box 38, folder 13, E. W. Scripps Papers, Alden Library, Ohio University, Athens (hereafter EWS Papers).

8. K. J. Murdoch to E. W. Scripps, December 28, 1915, subseries 1.1, box 35, folder 13, EWS Papers.

9. Ibid.

10. K. J. Murdoch to E. W. Scripps, January 4, 1916, subseries 1.1, box 36, folder 7, EWS Papers.

11. E. W. Scripps to Franklin K. Lane, November 4, 1915, subseries 1.2, box 16, folder, 15, EWS Papers.

12. E. W. Scripps to B. H. Canfield, August 29, 1915, subseries 1.2, box 16, folder 13, EWS Papers.

13. E. W. Scripps to J. C. Harper, July 13, 1915, subseries 1.2 box 16, folder 11, EWS Papers.

14. The income number is reported in Vance H. Trimble, *The Astonishing Mr. Scripps: The Turbulent Life of America's Penny Press Lord* (Ames: Iowa State University Press, 1992), 367, and the tax paid is reported in Scripps to Harper, July 13, 1915. Scripps claimed he probably paid $7,600 to the government, but the total was $10,000 after he accounted for taxes collected at the source and "indirect" taxes.

15. Scripps to Harper, July 13, 1915. Scripps asked Harper if any inquiry was made into his tax return. Harper answered that no personal returns of people working for the Concern had been audited, but some Scripps newspapers' corpo-

rate returns had been audited because of depreciation claims. See J. C. Harper to E. W. Scripps, August 19, 1915, subseries 1.1, box 35, folder 9, EWS Papers.

16. Ibid. See also *Annual Report of the Secretary of the Treasury: For the Fiscal Year Ended June 30, 1915* (Washington, D.C.: Government Printing Office), 16.

17. Scripps to Harper, July 13, 1915.

18. E. W. Scripps to Charles R. Crane, August 15, 1915, subseries 1.2, box 16, folder 12, EWS Papers.

19. Gilson Gardner to E. W. Scripps, August 26, 1915, subseries 1.1, box 35, folder 8, EWS Papers.

20. E. W. Scripps to B. H. Canfield, August 29, 1915, subseries 1.2, box 16, folder 13, EWS Papers.

21. B. H. Canfield to E. W. Scripps, September 14, 1915, subseries 1.1, box 15, folder 6, EWS Papers.

22. Ibid.

23. B. H. Canfield to E. W. Scripps, September 28, 1915, subseries 1.1 box 35, folder 6, EWS Papers.

24. Ibid.

25. See Graham Adams, Jr., *Age of Industrial Violence, 1910–1915: The Activities and Findings of the United States Commission on Industrial Relations* (New York: Columbia University Press, 1966).

26. The best biography of Manly is James Boylan, *Dictionary of American Biography*, supp. 4, 1946–50, ed. John Garraty and Edward James (New York: Scribner's, 1974), 543, which describes his role in the Industrial Relations Committee.

27. Boylan, *Dictionary of American Biography*, 543.

28. Gilson Gardner to E. W. Scripps, October 21, 1915, subseries 1.1, box 35, folder 8, EWS Papers.

29. Gilson Gardner to E. W. Scripps, October 12, 1915, subseries 1.1, box 35, folder 8, EWS Papers.

30. Gardner to Scripps, October 21, 1915.

31. Basil Manly to H. Burton, October 13, 1915, subseries 1.1, box 35, folder 6, EWS Papers.

32. Ibid.

33. Scripps to Gardner, October 21, 1915.

34. Gilson Gardner to E. W. Scripps, October 29, 1915, subseries 1.1, box 35, folder 8, EWS Papers.

35. E. W. Scripps to Amos Pinchot, November 10, 1915, subseries 1.2, box 16, folder 15, EWS Papers.

36. Basil Manly to S. T. Hughes, October 29, 1915, subseries 1.1, box 35, folder 6, EWS Papers.

37. E. W. Scripps to Gilson Gardner, November 9, 1915, subseries 1.2, box 16, folder 15, EWS Papers.

38. Scripps to Pinchot, November 10, 1915.

39. William McAdoo to E. W. Scripps, November 15, 1915, subseries 1.1, box 35, folder 13, EWS Papers.

40. Franklin Lane to E. W. Scripps November 15, 1915, subseries 1.1, box 35, folder 11, EWS Papers.

41. Gilson Gardner to E. W. Scripps, November 18, 1915, subseries 1.1, box 35, folder 8, EWS Papers.

42. Ibid.

43. E. W. Scripps to Basil Manly, November 21, 1915, subseries 1.2, box 16, folder 15, EWS Papers.

44. Basil M. Manly, "Proof $320,000,000 Is Stolen by Tax Frauds," *Cleveland Press*, April 26, 1916.

45. B. H. Canfield to E. W. Scripps, December 14, 1915, subseries 1.1, box 35, folder 6, EWS Papers.

46. Ibid.

47. E. W. Scripps to B. H. Canfield, December 21, 1915, subseries 1.2, box 17, folder 1, EWS Papers.

48. For a discussion of the 1916 revenue act, see Blakey and Blakey, *The Federal Income Tax*, 104–21.

49. Ibid., 107–8.

50. William McAdoo to E. W. Scripps, December 16, 1915, subseries 1.1, box 35, folder 13, EWS Papers.

51. *Annual Report, 1915*, 17.

52. Ibid., 18.

53. Ibid.

54. Basil Manly, "$320,000,000 Is Stolen from U.S.," *Cleveland Press*, April 24, 1916. To check for "inaccurate phrasing," the Scripps corporate attorneys, who did the Concern's corporate taxes and many of the Concern men's personal income taxes, volunteered to review Manly's articles in advance. See J. W. Curts to B. H. Canfield, March 29, 1916, subseries 3.1, box 47, folder 13, EWS Papers.

55. Ibid. This assertion is based on the *Press*'s layout of the Manly article.

56. Basil Manly, "Publicity Can Stop Tax Thefts," *Cleveland Press*, April 25, 1916.

57. Blakey and Blakey, *The Federal Income Tax*, 54.

58. Ibid., 57.

59. Manly, "Proof $320,000,000 Is Stolen."

60. Basil Manly, "Income Tax Law Allows Thefts," *Cleveland Press*, April 27, 1916. See also *Annual Report, 1915*, 19.

61. Basil Manly, "Manly Points Out Way to End Huge Tax Fraud," *Cleveland Press*, April 29, 1916.

62. Basil Manly, "Harkness Suit Bares How Tax Law Is Evaded," *Cleveland Press*, May 1, 1916.

63. "Publicity or Espionage," *Cleveland Press*, April 27, 1916.

64. "That Interesting, Inevitable Income Tax," *Everybody's*, February 1917, 254–55. It should be noted that this magazine was an easy mark because Howard Wheeler, a former Scripps employee, was its editor. Wheeler had pledged to "do everything possible personally to help," according to NEA president Canfield. See B. H. Canfield to E. W. Scripps, August 3, 1916, subseries 1.1, box 36, folder 7, EWS Papers.

65. "Publicity for Income Tax Returns," *New Republic*, August 12, 1916, 31–32.

66. "Income Tax Records Open," *New York Times*, September 9, 1916, 254–55.

67. Tenth Annual NEA Meeting, December 28, 1916, subseries 3.1, box 49, folder 4, EWS Papers.

68. As the largest newspaper in the Scripps chain during this time period, it can be assumed that the *Press* printed much more than most Scripps papers, which tended to be the second or third largest newspapers in their local markets.

69. Blakey and Blakey, *The Federal Income Tax*, 119. According to Blakey and Blakey, the issue would resurface again in income tax debates in 1921, 1924, 1928, and 1934. Senator Robert LaFollette of Wisconsin would be the biggest supporter of income tax publicity.

70. Contemporaries who credited the Scripps newspapers include then postmaster general Albert Burleson and progressive Amos Pinchot. See Gilson Gardner, *Lusty Scripps: The Life of E. W. Scripps* (Vanguard Press, 1932), 193; and Amos Pinchot, *History of the Progressive Party* (New York: New York University Press, 1958) 222–23. Progressive Supreme Court justice Louis Brandeis also told NEA political correspondent Gilson Gardner that the Scripps papers carried the election. See Gilson Gardner to E. W. Scripps, November 24, 1916, subseries 1.1, box 34, folder 8, EWS Papers. Progressive judge Ben Lindsey of Denver also told Scripps he thought the Scripps newspapers deserved "the chief credit" for Wilson's reelection. See Ben Lindsey to E. W. Scripps, December 7, 1916, series 2, letterbooks, vol. 32, box 29, EWS papers.

71. John Milton Cooper, Jr., *Pivotal Decades: The United States, 1900–1920* (New York: Norton, 1990), 253.

72. See Robert E. Burke, "The Scripps West Coast Newspapers and the Election of 1916," in *A Celebration of the Legacies of E. W. Scripps: His Life, Works, and Heritage* (Athens: Ohio University, 1990), 21.

73. In 1916 Wilson was the first Democratic presidential candidate since 1856 to win a majority of the votes cast in Ohio. He won by a large plurality in 1916, but he did not have more than 50 percent of the votes cast in the three-candidate race between him, William Taft, and Theodore Roosevelt. See Hoyt Landon Warner, *Progressivism in Ohio, 1897–1917* (Columbus: Ohio State University Press, 1964), 481.

74. Gilson Gardner to E. W. Scripps, November 10, 1916, subseries 1.1, box 36, folder 8, EWS Papers. For the election in California, see Burke, "The Scripps West Coast Papers," 21.

75. Microfilm of these newspapers from June through November 1916 was viewed for this discussion. The *Citizen* and *News-Bee* are available at the Ohio Historical Society, Columbus; the *Post* and *Cleveland Press* are available at Alden Library, Ohio University, Athens; and the *Akron Press* is available at Bierce Library, University of Akron.

76. Historians widely agree on the critical importance of Ohio for Wilson in 1916, especially because nearby states such as Illinois, Michigan, Pennsylvania, and Indiana went to Hughes. See Cooper, *Pivotal Decades*, 255, and S. D. Lovell, *The Presidential Election of 1916* (Carbondale: Southern Illinois Press, 1980), 88, 177.

77. Arthur S. Link, *Woodrow Wilson and the Progressive Era: 1910–1917* (New York: Harper and Row, 1954), 79.

78. Finnegan, *Against the Specter of a Dragon*, 193.

79. E. W. Scripps to William Kettner, March 11, 1916, subseries 1.2 box 17, folder 4, EWS Papers.

80. Ibid.

81. E. W. Scripps to Franklin K. Lane, March 11, 1916, subseries 1.2, box 17, folder 4, EWS Papers.
82. Warner, *Progressivism in Ohio*, 475.
83. Scripps to Lane, March 11, 1916.
84. Link, *Wilson and the Progressive Era*, 225–26.
85. Ibid., 226–28.
86. Cooper, *Pivotal Decades*, 214.
87. Link, *Wilson and the Progressive Era*, 229.
88. E. W. Scripps to John W. Hart, May 2, 1916, subseries 1.2, box 17, folder 4, EWS Papers.
89. For an overview of the 1916 election, see Sean Dennis Cashman, *America in the Age of Titans: The Progressive Era and World War I* (New York: New York University Press, 1988) 475–79. The definitive book on the 1916 election is Lovell, *The Presidential Election of 1916*.
90. R. F. Paine to James Scripps, July 5, 1916, subseries 3.1, box 48, folder 11, EWS Papers.
91. Ibid.
92. Ibid.
93. Gilson Gardner to E. W. Scripps, June 24, 1916, subseries 1.1, box 36, folder 8, EWS papers.
94. "Get Busy, McAdoo," *Columbus Citizen*, July 24, 1916.
95. William Kent to E. W. Scripps, July 16, 1916, series 2, letterbooks, vol. 32, box 29, EWS Papers.
96. E. W. Scripps to William Kent, July 16, 1916, series 2, letterbooks, vol. 32, box 29, EWS Papers.
97. Ibid. The letter and telegram can be found together in the letterbooks.
98. E. W. Scripps to B. H. Canfield, July 16, 1916, series 2, letterbooks, vol. 32, box 29, EWS Papers.
99. Ibid.
100. The Scripps archives do not reveal the exact date Rickey was assigned to this campaign. Rickey tells E.W. in an August letter, however, that NEA president B. H. Canfield asked Rickey to "take charge" of it. H. N. Rickey to E. W. Scripps, August 9, 1916, series 2, letterbooks, vol. 32, box 29, EWS papers.
101. Ibid.
102. Ibid.
103. Ibid.
104. Woodrow Wilson, August 10, 1916, quoted in H. N. Rickey to E. W. Scripps, August 14, 1916, series 2, letterbooks, vol. 32, box 29, EWS papers.
105. Rickey to Scripps, August 14, 1916.
106. R. F. Paine to E. W. Scripps, August 28, 1916, series 2, letterbooks, vol. 32, box 29, EWS papers.
107. See Michael Schudson, *Discovering the News: A Social History of American Newspapers* (New York: Basic Books, 1978). Although some historians say objectivity emerged earlier, Schudson says that the "objectivity" did not develop in American journalism until after World War I.
108. H. N. Rickey to Editors of Ohio Papers, *Oklahoma News, Des Moines News*, September 27, 1916, subseries 3.1, box 48, folder 14, EWS Papers.
109. Rickey to Editors of Ohio Papers, September 27, 1916.

110. Ibid.

111. Bureau of Census, *Thirteenth Census of the United States* (Washington, D.C.: Government Printing Office, 1910), 4:395.

112. See Lovell, *Presidential Election of 1916*, 60–70.

113. Ibid., 68.

114. George W. Knepper, *Ohio and Its People* (Kent, Ohio: Kent State University Press, 1989), 315.

115. H. N. Rickey to Robert W. Wooley, September 27, 1916, box 48, folder 14, EWS papers.

116. One example came immediately after the election. Excerpts from German press editorials supporting Hughes were reprinted as one editorial in Scripps-McRae newspapers. See "German Papers Lining Up for Charles E. Hughes," *Akron Press*, June 16, 1916. Another exception appeared in mid-October. The editorial "Why German-Americans Should Vote for Hughes," *Cleveland Press*, October 11, 1916, was a translation of an editorial from the German newspaper the *New York Herold*.

117. "Roosevelt Hits Hyphen in Talk to Help Hughes," *Cleveland Press*, September 1, 1916.

118. "B-R-R-! Yes. T. R. Went thru City," *Cincinnati Post*, October 18, 1916.

119. Shall the President Be Punished for His Americanism?" *Cleveland Press*, October 28, 1916.

120. "Hits at Teddy," *Cincinnati Post*, October 6, 1916.

121. "German American Writes," *Cincinnati Post*, November 6, 1996.

122. "Are We Stung?" *Cincinnati Post*, October 14, 1916.

123. See "Chief Asks Voting Indians to Rally to Support for Wilson," *Akron Press*, November 2, 1916; "Ten Cincinnati Progressive Leaders Are Out for Wilson," *Akron Press*, November 2, 1916; "Moose Leader in Connecticut Favors Wilson," *Cincinnati Post*, November 3, 1916; and "Progressive, for Wilson, Warns of Standpat Peril," *Cincinnati Post*, November 3, 1916.

124. "President Wilson Has Helped All," *Akron Press*, October 31, 1916.

125. "When It's America That's at Stake, Men Should Not Vote as Republicans or Democrats, Says Edison," *Akron Press*, November 1, 1916.

126. "Jane Addams Praises Laws Wilson Has Passed to Aid People," *Cleveland Press*, November 3, 1916.

127. "Shall the Nation Go Forward with Wilson or Shall It Go Backward with Hughes?" *Cleveland Press*, November 3, 1916.

128. Knepper, *Ohio and Its People*, 297.

129. Ibid., 303.

130. Ibid., 313–14. Ohio's population grew rapidly at this time, too. From 1910 to 1920, Akron's population grew 201 percent (to 208,435); Cincinnati's 10.4 percent (to 401,247); Cleveland's 42.1 percent (to 560,663); Columbus's 30.6 percent (to 237,031); and Toledo's 44.3 percent (to 243,164). Harvey J. Smith, *Ohio Fourteenth Federal Census: Statistics of Population, 1920–1910–1900* (Columbus: F. J. Heer, 1921), 6.

131. Merlo J. Pusey, *Charles Evans Hughes* (New York: MacMillan, 1952), 1:352–53.

132. "Labor and the Candidates," *Akron Press*, September 18, 1916.

133. "It Was a Condition, Not a Theory, That Confronted the President," *Toledo News-Bee*, September 26, 1916.

134. "Does Ford or Hughes Know More about the Eight-Hour Day?" *Toledo News-Bee,* September 28, 1916.
135. Lovell, *Presidential Election of 1916,* 136.
136. "Cheer for Wilson as Hughes Talks; Jurist Gets Stormy Reception at Overland," *Toledo News-Bee,* September 26, 1916.
137. Lovell, *Presidential Election of 1916,* 135.
138. "If You Think This Country Should Go to War—Read This." *Cleveland Press,* November 1, 1916.
139. "World War Likely to Go On Five Years," *Cleveland Press,* November 4, 1916.
140. "Peace or War—A Clearly Defined Issue of the Campaign," *Cleveland Press,* October 4, 1916.
141. "Hughes, the Boys of America, and the European Slaughterhouse," *Akron Press,* September 21, 1916.
142. "Would You Die to Save Europe?" *Columbus Citizen,* November 7, 1916.
143. "Hail to Ohio and the West," *Cleveland Press,* November 14, 1916.
144. Socialist candidate Allen L. Benson garnered 38,092 votes in the election. Prohibition candidate J. Frank Hanley received 8,080. Wilson finished with 604,161 votes; Hughes with 514,753. Ohio Secretary of State, *Annual Report of the Secretary of State to the Governor and General Assembly of the State of Ohio for Year Ending June 30, 1917,* July 20, 1917, 241–42.
145. Ibid.
146. "Votes of Women and Bull Moose Elected Wilson," *New York Times,* November 12, 1916.
147. Charles Evans Hughes, *The Autobiographical Notes of Charles Evans Hughes,* edited by David J. Danleski and Joseph S. Tulchin (Cambridge, Mass.: Harvard University Press, 1973), 184.
148. Lovell, *Presidential Election of 1916,* 177.
149. Ibid.
150. H. N. Rickey to E. W. Scripps, November 15, 1916, box 36, folder 12, EWS papers.
151. E. W. Scripps, "A Short Visit with the President," in Knight, *I Protest,* 570.
152. E. W. Scripps to Gilson Gardner, December 15, 1916, subseries 1.2, box 17, folder 8, EWS Papers.

Chapter 5: Democracy versus Autocracy

1. E. W. Scripps to Gilson Gardner, December 6, 1916, subseries 1.2, box 17, folder 8, E. W. Scripps Papers, Alden Library, Ohio University, Athens (hereafter EWS Papers).
2. E. W. Scripps to Gilson Gardner, December 26, 1916, subseries 1.2, box 17, folder 8, EWS Papers.
3. Gilson Gardner, *Lusty Scripps* (New York City: Vanguard Press, 1932), 182.
4. Vance Trimble, ed. *Scripps Howard Handbook,* 3d ed. (Cincinnati: Scripps, 1981), 70.

5. E. W. Scripps to Max Eastman, November 9, 1916, subseries 1.2, box 17, folder 8, EWS Papers.

6. Scripps to Gardner, December 26, 1916.

7. Ibid.

8. Ed Keen, "People of England Say 'No Peace on Germany's Terms,'" *Cleveland Press*, December 13, 1916.

9. Roy W. Howard to E. M. House, December 1, 1916, reel 2, Roy W. Howard Papers, Manuscript Division, Library of Congress, Washington, D.C. (hereafter RWH-LOC Papers).

10. Roy W. Howard to C. F. Mosher, December 14, 1916, Roy W. Howard Papers, Indiana University, Bloomington, Department of Journalism (hereafter RWH-IU Papers).

11. Lord Northcliffe, "Northcliffe's Opinion of Germany's Proposal," *Cleveland Press*, December 12, 1916.

12. "Sit Tight and Don't Rock the Boat!" *Cleveland Press*, December 15, 1916.

13. Quoted in John Milton Cooper, Jr., *Vanity of Power: American Isolationism and the First World War, 1914–1917* (Westport, Conn.: Greenwood, 1969), 133–34.

14. "The President's Peace Move," *Cleveland Press*, December 22, 1916.

15. Quoted in Ed L. Keen, "British Warmly Resent Wilson's Note of Peace," *Cleveland Press*, December 22, 1916.

16. "Shall the U.S. Guarantee Performance of Any Nation's Peace Pledges?" *Cleveland Press*, December 26, 1916.

17. "It Is the Supreme Duty of Every American to Know What Is Happening in the World," *Cleveland Press*, December 30, 1916.

18. "This Nation Should Not Try to Force Peace That Is Not Based upon Justice; Any Other Peace Is Worse Than War," *Cleveland Press*, January 8, 1917.

19. "The Answer of the Allies to the President's Note," *Cleveland Press*, January 13, 1917.

20. Quoted in August Heckscher, *Woodrow Wilson* (New York: Collier Books, 1991), 424–25.

21. "'The Federation of the World,'" *Cleveland Press*, January 23, 1917.

22. Cooper, *The Vanity of Power*, 146–62, gives an excellent description of the forces that formed to oppose Wilson in January and February.

23. Ibid., 160, 162.

24. "'A World Afire,'" *Cleveland Press*, February 1, 1917.

25. "Stand by the President," *Cleveland Press*, February 3, 1917.

26. Cooper, *The Vanity of Power*, 168.

27. Alfred K. Nippert to J. C. Harper, February 11, 1917, subseries 1.2, box 17, folder 10, EWS Papers.

28. Daniel Kiefer to E. W. Scripps, February 12, 1917, subseries 1.2, box 17, folder 10, EWS Papers.

29. E. W. Scripps to Daniel Kiefer, February 13, 1917, subseries 1.2, box 17, folder 10, EWS Papers.

30. Robert Paine to E. W. Scripps, February 15, 1917, subseries 1.1, box 37, folder 10, EWS Papers.

31. Cooper, *The Vanity of Power*, 175–76.

32. "Our Duty Now," *Cleveland Press*, February 5, 1917.
33. Charles Edward Russell, "We'd End War in Ninety Days—Russell," *Cleveland Press*, February 7, 1917.
34. B. H. Canfield to S. T. Hughes, February 12, 1917, subseries 3.1, box 49, folder 7, EWS Papers.
35. "Kaiser to Go to Limit in Frightfulness," *Cleveland Press*, February 8, 1917.
36. Mary Boyle O'Reilly, "Record Reporter Runs U Blockaide," *Los Angeles Record*, February 13, 1917; The quotation is from the editor's note prefacing the piece.
37. Neg Cochran to B. H. Canfield, February 23, 1916, subseries 3.1, box 49, folder 7, EWS Papers.
38. Neg Cochran to E. W. Scripps, February 24, 1917, subseries 1.2, box 37, folder 2, EWS Papers.
39. Barbara Tuchman, *The Zimmermann Telegram* (1958; reprint, New York: Ballantine Books, 1985), 175.
40. "Germany's Plot Foiled; Tried to Get Japs and Mexico to Invade U.S.," *Cleveland Press*, March 1, 1917.
41. Robert J. Bender, "Berlin Admits Plot," *Cleveland Press*, March 3, 1917.
42. "When the Germans Plot against America They Act True to Form," *Cleveland Press*, March 3, 1917.
43. William P. Simms, "One Day amid Ruin in France Cures Pacifism," *Cleveland Press*, March 27, 1917.
44. William Philip Simms, "French Women Are Made War Captives," *Cleveland Press*, March 23, 1917.
45. Henry Wood, "Old and Young Victims of Germans," *Cleveland Press*, March 26, 1917.
46. "An Interpretation of Pacifism and Some Remarks on Universal Military Training," *Cleveland Press*, March 24, 1917.
47. See: "Uncle Sam's Secret Service Men," *Cleveland Press*, March 3, 1917; Milton Bronner, "Full Story of Secret War Germany Has Waged against the United States for Thirty Months," *Cleveland Press*, March 12, 1917.
48. Harry B. Hunt to E. E. Martin, April 3, 1917, subseries 3.1, box 49, folder 9, EWS Papers.
49. Quoted in John Dos Passos, *Mr. Wilson's War* (Garden City, N.Y.: Doubleday, 1962), 201.
50. See John Milton Cooper, *Pivotal Decades: the United States: 1900–1920* (New York: Norton, 1990), 262, 264.
51. "Wilson Calls War Congress," *Cleveland Press*, March 21, 1917.
52. "United States Should Make Common Cause with Entente Nations against Germany," *Cleveland Press*, March 23, 1917.
53. B. H. Canfield to S. T. Hughes, March 29, 1917, subseries 3.1, box 49, folder 8, EWS Papers.
54. "Finley" to B. H. Canfield, March 29, 1917, subseries 3.1, box 49, folder 8, EWS Papers.
55. Eugene MacLean to B. H. Canfield, April 4, 1917, subseries 3.1, box 49, folder 9, EWS Papers.
56. Cooper, *Pivotal Decades*, 270,

57. MacLean to Canfield, April 4, 1917.
58. Cooper, *Pivotal Decades*, 267.
59. MacLean to Canfield, April 4, 1917.
60. Harry Rickey to J. C. Harper, April 16, 1917, subseries 3.1, box 49, folder 10, EWS Papers.
61. S. T. Hughes to J. W. T. Mason, April 6, 1917, subseries 3.1, box 49, folder 9, EWS Papers.
62. S. T. Hughes to W. W. Hawkins, April 10, 1917, subseries 3.1, box 49, folder 9, EWS Papers.
63. R. F. Paine to B. H. Canfield, April 17, 1917, subseries 3.1 box 49, folder 10, EWS Papers.
64. Gilson Gardner, *Lusty Scripps* (St. Clair Shores, Mich.: Vanguard Press, 1932), 200–201.
65. A. O. Andersson to B. H. Canfield, May 15, 1917, subseries 3.1, box 49, folder 12, EWS Papers.
66. B. H. Canfield to A. O. Andersson, May 23, 1917, subseries 3.1 box, 50, folder 1, EWS Papers.
67. R. F. Paine to B. H. Canfield, April 17, 1917, subseries 3.1 box 49, folder 10, EWS Papers.
68. J. C. Harper to B. H. Canfield, April 28, 1917, subseries 3.1, box 49, folder 11, EWS Papers.
69. B. H. Canfield to J. C. Harper, May 6, 1917, subseries 3.1, box 49, folder 12, EWS Papers.
70. J. C. Harper to B. H. Canfield, May 18, 1917, subseries 3.1, box 49, folder 12, EWS Papers.
71. Leroy Sanders to "Northwest Editors," subseries 3.1, box 49, folder 12, EWS Papers.
72. This exchange is recounted in E. W. Scripps to Robert P. Scripps, May 3, 1917, subseries 3.1, box 49, folder 12, EWS Papers.
73. E. W. Scripps to Bob Scripps, March 16, 1917, subseries 1.2, box 17, folder 12, EWS Papers.
74. Robert P. Scripps to James G. Scripps, April 21, 1917, subseries 3.1, box 49, folder 11, EWS Papers.
75. Cooper, *Vanity of Power*, 192.
76. "A Noble Message Which Meets the Approval of All Patriots," *Cleveland Press*, April 3, 1917.
77. "As the Poor Will Do the Fighting, Let the Rich Do the Paying," *Cleveland Press*, April 3, 1917.
78. Charles Edward Russell, "U.S. Has Chance to Revolutionize World Diplomacy, Says Russell," *Cleveland Press*, May 14, 1917.
79. See David M. Kennedy, *Over There: The First World War and American Society* (1980; reprint, Oxford: Oxford University Press, 1982), 26–27.
80. John A. Thompson, *Reformers and War: American Progressive Publicists and the First World War* (Cambridge: Cambridge University Press, 1987), 181.
81. "Lest We Forget," *Cleveland Press*, May 17, 1917.
82. "How Ruthlessness of Kaiser Forced U.S. in World War," *Cleveland Press*, April 6, 1917.
83. John Milton Cooper, *The Warrior and the Priest* (Cambridge, Mass.: Harvard University Press, 1985), 322–24.

84. "We Are All Soldiers in This Great War," *Cleveland Press*, April 20, 1917.

85. Seward W. Livermore, *Woodrow Wilson and the War Congress, 1916–1918* (originally published under the title *Politics Is Adjourned: Woodrow Wilson and the War Congress, 1916–1918*, 1966; reprint, Seattle: University of Washington Press, 1968), 17.

86. "An Extra Session of Congress at Once to Pass a Universal Military Training Law," *Cleveland Press*, March 9, 1917.

87. "Watch Your Congressman Closely," *Cleveland Press*, April 10, 1917.

88. If This Is Not Treason, in Heaven's Name What Is It?" *Cleveland Press*, April 11, 1917.

89. Charles Edward Russell, "Skulkers in Congress Best Aids to Kaiser," *Cleveland Press*, April 12, 1917.

90. E. W. Scripps to Woodrow Wilson, April 2, 1917, subseries 1.2, folder 12, box 17, EWS Papers.

91. Joseph Tumulty to E. W. Scripps, April 2, 1917, subseries 1.2, box 37, folder 9, EWS Papers.

92. Thompson, *Reformers and War*, 183. E. W. Scripps to Amos Pinchot, April 10, 1917, subseries 1.2, box 17, folder 12, EWS Papers.

93. Scripps stated that in an angry telegram to Pinchot. See E. W. Scripps to Amos Pinchot, April 11, 1917, subseries 1.2, box 17, folder 12, EWS Papers.

94. E. W. Scripps to Amos Pinchot, April 9, 1917, subseries 1.2, box 17, folder 12, EWS Papers.

95. A copy of this editorial can be found attached to H. N. Rickey to E. W. Scripps, April 12, 1917, subseries 1.1, box 37, folder 12, EWS Papers.

96. Rickey later apologized for the tone of his writings, saying that he was sorry E.W. might have taken them "as a reflection upon your intelligence." Rickey explained that he was just worked up about watching to "lick the Germans." See H. N. Rickey to E. W. Scripps, April 27, 1917, subseries 1.1, box 37, folder 12.

97. Amos Pinchot to E. W. Scripps, April 15, 1917, subseries 1.1, box 37, folder 12, EWS Papers.

98. E. W. Scripps to Edward Keating, April 16, 1917, subseries 1.2, box 17, folder 12.

99. Recalled in Robert Scripps to James Scripps, April 24, 1917, subseries 3.1, box 49, folder 11, EWS Papers.

100. E. W. Scripps to Robert Scripps, April 24, 1917, subseries 1.2, box 17, folder 12, EWS Papers.

101. Gilson Gardner, "Millionaires Ask That Their Big Incomes Be Conscripted," *Evansville Press*, April 30, 1917.

102. Gilson Gardner to E. W. Scripps, April 26, 1917, subseries 1.1, box 37, folder 6, EWS Papers.

103. Kennedy, *Over There*, 109.

104. Edward Keating to E. W. Scripps, April 16, 1917, subseries 1.1, box 37, folder 6, EWS Papers.

105. E. W. Scripps to Gilson Gardner, May 3, 1917, subseries 1.2, box 17, folder 13, EWS Papers.

106. E. W. Scripps to H. N. Rickey, B. H. Canfield, and E. E. Martin, May 3, 1917, subseries 1.2, box 17, folder 13, EWS Papers.

107. Ibid. Scripps felt his plan, backed in his papers, of paying soldiers the high

wage of three dollars a day would forestall any tendencies for soldiers to revolt in peacetime. He also felt that the rich should pay for the war through high income and inheritance taxes, another plan that was backed editorially by the NEA.

108. E. W. Scripps to Ellen Scripps, May 26, 1917, subseries 1.2, box 17, folder 13, EWS Papers.

109. E. W. Scripps to Bob Scripps, April 16, 1917, EWS Papers.

110. E. W. Scripps to Ellen Scripps, May 26, 1917.

111. E. W. Scripps to J. C. Harper, July 28, 1917, subseries 1.2, box 18, folder 3, EWS Papers.

112. B. H. Canfield to Robert P. Scripps, June 1, 1917, subseries 3.1, box 50, folder 2, EWS Papers.

113. R. F. Paine to B. H. Canfield, May 31, 1917, subseries 3.1, box 50, folder 1, EWS Papers.

114. *N. W. Ayers and Sons American Newspaper Annual and Directory* (Philadelphia: Ayers, 1917), 74–76. The *Record*'s circulation was 38,987. The *Herald* led all newspapers with a circulation of 116,143, followed by the *Times* at 66,906 and the *Examiner* at 66,843.

115. Charles Edward Russell, "No More Kings, No More War; On the Way to Coming True," *Los Angeles Record*, March 26, 1917.

116. See "Financing the War," *Los Angeles Record*, April 6, 1917; and Idah M'Glone Gibson, "President Endorses Army against Waste," *Los Angeles Record*, May 1, 1917.

117. "A Word to a Mad Pacifist," *Los Angeles Record*, April 12, 1917. This article contained the letter from Frank N. Fish and Sleeth's response.

118. Livermore, *Woodrow Wilson and the War Congress*, 49.

119. Ibid., 32–33.

120. Zechariah Chafee, Jr., *Free Speech in the United States* (1941; reprint, New York: Atheneum, 1969), 39.

121. George Juergens, *News from the White House* (Chicago: University of Chicago Press, 1981), 192–96.

122. "Short and Important," *Los Angeles Record*, May 29, 1917.

123. John Perry, "Why You Don't Care about War," *Los Angeles Record*, May 31, 1917. Perry was identified as a "newspaper lawyer" in his byline.

124. W. H. Porterfield to E. W. Scripps, June 1, 1917, subseries 1.1, box 37, folder 1, EWS Papers.

125. E. W. Scripps to James Scripps, June 5, 1917, subseries 1.2, box 17, folder 14, EWS Papers.

126. W. H. Porterfield to James G. Scripps, June 7, 1917, subseries 3.1, box 50, folder 2, EWS Papers.

127. John Perry to E. W. Scripps, June 7, 1917, subseries 1.1, box 37, folder 10, EWS Papers.

128. Robert P. Scripps to James G. Scripps, June 6, 1917, subseries 3.1, box 50, folder 2, EWS Papers.

129. E. W. Scripps to James G. Scripps, June 7, 1917, subseries 1.2, folder 14, box 17, EWS Papers.

130. E. W. Scripps to M. A. McRae, June 8, 1917, subseries 1.2, box 17, folder 14, EWS Papers.

131. E. W. Scripps to Robert Paine, June 14 1917, subseries 1.2, box 17, folder 14, EWS Papers.

132. E. W. Scripps to James G. Scripps, June 15, 1917, subseries 1.2, box 17, folder 14, EWS Papers. Begins "I urge you to wire . . ."
133. Ibid. Begins "Your telegram received . . ."
134. J. C. Harper to R. F. Paine, June 16, 1917, subseries 3.1, box 50, folder 2, EWS Papers.
135. E. W. Scripps to W. W. Thornton, June 16, 1917, subseries 1.2, box 17, folder 15, EWS Papers. Copies of all the original letters are in this folder. The letters are all the same except for their addressees.
136. Victor Morgan to E. W. Scripps, June 21, 1917, subseries 1.1 box 37, folder 9, EWS Papers.
137. G. B. Parker to E. W. Scripps, June 22, 1917, subseries 1.1, box 37, folder 10, EWS Papers.
138. Ralph Millett to E. W. Scripps, June 21, 1917, subseries 1.1, box 37, folder 9, EWS Papers.
139. F. R. Peters to E. W. Scripps, June 27, 1917, subseries 1.1, box 37, folder 10, EWS Papers.
140. S. T. Hughes to E. W. Scripps, June 21, 1917, subseries 1.1, box 37, folder 6, EWS Papers.
141. N. D. Cochran to E. W. Scripps, June 23, 1917, subseries 1.1, box 37, folder 2, EWS Papers.
142. J. C. Harper to E. W. Scripps, June 29, 1917, subseries 1.1 box 37, folder 4, EWS Papers.
143. Dana Sleeth to E. W. Scripps, June 26, 1917, subseries 1.1, box 37, folder 13, EWS Papers.
144. E. W. Scripps to J. C. Harper, July 7, 1917, subseries 1.2, box 18, folder 2, EWS Papers.
145. E. W. Scripps to Dana Sleeth, July 3, 1917, subseries 1.2, Both 18, folder 2, EWS Papers.
146. E. W. Scripps to H. N. Rickey, July 7, 1917, subseries 1.2, box 18, folder 2, EWS Papers.
147. Ibid.
148. E. W. Scripps to James Scripps, H. N. Rickey, and N. D. Cochran, July 12, 1917, subseries 2, box 18, folder 2, EWS papers.
149. J. C. Harper to N. D. Cochran, July 6, 1917, subseries 3.1, box 50, folder 4, EWS Papers.
150. "Shut Up or Be Locked Up," *Cleveland Press*, June 21, 1917.
151. Daniel Kiefer to editor of *Cincinnati Post*, July 13, 1917, subseries 3.1, box 50, folder 4, EWS Papers. Kiefer said a "citizen of Los Angeles" had sent him copies of some of the *Record*'s articles from May 31.
152. B. H. Canfield to S. T. Hughes, July 14, 1917, subseries 3.1, box 50, folder 4, EWS Papers.
153. Joseph L. Morrison, *Josephus Daniels: The Small-d Democrat* (Chapel Hill: University of North Carolina Press, 1966), 94.
154. Clarence H. Cramer, *Newton D. Baker: A Biography* (Cleveland: World, 1961), 99–100.
155. B. H. Canfield to S. T. Hughes, July 14, 1917, subseries 3.1, box 50, folder 4, EWS Papers.
156. "What You Think of the War," *Los Angeles Record*, June 4, 1917.

157. "T.R. as War Sec'y? Record Readers Ask," *Los Angeles Record*, June 12, 1917.

158. "Whose Flag Is This," *Los Angeles Record*, July 17, 1917.

159. W. H. Porterfield to B. H. Canfield, July 18, 1917, subseries 3.1, box 50, folder 4, EWS Papers.

160. Quoted in Juergens, *News from the White House*, 195.

161. Chafee, *Free Speech in the United States*, 51–60.

162. H. C. Peterson and Gilbert C. Fite, *Opponents of War, 1917–1918* (1957; reprint, Seattle: University of Washington Press, 1968), 94–95.

163. E. W. Scripps to H. N. Rickey and N. D. Cochran, July 18, 1917, subseries 1.2, box 18, folder 3, EWS Papers.

164. H. N. Rickey to Martin, Sanders, Andersson, Mayborn, Peters, McClain, Porterfield, and Sleeth, July 19, 1917, subseries 1.2, box 18, folder 3, EWS Papers.

165. James G. Scripps to E. W. Scripps, July 24, 1917, subseries 1.1 box 37, folder 14, EWS Papers.

166. James G. Scripps to E. W. Scripps, July 25, 1917, subseries 1.1, box 37, folder 14, EWS Papers.

167. Ibid.

168. E. W. Scripps to James G. Scripps, July 22, 1917, subseries 1.2, box 18, folder 3, EWS Papers.

169. James G. Scripps to E. W. Scripps, July 28, 1917, subseries 1.2, box 18, folder 3, EWS Papers.

170. Ibid.

171. Robert Scripps to J. W. Curts, June 1, 1917, subseries 3.1, box 50, folder 2, EWS Papers.

172. J. C. Harper to E. W. Scripps, June 11, 1917, subseries 1.1, box 37, folder 4, EWS Papers.

Chapter 6: "To Advocate a Policy and to Yourself Meet Its Requirements"

1. "Universal Training," *Cleveland Press*, December 4, 1916.

2. "Fallacies of the Opponents of Universal Military Service," *Cleveland Press*, March 21, 1917. See also: "If We Are Fighting for Democracy Let's Fight Democratically," *Cleveland Press*, April 26, 1917.

3. "To the Young Men Who Are 'Selected for Service,'" *Cleveland Press*, June 5, 1917.

4. "Tomorrow We Report for Duty to Our Country," *Cleveland Press*, June 4, 1917.

5. "Extreme Penalty for Those Who Are Fighting Selective Service Enrollment," *Cleveland Press*, June 2, 1917.

6. "Trustees Succeed Robert P. Scripps," *New York Times*, March 5, 1938.

7. E. W. Scripps to J. C. Harper, July 27, 1917, subseries 1.2, box 18, folder 3, E. W. Scripps Papers, Alden Library, Ohio University, Athens (hereafter referred to as EWS Papers).

8. E. W. Scripps to Howard Wheeler, August 3, 1917, subseries 1.2, box 18, folder 4, EWS Papers.

9. E. W. Scripps to Ellen Scripps, August 4, 1917, subseries 1.2, box 18, folder 4, EWS Papers.

10. E. W. Scripps to J. C. Harper, July 20, 1917, subseries 1.2, box 18, folder 3, EWS Papers.

11. Negley D. Cochran, *E. W. Scripps* (1933; reprint, Westport, Conn.: Greenwood Press, 1972), 171.

12. Ibid., 172. Cochran is quoting Scripps.

13. Ibid., 177.

14. Michael C. C. Adams, *The Great Adventure: Male Desire and the Coming of World War I* (Bloomington: Indiana University Press, 1990), 73–84.

15. E. W. Scripps to J. W. Curts, July 20, 1917, subseries 3.1, box 50, folder 5, EWS Papers.

16. J. W. Curts to E. W. Scripps, July 20, 1917, subseries 1.1, box 37, folder 3, EWS Papers.

17. J. C. Harper to E. W. Scripps, July 21, 1917, subseries 1.1, box 37, folder 4, EWS Papers.

18. J. C. Harper to E. W. Scripps, July 22, 1917, subseries 1.1, box 37, folder 4, EWS Papers.

19. Ibid.

20. J. W. Curts to E. W. Scripps, July 22, 1917, subseries 1.1, box 37, folder 3, EWS Papers.

21. Steven J. Diner, *A Very Different Age: Americans of the Progressive Era* (New York: Hill and Wang, 1998), 233.

22. Seward W. Livermore, *Woodrow Wilson and the War Congress, 1916–1918* (originally published under the title *Politics Is Adjourned: Woodrow Wilson and the War Congress, 1916–1918*, 1966; reprint, Seattle: University of Washington Press, 1968), 48–49.

23. Harry B. Hunt, "Congress Still Dawdles over Food Control," *Cleveland Press*, June 14, 1917.

24. "Remember the Date—July 1," *Cleveland Press*, June 23, 1917.

25. "A Precious Senatorial Trinity," *Cleveland Press*, June 27, 1917.

26. Gilson Gardner, "Publicity Will Mark War Tax," *Cleveland Press*, April 16, 1917.

27. Basil M. Manly, "Tax Publicity Held Vital to Victory by U.S.," *Cleveland Press*, April 18, 1917.

28. "Income Tax Increases Ineffective Unless Evasions Are Made Impossible," *Cleveland Press*, April 18, 1917.

29. "We Have Conscripted Men to Fight; Now Let's Conscript Wealth to Pay," *Cleveland Press*, May 4, 1917.

30. Charles Gilbert, *American Financing of World War I* (Westport, Conn.: Greenwood, 1970), 91.

31. Scripps recounts his involvement in the draft issue in E. W. Scripps to J. C. Harper, July 28, 1917, subseries 1.2, box 18, folder 3, EWS Papers.

32. Ibid.

33. Gilson Gardner to E. W. Scripps, July 27, 1917, subseries 1.2, box 37, folder 6, EWS Papers. Gardner, however, erroneously wrote in his biography of Scripps that Scripps gave Taylor $4,000, when E. W. reported he gave Taylor $5,000. E. W. Scripps to James Scripps, July 25, 1917, subseries 3.2, box 6, folder 11, EWS Pa-

pers. See also: Gilson Gardner, *Lusty Scripps: The Life of E. W. Scripps, 1854–1926* (New York: Vanguard Press, 1932), 199–200.

34. E. W. Scripps to Nackie Scripps, July 24, 1917, subseries 1.2, box 18, folder 3, EWS Papers.

35. E. W. Scripps to James Scripps, July 25, 1917.

36. E. W. Scripps to Neg Cochran, July 28, 1917, subseries 1.2, box 18, folder 3, EWS Papers.

37. E. W. Scripps to Hannis Taylor, July 28, 1917, subseries 1.1, box 37, folder 3, EWS Papers.

38. E. W. Scripps to Hannis Taylor, August 22, 1917, subseries 1.2, box 8, folder 5, EWS Papers.

39. J. C. Harper to E. W. Scripps, August 1, 1917, subseries 1.1, box 37, folder 4, EWS Papers.

40. Gilson Gardner, "Expert Says Law Governing S.-S. Is Constitutional," *Cleveland Press*, August 13, 1917. The other article is Gilson Gardner, "Want Court to Prevent Sending Boys to France," *Cleveland Press*, August 6, 1917.

41. Tennant S. McWilliams, *Hannis Taylor: The New Southerner as an American* (Tuscaloosa: University of Alabama Press, 1978), 80–81.

42. John Whiteclay Chambers II, *To Raise an Army: The Draft Comes to Modern America* (New York: Free Press, 1987), 221–22.

43. Gardner, *Lusty Scripps*, 199

44. Lyon had gained attention in Ohio after he went undercover as an inmate in the Ohio penitentiary and exposed poor conditions there. During the Mexican border problems with Pancho Villa, Lyon also joined the army and served at a army barracks in Columbus, Ohio.

45. C. C. Lyon, "What Life in Navy's Like," *Cleveland Press*, April 10, 1917. This was the first article in the series and briefly mentioned Lyon's background.

46. C. C. Lyon, "Lyon Tells How Men Are Made Over in Uncle Sam's Navy," *Cleveland Press*, April 11, 1917.

47. C. C. Lyon, "Rivalry in Navy Makes Work Seem Like Play—Lyon," *Cleveland Press*, April 12, 1917.

48. Mary Boyle O'Reilly, "Press Woman Makes Trip in War Airplane," *Cleveland Press*, May 1, 1917.

49. See C. C. Lyon, "Press Man Serves on G-4, One of U.S. Submarines," *Cleveland Press*, May 19, 1917; and C. C. Lyon, "On U.S. Battleship in War Zone," *Cleveland Press*, April 25, 1917.

50. The best description of Russell's role in the Root Commission can be found in Donald H. Bragaw, "Soldier for the Common Good: The Life and Career of Charles Edward Russell" (Ph.D. diss., Syracuse University, 1970), 370–414.

51. "Russell, Writer of Press Articles on Russia, Is World-Known Newspaper Man," *Cleveland Press*, August 16, 1917.

52. Charles Edward Russell, "Russell on Russia," *Cleveland Press*, August 16, 1917.

53. Charles Edward Russell, "Russell Says: Pro-Germans from America Spread Lies among Russians," *Cleveland Press*, August 18, 1917.

54. Charles Edward Russell, "Russell Says: Russia Fights Only for Ideal," *Cleveland Press*, August 21, 1917.

55. Bragaw, *Soldier for the Common Good*, 411–12.

56. Roy Howard to F. M. Heller, May 5, 1917, subseries. 3.1, box 58, folder 10, EWS Papers.
57. Ibid.
58. Roy Howard to E. E. Martin, May 19, 1917, subseries 3.1, box 58, folder 10, EWS Papers.
59. Finis Farr, *Fair Enough: The Life of Westbrook Pegler* (New Rochelle, N.Y.: Arlington House, 1975), 61.
60. "Pegler Assigned to Front with Pershing," *Editor and Publisher*, August 4, 1917, 14.
61. Oliver Pilat, *Pegler: Angry Man of the Press* (Boston: Beacon Press, 1963), 69.
62. Ibid., 73-74.
63. Roy Howard to Josephus Daniels, July 5, 1917, Press Relations File, Josephus Daniels Papers, Manuscript Division, Library of Congress (hereafter JD Papers).
64. Recounted in Josephus Daniels to Roy Howard, July 23, 1918, Press Relations File, JD Papers.
65. Roy Howard to Josephus Daniels, July 21, 1917, Press Relations, July File, JD Papers.
66. Roy Howard to Josephus Daniels, July 26, 1917, Roy W. Howard Papers, Indiana University, Bloomington, Department of Journalism (hereafter RWH-IU Papers).
67. Wilbur Forrest, *Behind the Front Page: Stories of Newspaper Stories in the Making* (New York: Appleton-Century, 1934), 112-13.
68. Ibid., 112.
69. John J. Pershing, *My Experiences in the World War* (New York: Frederick A. Stokes, 1931), 2:221-22.
70. Roy Howard to Josephus Daniels, September 12, 1917, Navy Files: Press Censorship, JD Papers.
71. Josephus Daniels to Roy Howard, September 21, 1917, Navy Files: Press Censorship, JD Papers.
72. Joseph J. Mathews, *Reporting the Wars* (Minneapolis: University of Minnesota Press, 1957), 156-58.
73. Forrest, *Behind the Front Page*, 108.
74. Ibid., 107.
75. Pilat, *Angry Man of the Press*, 80.
76. "Memorandum Dictated by E. W. Scripps," August 20, 1917, subseries 1.2, box 18, folder 5, EWS Papers.
77. Milton McRae to E. W. Scripps, August 23, 1917, subseries 1.1, box 37, folder 8, EWS Papers.
78. J. W. Curts to E. W. Scripps, August 25, 1917, subseries 1.1, box 37, folder 3, EWS Papers.
79. J. W. Curts to E. W. Scripps, August 31, 1917, subseries 1.1, box 37, folder 3, EWS Papers.
80. E. W. Scripps to Nackie Scripps, September 23, 1917, subseries 1.2, box 18, folder 7, EWS Papers.
81. E. W. Scripps to Nackie Scripps, September 18, 1917, subseries 1.2, box 18, folder 6, EWS Papers.

82. E. W. Scripps to Nackie Scripps, September 9, 1917, subseries 1.2, box 18, folder 6, EWS Papers.

83. E. W. Scripps to Ellen Scripps, September 19, 1917, subseries 1.2, box 18, folder 17, EWS Papers.

84. J. C. Harper to E. W. Scripps, August 25, 1917, subseries 1.1, box 37, folder 5, EWS Papers. This letter is marked "not sent."

85. J. C. Harper to E. W. Scripps, September 6, 1917, subseries 1.1, box 37, folder 5, EWS Papers.

86. E. W. Scripps to Nackie Scripps, August 27, 1917, subseries 1.2, box 19, folder 5, EWS Papers.

87. Neg Cochran to E. W. Scripps, September 6, 1917, subseries 1.1, box 37, folder 2, EWS Papers.

88. Milton McRae to E. W. Scripps, August 14, 19197, subseries 1.1, box 37, folder 8, EWS Papers.

89. Harry Rickey to James Scripps, September 5, 1917, subseries 1.2, box 18, folder 6, EWS Papers.

90. B. H. Canfield to S. T. Hughes, August 23, 1917, subseries 3.1, box 50, folder 8, EWS Papers.

91. E. W. Scripps to Nackie Scripps, September 23, 1917.

92. E. W. Scripps to Nackie Scripps, September 18, 1917.

93. E. W. Scripps to Nackie Scripps, October 1, 1917, subseries 1.2, box 18, folder 8, EWS Papers.

94. Roosevelt, one of the Scripps newspapers' favorite personalities, led blistering attacks on the administration throughout 1917. See Livermore, *Woodrow Wilson and the War Congress*, 62–65.

95. E. W. Scripps to Nackie Scripps, September 18, 1917.

96. E. W. Scripps to Nackie Scripps, September 23, 1917.

97. E. W. Scripps to Nackie Scripps, September 18, 1917.

98. E. W. Scripps to Nackie Scripps, September 24, 1917, subseries 1.2, box 18, folder 7, EWS Papers.

99. E. W. Scripps to Jim Scripps, September 29, 1917, subseries 1.2, box 18, folder 7, EWS Papers.

100. E. W. Scripps to Ellen Scripps, October 2, 1917, subseries.3.2, box 7, folder 1, EWS Papers.

101. Neg Cochran to E. W. Scripps, September 30, 1917, subseries 1.1, box 37, folder 2, EWS Papers.

102. "Scripps Appeals to Wilson," *Editor and Publisher*, September 29, 1917, 9. See also "Son of E. W. Scripps Seeks Draft Exemption," *Editor and Publisher*, September 22, 1917, 14.

103. Robert Scripps to Newton Baker, September 30, 1917, General Correspondence, S file, 1917, Newton D. Baker Papers, Manuscript Division, Library of Congress, Washington, D.C. (hereafter NDB Papers).

104. E. W. Scripps to Nackie Scripps, October 1, 1917.

105. E. W. Scripps to Jim Scripps, October 3, 1917, subseries 1.2, box 18, folder 8, EWS Papers.

106. Ibid.

107. See David M. Kennedy, *Over There: The First World War and American Society* (1980; reprint, Oxford: Oxford University Press, 1982), 147–18.

108. Quoted in John Whiteclay Chambers II, *To Raise an Army: The Draft Comes to Modern America* (New York: Free Press, 1987), 190.

109. Newton Baker to Tom Sidlo, November 6, 1917, Miscellaneous Personal Correspondence File, 1918 [misfiled], NDB Papers.

110. E. W. Scripps to Nackie Scripps, October 14, 1917, subseries 1.2, box 18, folder 8, EWS Papers.

111. Vance H. Trimble, *The Astonishing Mr. Scripps: The Turbulent Life of America's Penny Press Lord* (Ames: Iowa State University Press, 1992), 373-74.

112. J. W. Curts to E. W. Scripps, October 3, 1917, subseries 1.1, box 37, folder 3, EWS Papers.

113. J. W. Curts to E. W. Scripps, October 8, 1917, subseries 1.1, box 37, folder 3, EWS Papers.

114. E. W. Scripps to Nackie Scripps, October 7, 1917, subseries 1.2, box 18, folder 8, EWS Papers.

115. Ibid. Scripps said Peggy asked him if he could arrange for Bob to stay in the army "for several months."

116. "Wilson Exempts Scripps's Son," *Los Angeles Times,* October 10, 1917.

117. E. W. Scripps to Nackie Scripps, October 17, 1917, subseries 1.2, box 18, folder 9, EWS Papers.

118. E. W. Scripps to Nackie Scripps, October 1, 1917, subseries 1.2, box 18, folder 8, EWS Papers.

119. Ibid.

120. E. W. Scripps to Ellen Browning Scripps, October 5, 1917, subseries 1.2, box 18, folder 8, EWS Papers.

121. Jim Scripps to Bob Scripps, October 17, 1917, subseries. 3.1, box 50, folder 12, EWS Papers.

122. Cochran, *E. W. Scripps,* 177.

123. E. W. Scripps to Milton McRae, October 25, 1917, subseries 1.2, box 18, folder 9, EWS Papers.

124. E. W. to Nackie Scripps, October 21, 1917, subseries 1.2, box 18, folder 9, EWS Papers.

125. E. W. Scripps to Nackie Scripps, October 27, 1917, subseries 1.2, box 18, folder 9, EWS Papers.

126. Milton McRae to E. W. Scripps, October 16, 1917, subseries 1.1, box 37, folder 8, EWS Papers.

127. Both newspapers quoted in Trimble, *The Astonishing Mr. Scripps,* 387.

128. C. F. Mosher to E. W. Scripps, October 22, 1917, subseries 3.1, box 50, folder 18, EWS Papers.

129. Scripps to McRae, October 25, 1917.

130. E. W. Scripps to Robert Paine, October 27, 1917, subseries 1.2, box 18, folder 9, EWS Papers.

131. Trimble, *The Astonishing Mr. Scripps,* 387.

132. Milton McRae to E. W. Scripps, November 6, 1917, subseries 1.1, box 37, folder 8, EWS Papers.

133. E. W. Scripps to Ellen Scripps, November 12, 1917, subseries 1.2, box 18, folder 10, EWS Papers.

134. Scripps to Paine, October 27, 1917.

135. Ibid.

136. E. W. Scripps to Ellen Scripps, November 6, 1917, subseries 3.2, box 7, folder 2, EWS Papers.

137. E. W. Scripps to Ellen Scripps, November 12, 1917.

138. Jim Scripps to Bob Scripps, October 30, 1917, subseries 3.1, box 50, folder 13, EWS Papers.

139. George Creel, *How We Advertised America* (New York: Harper, 1920), 247–48.

140. "E. W. Scripps Statement," October 26, 1917, subseries 1.2, box 18, folder 9, EWS Papers. Because surviving copies of the *Cincinnati Post* are incomplete, it is not known if the letter actually was published, although it probably was because of the criticism being raised in Ohio.

141. Excess profits were calculated by comparing current income to average income before 1914. This sort of tax mechanism favored industries that had been doing well before the war and hurt those that had been in a slump before the war. Scripps disliked the excess profits tax and instead wanted steep increases solely in income taxes. He said the income tax proposal would have cost him much more money. See E. W. Scripps to J. C. Harper, October 24, 1917, subseries 1.2, box 18, folder 9, EWS Papers; for a discussion of the tax debate, see Kennedy, *Over There*, 108.

142. E. W. Scripps to Nackie Scripps, October 14, 1917, subseries 1.2, box 18, folder 8, EWS Papers.

143. Frank Luther Mott, *American Journalism: A History: 1690–1960*, 3d ed. (New York: MacMillan, 1962), 632.

144. E. W. Scripps to Julius Wangenheim, October 5, 1917, subseries 1.2, box 18, folder 8, EWS Papers.

145. J. C. Harper to E. W. Scripps, October 12, 1917, subseries 1.1, box 37, folder 5, EWS Papers.

146. "Bonds or Bondage?" *Cleveland Press*, May 26, 1917.

147. "Your Debt to Uncle Sam," *Cleveland Press*, May 21, 1917.

148. "Liberty Bonds Pay Way," *Cleveland Press*, May 23, 1917.

149. "Have You Made Your Sacrifice?" *Cleveland Press*, October 10, 1917.

150. Milton McRae to E. W. Scripps, October 16, 1917, subseries 1.1, box 37, folder 8, EWS Papers.

151. E. W. Scripps to J. C. Harper, October 24, 1917, subseries 1.2, box 18, folder 9, EWS Papers.

152. C. F. Mosher to E. W. Scripps, June 5, 1917, subseries 1.1, box 37, folder 9, EWS Papers.

153. Oliver Knight, "Scripps and His Adless Newspaper, the *Day Book*," *Journalism Quarterly* 41 (1964): 63–64.

154. E. W. Scripps to Thomas Sharp, November 10, 1917, subseries 1.2, box 8, folder 10, EWS Papers.

155. Milton McRae to E. W. Scripps, August 3, 1917, subseries 1.1, box 37, folder 8, EWS Papers.

156. Milton McRae to E. W. Scripps, September 17, 1917, subseries 1.1, box 37, folder 8, EWS Papers.

157. Alfred Andersson to J. A. Keefe, January 2, 1917, subseries 3.1, box 49, folder 5, EWS Papers.

158. W. W. Thornton to Milton McRae, May 2, 1917, subseries 3.1, box 49, folder 12, EWS Papers.

159. "May Soon Raise Price of Cleveland Dailies," *Editor and Publisher*, May 19, 1917, 25.

160. Neg Cochran to Jim Scripps, May 10, 1917, subseries 3.1, box 49, folder 12, EWS Papers.

161. J. T. Watters to Neg Cochran, August 20, 1917, subseries 3.1, box 50, box 8, EWS Papers.

162. Mott, *American Journalism*, 633.

163. LeRoy Sanders to W. S. Dayton, J. C. Flagg, L. H. LaRash, and C. M. Burrowes, July 11, 1917, subseries 3.1, box 50, folder 4, EWS Papers.

164. J. C. Harper to Bob Scripps, November 7, 1917, subseries 3.1, box 50, folder 15, EWS Papers.

165. Bob Scripps to J. C. Harper, November 15, 1917, subseries 1.2, box 18, folder 10, EWS Papers.

166. E. W. Scripps to Ben Lindsey, October 30, 1917, subseries 1.2, box 18, folder 9, EWS Papers.

167. For a description of the magazine and its battle for survival during the war, see Eugene E. Leach, "The Radicals of the *Masses*," in *1915, The Cultural Moment*, ed. Adele Heller and Lois Rudnick (New Brunswick, N.J.: Rutgers University Press, 1991), 27–47.

168. Paul L. Murphy, *World War I and the Origin of Civil Liberties in the United States* (New York: Norton, 1979), 55–56.

169. Bob Scripps to B. H. Canfield, October 25, 1917, subseries 3.1, box 50, folder 13, EWS Papers.

170. H. C. Peterson and Gilbert C. Fite, *Opponents of War, 1917–1918* (1957; reprint, Seattle: University of Washington Press, 1968), 93.

171. B. H. Canfield to Bob Scripps, October 29, 1917, subseries 3.1, box 50, folder 13, EWS Papers.

172. E. W. Scripps to Ellen Scripps, November 6, 1917, subseries 3.2, box 7, folder 2, EWS Papers.

173. E. W. Scripps to Ellen Scripps, October 2, 1917, subseries 3.2, box 7, folder 1, EWS Papers.

174. Gardner, *Lusty Scripps*, 201.

175. J. C. Harper to E. W. Scripps, November 15, 1917, subseries 1.1, box 37, folder 5, EWS Papers.

176. "History of the Fight," *Los Angeles Record*, December 11, 1917.

177. "Bossism of Earl Is Crushed," *Los Angeles Record*, December 1, 1917.

178. Quoted in Harper to Scripps, November 15, 1917.

179. "Editor Asks Right to Keep on Aiding Nation in War," *Los Angeles Evening Herald*, November 14, 1917.

180. See: Roy Howard to Jim Scripps, October 29, 1915, reel 3, Roy W. Howard Papers, Library of Congress, Washington, D.C. (hereafter RWH-LOC Papers); J. C. Harper to Roy Howard, September 18, 1915, subseries 3.1, box 58, folder 8, EWS Papers; Howard to Jim Scripps, October 11, 1915, RWH-LOC Papers; Roy Howard to E. W. Scripps, July 20, 1917, subseries 1.1, box 40, folder 32, EWS Papers.

181. Roy Howard to John Perry, March 31, 1917, subseries 3.1, box 58, folder 10, EWS Papers.

182. J. C. Harper to Roy Howard, April 6, 1917, subseries 3.1, box 58, folder 10, EWS Papers.

183. J. C. Harper to Roy Howard, June 28, 1917, subseries 3.1, box 50, folder 4, EWS Papers.

184. This latter point was made by Harper. See ibid.

185. Milton McRae to J. C. Harper, subseries 3.1, box 50, folder 15, EWS Papers.

186. "Oral Evidence of Milton A. McRae and J. C. Harper before Industrial Commissioner, H. W. Wright," November 1917, subseries 3.2, box 6, folder 12.

187. Quoted in "Scripps Must Go to Army, Says Appeal Body," *Los Angeles Tribune*, November 24, 1917.

188. Ed Fletcher to Woodrow Wilson, November 28, 1917, subseries 3.1, box 50, folder 15, EWS Papers.

189. Chambers, *To Raise an Army*, 191.

Chapter 7: Reconsidering an "Ostrich Type of Patriotism"

1. Negley Cochran to George Creel, January 24, 1918, subseries 3.1, box 51, folder 4, E. W. Scripps Papers, Alden Library, Ohio University, Athens (hereafter EWS Papers).

2. Bob Scripps to S. T. Hughes, January 25, 1918, subseries 3.1, box 51, folder 5, EWS Papers.

3. James P. Johnson, "The Wilsonians as War Managers: Coal and the 1917–18 Winter Crisis," *Prologue* 9 (1977): 205–7.

4. Ibid., 203.

5. "Doctor Garfield Is Giving Us Medicine out of Wrong Bottle," *Cleveland Press*, January 17, 1918.

6. "All Factories Must Be Shut at Midnight," *Cleveland Press*, January 17, 1918.

7. Earle Martin to Neg Cochran, January 28, 1918, subseries 3.1, box 51, folder 5, EWS Papers.

8. "'Coalless Monday,'" *Cleveland Press*, January 21, 1918.

9. Scripps to Hughes, January 25, 1918.

10. Seward W. Livermore, *Woodrow Wilson and the War Congress, 1916–1918* (originally published under the title *Politics Is Adjourned: Woodrow Wilson and the War Congress, 1916–1918*, 1966; reprint, Seattle: University of Washington Press, 1968), 88–89.

11. N. D. Cochran, "Wilson or Wall Street Is the Issue," *Cleveland Press*, February 9, 1918.

12. Bob Scripps to S. T. Hughes, January 29, 1918, subseries 3.1, box 51, folder 5, EWS Papers.

13. Ibid.

14. Quoted in Livermore, *Woodrow Wilson and the War Congress*, 101. Livermore said the "great offensive" against Wilson "petered out after February 15."

15. "The Show of Dirty Politics," *Cleveland Press*, January 23, 1918.

16. "Chamberlain Opens Attack on President," *Cleveland Press*, January 24, 1918.

17. N. D. Cochran, "Plotters Try to Make Roosevelt Dictator in War," *Cleveland Press*, January 25, 1918.

18. "Still Jawing, Not Lawing," *Cleveland Press*, February 8, 1918.

19. H. B. Hunt, "America's Record in the War," *Cleveland Press*, February 21, 1918.

20. "Just Where Uncle Sam Is At," *Cleveland Press*, February 21, 1918.

21. H. B. Hunt, "Every Soldier in U.S. Army Has His Rifle," *Cleveland Press*, February 27, 1918.

22. H. B. Hunt, "Machine Guns for Millions," *Cleveland Press*, February 28, 1918.

23. H. B. Hunt, "U.S. Is Ready to Shoot—And Straight, Too," *Cleveland Press*, March 7, 1918.

24. H. B. Hunt, "America Now Building Planes by Thousands," *Cleveland Press*, March 2, 1918.

25. H. B. Hunt, "U.S. Provides Army Best of Medical Care," *Cleveland Press*, March 12, 1918.

26. H. B. Hunt, "American Gets the Big Guns," *Cleveland Press*, February 25, 1918.

27. See Milton Bronner, "What America Is Doing to Build the Ships to Win War," *Cleveland Press*, March 11, 1918; and Milton Bronner, "U.S. Mobilizes 250,000 Men for Vast Shipbuilding Drive," *Cleveland Press*, March 18, 1918.

28. B. H. Canfield to Bob Scripps, November 19, 1917, subseries 3.1, box 50, folder 15, EWS Papers.

29. Earle Martin to E. E. Cook and M. B. Felber, November 23, 1917, subseries 3.1, box 50, folder 15, EWS Papers.

30. Ibid.

31. A discussion of Manly's leave can be found in Bob Scripps to S. T. Hughes, January 29, 1918, and S. T. Hughes to Bob Scripps, January 31, 1918, both in subseries 3.1, box 51, folder 5, EWS Papers. For information about the investigation, see N. D. Cochran, "Plan of Packers to Grab Food Control Shown by Heney," *Cleveland Press*, April 10, 1918.

32. Idah McGlone Gibson, "Author of 'Confessions of Wife' Interviews Pershing in France," *Cleveland Press*, January 18, 1918.

33. Idah McGlone Gibson, "'My Sweater Warms Heart as Well as Body,' Sammy Tells Idah M'Glone Gibson," *Cleveland Press*, March 12, 1918.

34. Victor Morgan, "Germany Today: Gold of the Kaiser Works Harder Than Valor; Treachery and Infamy Are Held in High Esteem," *Cleveland Press*, February 7, 1918.

35. Victor Morgan, "Germany Today: Militarists Do Not Deny Atrocities; They Advertise Them," *Cleveland Press*, February 11, 1918.

36. Morgan, "Germany Today: Gold of the Kaiser," *Cleveland Press*.

37. George Randolph Chester and Lillian Chester, "The Spirit of France," *Cleveland Press*, February 18, 1918.

38. George Randolph Chester and Lillian Chester, "France Today: Nation Toils to Save Babies," *Cleveland Press*, March 1, 1918.

39. "Russia Today: Bolsheviki's Peace Treaty Is Their Own Death Warrant," *Cleveland Press*, March 9, 1918.

268   *Notes to Pages 180–84*

40. Joseph Martinek, "Russia Today: America Is Beloved by Masses," *Cleveland Press*, March 13, 1918.

41. C. C. Arbuthnot, "Your Thrift Fights," *Cleveland Press*, February 14, 1918. Arbuthnot was a professor at Western Reserve University.

42. "Another War Sacrifice—The Patriotic Manicure," *Cleveland Press*, March 20, 1918.

43. "Plan Your War Garden Now; Press Will Tell You How to Increase Food Supply," *Cleveland Press*, February 13, 1918. The series began with this article.

44. "Everybody Who Can, Must Help," *Cleveland Press*, March 16, 1918.

45. For a description of German strategy and the success of the drives, see James Stokesbury, *A Short History of World War I* (New York: Morrow, 1981), 259–80.

46. For example, see "Official Statements," *Cleveland Press*, March 27, 1918.

47. "'We Hold the Enemy,'" *Cleveland Press*, March 22, 1918.

48. William Philip Simms, "British Drive Foe Back at Places," *Cleveland Press*, March 22, 1918.

49. Ed L. Keen, "London Warns of Undue Optimism," *Cleveland Press*, March 28, 1918.

50. J. W. T. Mason, "Climax of Drive Near," *Cleveland Press*, March 25, 1918.

51. J. W. T. Mason, "Sammies Block Foe," *Cleveland Press*, March 28, 1918.

52. J. W. T. Mason, "Foch Repels Huns as Drive Reopens," *Cleveland Press*, April 5, 1918.

53. "Morale of a Nation," *Cleveland Press*, April 30, 1918.

54. "Buy Today," *Cleveland Press*, April 16, 1918.

55. "Germans Shoot Down Mothers and Children," *Cleveland Press*, April 22, 1918.

56. "The Huns Did This," *Cleveland Press*, April 22, 1918.

57. "The Huns Did This," *Cleveland Press*, April 20, 1918. In the picture the girl's hands are at her side, but the her long hair, boyish figure, and downcast face look surprisingly like Christian representations of Jesus being crucified.

58. C. F. Mosher to E. E. Martin, October 5, 1918, subseries 3.1, box 52, folder 1, EWS Papers.

59. "How We Can Break the Heart of Autocracy," *Cleveland Press*, May 2, 1918.

60. Neg Cochran to A. O. Andersson, August 6, 1918, subseries 3.1, box 51, folder 11, EWS Papers.

61. See Earle Martin to Milton Bronner, August 26, 1918, box 11, folder 72, Records of the Committee for Public Information, Record Group 63, National Archives, Washington, D.C. (hereafter CPI-DC Papers).

62. Milton Bronner to Maurice Lyons, August 28, 1918, box 11, folder 72, CPI-DC Papers.

63. Earle Martin to Milton Bronner, October 1, 1918, box 11, folder 72, CPI-DC Papers.

64. Milton Bronner to George Creel, undated, box 11, folder 72, CPI-DC Papers. From the references in the letter and the context of the other letters, the letter was written in early October.

65. Maurice Lyons to George Creel, October 7, 1918, box 11, folder 72, CPI-DC Papers.

66. Earle Martin to Milton Bronner, August 26, 1918, box 11, folder 72, CPI-DC Papers.
67. George Creel, *How We Advertised America* (1920; reprint, New York: Arno Press, 1972), 74–75.
68. James R. Mock and Cedric Larson, *Words That Won the War: The Story of the Committee on Public Information, 1917–1919* (Princeton: Princeton University Press, 1939), 92.
69. Ibid., 6.
70. For a discussion of the news division, see Stephen Vaughn, *Holding Fast the Inner Lines: Democracy, Nationalism, and the Committee on Public Information* (Chapel Hill: University of North Carolina Press, 1980), 193–213.
71. Robert Paine to C. F. Mosher, August 14, 1918, subseries 3.1, box 51, folder 12, EWS Papers.
72. Quoted in Livermore, *Woodrow Wilson and the War Congress*, 119.
73. For an analysis of the controversy, see ibid., 125–34.
74. See ibid., 134–37.
75. Zechariah Chafee, Jr., *Free Speech in the United States* (1941; reprint, New York: Atheneum, 1969), 39.
76. C. F. Mosher to Milton McRae, July 24, 1918, subseries 3.1, box 51, folder 11, EWS Papers.
77. See memos in E. E. Cook to Earle Martin, undated, subseries 3.1, box 51, folder 6, EWS Papers, and V. Morgan to Earle Martin, undated, subseries 3.1, box 51, folder 6, EWS Papers.
78. Neg Cochran to E. W. Scripps, July 16, 1918, subseries 1.1, box 38, folder 2, EWS Papers.
79. "Second Son of Scripps Still Evades War Draft," *Cleveland News*, January 9, 1918.
80. Robert Scripps to *Cleveland Press*, January 1918, subseries 3.1, box 51, folder 5, EWS Papers. This is a telegram sent generically to the offices of the Cleveland newspaper. The exact date in January is not recorded.
81. Milton McRae, memorandum of conversation, January 8, 1918,. The man being quoted is a district-level official for San Diego County. The district board serving Los Angeles ultimately looked at Jim's case.
82. R. C. Allen to chairman of the District Exemption Board No. 3, January 30, 1918, subseries 3.1, box 51, folder 5, EWS Papers.
83. Milton McRae to Robert Scripps, January 30, 1918, subseries 3.1, box 51, folder 5, EWS Papers.
84. J. W. Curts to Neg Cochran, July 26, 1918, subseries 3.1, box 51, folder 11, EWS Papers. This letter provides an excellent timeline of the battle to get Bob exempted.
85. Unsigned and apparently unsent letter to Woodrow Wilson, undated (apparently, to judge by the time references in it, written in March or April 1918), subseries 3.1, box 51, folder 11, EWS Papers. This letter provides a good summary of Jim's fight to get exempted. The archival material does not explain how or why the deadlock came to be broken and Jim placed in Class IV. Cochran mentioned in a later letter that Jim was placed in Class IV "by the draft machinery without the President or the Secretary of War." Negley Cochran to Jay Curts, July 29, 1918, box 4, Negley Cochran Papers, Toledo-Lucas County Public Library, Toledo, Ohio (hereafter NC Papers).

86. "Newspaper Men Not to Be Exempted," *Editor and Publisher*, August 17, 1918, 82.

87. E. W. Scripps to Jim Scripps, June 26, 1918, series 2, letterbooks, box 31, EWS Papers.

88. E. W. Scripps to Ellen Scripps, August 8, 1918, series 2, letterbooks, box 31, EWS Papers.

89. Ibid.

90. Bob Scripps to S. T. Hughes, January 29, 1918, subseries 3.1, box 51, folder 5, EWS Papers.

91. E. W. Scripps to Negley Cochran, December 29, 1917, subseries 1.2, box 18, folder 11, EWS Papers.

92. The 1917 circulation of the *News-Bee* was 89,223, outdistancing the *Blade* with 50,726. See *N. W. Ayers and Sons American Newspaper Annual and Directory* (Philadelphia: Ayers, 1917), 771.

93. "Scripps Patriotism," *Toledo Times*, July 21, 1918.

94. "The Nerve of Scripps," *Toledo Times*, August 29, 1918.

95. "You're Wrong, Senator Sherman; Scripps Is the Original Slacker, and Not Ford," *Toledo Times*, September 5, 1918.

96. "They're Rounding Up Slackers in New York; When Will They Round Up the Scripps Herd?" *Toledo Times*, September 7, 1918.

97. "There Is No Idea among Patriots That We Must Let Up Our Efforts," *Toledo Times*, September 12, 1918.

98. Neg Cochran to N. C. Wright, August 7, 1918, subseries 3.1, box 51, folder 11, EWS Papers.

99. Neg Cochran to E. E. Martin, September 20, 1918, box 5, NC Papers.

100. The *Toledo Times* apparently began its campaign of encouraging its solicitors to spread rumors after the July 21 editorial in the *Times*. See Earle Martin to Neg Cochran, August 5, 1918, box 3, NC Papers.

101. F. M. Heller to Neg Cochran, September 16, 1918, box 3, NC Papers.

102. F. M. Heller to Neg Cochran, September 2, 1918, box 4, NC Papers. A copy of the advertising man's report can be found in W. G. Chandler to Neg Cochran, November 4, 1918, box 3, NC Papers.

103. Jim Scripps, Memorandum: Robert P. Scripps, October 7, 1918, subseries 3.1, box 52, folder 1, EWS Papers.

104. Neg Cochran to Bob Scripps, December 16, 1918, subseries 3.1, box 52, folder 6, EWS Papers.

105. Robert Mosher to C. F. Mosher, October 21, 1918, subseries 3.1, box 52, folder 3, EWS Papers.

106. Cochran to Scripps, December 16, 1918.

107. Jim Scripps to J. C. Harper, June 17, 1918, subseries 3.2, box 7, folder 3, EWS Papers.

108. For a discussion of the New York situation, see "New York Newspapers in Line," *Editor and Publisher*, January 26, 1918, 20. For the situation in other cities, see "Two-Cent Policy Greatest Forward Step of the Year," *Editor and Publisher*, January 19, 1918, 22.

109. Quoted in "One Cent Newspaper Is Disappearing," *Editor and Publisher*, April 6, 1918, 27.

110. W. W. Thornton to Milton McRae, July 3, 1918, subseries 3.1, box 51, folder 9, EWS Papers.

111. W. H. Dodge to W. W. Thornton, June 14, 1918, subseries 3.1, box 51, folder 6, EWS Papers.

112. Sam T. Hughes, "High Class Feature Matter in Favor," *Editor and Publisher*, January 19, 1918, 27.

113. Livermore, *Woodrow Wilson and the War Congress*, 88–89.

114. B. H. Canfield to Sam Hughes, May 25, 1918, subseries 3.1, box 51, folder 6, EWS Papers.

115. B. H. Canfield to Bob Scripps, June 8, 1918, subseries 3.1, box 51, folder 5, EWS Papers.

116. "War News by Mail, War News by Cable," *Editor and Publisher*, July 13, 1918, 3.

117. B. H. Canfield to Bob Scripps, June 8, 1918, subseries 3.1, box 51, folder 6, EWS Papers. See also: B. H. Canfield to Sam Hughes, May 25, 1918, subseries 3.1, box 51, folder 6, EWS Papers.

118. First seen in advertisements "Ideas," *Editor and Publisher*, April 20, 1918, 3.

119. See "NEA Reporter Covers Japan," *Editor and Publisher*, June 15, 1918, 3; "NEA Gets the Big Ones," *Editor and Publisher*, June 29, 1918, 15."How's War Business," *Editor and Publisher*, July 27, 1918, 8.

120. Jim Scripps to J. C. Harper, June 17, 1918, subseries 3.2, box 7, folder 3, EWS Papers.

121. Negley Dakin Cochran, *E. W. Scripps* (1933; reprint, Westport, Conn.: Greenwood Press, 1972), 171–78.

122. Ibid., 172–73.

123. Jim Scripps, "Robert P. Scripps," November 11, 1918, subseries 3.1, box 52, folder 4, EWS Papers.

124. Jim Scripps to J. C. Harper, June 17, 1918, subseries 3.2, box 7, folder 3, EWS Papers.

125. Jim Scripps, Memorandum: Robert P. Scripps, October 7, 1918, subseries 3.1, box 52, folder 1, EWS Papers.

126. Robert Scripps, Memorandum, October 7, 1918, subseries 3.1, box 52, folder 3, EWS Papers. The memorandum was intended for E. W. and was mailed with a short cover letter, Robert Scripps to Gilson Gardner, October 29, 1918, subseries 3.1, box 52, folder 3, EWS Papers. Gardner was accompanying E. W. at the time.

127. B. H. Canfield to Bob Scripps, June 8, 1918, subseries 3.1, box 51, folder 5, EWS Papers.

128. Robert Scripps, Memorandum, June 7, 1918.

129. Robert Scripps, Memorandum, October 7, 1918, subseries 3.1, box 52, folder 3, EWS Papers.

130. Bob Scripps to B. H. Canfield, June 10, 1918, subseries 3.1, box 51, folder 7, EWS Papers.

131. C. F. Mosher to Earle Martin, June 17, 1918, subseries 3.1, box 51, folder 8, EWS Papers.

132. C. F. Mosher to Earle Martin, August 7, 1918, subseries 3.1, box 51, folder 11, EWS Papers.

133. Earle Martin to Neg Cochran and B. H. Canfield, June 27, 1918, subseries 3.1, box 51, folder 6, EWS Papers.

134. S. T. Hughes to Tom Johnstone, E. C. Rodgers, and A. Geldhoff, October 2, 1918, subseries 3.1, box 52, folder 1, EWS Papers.

135. Jim Scripps, Memorandum: Robert P. Scripps, October 7, 1918.

136. S. T. Hughes to Gilson Gardner, October 2, 1918, subseries 3.1, box 52, folder 1, EWS Papers.

137. B. H. Canfield to S. T. Hughes, October 19, 1918, subseries 3.1, box 52, folder 3, EWS Papers.

138. C. F. Mosher to J. C. Harper, October 16, 1918, subseries 3.1, box 52, folder 3, EWS Papers.

139. B. H. Canfield to E. E. Martin, October 28, 1918, subseries 3.1, box 52, folder 3, EWS Papers.

140. Jim Scripps, Memorandum: Robert P. Scripps, October 7, 1918.

141. Jim Scripps to E. W. Scripps, October 26, 1918, subseries 1.2, box 38, folder 5, EWS Papers.

142. Bob Scripps to Jim Scripps, November 1, 1918, subseries 3.1, box 52, folder 4, EWS Papers.

143. Jim Scripps, Memorandum regarding Robert P. Scripps, November 11, 1918, subseries 3.1, box 52, folder 4, EWS Papers.

144. J. C. Harper to Ellen Scripps, November 11, 1918, subseries 3.1, box 52, folder 4, EWS Papers.

145. Bob Scripps to B. H. Canfield, November 12, 1918, subseries 3.1, box 52, folder 4, EWS Papers.

146. James Scripps, announcement, November 14, 1918, subseries 3.1, box 52, folder 4, EWS Papers.

147. Joseph Shaplen, "Trotsky Answers U.S., Gives Peace Plan," *Cleveland Press*, February 1, 1918.

148. Roy Howard to Ham Clark, January 26, 1918, Roy W. Howard Papers, Indiana University, Bloomington, Department of Journalism (hereafter RWH-IU Papers).

149. Roy Howard to Mrs. Frank Zuber, June 13, 1918, RWH-IU Papers.

150. Ibid.

151. Joe Alex Morris, *Deadline Every Minute: The Story of the United Press* (Garden City, N.Y.: Doubleday, 1957), 106. See also: W. W. Hawkins to C. F. Mosher, August 8, 1918, subseries 3.1, box 58, folder 12, EWS Papers. United Press did regain its strength and overtook AP within a few years. See Terhi Rantanen, *Mr. Howard Goes to South America: The United Press Associations and Foreign Expansion*, Roy W. Howard Monographs in Journalism and Mass Communication Research, no. 2 (Indiana University School of Journalism, May 15, 1992), 18–19.

152. Roy W. Howard to George Creel, September 12, 1918, Record Group 63, box 11, folder 314, CPI-DC Papers.

153. Emmet Crozier, *American Reporters on the Western Front* (New York: Oxford University Press, 1959), 27–228.

154. Ibid., 246.

155. Ferguson, an Indiana native, was a ten-year employee of UP; he most recently had been news manager of its New York bureau. See "Fred Ferguson Sent Abroad for U.P.," *Editor and Publisher*, February 23, 1918, 18.

156. Fred Ferguson, "U.S. Artillery Pounds Hun Line Back of Captured Pocket," *Cleveland Press*, September 14, 1918.

157. For a full description of Ferguson's scoop, see: Webb Miller, *I Found No Peace: The Journal of a Foreign Correspondent* (New York: Literary Guild, 1936), 85–87.

158. "Most Astounding Scoop," *Editor and Publisher*, September 28, 1918, 15. See also: "Biggest Beat of War," *Editor and Publisher*, September 14, 1918, 17.

159. Robert Scripps to Gilson Gardner, October 29, 1918, subseries 3.1, box 52, folder 3, EWS Papers.

160. Miller, *I Found No Peace*, 81–83.

161. A story in *Editor and Publisher* noted that the American intervention in the war made the cost of cable tolls greater because wire services were more likely to send stories immediately because of their increased importance. Instead of sending at the seven-cents-per-word regular press rate, which was slower, wire services sent at the 25-cent full rate as a matter of routine. See "Cost of War News Takes Big Jump," *Editor and Publisher*, April 6, 1918, 5.

162. William Philip Simms to Ed Keen, December 27, 1917, reel 2, Roy W. Howard Papers, Manuscript Division, Library of Congress, Washington, D.C. (hereafter RWH-LOC Papers).

163. Crozier, *American Reporters on the Western Front*, 228–29.

164. For a discussion of Wilson's dealings with Japan, see Kendrick Clements, *The Presidency of Woodrow Wilson* (Lawrence: University Press of Kansas, 1992) 107–12.

165. For a discussion of Wilson's thinking before committing American troops to Russia, see Thomas Knock, *To End All Wars: Woodrow Wilson and the Quest for a New World Order* (Princeton: Princeton University Press, 1992), 155–56. For an excellent overview of the Allied military intervention in Russia in 1918, see Byron Farwell, *Over There: The United States in the Great War, 1917–1918* (New York: Norton, 1999), 273–84.

166. See: Burton Knisely, "Japan Today: People Live in 'Horseless Age,'" *Cleveland Press*, July 11, 1918; Burton Knisely, "Japan Today: Tokyo Will Be Made an Ocean Port,'" *Cleveland Press*, July 12, 1918; Burton Knisely, "Japan Today: Darned Socks and the Rich," *Cleveland Press*, July 22, 1918; Burton Knisely, "Japan Today: Shoes at Twenty-Five Cents a Pair," *Cleveland Press*, July 15, 1918.

167. Burton Knisely, "That Yellow Peril—Knisely Tells What It Is," *Cleveland Press*, July 18, 1918.

168. Chairman, Censorship Committee, to Chairman, Censorship Board, August 29, 1918, box 3, folder 95, CPI-DC Papers.

169. Burton Knisely, "Look Out, Mr. Laboringman, Businessman, Storekeeper, Japan's After Your Bread and Butter," *San Francisco Daily News*, August 21, 1918.

170. Thomas P. Bryan to George Creel, September 6, 1918, box 3, folder 95, CPI-DC Papers.

171. Thomas Bryan to George Creel, August 30, 1918, box 3, folder 95, CPI-DC Papers.

172. B. H. Canfield to George Creel, September 11, 1918, box 3, folder 95, CPI-DC Papers.

173. George Creel to B. H. Canfield, September 17, 1918, box 3, folder 95, CPI-DC Papers.

174. Mark Sullivan, *Over There*, vol. 5 of *Our Times: 1900–1925* (New York: Scribner's, 1939), 513.

175. "Roy W. Howard Tells Full Story of Premature Peace Rumor," *Editor and Publisher*, November 23, 1918, 18.

176. Quoted in Morris, *Deadline Every Minute*, 95.

177. Ibid.

178. Emmett King to W.F.L., December 19, 1918, RWH-IU Papers. In this letter, King, stationed in Paris, said he got the same message as Admiral Wilson and also thought it was genuine.

179. "Always First!" *Cleveland Press*, November 7, 1918.

180. Sullivan, *Over There*, 513–14.

181. "Country from New York to San Francisco Went Wild over False Peace News," *St. Louis Post-Dispatch*, November 8, 1918. For a long description of the reaction in New York and elsewhere, see "City Goes Wild with Joy," *New York Times*, November 8, 1918.

182. "Plants Close, Throngs Parade in Peace Joy," *Cleveland Plain-Dealer*, November 8, 1918.

183. "Wild Crowds Howl Kaiser's Dirge in Loop," *Chicago Daily Tribune*, November 8, 1918.

184. "Nation Joy-Mad at Peace Report," *Washington Post*, November 8, 1918.

185. "Public Is Victim of Great Hoax of Recent Years," *Atlanta Constitution*, November 8, 1918.

186. Ibid., 516.

187. For a description of the UP office reaction, see Morris, *Deadline Every Minute*, 97.

188. Ibid., 98–99.

189. "Roy W. Howard Tells Full Story," *Editor and Publisher*, 18.

190. "Fighting Goes On: Allies Advance on Long Front," *Cleveland Press*, November 8, 1918.

191. "That Colossal News Hoax," *St. Louis Post-Dispatch*, November 8, 1918.

192. "The *St. Louis Post-Dispatch*," *St. Louis Post-Dispatch*, November 8, 1918.

193. "The Judas in Toledo," *Toledo Times*, November 8, 1918.

194. "Nailing the *News-Bee* Lie," *Toledo Times*, November 9, 1918.

195. "Reprehensible Journalism," *Toledo Blade*, November 8, 1918.

196. "The Associated Press," *Columbus Evening Dispatch*, November 9, 1918.

197. "Who Did It?" *New York Times*, November 8, 1918. Admiral Wilson was just one of several military officials who received word on November 7 that the armistice had been signed. The rumor was rampant and was accepted as fact in many circles. See John Toland, *No Man's Land: 1918, the Last Year of the Great War* (New York: Konecky and Konecky, 1980), 547–48.

198. "The Day," *New York Times*, November 9, 1918. Other newspapers' reactions to the armistice story can be found in Morris, *Deadline Every Minute*, 99–100.

199. Neg Cochran to Bob Scripps, November 12, 1918, subseries 3.1, box 52, folder 4, EWS Papers.

200. Robert Paine to J. C. Harper, November 19, 1918, subseries 3.1, box 52, folder 5, EWS Papers.

201. "Big Enough to Be Fair," *Editor and Publisher*, November 23, 1918, 21.
202. Morris, *Deadline Every Minute*, 101.
203. Miller, *I Found No Peace*, 105, 108.
204. A. O. Andersson to Sam T. Hughes, November 4, 1918, subseries 3.1, box 52, folder 4, EWS Papers.

Conclusion: "Harder . . . to Be of Public Service"

1. E. W. Scripps to Gentlemen of the Editorial Conference, July 5, 1919, subseries 1.2, box 19, folder 6, E. W. Scripps Papers, Alden Library, Ohio University, Athens (hereafter EWS Papers). The letter is dated July 5 but is mentioned in the July 3 minutes. Thus it can be assumed E. W.'s letter was dated incorrectly.
2. Joe Alex Morris, *Deadline Every Minute: The Story of the United Press* (Garden City, N.Y.: Doubleday, 1957), 119.
3. Roy Howard to E. W. Scripps, subseries 1.2, box 4, folder 36, EWS Papers.
4. Minutes of Editorial Conference, July 7, 1919, subseries 3.1, box 53, folder 3, EWS Papers.
5. Edward E. Adams, "Market Subordination and Competition: A Historical Analysis of Combinations, Consolidation, and Joint Operating Agreements through an Examination of the E. W. Scripps Newspaper Chain, 1877–1993" (Ph.D. diss., Ohio University, 1993), 59.
6. All figures from *N. W. Ayers and Sons American Newspaper Annual and Directory* (Philadelphia: Ayers, 1915); and *N. W. Ayers and Sons American Newspaper Annual and Directory* (Philadelphia: Ayers, 1920). It is assumed the 1915 Ayers edition reflected 1914 circulation figures, although the directory was unclear about this.
7. Stewart Halsey Ross, *Propaganda for War: How the United States Was Conditioned to Fight the Great War of 1914–1918* (Jefferson, N.C.: McFarland, 1996), 15, 20.
8. Phillip Knightley, *The First Casualty: From the Crimea to Vietnam: The War Correspondent as Hero, Propagandist, and Myth Maker* (New York: Harcourt Brace Jovanovich, 1975) 121.
9. H. C. Peterson, *Propaganda for War: The Campaign against American Neutrality, 1914–1917* (Norman: University of Oklahoma Press, 1939), 163.
10. Stephen Ponder, *Managing the Press: Origins of the Media Presidency, 1897–1933* (New York: St. Martin's Press, 1998), 96.
11. The NEA was based in Chicago until 1916, when it moved to Cleveland after a fire.
12. Bob Scripps to Jim Scripps, June 28, 1919, subseries 3.1, box 53, folder 2, EWS Papers.
13. Ibid.
14. Minutes of Editorial Conference, July 1, 1919, subseries 3.1, box 53, folder 3, EWS Papers.
15. E. W. Scripps to Gentlemen of the Editorial Conference, July 5, 1919.
16. E. W. Scripps to Gilson Gardner, July 27, 1919, subseries 1.2, box 19, folder 6, EWS Papers.
17. Scripps to Gardner, July 27, 1919.

18. Robert K. Murray, *Red Scare: A Study of National Hysteria, 1919–1920* (New York: McGraw-Hill, 1955), 9.

19. John Milton Cooper, *Pivotal Decades: the United States: 1900–1920* (New York: Norton, 1990), 325–26. Cooper provides an excellent overview of the Red Scare, 320–33. The definitive book on this period is Murray, *Red Scare*.

20. See Murray, *Red Scare*, 13–17.

21. Tom Sidlo to E. W. Scripps, October 1, 1919, subseries 1.1, box 38, folder 9, EWS Papers.

22. Vance H. Trimble, *The Astonishing Mr. Scripps: The Turbulent Life of America's Penny Press Lord* (Ames: Iowa State University Press, 1992), 400, 408.

23. E. W. Scripps to E. M. House, May 16, 1919, subseries 1.2, box 19, folder 5, EWS Papers.

24. See E. W. Scripps to Gilson Gardner, April 5, 1919, subseries 1.2, box 19, folder 5, EWS Papers; Gilson Gardner to E. W. Scripps, May 7, 1919, subseries 1.1, box 38, folder 7, EWS Papers; E. W. Scripps to Woodrow Wilson, May 6, 1919, subseries 1.2, box 19, folder 5, EWS Papers; Gilson Gardner to E. W. Scripps, May 23, 1919 (two letters), and Gilson Gardner to E. W. Scripps, June 4, 1919, both in subseries 1.1, box 38, folder 7, EWS Papers.

25. Cooper, *Pivotal Decades*, 327.

26. Minutes of Editorial Conference, July 7, 1919.

27. E. W. Scripps to Gilson Gardner, January 28, 1920, subseries 1.2, box 19, folder 8, EWS Papers.

28. "Promotions Reward Scripps Men," *Editor and Publisher*, September 18, 1919, 82.

29. Tom Sidlo to E. W. Scripps, June 13, 1919, subseries 1.1, box 38, folder 9, EWS Papers.

30. See Edward Adams, "An Early Hostile Corporate Takeover: The Split of the Scripps Newspaper Empire, 1920–1922," paper presented at the annual meeting of the Association for Education in Journalism and Mass Communication, Chicago, July 30, 1997. The Scripps League of newspapers (Jim's new company) was sold to the Pulitzer Company in 1996. It consisted of sixteen daily and thirty nondaily newspapers.

31. A. J. Liebling, *The Telephone Booth Indian* (1941; reprint, with an introduction by Luc Sante, New York: Broadway Books, 2004).

32. Minutes of Editorial Conference, July 3, 1919, subseries 3.1, box 53, folder 3, EWS Papers.

33. Minutes of Editorial Conference, July 5, 1919, subseries 3.1, box 53, folder 3, EWS Papers.

34. Minutes of Editorial Conference, July 2, 1919, subseries 3.1, box 53, folder 3, EWS Papers.

35. Ibid. A national referendum idea was championed by Idaho senator William Borah, an opponent of the League of Nations, as a way to buy time so opposition could be built against it. See Ralph Stone, *The Irreconcilables: The Fight against the League of Nations* (Lexington: University Press of Kentucky, 1970), 91. Killing the League was not Bob's intention, however.

36. Declaration of Principles, July 8, 1919, subseries 3.1, box 53, folder 3, EWS Papers.

37. Murray, *Red Scare*, 4.

38. E. W. Scripps to Gilson Gardner, January 10, 1920, subseries 1.2, box 19, folder 8, EWS Papers.
39. Scripps to Gardner, January 10, 1920.
40. E. W. Scripps, "A Blind Leader of the Blind," in *I Protest: Selected Disquisitions of E. W. Scripps*, ed. Oliver Knight (Madison: University of Wisconsin Press, 1966), 145.
41. E. W. Scripps to Amos Pinchot, February 26, 1920, subseries 1.2, box 19, folder 9, EWS Papers.
42. E. W. Scripps, "Two Presidents," in Knight, *I Protest*, 503.
43. Ibid., 504.

BIBLIOGRAPHY

Unpublished Documents

The archives of the E. W. Scripps papers in the Archives and Special Collections Department at Alden Library at Ohio University in Athens, Ohio, provided the vast majority of the documents in this study. These archives contain substantial information about the Scripps Concern. The collection centers on correspondence involving E. W. Scripps, but contains hundreds of letters exchanged among others in the Concern. Documents relating to the Newspaper Enterprise Association, for example, form a large portion. Financial information for the Concern is disappointingly sparse in the collection for the years studied, however. Alden Library archivists are in the process of revamping the classification system and finding aids, but the citations used in this study still will be able to be used to locate sources in the collection.

The Roy Howard papers provided the best information about the operations of United Press. The Howard papers are split between the Manuscript Division of the Library of Congress and the School of Journalism at Indiana University in Bloomington. Although the Bloomington collection is much smaller, it did provide important letters not found elsewhere.

Various archival collections at the Manuscript Division of the Library Congress provided small but useful amounts of material for this study. The most valuable included the papers of Newton Baker and Josephus Daniels. The collections of George Creel, William Gibbs McAdoo, Carl Ackerman, and Charles Russell, also housed in the Manuscript Division, were consulted but contained little or nothing relevant for this study. The papers of Woodrow Wilson were also examined at the Manuscript Division, but all of its relevant correspondence for this study already had been located at the Scripps collection in Ohio. The employees of the Concern seemed to have maintained a wonderful habit of keeping letters written by the noteworthy for posterity, making the Ohio University collection surprisingly complete.

Scripps historians will find an interesting collection of correspondence as part of the Negley Cochran papers at the Toledo-Lucas County Public Library in Toledo, Ohio. A finding aid for the collection did not exist while this study was being written, however, which hurt its usefulness. Still, valuable letters pertaining to the problems the *Toledo News-Bee* faced during the Scripps exemption fights were found. As one of the Concern's top editorial men, Cochran's collection of personal and business correspondence should not be overlooked, although many of the same letters were found in the Scripps collection at Ohio University.

Two collections were consulted at National Archives in Washington D.C., and its extension, the Washington National Records Center in Suitland, Maryland. First, the remaining records of the Committee on Public Information were consulted in Washington, and provided small, but significant parts of the material used to describe the censorship restrictions of 1917. Most of the information relating to how the Concern interacted with the CPI was found in the Scripps papers, however. Internal Revenue Service files at Suitland were consulted in hope of finding information relating to the 1915–16 discussion of income tax publicity, but nothing relevant was found.

INDEX

Ackerman, Carl, 70–73
Andersson, Alfred O., 26, 54, 119, 164, 220; discusses news policy, 45, 58, 62–63, 209; as editor in chief, 26
armistice, false, 204–6; media criticism of, 207–8; public reaction to, 206–7; United Press after, 208–9
Associated Press (AP), 37, 50; catches up to United Press in 1915, 68–70; comparisons to UP, 19–21; competes with UP, 6, 51, 61, 114, 146, 178, 199, 208; German preferential treatment of, 71–73; sues INS over copyright, 75
atrocity stories: as discussed by historians, 4–5; in early years of war, 45–47; use after war declared, 115, 179, 182–83, 197–98, 213

Baker, Newton, 149–50, 152, 157, 206, 215, 219; criticized by Concern, 133–34; criticized for war management, 172, 176; and exemption of Bob Scripps, 154–56, 188, 190
Boalt, Fred, 131
Boyle O'Reilly, Mary, 46–47, 113, 144, 198
Bryan, Williams Jennings: asked to help United Press, 38, 69–70; asked to propose publicity help for Wilson, 33–34, 55; criticized for isolationism, 66, 111–12

Canfield, Byron, 25, 28; advocates centralized control of NEA, 45, 63–64, 98, 116–19; advocates preparedness in NEA, 48–49, 55–57, 62, 66–67, 126; changes NEA focus to factual news, 192–94; criticizes Wilson administration, 133–35; helps direct 1917 war coverage, 113, 126, 167; as possible editor-in-chief of Concern, 129, 136, 151–53, 216; as president and general manager of NEA, 45, 47, 60, 77, 178; promoted to assistant chairman of board, 220; supports Wilson, 58, 62, 67; works with E.W. on tax publicity campaign, 83, 85–86, 89–90, 93
censorship, 21, 138, 146–47, 181; accepted by most journalists, 148–49; as discussed by historians, 4–5, 213–14; in Espionage Act, 127–28, 134–35; fails to stop false armistice story, 205, 207–8; imposed by the Germans, 71–73; loosening of, 60, 75–76; monitored by Bob Scripps, 166–67, 195; of NEA stories, 197, 202–4; to save costs, 50, 214; stories written poorly because of, 145–46; of UP stories, 37–39, 41–43, 115, 200–202
Chester, George Randolph, 180
Churchill, Winston, 42–43
Clark, Hamilton, 69
Cochran, Negley, 25, 142; ad-hoc editorial leadership of, 128–29, 131, 151; assesses personalities of Jim and Bob Scripps, 139, 154, 194; as defender of Wilson war effort, 176–77, 186; as editor-in-chief, 195, 216; as editor of *Day Book*, 163; as editor of *Toledo News-Bee*,

281

164, 175, 189–94; as mentor for Bob Scripps, 157–59, 173–74, 216; opposed to centralized editorial control, 64; as possible secretary of the people, 54–55, 68, 173; prewar assessment of military by, 113–14; on Scripps Editorial Board, 198–99
Committee for Public Information (CPI): cooperates with NEA, 173–74, 176–78; influence on journalists, 6; Scripps newspapers problems with, 183–86, 214; as target of *Los Angeles Record* criticism, 127–28
Concern. *See* Scripps Concern
conscription. *See* draft, military
copyright infringement: by International News Service (INS), 52, 169; of Karl Von Wiegand stories, 51–53; Scripps discussions of legal parameters of, 74–75
Crane, Charles, 54–55, 84, 113
Creel, George, 150, 203–4, 214; handles complaints about CPI mailings, 183–85; works with NEA, 172–73, 176
Curts, Jay W., 59; helps Bob Scripps with draft, 136, 139–40, 149–50, 156, 187; legal work of, 52–53, 74–75

Daniels, Josephus, 78, 176, 215; Concern seeks help from, 69, 147–48, 219; newspaper criticism of, 133–34
draft, military: E. W. Scripps to oppose, 142–44; as proposed as universal training, 78–79; Scripps Concern criticizes opponents of, 122
Durborough, Wilbur H., 77

Eastman, Max, 26, 107, 166
election of 1916: appeals to ethnic vote during, 100–102; appeals to progressives before, 95; consideration of Republican nominee by Scripps Concern, 96–97; importance of Ohio during, 94, 104–5; importance of Scripps Concern in, 8, 93–94, 104–5, 173, 248n70; peace appeals during, 103–4; results of, 104–5

Ferdinand, Franz (Archduke of Austria-Hungary), 33–36
Ferguson, Fred, 36–37, 200–201
Food Control Bill, 127, 141
Forrest, Wilbur, 60–61, 147–49

Gardner, Gilson, 106; as head of NEA Washington bureau, 197; as NEA writer, 48, 54, 57, 124, 141, 143–44; as political operative, 29, 34, 97, 142, 219; as Scripps biographer, 107, 167; suppressed by NEA, 119; works on income tax publicity, 84–88
Gibson, Idah McGlone, 67, 179

Harper, Jacob C., 14–15, 25, 53, 165; comments on centralized control of NEA, 49, 64, 131, 133, 151; comments on coverage of President Wilson, 67, 119; comments on election strategy, 29–30; comments on war, 44–45, 47, 65–66, 77; confronts E. W. on draft and bond purchases, 143, 162; as intermediary for Jim Scripps, 130, 136, 140, 149, 168–70, 187, 194
Hawkins, William W., 54, 207
Hearst, William Randolph, 6, 20, 135, 168–70
House, Edward M., 108, 153, 219
Howard, Roy, 19–20, 22–23, 108, 129, 158; and copyright concerns, 52, 74–76, 169; as critic of war censors, 38–39, 42, 146–47; criticizes atrocity stories, 47; describes role of war reporters, 44; expands UP globally, 73, 199–200; and management issues, 68–73, 145, 162; as part of false armistice story, 204–9; promoted to chairman of Concern, 220–21; raises UP rates, 50–51
Hughes, Charles Evans, 94, 185; 1916 campaign of, 100–104; reasons for

losing election, 104–5; wins Republican nomination, 96–97
Hughes, Sam T., 87, 113, 131, 209; as leader in war coverage, 118–19, 133–34, 152; promotes NEA bureau and service, 192–93, 197
Hunt, Harry, 115, 141; defends Wilson war effort, 173, 176–78

income tax, publicity of: as boost to circulation and influence, 82–83, 85; calls for Wilson administration support of, 87–88; as conceived by Scripps, 84–85, 89–90; investigation by Basil Manly, 86–91; news articles published supporting, 91–93; public reaction to campaign for, 92–93; threat to link support for Wilson to, 97–99; as way to pay for war, 141–42
International News Service (INS), 6, 20, 37, 61, 169; copyright complaints against, 52, 75, 169

Johnson, Hiram, 19, 130

Keen, Ed: dealings with censorship, 75–76, 202; as head of UP European operations, 37–39, 71; as UP writer, 55, 109, 181
Knisely, Burton, 202–4

Lane, Franklin, 24, 69, 113, 215, 233n9; as intermediary for income tax publicity, 87–88, 95; as supporter of secretary of the people, 34, 54, 68
Lee, C. D., 50
Liberty Loans, 162–63, 183
Lyon, C. C., 144, 193
Lusitania, sinking of, 60–62

MacLean, Eugene, 64, 117–18
Manly, Basil, 124, 141, 178–79, 185; researches income tax publicity, 85–93
Martin, Earle E., 175, 184; as editor of Ohio papers, 56, 60, 118, 146, 178–79, 186; as leader in Concern war policy, 120, 125, 129, 196–97, 220
Martinek, Joseph, 180
Mason, Jason W. T., 39, 47, 118, 181–82
McAdoo, Williams G., 84–88, 90–93
McRae, Milton, 129, 149, 152, 163–64; helps with draft exemption, 159–60, 168–70, 186–88
Mellett, Lowell, 202
Miller, Webb, 201–2
Millett, Ralph, 131
Morgan, Victor, 77–78, 131, 179
Mosher, Charles F., 49, 136; as editorial writer, 183, 196; input on editorial policy, 66, 77, 185–86, 197–98, 218
Murdoch, K. J., 83
"Must Copy" authority, 24; as advocated after *Lusitania* sinking, 63–64; attempts by E. W. to implement in 1917, 129–36, 150–53; discussion during "Greatest Navy" campaign launch, 56; discussions during preparedness debate, 48–49; during 1917 war coverage, 116–18; as enacted during 1916 election, 98–100

Newspaper Enterprise Association (NEA), 23–25; bans use of war jargon, 77–78; and censorship issues, 203–4; coverage influenced by Washington-center newsgathering, 215; defends Wilson's war management, 176–78; neutrality of war coverage, 44–47, 213–14; remakes mission and hires staff, 192–94, 196–99; uses photography to cover the war, 77; uses stunts and series to cover war effort, 144–45, 179–80

objectivity, journalistic, 9, 99, 148

Paine, Robert, 15, 18, 45, 112; and centralized control of NEA, 119, 129–30; criticizes Committee for

Public Information, 185; criticizes false armistice story, 208; as political observer, 29, 96–97, 99; as supporter of preparedness, 48–49, 55–56; as top editorial writer, 24–25, 66, 126, 198
Parker, George, 131
Pegler, Westbrook, 146–47, 149
Perry, John, 128, 135
Peters, Frederick R., 26, 64
Pinchot, Amos, 87, 123, 223
Porterfield, William H., 20, 27, 128, 134
preparedness, military, 79; cooperation with Army and Navy Leagues on issue of, 66–67; disputes with previous Scripps allies over, 65–66; "The Greatest Navy" campaign for, 55–57, 78–79; and international isolationism, 65, 109–11; NEA discussions in 1914 about, 48–49. *See also* draft, military
progressivism, 16–17
Pulitzer, Joseph, II, 38; and his newspapers, 51, 53–54, 68, 207

Rickey, Harry, 25; as coordinator of 1916 election coverage, 98–105; as coordinator of 1917 war coverage, 116–17, 131–36, 151–52; offered role in Wilson administration, 105; as possible secretary of the people, 54; resigns from Concern, 161
Roosevelt, Franklin D., 79
Roosevelt, Theodore, 82; criticizes war management, 175, 177; in 1912 election, 29–30; in 1916 election, 96, 100–101, 103; in preparedness debate, 56–57, 66; as progressive leader, 17
Russell, Charles Edward, 60, 113, 144–45

Sanders, LeRoy, 59, 119, 165, 220
Scripps Concern, 2; begins to criticize Wilson administration in 1918, 174–75; corporate split in 1920 of, 2, 7–8, 220; disagreements over peace issues with progressives, 111–12; experiments with hemp paper, 163–64; finances during war, 49–51, 162–64, 191–92; as independent progressive advocate, 8, 15, 18–19, 29–30; internal disagreements over coverage of 1917 war effort, 126–36; ownership and management structure of, 25–27; postwar circulation and finances of, 212–13; working class reader focus of, 14–15. *See also* Newspaper Enterprise Association; United Press
Scripps Editorial Board, 198–99
Scripps, Edward Willis (E.W.): advocates amnesty for political prisoners, 219; disappointment with conservative postwar editorial direction, 218–23; early life of, 16–18; editorial philosophy of, 1–2; fights over sons' roles, 157–58, 188–89; moves to Washington in 1917, 106–8, 124–25; suffers stroke, 167; worries about sons as successors, 7, 27–28, 153
Scripps, Ellen Browning (E.W.'s half sister), 25, 163
Scripps, James E. (E.W.'s older brother), 17–18
Scripps, James "Jim" G. (E.W.'s son): argues with E.W. for editorial control, 7, 107–8, 135, 218, 221; considers volunteering for government service, 149–50, 153; controversy created by exemption for, 186, 189–91; early career of, 27; editorial philosophy of, 14, 30, 64, 120, 194; as leader of criticism of Wilson in *Los Angeles Record*, 126–29, 134–36, 151–53; the military draft process for, 136, 140, 167–70, 186–88
Scripps, John Paul (E.W.'s son), 27, 160
Scripps, Nackie (E.W's wife), 35, 159; and draft worries, 139, 142–43, 156
Scripps newspapers. *See* Scripps Concern

Scripps, Robert "Bob" P. (E.W.'s son): controversy created by exemption of, 159–61, 213; early career of, 27–28, 107–8; goes to training camp, 153–57; in the military draft process, 136, 139–40, 149–50, 170–71, 187–88; in Washington after war declared, 120, 124; named to Scripps Editorial Board, 198–99; removed as editorial chief, 194–95; visits Europe in 1918, 195–96; as successor to E.W., 7, 125, 139, 194–95, 221; works as editorial chief, 157–59, 165–67, 188–89
secretary of the people, 33–35, 54–55, 68
Shepherd, William G., 39, 42–44
Sidlow, Thomas, 1, 154–55, 219–20
Simms, William Phillip, 14, 115, 181, 202, 207; as early advocate for war news, 36–37; as reporter with French army, 40
Sleeth, Dana, 67, 127, 131–32, 135
Steffens, Lincoln, 28

Taylor, Hannis, 142–44
Thornton, Willis, 164, 191–92

United Press (UP): coverage of 1918 German offensives, 181–82; dealing with censors and competition in 1918, 200–202; difficulty in finding news scoops, 76, 145–49; expansion into South America and Europe by, 73, 214; history of, 19–23; loses South American clients, 199–200; success in early war stages, 37, 39

Von Wiegand, Karl, 41; as reporter within Germany, 40–42, 51–53; leaves the UP, 53–54, 68–69

war finances, U.S., 122–24
war, U.S. declaration of: disagreement over tone of Scripps newspapers after, 118–20; Scripps Concern support for, 112–14, 116; stated war aims after, 120–22
Wheeler, Howard, 247n64
Wilson, Woodrow: Concern's postwar frustration with, 219–22; criticism of postelection peace maneuvers of, 108–11; early progressive attraction to, 28–29; feature stories written about, 67–68; grants exemption to Bob Scripps, 155–56; growing support in 1915 of, 58–59; support in 1912 of, 29–30. *See also* election of 1916
World War I journalism, postwar critique of, 4–5

Zimmerman, Arthur, 71, 114
Zimmerman telegram, 114

DALE ZACHER is an assistant professor in the School of Mass Communication at the University of Arkansas at Little Rock. A Rugby, North Dakota, native, Zacher has worked in radio and television journalism, and in government and political public relations. He earned his master's and Ph.D. degrees from the E. W. Scripps School of Journalism at Ohio University. His dissertation, "News and Editorial Policy of the Scripps Newspapers during World War I," won the American Journalism Historian's Association's Outstanding Dissertation Award in 2000. Zacher lives in the Little Rock, Arkansas, area with his wife and two boys.

THE HISTORY OF COMMUNICATION

Selling Free Enterprise: The Business Assault on Labor and Liberalism, 1945–60   *Elizabeth A. Fones-Wolf*
Last Rights: Revisiting *Four Theories of the Press*   Edited by *John C. Nerone*
"We Called Each Other Comrade": Charles H. Kerr & Company, Radical Publishers   *Allen Ruff*
WCFL, Chicago's Voice of Labor, 1926–78   *Nathan Godfried*
Taking the Risk Out of Democracy: Corporate Propaganda versus Freedom and Liberty   *Alex Carey; edited by Andrew Lohrey*
Media, Market, and Democracy in China: Between the Party Line and the Bottom Line   *Yuezhi Zhao*
Print Culture in a Diverse America   Edited by *James P. Danky and Wayne A. Wiegand*
The Newspaper Indian: Native American Identity in the Press, 1820–90   *John M. Coward*
E. W. Scripps and the Business of Newspapers   *Gerald J. Baldasty*
Picturing the Past: Media, History, and Photography   Edited by *Bonnie Brennen and Hanno Hardt*
Rich Media, Poor Democracy: Communication Politics in Dubious Times   *Robert W. McChesney*
Silencing the Opposition: Antinuclear Movements and the Media in the Cold War   *Andrew Rojecki*
Citizen Critics: Literary Public Spheres   *Rosa A. Eberly*
Communities of Journalism: A History of American Newspapers and Their Readers   *David Paul Nord*
From Yahweh to Yahoo!: The Religious Roots of the Secular Press   *Doug Underwood*
The Struggle for Control of Global Communication: The Formative Century   *Jill Hills*
Fanatics and Fire-Eaters: Newspapers and the Coming of the Civil War   *Lorman A. Ratner and Dwight L. Teeter Jr.*
Media Power in Central America   *Rick Rockwell and Noreene Janus*
The Consumer Trap: Big Business Marketing in American Life   *Michael Dawson*
How Free Can the Press Be?   *Randall P. Bezanson*
Cultural Politics and the Mass Media: Alaska Native Voices   *Patrick J. Daley and Beverly A. James*
Journalism in the Movies   *Matthew C. Ehrlich*
Democracy, Inc.: The Press and Law in the Corporate Rationalization of the Public Sphere   *David S. Allen*
Investigated Reporting: Television Muckraking and Regulation   *Chad Raphael*

Women Making News: Gender and the Women's Periodical Press
  in Britain   *Michelle Tusan*
Advertising on Trial: Consumer Activism and Corporate Public Relations
  in the 1930s   *Inger Stole*
Speech Rights in America: The First Amendment, Democracy,
  and the Media   *Laura Stein*
Freedom from Advertising: E. W. Scripps's Chicago Experiment
  Duane C. S. Stoltzfus
Waves of Opposition: The Struggle for Democratic Radio, 1933–58
  Elizabeth Fones-Wolf
Prologue to a Farce: Democracy and Communication in America
  Mark Lloyd
Outside the Box: Corporate Media, Globalization, and the UPS Strike
  Deepa Kumar
The Scripps Newspapers Go to War, 1914–1918   *Dale E. Zacher*

The University of Illinois Press
is a founding member of the
Association of American University Presses.

Composed in 9.5/12.5 Trump Mediaeval
by Jim Proefrock
at the University of Illinois Press
Manufactured by Thomson-Shore, Inc.

University of Illinois Press
1325 South Oak Street
Champaign, IL 61820-6903
www.press.uillinois.edu

Descendants of Totoliguoqui

Ethnicity and Economics
in the Mayo Valley

Mary I. O'Connor

UNIVERSITY OF CALIFORNIA PRESS
Berkeley • Los Angeles • London

UNIVERSITY OF CALIFORNIA PUBLICATIONS IN ANTHROPOLOGY

Editorial Board: Robert L. Bettinger, Robert Boyd, Michael A. Jochim,
Katharina J. Schreiber, William A. Shack, Marc J. Swartz

Volume 19

UNIVERSITY OF CALIFORNIA PRESS
BERKELEY AND LOS ANGELES, CALIFORNIA

UNIVERSITY OF CALIFORNIA PRESS, LTD.
LONDON, ENGLAND

ISBN 0-520-09742-4
LIBRARY OF CONGRESS CATALOG CARD NUMBER: 88-32908

© 1989 BY THE REGENTS OF THE UNIVERSITY OF CALIFORNIA
PRINTED IN THE UNITED STATES OF AMERICA

Library of Congress Cataloging-in-Publication Data

O'Connor, Mary I.
   Descendants of Totoliguoqui: ethnicity and economics in the Mayo valley / Mary I. O'Connor
      p.   cm. — (University of California publications in anthropology; v. 19)
   Bibliography: p.
   ISBN 0-520-09742-4
   1. Mayo Indians—Ethnic identity. 2. Mayo Indians—Economic conditions. 3. Indians of Mexico—Sonora (State)—Ethnic identity. 4. Indians of Mexico—Sonora (State)—Economic conditions.
I. Title. II. Series.
F1221.M3O28 1989
305.8'97—dc19   88-32908
                                                            CIP

To Charles J. Erasmus and Edward W. Loomis

Contents

Introduction   1
    The Legacy of Totoliguoqui, 1
    Why the Mayo Valley?, 3
    The Anthropologist as Female, 5
    Field Methods, 8
    Analysis of Data, 9

Chapter One: History of the Mayo Region   11
    Introduction, 11
    The Mayos and Spanish Contact, 11
    The Spanish Colonial Period, 13
    The Long Struggle for Autonomy, 17
    Peons and Revolutionaries, 24
    The Legacy of the Revolution, 27
    Conclusion, 29

Chapter Two: Theoretical Perspectives on Economic
    Development and Ethnic Identity   31
    Theories of Economic Development and Ethnic
    Identity, 31
    Economic Development in the Mayo Region, 38
    Ethnic Identity in the Mayo Valley, 43
    Conclusion: Development, Marginality and
    Ethnic Identity, 49

Contents

Chapter Three: Ethnic Symbols in the Mayo Valley — 53
    Ethnic Symbols and Social Behavior, 53
    Mayo and Orthodox Catholicism, 56
        Major Participants and Ceremonies, 57
        Minor Promises and Ceremonies, 60
        Church Leadership and Structure, 61
        The Fiesta System, 62
        Lent and Easter Ceremonies, 64
    Conclusion, 66

Chapter Four: Ecology, Politics and Economy in the Mayo Area — 69
    Introduction, 69
    Political Organization, 70
    Three Areas of Economic Development, 72
    The Occupational Structure, 75
    Conclusion: Ecology and Economy in Southern Sonora, 76

Chapter Five: Júpare: Village on the Lower Mayo — 79
    Introduction, 79
    Ethnic Mixing, 80
    Ethnic Cleavage, 84
    Situational Ethnicity, 85
    Ethnic Change, 87
    Social and Economic Opportunities, 89
    Conclusion, 91

Chapter Six: Buaysiacobe, a New Community — 93
    Introduction, 93
    Ethnic Homogeneity, 95
    Economic Homogeneity, 95
    Religion and Ethnic Expression, 96
    Ethnic Continuity and Economic Mobility, 99
    Situational Ethnicity, 102
    Conclusion, 103

Chapter Seven: The Masiaca Comunidad — 105
    Introduction, 106
    Role of the Instituto Nacional Indigenista, 107
    Three Hamlets, 108
        San Pedrito, 108
        Jopopaco, 109
        Las Bocas, 111

Contents

    Ethnic Cleavage and Situational Ethnicity, 113
    Economics and Ethnicity in the Masiaca
    Comunidad, 116

Conclusion   119
    Economic Development in the Mayo Valley, 119
    Ethnic Identity in the Mayo Valley, 120
    The Future of the Mayo Valley, 122

Bibliography, 125

Plates, 137

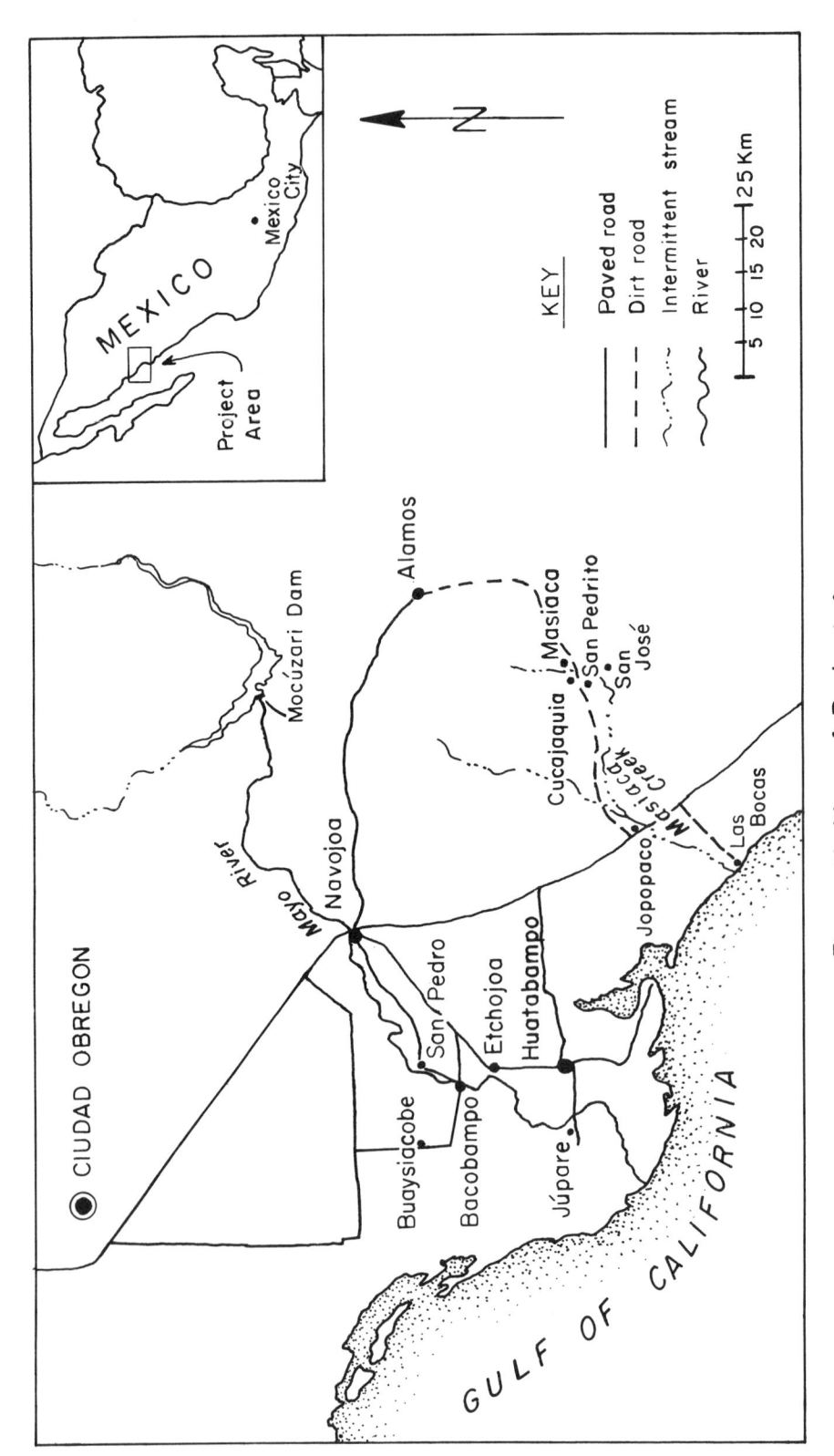

Figure 1: Map of Project Area